THE J2EE™ Tutorial

The Java™ Series

Lisa Friendly, Series Editor
Tim Lindholm, Technical Editor
Ken Arnold, Technical Editor of The Jini™ Technology Series
Jim Inscore, Technical Editor of The Java™ Series, Enterprise Edition

http://www.javaseries.com

Eric Armstrong, Stephanie Bodoff, Debbie Carson, Maydene Fisher, Dale Green, Kim Haase
The Java™ Web Services Tutorial

Ken Arnold, James Gosling, David Holmes
The Java™ Programming Language, Third Edition

Joshua Bloch
Effective Java™ Programming Language Guide

Mary Campione, Kathy Walrath, Alison Huml
The Java™ Tutorial, Third Edition: A Short Course on the Basics

Mary Campione, Kathy Walrath, Alison Huml,Tutorial Team
The Java™ Tutorial Continued: The Rest of the JDK™

Patrick Chan
The Java™ Developers Almanac 1.4, Volume 1

Patrick Chan
The Java™ Developers Almanac 1.4, Volume 2

Patrick Chan, Rosanna Lee
The Java™ Class Libraries, Second Edition, Volume 2: java.applet, java.awt, java.beans

Patrick Chan, Rosanna Lee, Doug Kramer
The Java™ Class Libraries, Second Edition, Volume 1: java.io, java.lang, java.math, java.net, java.text, java.util

Patrick Chan, Rosanna Lee, Doug Kramer
The Java™ Class Libraries, Second Edition, Volume 1: Supplement for the Java™ 2 Platform, Standard Edition, v1.2

Kirk Chen, Li Gong
Programming Open Service Gateways with Java™ Embedded Server

Zhiqun Chen
Java Card™ Technology for Smart Cards: Architecture and Programmer's Guide

Li Gong
Inside Java™ 2 Platform Security: Architecture, API Design, and Implementation

James Gosling, Bill Joy, Guy Steele, Gilad Bracha
The Java™ Language Specification, Second Edition

Doug Lea
Concurrent Programming in Java™, Second Edition: Design Principles and Patterns

Rosanna Lee, Scott Seligman
JNDI API Tutorial and Reference: Building Directory-Enabled Java™ Applications

Sheng Liang
The Java™ Native Interface: Programmer's Guide and Specification

Tim Lindholm, Frank Yellin
The Java™ Virtual Machine Specification, Second Edition

Roger Riggs, Antero Taivalsaari, Mark VandenBrink
Programming Wireless Devices with the Java™ 2 Platform, Micro Edition

Henry Sowizral, Kevin Rushforth, Michael Deering
The Java 3D™ API Specification, Second Edition

Sun Microsystems, Inc.
Java™ Look and Feel Design Guidelines: Advanced Topics

Kathy Walrath, Mary Campione
The JFC Swing Tutorial: A Guide to Constructing GUIs

Seth White, Maydene Fisher, Rick Cattell, Graham Hamilton, Mark Hapner
JDBC™ API Tutorial and Reference, Second Edition: Universal Data Access for the Java™ 2 Platform

Steve Wilson, Jeff Kesselman
Java™ Platform Performance: Strategies and Tactics

The Jini™ Technology Series

Eric Freeman, Susanne Hupfer, Ken Arnold
JavaSpaces™ Principles, Patterns, and Practice

Jim Waldo/Jini™ Technology Team
The Jini™ Specifications, Second Edition, edited by Ken Arnold

The Java™ Series, Enterprise Edition

Stephanie Bodoff, Dale Green, Kim Haase, Eric Jendrock, Monica Pawlan, Beth Stearns
The J2EE™ Tutorial

Rick Cattell, Jim Inscore, Enterprise Partners
J2EE™ Technology in Practice: Building Business Applications with the Java™ 2 Platform, Enterprise Edition

Mark Hapner, Rich Burridge, Rahul Sharma, Joseph Fialli, Kim Haase
Java™ Message Service API Tutorial and Reference: Messaging for the J2EE™ Platform

Inderjeet Singh, Beth Stearns, Mark Johnson, Enterprise Team
Designing Enterprise Applications with the Java™ 2 Platform, Enterprise Edition

Vlada Matena and Beth Stearns
Applying Enterprise JavaBeans™: Component-Based Development for the J2EE™ Platform

Bill Shannon, Mark Hapner, Vlada Matena, James Davidson, Eduardo Pelegri-Llopart, Larry Cable, Enterprise Team
Java™ 2 Platform, Enterprise Edition: Platform and Component Specifications

Rahul Sharma, Beth Stearns, Tony Ng
J2EE™ Connector Architecture and Enterprise Application Integration

THE J2EE™ Tutorial

Stephanie Bodoff
Dale Green
Kim Haase
Eric Jendrock
Monica Pawlan
Beth Stearns

Addison-Wesley

Boston • San Francisco • New York • Toronto • Montreal
London • Munich • Paris • Madrid
Capetown • Sydney • Tokyo • Singapore • Mexico City

Duke™ designed by Joe Palrang.

Pearson Education Corporate Sales Division
201 W. 103rd Street
Indianapolis, IN 46290
(800) 428-5331
corpsales@pearsoned.com

Visit AW on the Web: www.awprofessional.com

Library of Congress Control Number: 2002102527

Text printed on recycled and acid-free paper.

ISBN 0201791684

3 4 5 6 7 8 MA 05 04 03 02

3rd Printing June 2002

Contents

Foreword

I joined Sun—actually, a small Sun spin-off called FirstPerson—in August 1993. I knew about the company because a few of my favorite coworkers had left NeXT to work at FirstPerson. But my main reason for joining was that I loved the cartoony user interfaces FirstPerson was developing, interfaces that featured a character nicknamed Duke.[1]

Figure F–1 Duke, the Unofficial Mascot of the Java™ Platform

FirstPerson's first demo, called Star 7, was a household remote control with a small touchscreen. By the time I arrived, they were working on a demo for video on demand.

The wonderfully loony animation for the video-on-demand demo was created by a San Francisco studio called Colossal Pictures (where, incidentally, my husband had gotten his start in the animation industry). Both demos were written using a programming language that was then called Oak.

My first task was to help the creator of the Oak language, James Gosling, write the language specification. What I really wanted to do, though, was to write task-oriented documentation aimed at ordinary programmers.

---

1 You can get more information about Duke in the article "It's Duke's Birthday, Too!": `http://java.sun.com/features/1999/05/duke.html`.

By July 1994, FirstPerson was in turmoil, having failed to convince cable companies that their video-on-demand solution was what customers needed. I stayed at the company only because I was about to go on maternity leave.

Programming for the Internet

When I returned to work in the fall of 1994, the company's dynamic and vision had completely changed. They had decided that the Oak language—with its ability to produce platform-independent, secure, easily transported code—was ideal for the Internet. And they were creating a Web browser called WebRunner that showcased the ability to deliver Oak code, packaged in a form they called applets, over the Internet.

I set to work writing a guide to help people write and use applets. When the WebRunner browser was first released in early 1995, the guide was part of the small set of documentation included with the browser. That guide was the granddaddy of *The J2EE™ Tutorial*.

The guide was the first documentation to include applets. It looked somewhat similar to *The Java™ Tutorial*, and in fact *The Java™ Tutorial* probably still has some of the text originally published in the guide. Because we had no HTML tools, however, I had to generate the guide completely by hand. Let me tell you, hand coding navigation links for a document in progress is not fun, even for a small document. Much less painful was making name changes: The language name changed from Oak to Java™, and the name of the browser from WebRunner to HotJava.

Mary Enters the Picture

In early 1995, we hired a contract writer named Mary Campione. She and I knew of each other from her time in NeXT developer support. Mary's job was to help programmers use platform features such as threads. We soon realized that our work was too similar for us to do it separately, and we started working together on a programmer's guide for the Java platform.

On May 18, 1995, Mary Campione and I released the first version of our guide, which we called *The Java™ Programmer's Guide*. It was an incomplete first draft—nothing pretty—but it provided people with the information they needed to get started programming for the Java platform.

The next week, Sun officially announced the Java platform at a show called SunWorld. The best part of the show for us was the announcement that Netscape had agreed (just hours before) to support applets in their Web browser.

In the following months, Mary and I continued to add to and refine our programmer's guide.[2] We worked together closely, sharing the same office and even the same train commute from San Francisco to Palo Alto. By coincidence, we even got pregnant within days of each other.

By late 1995, the first wave of books in The Java Series was being developed. The Java Series was a group of books published by Addison-Wesley and written mainly by employees of what used to be FirstPerson. By that time, FirstPerson had been absorbed back into Sun, in the form of a division called JavaSoft. The Series Editor was JavaSoft technical publications manager Lisa Friendly.[3]

Our programmer's guide was slated to be one of the books in The Java Series, but the publisher wanted it to have a less intimidating name. So we changed its name to *The Java™ Tutorial.* There we were, two increasingly large women working insanely long hours to finish the book before the babies arrived in mid-1996. We managed—just barely—to get the book to our publisher in time. We couldn't have done it without the help of yet another ex-NeXTer, Randy Nelson, who took care of all the final details of the book and Web site.

The Tutorial Team Grows

When Mary and I returned from maternity leave, we felt completely overwhelmed. Our book and Web site covered the 1.0 version of the Java platform (JDK 1.0), but JDK 1.1 was scheduled to be released soon and work had already started on JDK 1.2 (which would be renamed to the Java 2 Platform, Standard Edition, Version 1.2—J2SE™ v 1.2, for short). We would be able to update our existing documentation to 1.1, but for 1.2 we'd need help.

Help arrived in the form of guest authors and Alison Huml. The guest authors were writers and engineers on the teams developing the new 1.2 features. Alison was a postgraduate student with experience in both software and publishing. She did whatever was necessary to make the Tutorial succeed, ranging from producing camera-ready copy for books to writing text and examples.

---

[2] By looking at `http://java.sun.com/docs/books/tutorial/information/history.html`, you can see what was in each of our updates.

[3] Lisa has some great anecdotes about the early days of FirstPerson. You can read some of them at `http://java.sun.com/features/1998/05/birthday.html`.

Between 1998 and 2000, the Tutorial team updated the Web site many times and produced two completely new books, as well as two major revisions of the original book. In mid-2000, Mary retired from paid work. Alison and I still work on *The Java™ Tutorial*, in both its Web and book forms. Although we rely on guest authors from time to time, the rate of change has become less frantic as the J2SE platform matures.

The J2EE Tutorial

Now there's a new platform—and a new tutorial—in town. The success of the Java 2 Platform, Enterprise Edition (J2EE™) has been phenomenal. Developers are clamoring for information about how to write applications using this new Java platform for the server. And this book helps, continuing the tradition of *The Java™ Tutorial*, but this time for the J2EE platform. Like the original Tutorial, this is an example-filled, easy-to-use entry point and quick reference for programming with the J2EE platform. And I'm sure, like the original tutorial team, Stephanie, Dale, Eric, Kim, and Beth all have stories to tell about the time they've spent working on the J2EE platform and bringing you this book.

Just a note—Because the J2EE platform sits on top of the J2SE platform, you need to be comfortable writing programs for the J2SE platform before you can make full use of this book. If you're not comfortable with the J2SE platform, go to *The Java™ Tutorial*[4] and learn!

Then come back here, so you can find out all about developing and deploying applications for the J2EE platform.

Kathy Walrath
Sun Microsystems
San Francisco, CA
December 21, 2001

---

4 On the Web at `http://java.sun.com/docs/books/tutorial/`, or in book form as *The Java™ Tutorial: A Short Course on the Basics*.

Preface

The Java™ Tutorial has been an indispensable resource for many programmers learning the Java programming language. This tutorial hopes to serve the same role for developers encountering the Java™ 2 Platform, Enterprise Edition (J2EE™) for the first time. It follows an example-oriented focus similar to *The Java™ Tutorial.*

Who Should Use This Tutorial

This tutorial is intended for programmers interested in developing and deploying J2EE applications. It covers the technologies comprising the J2EE platform and describes how to develop J2EE components and deploy them on the J2EE Software Development Kit (SDK).

This tutorial is not intended for J2EE server or tool vendors. It does not explain how to implement the J2EE architecture, nor does it explain the internals of the J2EE SDK. The J2EE specifications describe the J2EE architecture and can be downloaded from

```
http://java.sun.com/j2ee/docs.html#specs
```

About the Examples

This tutorial includes many complete, working examples. See Examples (page 445) for a list of the examples and the chapters where they appear.

Prerequisites for the Examples

To understand the examples, you will need a good knowledge of the Java programming language, SQL, and relational database concepts. The topics in *The Java™ Tutorial* listed in Table P–1 are particularly relevant.

Table P–1 Prerequisite Topics

Topic	Java Tutorial
JDBC™	`http://java.sun.com/docs/books/tutorial/jdbc`
Threads	`http://java.sun.com/docs/books/tutorial/essential/threads`
JavaBeans™	`http://java.sun.com/docs/books/tutorial/javabeans`
Security	`http://java.sun.com/docs/books/tutorial/security1.2`

Downloading the Examples

If you are viewing this online and you want to build and run the examples, you need to download the tutorial bundle from

```
http://java.sun.com/j2ee/download.html#tutorial
```

Once you have installed the bundle, the example source code is in the `j2eetutorial/examples/src` directory, with subdirectories `ejb` for enterprise bean technology examples, `web` for Web technology examples, and `connector` for connector technology examples. For most of the examples, the bundle also includes J2EE application Enterprise Archive (EAR) files, which are located in the `j2eetutorial/examples/ears` directory.

How to Build and Run the Examples

This tutorial documents the J2EE SDK version 1.3. To build, deploy, and run the examples you need a copy of the J2EE SDK 1.3 and the Java 2 Platform, Standard Edition (J2SE™) SDK 1.3.1 (earlier versions were called JDK). You can download the J2EE SDK from

```
http://java.sun.com/j2ee/download.html#sdk
```

and the J2SE 1.3.1 from

```
http://java.sun.com/j2se/1.3/
```

The examples are distributed with a configuration file for version 1.3 of `ant`, a portable make tool. The `ant` utility is hosted by the Jakarta project at the Apache Software Foundation. You can download `ant` from

```
http://jakarta.apache.org/builds/jakarta-ant/release/v1.3/bin
```

To build the tutorial examples, follow these steps:

1. Download and install the J2SE SDK 1.3.1, J2EE SDK 1.3, and `ant`.
2. The installation instructions for the J2SE SDK, J2EE SDK, and `ant` explain how to set the required environment variables. Verify that the environment variables have been set to the values noted in the Table P–2.

Table P–2 Settings for Environment Variables

Environment Variable	Value
`JAVA_HOME`	The location of the J2SE SDK installation.
`J2EE_HOME`	The location of the J2EE SDK installation.
`ANT_HOME`	The location of the `ant` installation.
`PATH`	Should include the `bin` directories of the J2EE SDK, J2SE SDK, and `ant` installations.

3. Go to the `j2eetutorial/examples` directory.
4. Execute `ant` *`target`*. For example, to build all the examples, execute `ant all`; to build the Web layer examples, execute `ant web`. The build process deposits the output into the directory `j2eetutorial/examples/build`.

Related Information

This tutorial provides a concise overview of how to use the central component technologies in the J2EE platform. For more information about these technologies, see the Web sites listed in Table P–3.

Table P–3 Information Sources

Component Technology	Web Site
Enterprise JavaBeans™ (EJB™)	`http://java.sun.com/products/ejb`
Java Servlet	`http://java.sun.com/products/servlets`
JavaServer Pages™ (JSP™)	`http://java.sun.com/products/jsp`

The J2EE platform includes a wide variety of APIs that this tutorial only briefly touches on. Some of these technologies have their own tutorials, which are listed in Table P–4.

Table P–4 Other Tutorials

API	Tutorial
Java Message Service (JMS)	`http://java.sun.com/products/jms/tutorial/`
Java Naming and Directory Interface™ (JNDI)	`http://java.sun.com/products/jndi/tutorial/`
Java API for XML Processing (JAXP)	`http://java.sun.com/xml/jaxp/dist/1.1/docs/tutorial/index.html`

For complete information on these topics, see the Web sites listed in Table P–5.

Table P–5 Other Web Sites

API	Web Site
J2EE Connector	`http://java.sun.com/j2ee/connector`
JAXP	`http://java.sun.com/products/jaxp`
JavaMail™	`http://java.sun.com/products/javamail`
JMS	`http://java.sun.com/products/jms`
JNDI	`http://java.sun.com/products/jndi`
JDBC™	`http://java.sun.com/products/jdbc`

Once you have become familiar with the J2EE technologies described in this tutorial, you may be interested in guidelines for architecting J2EE applications. The Java BluePrints illustrate best practices for developing and deploying J2EE applications. You can obtain the Java BluePrints from

```
http://java.sun.com/blueprints
```

How to Print This Tutorial

To print this tutorial, follow these steps:

1. Ensure that Adobe Acrobat Reader is installed on your system.
2. Download the PDF version of this book from

   ```
   http://java.sun.com/j2ee/download.html#tutorial
   ```

3. Click the printer icon in Adobe Acrobat Reader.

Typographical Conventions

Table P–6 lists the typographical conventions used in this tutorial.

Table P–6 Typographical Conventions

Font Style	Uses
Italic	Emphasis, titles, first occurrence of terms
`Monospace`	URLs, code examples, file names, command names, programming language keywords
`Italic monospace`	Programming variables, variable file names

Menu selections indicated with the right-arrow character →, for example, First→Second, should be interpreted as: select the First menu, then choose Second from the First submenu.

Acknowledgments

The J2EE tutorial team would like to thank the J2EE SDK team for their technical advice.

We are extremely grateful to the many internal and external reviewers who provided feedback on the tutorial. This helped us to improve the presentation, correct errors, and eliminate bugs.

We would also like to thank our manager, Jim Inscore, for his support and steadying influence.

The chapters on Web components use an example and some material that first appeared in the servlet trail of *The Java™ Tutorial*. The chapters on custom tags and the Duke's Bank application use a template tag library that first appeared in the Java BluePrints.

1 Overview

Monica Pawlan

TODAY, more and more developers want to write distributed transactional applications for the enterprise and leverage the speed, security, and reliability of server-side technology. If you are already working in this area, you know that in today's fast-moving and demanding world of e-commerce and information technology, enterprise applications have to be designed, built, and produced for less money, with greater speed, and with fewer resources than ever before.

To reduce costs and fast-track enterprise application design and development, the Java™ 2 Platform, Enterprise Edition (J2EE™) technology provides a component-based approach to the design, development, assembly, and deployment of enterprise applications. The J2EE platform offers a multitiered distributed application model, the ability to reuse components, integrated Extensible Markup Language (XML)-based data interchange, a unified security model, and flexible transaction control. Not only can you deliver innovative customer solutions to market faster than ever, but your platform-independent J2EE component-based solutions are not tied to the products and application programming interfaces (APIs) of any one vendor. Vendors and customers enjoy the freedom to choose the products and components that best meet their business and technological requirements.

This tutorial takes an examples-based approach to describing the features and functionalities available in J2EE Software Development Kit (SDK) version 1.3. Whether you are a new or an experienced enterprise developer, you should find the examples and accompanying text a valuable and accessible knowledge base for creating your own enterprise solutions.

If you are new to J2EE applications development, this chapter is a good place to start. Here you will learn the J2EE architecture, become acquainted with important terms and concepts, and find out how to approach J2EE application programming, assembly, and deployment.

In This Chapter

Distributed Multitiered Applications

The J2EE platform uses a multitiered distributed application model. Application logic is divided into components according to function, and the various application components that make up a J2EE application are installed on different machines depending on the tier in the multitiered J2EE environment to which the application component belongs. Figure 1–1 shows two multitiered J2EE applications divided into the tiers described in the following list. The J2EE application parts shown in Figure 1–1 are presented in J2EE Components (page 3).

- Client-tier components run on the client machine.
- Web-tier components run on the J2EE server.

- Business-tier components run on the J2EE server.
- Enterprise information system (EIS)-tier software runs on the EIS server.

Although a J2EE application can consist of the three or four tiers shown in Figure 1–1, J2EE multitiered applications are generally considered to be three-tiered applications because they are distributed over three different locations: client machines, the J2EE server machine, and the database or legacy machines at the back end. Three-tiered applications that run in this way extend the standard two-tiered client and server model by placing a multithreaded application server between the client application and back-end storage.

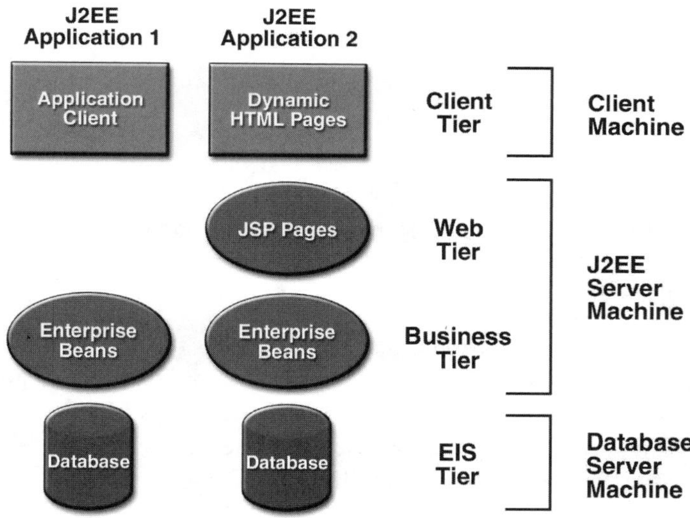

Figure 1–1 Multitiered Applications

J2EE Components

J2EE applications are made up of components. A *J2EE component* is a self-contained functional software unit that is assembled into a J2EE application with its related classes and files and that communicates with other components. The J2EE specification defines the following J2EE components:

- Application clients and applets are components that run on the client.

- Java Servlet and JavaServer Pages™ (JSP™) technology components are Web components that run on the server.
- Enterprise JavaBeans™ (EJB™) components (enterprise beans) are business components that run on the server.

J2EE components are written in the Java programming language and are compiled in the same way as any program in the language. The difference between J2EE components and "standard" Java classes is that J2EE components are assembled into a J2EE application, verified to be well formed and in compliance with the J2EE specification, and deployed to production, where they are run and managed by the J2EE server.

J2EE Clients

A J2EE client can be a Web client or an application client.

Web Clients

A Web client consists of two parts: dynamic Web pages containing various types of markup language (HTML, XML, and so on), which are generated by Web components running in the Web tier, and a Web browser, which renders the pages received from the server.

A Web client is sometimes called a *thin client*. Thin clients usually do not do things like query databases, execute complex business rules, or connect to legacy applications. When you use a thin client, heavyweight operations like these are off-loaded to enterprise beans executing on the J2EE server where they can leverage the security, speed, services, and reliability of J2EE server-side technologies.

Applets

A Web page received from the Web tier can include an embedded applet. An applet is a small client application written in the Java programming language that executes in the Java virtual machine installed in the Web browser. However, client systems will likely need the Java Plug-in and possibly a security policy file in order for the applet to successfully execute in the Web browser.

Web components are the preferred API for creating a Web client program because no plug-ins or security policy files are needed on the client systems. Also, Web components enable cleaner and more modular application design because they provide a way to separate applications programming from Web page design. Personnel involved in Web page design thus do not need to understand Java programming language syntax to do their jobs.

Application Clients

A J2EE application client runs on a client machine and provides a way for users to handle tasks that require a richer user interface than can be provided by a markup language. It typically has a graphical user interface (GUI) created from Swing or Abstract Window Toolkit (AWT) APIs, but a command-line interface is certainly possible.

Application clients directly access enterprise beans running in the business tier. However, if application requirements warrant it, a J2EE application client can open an HTTP connection to establish communication with a servlet running in the Web tier.

JavaBeans™ Component Architecture

The server and client tiers might also include components based on the JavaBeans component architecture (JavaBeans component) to manage the data flow between an application client or applet and components running on the J2EE server or between server components and a database. JavaBeans components are not considered J2EE components by the J2EE specification.

JavaBeans components have instance variables and `get` and `set` methods for accessing the data in the instance variables. JavaBeans components used in this way are typically simple in design and implementation, but should conform to the naming and design conventions outlined in the JavaBeans component architecture.

J2EE Server Communications

Figure 1–2 shows the various elements that can make up the client tier. The client communicates with the business tier running on the J2EE server either directly or, as in the case of a client running in a browser, by going through JSP pages or servlets running in the Web tier.

Your J2EE application uses a thin browser-based client or thick application client. In deciding which one to use, you should be aware of the trade-offs between keeping functionality on the client and close to the user (thick client) and offloading as much functionality as possible to the server (thin client). The more functionality you off-load to the server, the easier it is to distribute, deploy, and manage the application; however, keeping more functionality on the client can make for a better perceived user experience.

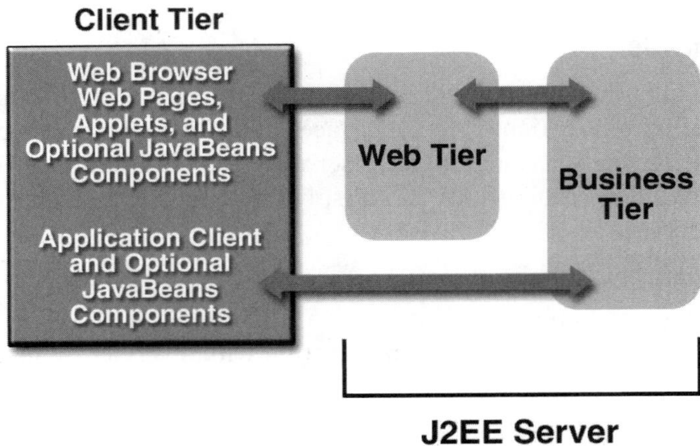

Figure 1–2 Server Communications

Web Components

J2EE Web components can be either servlets or JSP pages. *Servlets* are Java programming language classes that dynamically process requests and construct responses. *JSP pages* are text-based documents that execute as servlets but allow a more natural approach to creating static content.

Static HTML pages and applets are bundled with Web components during application assembly, but are not considered Web components by the J2EE specification. Server-side utility classes can also be bundled with Web components and, like HTML pages, are not considered Web components.

Like the client tier and as shown in Figure 1–3, the Web tier might include a JavaBeans component to manage the user input and send that input to enterprise beans running in the business tier for processing.

Business Components

Business code, which is logic that solves or meets the needs of a particular business domain such as banking, retail, or finance, is handled by enterprise beans running in the business tier. Figure 1–4 shows how an enterprise bean receives data from client programs, processes it (if necessary), and sends it to the enterprise information system tier for storage. An enterprise bean also retrieves data from storage, processes it (if necessary), and sends it back to the client program.

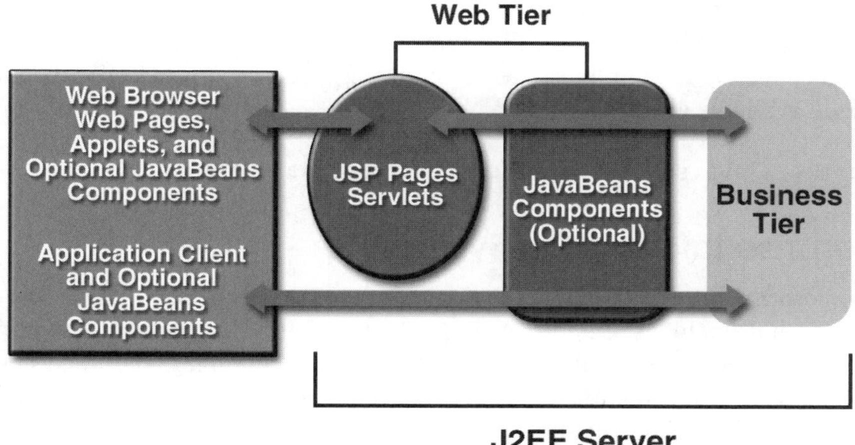

Figure 1–3 Web Tier and J2EE Application

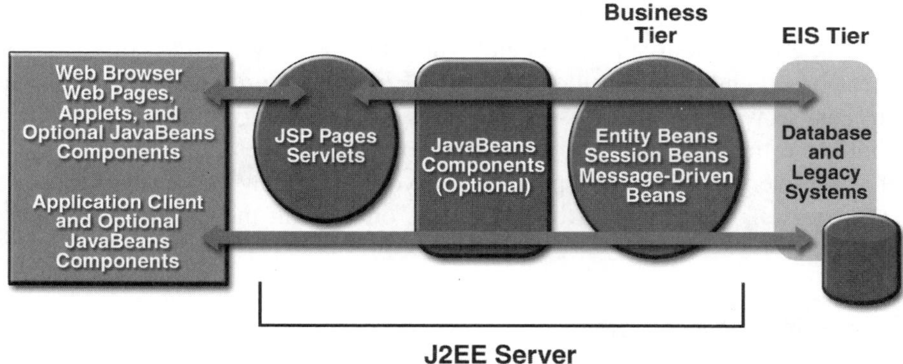

Figure 1–4 Business and EIS Tiers

There are three kinds of enterprise beans: session beans, entity beans, and message-driven beans. A *session bean* represents a transient conversation with a client. When the client finishes executing, the session bean and its data are gone. In contrast, an *entity bean* represents persistent data stored in one row of a database table. If the client terminates or if the server shuts down, the underlying services ensure that the entity bean data is saved.

A *message-driven bean* combines features of a session bean and a Java Message Service ("JMS") message listener, allowing a business component to receive JMS messages asynchronously. This tutorial describes entity beans and session beans. For information on message-driven beans, see *The Java Message Service Tutorial*, available at

```
http://java.sun.com/products/jms/tutorial/index.html
```

Enterprise Information System Tier

The enterprise information system tier handles enterprise information system software and includes enterprise infrastructure systems such as enterprise resource planning (ERP), mainframe transaction processing, database systems, and other legacy information systems. J2EE application components might need access to enterprise information systems for database connectivity, for example.

J2EE Containers

Normally, thin-client multitiered applications are hard to write because they involve many lines of intricate code to handle transaction and state management, multithreading, resource pooling, and other complex low-level details. The component-based and platform-independent J2EE architecture makes J2EE applications easy to write because business logic is organized into reusable components. In addition, the J2EE server provides underlying services in the form of a container for every component type. Because you do not have to develop these services yourself, you are free to concentrate on solving the business problem at hand.

Container Services

Containers are the interface between a component and the low-level platform-specific functionality that supports the component. Before a Web, enterprise bean, or application client component can be executed, it must be assembled into a J2EE application and deployed into its container.

The assembly process involves specifying container settings for each component in the J2EE application and for the J2EE application itself. Container settings customize the underlying support provided by the J2EE server, which includes services such as security, transaction management, Java Naming and Directory

Interface™ (JNDI) lookups, and remote connectivity. Here are some of the highlights:

- The J2EE security model lets you configure a Web component or enterprise bean so that system resources are accessed only by authorized users.
- The J2EE transaction model lets you specify relationships among methods that make up a single transaction so that all methods in one transaction are treated as a single unit.
- JNDI lookup services provide a unified interface to multiple naming and directory services in the enterprise so that application components can access naming and directory services.
- The J2EE remote connectivity model manages low-level communications between clients and enterprise beans. After an enterprise bean is created, a client invokes methods on it as if it were in the same virtual machine.

The fact that the J2EE architecture provides configurable services means that application components within the same J2EE application can behave differently based on where they are deployed. For example, an enterprise bean can have security settings that allow it a certain level of access to database data in one production environment and another level of database access in another production environment.

The container also manages nonconfigurable services such as enterprise bean and servlet life cycles, database connection resource pooling, data persistence, and access to the J2EE platform APIs described in the section J2EE APIs (page 15). Although data persistence is a nonconfigurable service, the J2EE architecture lets you override container-managed persistence by including the appropriate code in your enterprise bean implementation when you want more control than the default container-managed persistence provides. For example, you might use bean-managed persistence to implement your own finder (search) methods or to create a customized database cache.

Container Types

The deployment process installs J2EE application components in the J2EE containers illustrated in Figure 1–5.

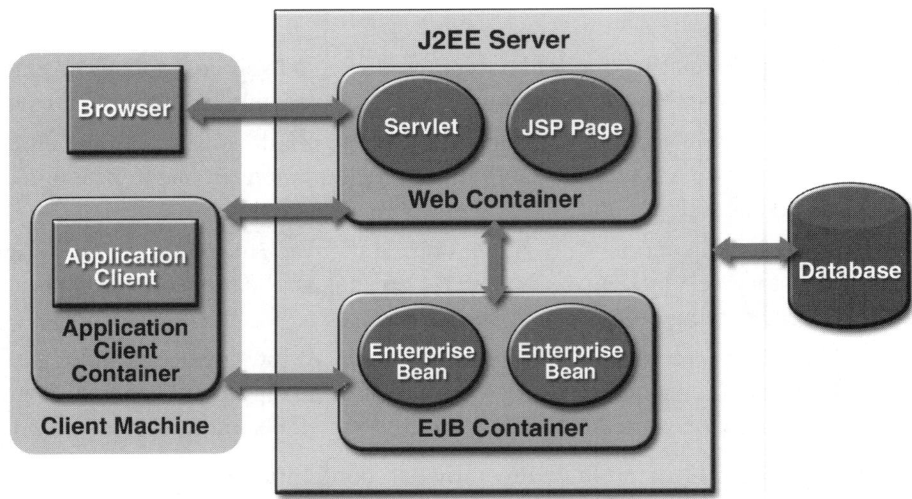

Figure 1–5 J2EE Server and Containers

J2EE server
The runtime portion of a J2EE product. A J2EE server provides EJB and Web containers.

Enterprise JavaBeans (EJB) container
Manages the execution of enterprise beans for J2EE applications. Enterprise beans and their container run on the J2EE server.

Web container
Manages the execution of JSP page and servlet components for J2EE applications. Web components and their container run on the J2EE server.

Application client container
Manages the execution of application client components. Application clients and their container run on the client.

Applet container
Manages the execution of applets. Consists of a Web browser and Java Plug-in running on the client together.

Packaging

J2EE components are packaged separately and bundled into a J2EE application for deployment. Each component, its related files such as GIF and HTML files or server-side utility classes, and a deployment descriptor are assembled into a module and added to the J2EE application. A J2EE application is composed of one or more enterprise bean, Web, or application client component modules. The final enterprise solution can use one J2EE application or be made up of two or more J2EE applications, depending on design requirements.

A J2EE application and each of its modules has its own deployment descriptor. A deployment descriptor is an XML document with an `.xml` extension that describes a component's deployment settings. An enterprise bean module deployment descriptor, for example, declares transaction attributes and security authorizations for an enterprise bean. Because deployment descriptor information is declarative, it can be changed without modifying the bean source code. At run time, the J2EE server reads the deployment descriptor and acts upon the component accordingly.

A J2EE application with all of its modules is delivered in an Enterprise Archive (EAR) file. An EAR file is a standard Java Archive (JAR) file with an `.ear` extension. In the GUI version of the J2EE SDK application deployment tool, you create an EAR file first and add JAR and Web Archive (WAR) files to the EAR. If you use the command line packager tools, however, you create the JAR and WAR files first and then create the EAR. The J2EE SDK tools are described in the section Tools (page 19).

- Each EJB JAR file contains a deployment descriptor, the enterprise bean files, and related files.
- Each application client JAR file contains a deployment descriptor, the class files for the application client, and related files.
- Each WAR file contains a deployment descriptor, the Web component files, and related resources.

Using modules and EAR files makes it possible to assemble a number of different J2EE applications using some of the same components. No extra coding is needed; it is just a matter of assembling various J2EE modules into J2EE EAR files.

Development Roles

Reusable modules make it possible to divide the application development and deployment process into distinct roles so that different people or companies can perform different parts of the process.

The first two roles involve purchasing and installing the J2EE product and tools. Once software is purchased and installed, J2EE components can be developed by application component providers, assembled by application assemblers, and deployed by application deployers. In a large organization, each of these roles might be executed by different individuals or teams. This division of labor works because each of the earlier roles outputs a portable file that is the input for a subsequent role. For example, in the application component development phase, an enterprise bean software developer delivers EJB JAR files. In the application assembly role, another developer combines these EJB JAR files into a J2EE application and saves it in an EAR file. In the application deployment role, a system administrator at the customer site uses the EAR file to install the J2EE application into a J2EE server.

The different roles are not always executed by different people. If you work for a small company, for example, or if you are prototyping a sample application, you might perform the tasks in every phase.

J2EE Product Provider

The J2EE product provider is the company that designs and makes available for purchase the J2EE platform, APIs, and other features defined in the J2EE specification. Product providers are typically operating system, database system, application server, or Web server vendors who implement the J2EE platform according to the Java 2 Platform, Enterprise Edition Specification.

Tool Provider

The tool provider is the company or person who creates development, assembly, and packaging tools used by component providers, assemblers, and deployers. See the section Tools (page 19) for information on the tools available with J2EE SDK version 1.3.

Application Component Provider

The application component provider is the company or person who creates Web components, enterprise beans, applets, or application clients for use in J2EE applications.

Enterprise Bean Developer

An enterprise bean developer performs the following tasks to deliver an EJB JAR file that contains the enterprise bean:

- Writes and compiles the source code
- Specifies the deployment descriptor
- Bundles the `.class` files and deployment descriptor into an EJB JAR file

Web Component Developer

A Web component developer performs the following tasks to deliver a WAR file containing the Web component:

- Writes and compiles servlet source code
- Writes JSP and HTML files
- Specifies the deployment descriptor for the Web component
- Bundles the `.class`, `.jsp`, `.html`, and deployment descriptor files in the WAR file

J2EE Application Client Developer

An application client developer performs the following tasks to deliver a JAR file containing the J2EE application client:

- Writes and compiles the source code
- Specifies the deployment descriptor for the client
- Bundles the `.class` files and deployment descriptor into the JAR file

Application Assembler

The application assembler is the company or person who receives application component JAR files from component providers and assembles them into a J2EE application EAR file. The assembler or deployer can edit the deployment descriptor directly or use tools that correctly add XML tags according to interactive selections. A software developer performs the following tasks to deliver an EAR file containing the J2EE application:

- Assembles EJB JAR and WAR files created in the previous phases into a J2EE application (EAR) file
- Specifies the deployment descriptor for the J2EE application
- Verifies that the contents of the EAR file are well formed and comply with the J2EE specification

Application Deployer and Administrator

The application deployer and administrator is the company or person who configures and deploys the J2EE application, administers the computing and networking infrastructure where J2EE applications run, and oversees the runtime environment. Duties include such things as setting transaction controls and security attributes and specifying connections to databases.

During configuration, the deployer follows instructions supplied by the application component provider to resolve external dependencies, specify security settings, and assign transaction attributes. During installation, the deployer moves the application components to the server and generates the container-specific classes and interfaces.

A deployer/system administrator performs the following tasks to install and configure a J2EE application:

- Adds the J2EE application (EAR) file created in the preceding phase to the J2EE server
- Configures the J2EE application for the operational environment by modifying the deployment descriptor of the J2EE application
- Verifies that the contents of the EAR file are well formed and comply with the J2EE specification
- Deploys (installs) the J2EE application EAR file into the J2EE server

Reference Implementation Software

The J2EE SDK is a noncommercial operational definition of the J2EE platform and specification made freely available by Sun Microsystems for demonstrations, prototyping, and educational use. It comes with the J2EE application server, Web server, relational database, J2EE APIs, and complete set of development and deployment tools. You can download the J2EE SDK from

```
http://java.sun.com/j2ee/download.html#sdk
```

The purpose of the J2EE SDK is to allow product providers to determine what their implementations must do under a given set of application conditions, and to run the J2EE Compatibility Test Suite to test that their J2EE products fully comply with the specification. It also allows application component developers to run their J2EE applications on the J2EE SDK to verify that applications are fully portable across all J2EE products and tools.

Database Access

The relational database provides persistent storage for application data. A J2EE implementation is not required to support a particular type of database, which means that the database supported by different J2EE products can vary. See the Release Notes included with the J2EE SDK download for a list of the databases currently supported by the reference implementation.

J2EE APIs

The Java 2 Platform, Standard Edition (J2SE™) SDK is required to run the J2EE SDK and provides core APIs for writing J2EE components, core development tools, and the Java virtual machine. The J2EE SDK provides the following APIs to be used in J2EE applications.

Enterprise JavaBeans Technology 2.0

An *enterprise bean* is a body of code with fields and methods to implement modules of business logic. You can think of an enterprise bean as a building block that can be used alone or with other enterprise beans to execute business logic on the J2EE server.

There are three kinds of enterprise beans: session beans, entity beans, and message-driven beans. Enterprise beans often interact with databases. One of the benefits of entity beans is that you do not have to write any SQL code or use the JDBC™ API directly to perform database access operations; the EJB container handles this for you. However, if you override the default container-managed persistence for any reason, you will need to use the JDBC API. Also, if you choose to have a session bean access the database, you have to use the JDBC API.

JDBC API 2.0

The JDBC API lets you invoke SQL commands from Java programing language methods. You use the JDBC API in an enterprise bean when you override the default container-managed persistence or have a session bean access the database. With container-managed persistence, database access operations are handled by the container, and your enterprise bean implementation contains no JDBC code or SQL commands. You can also use the JDBC API from a servlet or JSP page to access the database directly without going through an enterprise bean.

The JDBC API has two parts: an application-level interface used by the application components to access a database, and a service provider interface to attach a JDBC driver to the J2EE platform.

Java Servlet Technology 2.3

Java Servlet technology lets you define HTTP-specific servlet classes. A servlet class extends the capabilities of servers that host applications accessed by way of a request-response programming model. Although servlets can respond to any type of request, they are commonly used to extend the applications hosted by Web servers.

JavaServer Pages Technology 1.2

JavaServer Pages technology lets you put snippets of servlet code directly into a text-based document. A JSP page is a text-based document that contains two types of text: static template data, which can be expressed in any text-based format such as HTML, WML, and XML, and JSP elements, which determine how the page constructs dynamic content.

Java Message Service 1.0

The JMS is a messaging standard that allows J2EE application components to create, send, receive, and read messages. It enables distributed communication that is loosely coupled, reliable, and asynchronous. For more information on JMS, see the online Java Message Service Tutorial:

```
http://java.sun.com/products/jms/tutorial/index.html
```

Java Naming and Directory Interface 1.2

The JNDI provides naming and directory functionality. It provides applications with methods for performing standard directory operations, such as associating attributes with objects and searching for objects using their attributes. Using JNDI, a J2EE application can store and retrieve any type of named Java object.

Because JNDI is independent of any specific implementations, applications can use JNDI to access multiple naming and directory services, including existing naming and directory services such as LDAP, NDS, DNS, and NIS. This allows J2EE applications to coexist with legacy applications and systems. For more information on JNDI, see the online JNDI Tutorial:

```
http://java.sun.com/products/jndi/tutorial/index.html
```

Java Transaction API 1.0

The Java Transaction API ("JTA") provides a standard interface for demarcating transactions. The J2EE architecture provides a default auto commit to handle transaction commits and rollbacks. An auto commit means that any other applications viewing data will see the updated data after each database read or write operation. However, if your application performs two separate database access operations that depend on each other, you will want to use the JTA API to demarcate where the entire transaction, including both operations, begins, rolls back, and commits.

JavaMail™ API 1.2

J2EE applications can use the JavaMail™ API to send e-mail notifications. The JavaMail API has two parts: an application-level interface used by the application components to send mail, and a service provider interface. The J2EE platform includes JavaMail with a service provider that allows application components to send Internet mail.

JavaBeans Activation Framework 1.0

The JavaBeans Activation Framework ("JAF") is included because JavaMail uses it. It provides standard services to determine the type of an arbitrary piece of data, encapsulate access to it, discover the operations available on it, and create the appropriate JavaBeans component to perform those operations.

Java API for XML Processing 1.1

XML is a language for representing text-based data so the data can be read and handled by any program or tool. Programs and tools can generate XML documents that other programs and tools can read and handle. The Java API for XML Processing ("JAXP") supports processing of XML documents using DOM,

SAX, and XSLT. JAXP enables applications to parse and transform XML documents independent of a particular XML processing implementation.

For example, a J2EE application can use XML to produce reports, and different companies that receive the reports can handle the data in a way that best suits their needs. One company might put the XML data through a program to translate the XML to HTML so it can post the reports to the Web, another company might put the XML data through a tool to create a marketing presentation, and yet another company might read the XML data into its J2EE application for processing.

J2EE Connector Architecture 1.0

The J2EE Connector architecture is used by J2EE tools vendors and system integrators to create resource adapters that support access to enterprise information systems that can be plugged into any J2EE product. A *resource adapter* is a software component that allows J2EE application components to access and interact with the underlying resource manager. Because a resource adapter is specific to its resource manager, there is typically a different resource adapter for each type of database or enterprise information system.

Java Authentication and Authorization Service 1.0

The Java Authentication and Authorization Service ("JAAS") provides a way for a J2EE application to authenticate and authorize a specific user or group of users to run it.

JAAS is a Java programing language version of the standard Pluggable Authentication Module (PAM) framework that extends the Java 2 Platform security architecture to support user-based authorization.

Simplified Systems Integration

The J2EE platform is a platform-independent, full systems integration solution that creates an open marketplace in which every vendor can sell to every customer. Such a marketplace encourages vendors to compete, not by trying to lock customers into their technologies but by trying to outdo each other by providing products and services that benefit customers, such as better performance, better tools, or better customer support.

The J2EE APIs enable systems and applications integration through the following:

- Unified application model across tiers with enterprise beans

- Simplified response and request mechanism with JSP pages and servlets
- Reliable security model with JAAS
- XML-based data interchange integration with JAXP
- Simplified interoperability with the J2EE Connector Architecture
- Easy database connectivity with the JDBC API
- Enterprise application integration with message-driven beans and JMS, JTA, and JNDI

You can learn more about using the J2EE platform to build integrated business systems by reading *J2EE Technology in Practice*:

```
http://java.sun.com/j2ee/inpractice/aboutthebook.html
```

Tools

The J2EE reference implementation provides an application deployment tool and an array of scripts for assembling, verifying, and deploying J2EE applications and managing your development and production environments. See Appendix B for a discussion of the tools.

Application Deployment Tool

The J2EE reference implementation provides an application deployment tool (`deploytool`) for assembling, verifying, and deploying J2EE applications. There are two versions: command line and GUI.

The GUI tool includes wizards for:

- Packaging, configuring, and deploying J2EE applications
- Packaging and configuring enterprise beans
- Packaging and configuring Web components
- Packaging and configuring application clients
- Packaging and configuring resource adaptors

In addition, configuration information can be set for each component and module type in the tabbed inspector panes.

Scripts

Table 1–1 lists the scripts included with the J2EE reference implementation that let you perform operations from the command line.

Table 1–1 J2EE Scripts

Script	Description
`j2ee`	Start and stop the J2EE server
`cloudscape`	Start and stop the default database
`j2eeadmin`	Add JDBC drivers, JMS destinations, and connection factories for various resources
`keytool`	Create public and private keys and generate X509 self-signed certificate
`realmtool`	Import certificate files, add J2EE users to and remove J2EE users from the authentication and authorization list for a J2EE application
`packager`	Package J2EE application components into EAR, EJB JAR, application client JAR, and WAR files
`verifier`	Verify that EAR, EJB JAR, application client JAR, and WAR files are well-formed and comply with the J2EE specification
`runclient`	Run a J2EE application client
`cleanup`	Remove all deployed applications from the J2EE server

2

Getting Started

Dale Green

THIS chapter shows how to develop, deploy, and run a simple client-server application that consists of a currency conversion enterprise bean and two clients: a J2EE application client and a Web client that consists of a JSP page.

In This Chapter

Setting Up

Before you start developing the example application, you should follow the instructions in this section.

Getting the Example Code

The source code for the components is in `j2eetutorial/examples/src/ejb/converter`, a directory that is created when you unzip the tutorial bundle. If you are viewing this tutorial online, you need to download the tutorial bundle from

```
http://java.sun.com/j2ee/download.html#tutorial
```

Getting the Build Tool (ant)

To build the example code, you'll need installations of the J2EE SDK and `ant`, a portable make tool. For more information, see the section How to Build and Run the Examples (page xxii).

Checking the Environment Variables

The installation instructions for the J2EE SDK and `ant` explain how to set the required environment variables. Verify that the environment variables have been set to the values noted in Table 2–1.

Table 2–1 Required Environment Variables

Environment Variable	Value
JAVA_HOME	The location of the J2SE SDK installation
J2EE_HOME	The location of the J2EE SDK installation
ANT_HOME	The location of the `ant` installation
PATH	Should include the `bin` directories of the J2EE SDK, J2SE, and `ant` installations

Starting the J2EE Server

To launch the J2EE server, open a terminal window and type this command:

```
j2ee -verbose
```

Although not required, the `verbose` option is useful for debugging.

To stop the server, type the following command:

```
j2ee -stop
```

Starting the deploytool

The `deploytool` utility has two modes: command line and GUI. The instructions in this chapter refer to the GUI version. To start the `deploytool` GUI, open a terminal window and type this command:

```
deploytool
```

To view the tool's context-sensitive help, press the `F1` key.

Creating the J2EE Application

The sample application contains three J2EE components: an enterprise bean, a J2EE application client, and a Web component. Before building these components, you will create a new J2EE application called `ConverterApp` and will store it in an EAR file named `ConverterApp.ear`.

1. In `deploytool`, select File→New→Application.
2. Click Browse.
3. In the file chooser, navigate to `j2eetutorial/examples/src/ejb/converter`.
4. In the File Name field, enter `ConverterApp.ear`.
5. Click New Application.
6. Click OK.

Creating the Enterprise Bean

An *enterprise bean* is a server-side component that contains the business logic of an application. At runtime, the application clients execute the business logic by invoking the enterprise bean's methods. The enterprise bean in our example is a stateless session bean called `ConverterEJB`. The source code for `ConverterEJB` is in the `j2eetutorial/examples/src/ejb/converter` directory.

Coding the Enterprise Bean

The enterprise bean in this example requires the following code:

- Remote interface
- Home interface
- Enterprise bean class

Coding the Remote Interface

A *remote interface* defines the business methods that a client may call. The business methods are implemented in the enterprise bean code. The source code for the `Converter` remote interface follows.

```
import javax.ejb.EJBObject;
import java.rmi.RemoteException;
import java.math.*;
```

```
public interface Converter extends EJBObject {
   public BigDecimal dollarToYen(BigDecimal dollars)
      throws RemoteException;
   public BigDecimal yenToEuro(BigDecimal yen)
      throws RemoteException;
}
```

Coding the Home Interface

A *home interface* defines the methods that allow a client to create, find, or remove an enterprise bean. The ConverterHome interface contains a single create method, which returns an object of the remote interface type. Here is the source code for the ConverterHome interface:

```
import java.io.Serializable;
import java.rmi.RemoteException;
import javax.ejb.CreateException;
import javax.ejb.EJBHome;

public interface ConverterHome extends EJBHome {
   Converter create() throws RemoteException, CreateException;
}
```

Coding the Enterprise Bean Class

The enterprise bean class for this example is called ConverterBean. This class implements the two business methods, dollarToYen and yenToEuro, that the Converter remote interface defines. The source code for the ConverterBean class follows.

```
import java.rmi.RemoteException;
import javax.ejb.SessionBean;
import javax.ejb.SessionContext;
import java.math.*;

public class ConverterBean implements SessionBean {

   BigDecimal yenRate = new BigDecimal("121.6000");
   BigDecimal euroRate = new BigDecimal("0.0077");

   public BigDecimal dollarToYen(BigDecimal dollars) {
      BigDecimal result = dollars.multiply(yenRate);
      return result.setScale(2,BigDecimal.ROUND_UP);
   }

   public BigDecimal yenToEuro(BigDecimal yen) {
      BigDecimal result = yen.multiply(euroRate);
```

```
        return result.setScale(2,BigDecimal.ROUND_UP);
    }

    public ConverterBean() {}
    public void ejbCreate() {}
    public void ejbRemove() {}
    public void ejbActivate() {}
    public void ejbPassivate() {}
    public void setSessionContext(SessionContext sc) {}
}
```

Compiling the Source Files

Now you are ready to compile the remote interface (`Converter.java`), home interface (`ConverterHome.java`), and the enterprise bean class (`ConverterBean.java`).

1. In a terminal window, go to the `j2eetutorial/examples` directory.
2. Type the following command:

```
ant converter
```

This command compiles the source files for the enterprise bean and the J2EE application client. It places the resulting class files in the `j2eetutorial/examples/`**`build`**`/ejb/converter` directory (not the `src` directory). For more information about `ant`, see How to Build and Run the Examples (page xxii).

Note: When compiling the code, the preceding `ant` task includes the `j2ee.jar` file in the classpath. This file resides in the `lib` directory of your J2EE SDK installation. If you plan on using other tools to compile the source code for J2EE components, make sure that the classpath includes the `j2ee.jar` file.

Packaging the Enterprise Bean

To package an enterprise bean, you run the New Enterprise Bean wizard of the `deploytool` utility. During this process, the wizard performs the following tasks:

- Creates the bean's deployment descriptor
- Packages the deployment descriptor and the bean's classes in an EJB JAR file
- Inserts the EJB JAR file into the application's `ConverterApp.ear` file

After the packaging process, you can view the deployment descriptor by selecting Tools→Descriptor Viewer.

To start the New Enterprise Bean wizard, select File→New→Enterprise Bean. The wizard displays the following dialog boxes.

1. Introduction dialog box
   a. Read the explanatory text for an overview of the wizard's features.
   b. Click Next.
2. EJB JAR dialog box
   a. Select the Create New JAR File In Application button.
   b. In the combo box, select `ConverterApp`.
   c. In the JAR Display Name field, enter `ConverterJAR`.
   d. Click Edit.
   e. In the tree under Available Files, locate the `j2eetutorial/examples/build/ejb/converter` directory. (If the `converter` directory is many levels down in the tree, you can simplify the tree view by entering all or part of the `converter` directory's path name in the Starting Directory field.)
   f. Select the following classes from the Available Files tree and click Add: `Converter.class`, `ConverterBean.class`, and `ConverterHome.class`. (You may also drag and drop these class files to the Contents text area.)
   g. Click OK.
   h. Click Next.
3. General dialog box
   a. Under Bean Type, select the Session radio button.
   b. Select the Stateless radio button.
   c. In the Enterprise Bean Class combo box, select `ConverterBean`.
   d. In the Enterprise Bean Name field, enter `ConverterEJB`.
   e. In the Remote Home Interface combo box, select `ConverterHome`.
   f. In the Remote Interface combo box, select `Converter`.
   g. Click Next.
4. Transaction Management dialog box
   a. Because you may skip the remaining dialog boxes, click Finish.

Creating the J2EE Application Client

A J2EE application client is a program written in the Java programming language. At runtime, the client program executes in a different virtual machine than the J2EE server.

The J2EE application client in this example requires two different JAR files. The first JAR file is for the J2EE component of the client. This JAR file contains the client's deployment descriptor and its class files. When you run the New Application Client wizard, the `deploytool` utility automatically creates the JAR file and stores it in the application's EAR file. Defined by the J2EE Specification, the JAR file is portable across all compliant J2EE servers.

The second JAR file contains stub classes that are required by the client program at runtime. These stub classes enable the client to access the enterprise beans that are running in the J2EE server. Because this second JAR file is not covered by the *J2EE Specification*, it is implementation specific, intended only for the J2EE SDK.

The J2EE application client source code is in `j2eetutorial/examples/src/ejb/converter/ConverterClient.java`. You already compiled this code along with the enterprise bean code in the section Compiling the Source Files (page 26).

Coding the J2EE Application Client

The `ConverterClient.java` source code illustrates the basic tasks performed by the client of an enterprise bean:

- Locating the home interface
- Creating an enterprise bean instance
- Invoking a business method

Locating the Home Interface

The `ConverterHome` interface defines life-cycle methods such as `create`. Before the `ConverterClient` can invoke the `create` method, it must locate and instantiate an object whose type is `ConverterHome`. This is a four-step process.

1. Create an initial naming context.

```
Context initial = new InitialContext();
```

The `Context` interface is part of the Java Naming and Directory Interface (JNDI). A *naming context* is a set of name-to-object bindings. A name that is bound within a context is the *JNDI name* of the object.

An `InitialContext` object, which implements the `Context` interface, provides the starting point for the resolution of names. All naming operations are relative to a context.

2. Obtain the environment naming context of the application client.

```
Context myEnv = (Context)initial.lookup("java:comp/env");
```

The `java:comp/env` name is bound to the environment naming context of the `ConverterClient` component.

3. Retrieve the object bound to the name `ejb/SimpleConverter`.

```
Object objref = myEnv.lookup("ejb/SimpleConverter");
```

The `ejb/SimpleConverter` name is bound to an *enterprise bean reference*, a logical name for the home of an enterprise bean. In this case, the `ejb/SimpleConverter` name refers to the `ConverterHome` object. The names of enterprise beans should reside in the `java:com/env/ejb` subcontext.

4. Narrow the reference to a `ConverterHome` object.

```
ConverterHome home =
   (ConverterHome) PortableRemoteObject.narrow(objref,
      ConverterHome.class);
```

Creating an Enterprise Bean Instance

To create the bean instance, the client invokes the `create` method on the `ConverterHome` object. The `create` method returns an object whose type is `Converter`. The remote `Converter` interface defines the business methods of the bean that the client may call. When the client invokes the `create` method, the EJB container instantiates the bean and then invokes the `ConverterBean.ejbCreate` method. The client invokes the `create` method as follows:

```
Converter currencyConverter = home.create();
```

Invoking a Business Method

Calling a business method is easy—you simply invoke the method on the `Converter` object. The EJB container will invoke the corresponding method on the `ConverterEJB` instance that is running on the server. The client invokes the `dollarToYen` business method in the following lines of code.

```
BigDecimal param = new BigDecimal ("100.00");
BigDecimal amount = currencyConverter.dollarToYen(param);
```

ConverterClient Source Code

The full source code for the `ConverterClient` program follows.

```
import javax.naming.Context;
import javax.naming.InitialContext;
import javax.rmi.PortableRemoteObject;
import java.math.BigDecimal;

public class ConverterClient {

   public static void main(String[] args) {

      try {
         Context initial = new InitialContext();
         Object objref = initial.lookup
            ("java:comp/env/ejb/SimpleConverter");

         ConverterHome home =
            (ConverterHome)PortableRemoteObject.narrow(objref,
                                       ConverterHome.class);

         Converter currencyConverter = home.create();

         BigDecimal param = new BigDecimal ("100.00");
         BigDecimal amount =
            currencyConverter.dollarToYen(param);
         System.out.println(amount);
         amount = currencyConverter.yenToEuro(param);
         System.out.println(amount);

         System.exit(0);

      } catch (Exception ex) {
         System.err.println("Caught an unexpected exception!");
```

```
            ex.printStackTrace();
        }
    }
}
```

Compiling the Application Client

The application client files are compiled at the same time as the enterprise bean files, as described in Compiling the Source Files (page 26).

Packaging the J2EE Application Client

To package an application client component, you run the New Application Client wizard of the `deploytool`. During this process the wizard performs the following tasks.

- Creates the application client's deployment descriptor
- Puts the deployment descriptor and client files into a JAR file
- Adds the JAR file to the application's `ConverterApp.ear` file

After the packaging process you can view the deployment descriptor by selecting Tools→Descriptor Viewer.

To start the New Application Client wizard, select File→New→Application Client. The wizard displays the following dialog boxes.

1. Introduction dialog box
   a. Read the explanatory text for an overview of the wizard's features.
   b. Click Next.
2. JAR File Contents dialog box
   a. In the combo box, select `ConverterApp`.
   b. Click Edit.
   c. In the tree under Available Files, locate the `j2eetutorial/examples/build/ejb/converter` directory.
   d. Select the `ConverterClient.class` file and click Add.
   e. Click OK.
   f. Click Next.
3. General dialog box
   a. In the Main Class combo box, select `ConverterClient`.
   b. Verify that the entry in the Display Name field is `ConverterClient`.

c. In the Callback Handler Class combo box, select container-managed authentication.
d. Click Next.
e. Click Finish.

Specifying the Application Client's Enterprise Bean Reference

When it invokes the `lookup` method, the `ConverterClient` refers to the home of an enterprise bean:

```
Object objref = myEnv.lookup("ejb/SimpleConverter");
```

You specify this reference as follows.

1. In the tree, select `ConverterClient`.
2. Select the EJB Refs tab.
3. Click Add.
4. In the Coded Name column, enter `ejb/SimpleConverter`.
5. In the Type column, select Session.
6. In the Interfaces column, select Remote.
7. In the Home Interface column, enter `ConverterHome`.
8. In the Local/Remote Interface column, enter `Converter`.

Creating the Web Client

The Web client is contained in the JSP page `j2eetutorial/examples/src/ejb/converter/index.jsp`. A JSP page is a text-based document that contains static template data, which can be expressed in any text-based format such as HTML, WML, and XML; and JSP elements, which construct dynamic content.

Coding the Web Client

The statements (in bold in the following code) for locating the home interface, creating an enterprise bean instance, and invoking a business method are nearly identical to those of the J2EE application client. The parameter of the `lookup` method is the only difference; the motivation for using a different name is discussed in Specifying the JNDI Names (page 35).

The classes needed by the client are declared with a JSP `page` directive (enclosed within the `<%@ %>` characters). Because locating the home interface and creating the enterprise bean are performed only once, this code appears in a JSP declaration (enclosed within the `<%! %>` characters) that contains the initialization method, `jspInit`, of the JSP page. The declaration is followed by standard HTML markup for creating a form with an input field. A scriptlet (enclosed within the `<% %>` characters) retrieves a parameter from the request and converts it to a `BigDecimal` object. Finally, JSP expressions (enclosed within `<%= %>` characters) invoke the enterprise bean's business methods and insert the result into the stream of data returned to the client.

```
<%@ page import="Converter,ConverterHome,javax.ejb.*,
javax.naming.*, javax.rmi.PortableRemoteObject,
java.rmi.RemoteException" %>
<%!
   private Converter converter = null;
   public void jspInit() {
      try {
         InitialContext ic = new InitialContext();
         Object objRef = ic.lookup("
            java:comp/env/ejb/TheConverter");
         ConverterHome home =
         (ConverterHome)PortableRemoteObject.narrow(
         objRef, ConverterHome.class);
         converter = home.create();
      } catch (RemoteException ex) {
         ...
      }
   }
   ...
%>
<html>
<head>
    <title>Converter</title>
</head>

<body bgcolor="white">
<h1><center>Converter</center></h1>
<hr>
<p>Enter an amount to convert:</p>
<form method="get">
<input type="text" name="amount" size="25">
<br>
<p>
<input type="submit" value="Submit">
<input type="reset" value="Reset">
```

```
</form>
<%
   String amount = request.getParameter("amount");
   if ( amount != null && amount.length() > 0 ) {
      BigDecimal d = new BigDecimal (amount);
%>
   <p><%= amount %> dollars are
      <%= converter.dollarToYen(d) %>  Yen.
   <p><%= amount %> Yen are
      <%= converter.yenToEuro(d) %>  Euro.
<%
    }
%>
</body>
</html>
```

Compiling the Web Client

The J2EE server automatically compiles Web clients that are JSP pages. If the Web client were a servlet, you would have to compile it.

Packaging the Web Client

To package a Web client, you run the New Web Component wizard of the `deploytool` utility. During this process the wizard performs the following tasks.

- Creates the Web application deployment descriptor
- Adds the component files to a WAR file
- Adds the WAR file to the application's `ConverterApp.ear` file

After the packaging process, you can view the deployment descriptor by selecting Tools→Descriptor Viewer.

To start the New Web Component wizard, select File→New→Web Component. The wizard displays the following dialog boxes.

1. Introduction dialog box
   a. Read the explanatory text for an overview of the wizard's features.
   b. Click Next.
2. WAR File dialog box
   a. Select Create New WAR File In Application.
   a. In the combo box, select `ConverterApp`.
   b. In the WAR Display Name field, enter `ConverterWAR`.

c. Click Edit.
d. In the tree under Available Files, locate the `j2eetutorial/examples/build/ejb/converter` directory.
e. Select `index.jsp` and click Add.
f. Click OK.
g. Click Next.

3. Choose Component Type dialog box
   a. Select the JSP radio button.
   b. Click Next.
4. Component General Properties dialog box
   a. In the JSP Filename combo box, select `index.jsp`.
   b. Click Finish.

Specifying the Web Client's Enterprise Bean Reference

When it invokes the `lookup` method, the Web client refers to the home of an enterprise bean:

```
Object objRef = ic.lookup("java:comp/env/ejb/TheConverter");
```

You specify this reference as follows:

1. In the tree, select `ConverterWAR`.
2. Select the EJB Refs tab.
3. Click Add.
4. In the Coded Name column, enter `ejb/TheConverter`.
5. In the Type column, select Session.
6. In the Interfaces column, select Remote.
7. In the Home Interface column, enter `ConverterHome`.
8. In the Local/Remote Interface column, enter `Converter`.

Specifying the JNDI Names

Although the J2EE application client and the Web client access the same enterprise bean, their code refers to the bean's home by different names. The J2EE application client refers to the bean's home as `ejb/SimpleConverter`, but the Web client refers to it as `ejb/TheConverter`. These references are in the parameters of the `lookup` calls. In order for the `lookup` method to retrieve the home object, you must map the references in the code to the enterprise bean's JNDI name. Although this mapping adds a level of indirection, it decouples the clients from the beans, making it easier to assemble applications from J2EE components.

To map the enterprise bean references in the clients to the JNDI name of the bean, follow these steps.

1. In the tree, select `ConverterApp`.
2. Select the JNDI Names tab.
3. To specify a JNDI name for the bean, in the Application table locate the ConverterEJB component and enter `MyConverter` in the JNDI Name column.
4. To map the references, in the References table enter `MyConverter` in the JNDI Name for each row.

Figure 2–1 shows what the JNDI Names tab should look like after you've performed the preceding steps.

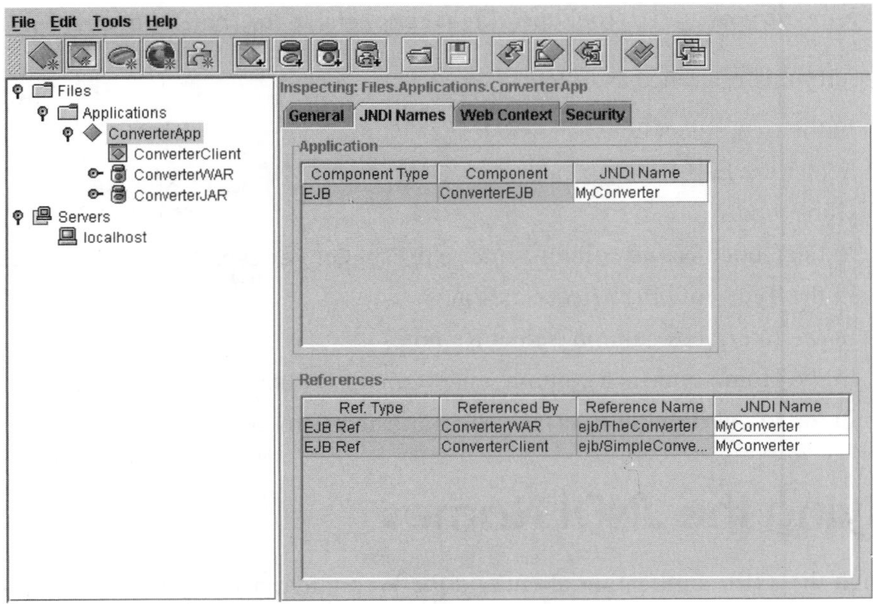

Figure 2–1 ConverterApp JNDI Names

Deploying the J2EE Application

Now that the J2EE application contains the components, it is ready for deployment.

1. Select the `ConverterApp` application.
2. Select Tools→Deploy.
3. In the Introduction dialog box, confirm that `ConverterApp` is shown for the Object To Deploy and that `localhost` is shown for the Target Server.
4. Select the checkbox labeled Return Client Jar.
5. In the text field that appears, enter the full path name for the file `ConverterAppClient.jar` so that it will reside in the `j2eetutorial/examples/src/ejb/converter` subdirectory. The `ConverterAppClient.jar` file contains the stub classes that enable remote access to `ConverterEJB`.
6. Click Next.
7. In the JNDI Names dialog box, verify the names you entered in the previous section.
8. Click Next.
9. In the WAR Context Root dialog box, enter `converter` in the Context Root field. When you run the Web client, the `converter` context root will be part of the URL.
10. Click Next.
11. In the Review dialog box, click Finish.
12. In the Deployment Progress dialog box, click OK when the deployment completes.

Running the J2EE Application Client

To run the J2EE application client, perform the following steps.

1. In a terminal window, go to the `j2eetutorial/examples/src/ejb/converter` directory.
2. Verify that this directory contains the `ConverterApp.ear` and `ConverterAppClient.jar` files.
3. Set the `APPCPATH` environment variable to `ConverterAppClient.jar`.

4. Type the following command (on a single line):

```
runclient -client ConverterApp.ear -name ConverterClient
-textauth
```

5. The client container prompts you to log in. Enter `guest` for the user name and `guest123` for the password.
6. In the terminal window, the client displays these lines:

```
Binding name:'java:comp/env/ejb/SimpleConverter'
12160.00
0.77
Unbinding name:'java:comp/env/ejb/SimpleConverter'
```

Running the Web Client

To run the Web client, point your browser at the following URL. Replace *<host>* with the name of the host running the J2EE server. If your browser is running on the same host as the J2EE server, you may replace *<host>* with `localhost`.

```
http://<host>:8000/converter
```

You should see the screen shown in Figure 2–2 after entering `100` in the input field and clicking Submit.

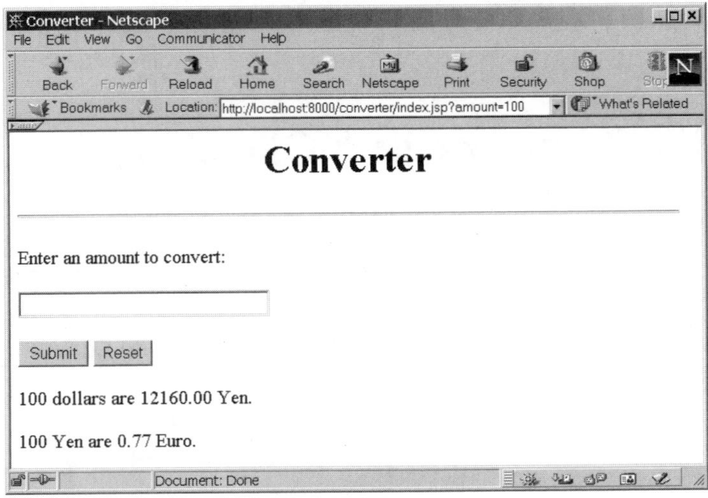

Figure 2–2 Converter Web Client

Modifying the J2EE Application

Since the J2EE SDK is intended for experimentation, it supports iterative development. Whenever you make a change to a J2EE application, you must redeploy the application.

Modifying a Class File

To modify a class file in an enterprise bean, you change the source code, recompile it, and redeploy the application. For example, if you want to change the exchange rate in the `dollarToYen` business method of the `ConverterBean` class, you would follow these steps.

1. Edit `ConverterBean.java`.
2. Recompile `ConverterBean.java` by typing `ant converter`.
3. In `deploytool`, select Tools→Update Files.
4. The Update Files dialog box appears. If the modified files are listed at the top of the dialog, click OK and go to step 6. If the files are listed at the bottom, they have not been found. Select one of those files and click Edit Search Paths.
5. In the Edit Search Paths dialog, specify the directories where the Update Files dialog will search for modified files.
   a. In the Search Root field, enter the fully-qualified name of the directory from which the search will start.
   b. In the Path Directory list, add a row for each directory that you want searched. Unless fully-qualified, these directory names are relative to the Search Root field.
   c. Click OK.
6. Select Tools→Deploy. Make sure the checkbox labeled Save Object Before Deploying is checked. If you do not want to deploy at this time, select Tools→Save to save the search paths specified in step 5.

As a shortcut, you can select Tools→Update And Redeploy. With this shortcut, the Update Files dialog box does not appear unless the files are not found.

To modify the contents of a WAR file you follow the preceding steps. The Update Files operation checks to see if any files have changed, including HTML files and JSP pages. If you change the `index.jsp` file of `ConverterApp`, be sure to type `ant converter`. The `converter` task copies the `index.jsp` file from the `src` to the `build` directory.

Adding a File

To add a file to the EJB JAR or WAR of the application, perform these steps.

1. In `deploytool`, select the JAR or WAR in the tree.
2. Select the General tab.
3. Click Edit.
4. In the tree of the Available Files field, locate the file and click Add.
5. Click OK.
6. From the main toolbar, select Tools→Update And Redeploy.

Modifying a Deployment Setting

To modify a deployment setting of `ConverterApp`, you edit the appropriate field in a tabbed pane and redeploy the application. For example, to change the JNDI name of the `ConverterBean` from `ATypo` to `MyConverter`, you would follow these steps.

1. In `deploytool`, select `ConverterApp` in the tree.
2. Select the JNDI Names tab.
3. In the JNDI Name field, enter `MyConverter`.
4. From the main toolbar, select File→Save.
5. Select Tools→Update And Redeploy.

Common Problems and Their Solutions

Cannot Start the J2EE Server

Naming and Directory Service Port Conflict

Symptom: When you start the J2EE server with the `-verbose` option, it displays these lines:

```
J2EE server listen port: 1050
RuntimeException: Could not initialize server...
```

Solution: Another process is using port 1050. If the J2EE server is already running, you can stop it by typing `j2ee -stop`. If some other program is using the port, then you can change the default port number (1050) by editing the `config/orb.properties` file of your J2EE SDK installation.

For more information about default port numbers, see the Configuration Guide in the download bundle of the J2EE SDK.

Web Service Port Conflict

Symptom: When you start the J2EE server with the `-verbose` option, it displays these lines:

```
LifecycleException: HttpConnector[8000].open:
java.net.BindException: Address in use...
```

Solution: Another process is using port 8000. You can change the default port number (8000) by editing the `config/web.properties` file of your J2EE SDK installation.

Incorrect XML Parser

Symptom: When you start the J2EE server with the `-verbose` option, it displays these lines:

```
Exception in thread "main"
javax.xml.parsers.FactoryConfigurationError:
org.apache.xerces.jaxp.SAXParserFactoryImpl at ...
```

Solution: Remove the `jre/lib/jaxp.properties` file from your J2SE installation.

Compilation Errors

ant Cannot Locate the Build File

Symptom: When you type `ant converter`, these messages appear:

```
Buildfile: build.xml does not exist!
Build failed.
```

Solution: Before running `ant`, go to the `j2eetutorial/examples/src` directory. If you want to run `ant` from your current directory, you must specify the build file on the command line. For example, on Windows you would type this command on a single line:

```
ant -buildfile C:\j2eetutorial\examples\src\build.xml
  converter
```

The Compiler Cannot Resolve Symbols

Symptom: When you type `ant converter`, the compiler reports many errors, including these:

```
cannot resolve symbol
...
BUILD FAILED
...
Compile failed, messages should have been provided
```

Solution: Make sure that you've set the J2EE_HOME environment variable correctly. See Checking the Environment Variables (page 23).

ant 1.4 Will Not Compile the Example after You Run the Client

Symptom: ant 1.4 displays this error:

```
The filename, directory name, or volume label syntax is
incorrect.
```

Solution: Use version 1.3 of `ant`. The 1.4 version of the `ant.bat` script and the scripts of the J2EE SDK all use the `JAVACMD` environment variable. The SDK's `runclient.bat` script, for example, sets `JAVACMD` to a value that causes problems for `ant.bat`.

Deployment Errors

The Incorrect XML Parser Is in Your Classpath

Symptom: The error displayed has the following text:

```
...
[]java.rmi.RemoteException:Error saving/opening

Deployment Error:Bad mapping of key{0}  class{1},
not found: com.sum.enterprise.deployment.xml.ApplicationNode
```

Solution: Remove the `jaxp.jar` file from the `jre/lib/ext` directory of your J2SE installation. This JAR file contains XML parsing routines that are incompatible with the J2EE server. If you do not have a `jaxp.jar` file, then perhaps your classpath refers to the XML routines of a Tomcat installation. In this case, you should remove that reference from your classpath.

The Remote Home Interface Was Specified as a Local Home Interface

Symptom: An error such as the following is displayed:

```
LocalHomeImpl must be declared abstract.
It does not define javax.ejb.HomeHandle getHomeHandle()
from interface javax.ejb.EJBHome.
```

Solution: Remove the enterprise bean from the EAR file (Edit→Delete) and create a new bean with the New Enterprise Bean wizard. In the General dialog box of the wizard, select values from the Remote Home Interface and Remote Interface combo boxes.

J2EE Application Client Runtime Errors

The Client Throws a NoClassDefFoundError

Symptom: The client reports this exception:

```
java.lang.NoClassDefFoundError:converter.ConverterHome
```

Solution: This error occurs if the client cannot find the classes in the `ConverterAppClient.jar` file. Make sure that you've correctly followed the steps outlined in Running the J2EE Application Client (page 37).

The Client Cannot Find ConverterApp.ear

Symptom: The client reports this exception:

```
IOException: ConverterApp.ear does not exist
```

Solution: Ensure that the `ConverterApp.ear` file exists and that you've specified it with the `-client` option:

```
runclient -client ConverterApp.ear -name ConverterClient
```

You created the `ConverterApp.ear` file in the section Creating the J2EE Application (page 24). See also the section Running the J2EE Application Client (page 37).

The Client Cannot Find the ConverterClient Component

Symptom: The client displays this line:

```
No application client descriptors defined for: ...
```

Solution: Verify that you've created the `ConverterClient` component and that you've specified it for the `-name` option of the `runclient` command. You created the `ConverterClient` component in the section Packaging the J2EE Application Client (page 31).

The Login Failed

Symptom: After you log in, the client displays this line:

```
Incorrect login and/or password
```

Solution: At the login prompts, enter `guest` as the user name and `guest123` as the password.

The J2EE Application Has Not Been Deployed

Symptom: The client reports the following exception:

```
NameNotFoundException. Root exception is org.omg.CosNaming...
```

Solution: Deploy the application. For instructions, see Deploying the J2EE Application (page 37).

The JNDI Name Is Incorrect

Symptom: The client reports the following exception:

```
NameNotFoundException. Root exception is org.omg.CosNaming...
```

Solution: In the JNDI Names tabbed pane of the `ConverterApp`, make sure that the JNDI names for the `ConverterBean` and the `ejb/SimpleConverter` match. Edit the appropriate JNDI Name field and then redeploy the application.

Web Client Runtime Errors

The Web Context in the URL Is Incorrect

Symptom: The browser reports that the page cannot be found (HTTP 404).

Solution: Verify that the Web context (`converter`) in the URL matches the one you specified in the Component General Properties dialog box (see the section Packaging the Web Client, page 34). The case (upper or lower) of the Web context *is* significant.

The J2EE Application Has Not Been Deployed

Symptom: The browser reports that the page cannot be found (HTTP 404).

Solution: Deploy the application.

The JNDI Name Is Incorrect

Symptom: When you click Submit on the Web page, the browser reports

```
A Servlet Exception Has Occurred.
```

Solution: In the JNDI Names tabbed pane of the `ConverterApp`, make sure that the JNDI names for the `ConverterBean` and the `ConverterWAR` match. Edit the appropriate JNDI Name field and then redeploy the application.

Detecting Problems With the Verifier Tool

The verifier tool (`verifier`) can detect inconsistencies in deployment descriptors and method signatures. These inconsistencies often cause deployment or runtime errors. From `deploytool`, you can run the GUI version of `verifier` by selecting Tools→Verifier. You can also run a stand-alone GUI or command-line version of `verifier`. For more information, see Appendix B.

Comparing Your EAR Files with Ours

For most of the examples, the download bundle of the tutorial includes J2EE application EAR files, which are located in the `j2eetutorial/examples/ears` directory.

When All Else Fails

If none of these suggestions fixes the problem, you can uninstall the application and clean out the server's repository by running the `cleanup` script. You'll also need to shut down and restart the server:

```
j2ee -stop
cleanup
j2ee -verbose
```

3

Enterprise Beans

Dale Green

ENTERPRISE beans are the J2EE components that implement Enterprise JavaBeans (EJB) technology. Enterprise beans run in the EJB container, a runtime environment within the J2EE server (see Figure 1–5, page 10). Although transparent to the application developer, the EJB container provides system-level services such as transactions to its enterprise beans. These services enable you to quickly build and deploy enterprise beans, which form the core of transactional J2EE applications.

In This Chapter

What Is an Enterprise Bean?

Written in the Java programming language, an *enterprise bean* is a server-side component that encapsulates the business logic of an application. The business logic is the code that fulfills the purpose of the application. In an inventory control application, for example, the enterprise beans might implement the business logic in methods called `checkInventoryLevel` and `orderProduct`. By invoking these methods, remote clients can access the inventory services provided by the application.

Benefits of Enterprise Beans

For several reasons, enterprise beans simplify the development of large, distributed applications. First, because the EJB container provides system-level services to enterprise beans, the bean developer can concentrate on solving business problems. The EJB container—not the bean developer—is responsible for system-level services such as transaction management and security authorization.

Second, because the beans—and not the clients—contain the application's business logic, the client developer can focus on the presentation of the client. The client developer does not have to code the routines that implement business rules or access databases. As a result, the clients are thinner, a benefit that is particularly important for clients that run on small devices.

Third, because enterprise beans are portable components, the application assembler can build new applications from existing beans. These applications can run on any compliant J2EE server.

When to Use Enterprise Beans

You should consider using enterprise beans if your application has any of the following requirements:

- The application must be scalable. To accommodate a growing number of users, you may need to distribute an application's components across multiple machines. Not only can the enterprise beans of an application run on different machines, but their location will remain transparent to the clients.
- Transactions are required to ensure data integrity. Enterprise beans support transactions, the mechanisms that manage the concurrent access of shared objects.
- The application will have a variety of clients. With just a few lines of code, remote clients can easily locate enterprise beans. These clients can be thin, various, and numerous.

Types of Enterprise Beans

Table 3–1 summarizes the three different types of enterprise beans. The following sections discuss each type in more detail.

Table 3–1 Summary of Enterprise Bean Types

Enterprise Bean Type	Purpose
Session	Performs a task for a client
Entity	Represents a business entity object that exists in persistent storage
Message-Driven	Acts as a listener for the Java Message Service API, processing messages asynchronously

What Is a Session Bean?

A *session bean* represents a single client inside the J2EE server. To access an application that is deployed on the server, the client invokes the session bean's methods. The session bean performs work for its client, shielding the client from complexity by executing business tasks inside the server.

As its name suggests, a session bean is similar to an interactive session. A session bean is not shared—it may have just one client, in the same way that an interactive session may have just one user. Like an interactive session, a session bean is not persistent. (That is, its data is not saved to a database.) When the client terminates, its session bean appears to terminate and is no longer associated with the client.

For code samples, see Chapter 4.

State Management Modes

There are two types of session beans: stateful and stateless.

Stateful Session Beans

The state of an object consists of the values of its instance variables. In a stateful session bean, the instance variables represent the state of a unique client-bean session. Because the client interacts ("talks") with its bean, this state is often called the *conversational state*.

The state is retained for the duration of the client-bean session. If the client removes the bean or terminates, the session ends and the state disappears. This transient nature of the state is not a problem, however, because when the conversation between the client and the bean ends there is no need to retain the state.

Stateless Session Beans

A stateless session bean does not maintain a conversational state for a particular client. When a client invokes the method of a stateless bean, the bean's instance variables may contain a state, but only for the duration of the invocation. When the method is finished, the state is no longer retained. Except during method invocation, all instances of a stateless bean are equivalent, allowing the EJB container to assign an instance to any client.

Because stateless session beans can support multiple clients, they can offer better scalability for applications that require large numbers of clients. Typically, an application requires fewer stateless session beans than stateful session beans to support the same number of clients.

At times, the EJB container may write a stateful session bean to secondary storage. However, stateless session beans are never written to secondary storage. Therefore, stateless beans may offer better performance than stateful beans.

When to Use Session Beans

In general, you should use a session bean if the following circumstances hold:

- At any given time, only one client has access to the bean instance.
- The state of the bean is not persistent, existing only for a short period of time (perhaps a few hours).

Stateful session beans are appropriate if any of the following conditions are true:

- The bean's state represents the interaction between the bean and a specific client.
- The bean needs to hold information about the client across method invocations.
- The bean mediates between the client and the other components of the application, presenting a simplified view to the client.
- Behind the scenes, the bean manages the work flow of several enterprise beans. For an example, see the `AccountControllerEJB` session bean in Chapter 18.

To improve performance, you might choose a stateless session bean if it has any of these traits:

- The bean's state has no data for a specific client.
- In a single method invocation, the bean performs a generic task for all clients. For example, you might use a stateless session bean to send an e-mail that confirms an online order.
- The bean fetches from a database a set of read-only data that is often used by clients. Such a bean, for example, could retrieve the table rows that represent the products that are on sale this month.

What Is an Entity Bean?

An *entity bean* represents a business object in a persistent storage mechanism. Some examples of business objects are customers, orders, and products. In the J2EE SDK, the persistent storage mechanism is a relational database. Typically, each entity bean has an underlying table in a relational database, and each instance of the bean corresponds to a row in that table. For code examples of entity beans, please refer to Chapters 5 and 6.

What Makes Entity Beans Different from Session Beans?

Entity beans differ from session beans in several ways. Entity beans are persistent, allow shared access, have primary keys, and may participate in relationships with other entity beans.

Persistence

Because the state of an entity bean is saved in a storage mechanism, it is persistent. *Persistence* means that the entity bean's state exists beyond the lifetime of the application or the J2EE server process. If you've worked with databases, you're familiar with persistent data. The data in a database is persistent because it still exists even after you shut down the database server or the applications it services.

There are two types of persistence for entity beans: bean-managed and container-managed. With *bean-managed persistence*, the entity bean code that you write contains the calls that access the database. If your bean has container-managed persistence, the EJB container automatically generates the necessary database access calls. The code that you write for the entity bean does not include these calls. For additional information, see the section Container-Managed Persistence (page 53).

Shared Access

Entity beans may be shared by multiple clients. Because the clients might want to change the same data, it's important that entity beans work within transactions. Typically, the EJB container provides transaction management. In this case, you specify the transaction attributes in the bean's deployment descriptor. You do not have to code the transaction boundaries in the bean—the container marks the boundaries for you. See Chapter 14 for more information.

Primary Key

Each entity bean has a unique object identifier. A customer entity bean, for example, might be identified by a customer number. The unique identifier, or *primary key*, enables the client to locate a particular entity bean. For more information see the section Primary Keys for Bean-Managed Persistence (page 113).

Relationships

Like a table in a relational database, an entity bean may be related to other entity beans. For example, in a college enrollment application, `StudentEJB` and `CourseEJB` would be related because students enroll in classes.

You implement relationships differently for entity beans with bean-managed persistence and those with container-managed persistence. With bean-managed persistence, the code that you write implements the relationships. But with container-managed persistence, the EJB container takes care of the relationships for you. For this reason, relationships in entity beans with container-managed persistence are often referred to as *container-managed relationships*.

Container-Managed Persistence

The term *container-managed persistence* means that the EJB container handles all database access required by the entity bean. The bean's code contains no database access (SQL) calls. As a result, the bean's code is not tied to a specific persistent storage mechanism (database). Because of this flexibility, even if you redeploy the same entity bean on different J2EE servers that use different databases, you won't need to modify or recompile the bean's code. In short, your entity beans are more portable.

In order to generate the data access calls, the container needs information that you provide in the entity bean's abstract schema.

Abstract Schema

Part of an entity bean's deployment descriptor, the *abstract schema* defines the bean's persistent fields and relationships. The term *abstract* distinguishes this schema from the physical schema of the underlying data store. In a relational database, for example, the physical schema is made up of structures such as tables and columns.

You specify the name of an abstract schema in the deployment descriptor. This name is referenced by queries written in the Enterprise JavaBeans Query Language ("EJB QL"). For an entity bean with container-managed persistence, you must define an EJB QL query for every finder method (except `findByPrimaryKey`). The EJB QL query determines the query that is executed by the EJB container when the finder method is invoked. To learn more about EJB QL, see Chapter 8.

You'll probably find it helpful to sketch the abstract schema before writing any code. Figure 3–1 represents a simple abstract schema that describes the relationships between three entity beans. These relationships are discussed further in the sections that follow.

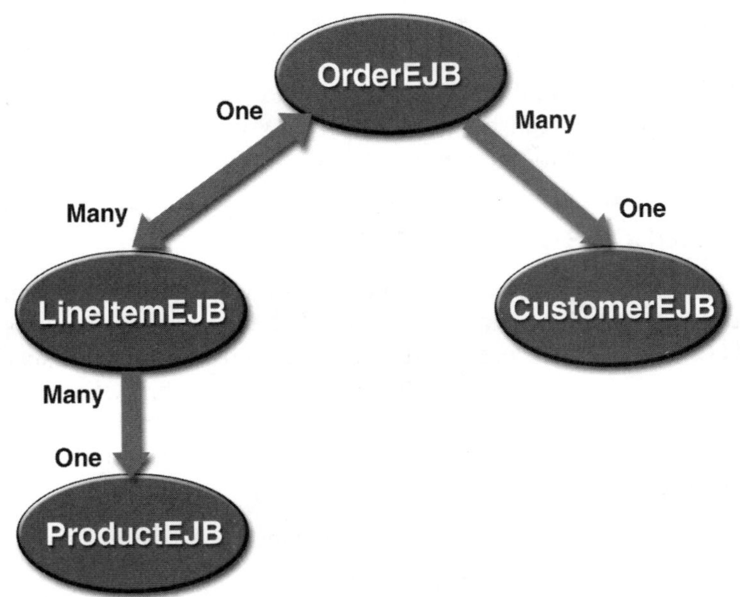

Figure 3–1 A High-Level View of an Abstract Schema

Persistent Fields

The persistent fields of an entity bean are stored in the underlying data store. Collectively, these fields constitute the state of the bean. At runtime, the EJB container automatically synchronizes this state with the database. During deployment, the container typically maps the entity bean to a database table and maps the persistent fields to the table's columns.

A `CustomerEJB` entity bean, for example, might have persistent fields such as `firstName`, `lastName`, `phone`, and `emailAddress`. In container-managed persistence, these fields are virtual. You declare them in the abstract schema, but you do not code them as instance variables in the entity bean class. Instead, the persistent fields are identified in the code by access methods (getters and setters).

Relationship Fields

A *relationship field* is like a foreign key in a database table—it identifies a related bean. Like a persistent field, a relationship field is virtual and is defined in the enterprise bean class with access methods. But unlike a persistent field, a relationship field does not represent the bean's state. Relationship fields are discussed further in Direction in Container-Managed Relationships (page 55).

Multiplicity in Container-Managed Relationships

There are four types of multiplicities:

One-to-one: Each entity bean instance is related to a single instance of another entity bean. For example, to model a physical warehouse in which each storage bin contains a single widget, `StorageBinEJB` and `WidgetEJB` would have a one-to-one relationship.

One-to-many: An entity bean instance may be related to multiple instances of the other entity bean. A sales order, for example, can have multiple line items. In the order application, `OrderEJB` would have a one-to-many relationship with `LineItemEJB`.

Many-to-one: Multiple instances of an entity bean may be related to a single instance of the other entity bean. This multiplicity is the opposite of a one-to-many relationship. In the example mentioned in the previous item, from the perspective of `LineItemEJB` the relationship to `OrderEJB` is many-to-one.

Many-to-many: The entity bean instances may be related to multiple instances of each other. For example, in college each course has many students, and every student may take several courses. Therefore, in an enrollment application, `CourseEJB` and `StudentEJB` would have a many-to-many relationship.

Direction in Container-Managed Relationships

The direction of a relationship may be either bidirectional or unidirectional. In a *bidirectional* relationship, each entity bean has a relationship field that refers to the other bean. Through the relationship field, an entity bean's code can access its related object. If an entity bean has a relative field, then we often say that it "knows" about its related object. For example, if `OrderEJB` knows what `LineItemEJB` instances it has and if `LineItemEJB` knows what `OrderEJB` it belongs to, then they have a bidirectional relationship.

In a *unidirectional* relationship, only one entity bean has a relationship field that refers to the other. For example, `LineItemEJB` would have a relationship field that identifies `ProductEJB`, but `ProductEJB` would not have a relationship field for `LineItemEJB`. In other words, `LineItemEJB` knows about `ProductEJB`, but `ProductEJB` doesn't know which `LineItemEJB` instances refer to it.

EJB QL queries often navigate across relationships. The direction of a relationship determines whether a query can navigate from one bean to another. For example, a query can navigate from `LineItemEJB` to `ProductEJB`, but cannot navigate in the opposite direction. For `OrderEJB` and `LineItemEJB`, a query could navigate in both directions, since these two beans have a bidirectional relationship.

When to Use Entity Beans

You should probably use an entity bean under the following conditions:

- The bean represents a business entity, not a procedure. For example, `CreditCardEJB` would be an entity bean, but `CreditCardVerifierEJB` would be a session bean.
- The bean's state must be persistent. If the bean instance terminates or if the J2EE server is shut down, the bean's state still exists in persistent storage (a database).

What Is a Message-Driven Bean?

Note: This section contains text from *The Java Message Service Tutorial*. Because message-driven beans rely on Java Message Service (JMS) technology, to fully understand how these beans work you should consult the tutorial at this URL:

`http://java.sun.com/products/jms/tutorial/index.html`

A *message-driven bean* is an enterprise bean that allows J2EE applications to process messages asynchronously. It acts as a JMS message listener, which is similar to an event listener except that it receives messages instead of events. The messages may be sent by any J2EE component—an application client, another enterprise bean, or a Web component—or by a JMS application or system that does not use J2EE technology.

Message-driven beans currently process only JMS messages, but in the future they may be used to process other kinds of messages.

For a code sample, see Chapter 7.

What Makes Message-Driven Beans Different from Session and Entity Beans?

The most visible difference between message-driven beans and session and entity beans is that clients do not access message-driven beans through interfaces. Interfaces are described in the section Defining Client Access with Interfaces (page 58). Unlike a session or entity bean, a message-driven bean has only a bean class.

In several respects, a message-driven bean resembles a stateless session bean.

- A message-driven bean's instances retain no data or conversational state for a specific client.
- All instances of a message-driven bean are equivalent, allowing the EJB container to assign a message to any message-driven bean instance. The container can pool these instances to allow streams of messages to be processed concurrently.
- A single message-driven bean can process messages from multiple clients.

The instance variables of the message-driven bean instance can contain some state across the handling of client messages—for example, a JMS API connection, an open database connection, or an object reference to an enterprise bean object.

When a message arrives, the container calls the message-driven bean's `onMessage` method to process the message. The `onMessage` method normally casts the message to one of the five JMS message types and handles it in accordance with the application's business logic. The `onMessage` method may call helper methods, or it may invoke a session or entity bean to process the information in the message or to store it in a database.

A message may be delivered to a message-driven bean within a transaction context, so that all operations within the `onMessage` method are part of a single transaction. If message processing is rolled back, the message will be redelivered. For more information, see Chapter 7.

When to Use Message-Driven Beans

Session beans and entity beans allow you to send JMS messages and to receive them synchronously, but not asynchronously. To avoid tying up server resources, you may prefer not to use blocking synchronous receives in a server-side component. To receive messages asynchronously, use a message-driven bean.

Defining Client Access with Interfaces

Note: The material in this section applies only to session and entity beans, not to message-driven beans. Because they have a different programming model, message-driven beans do not have interfaces that define client access.

A client may access a session or an entity bean only through the methods defined in the bean's interfaces. These interfaces define the client's view of a bean. All other aspects of the bean—method implementations, deployment descriptor settings, abstract schemas, and database access calls—are hidden from the client.

Well-designed interfaces simplify the development and maintenance of J2EE applications. Not only do clean interfaces shield the clients from any complexities in the EJB tier, but they also allow the beans to change internally without affecting the clients. For example, even if you change your entity beans from bean-managed to container-managed persistence, you won't have to alter the client code. But if you were to change the method definitions in the interfaces, then you might have to modify the client code as well. Therefore, to isolate your clients from possible changes in the beans, it is important that you design the interfaces carefully.

When you design a J2EE application, one of the first decisions you make is the type of client access allowed by the enterprise beans: remote or local.

Remote Access

A remote client of an enterprise bean has the following traits:

- It may run on a different machine and a different Java virtual machine (JVM) than the enterprise bean it accesses. (It is not required to run on a different JVM.)
- It can be a Web component, a J2EE application client, or another enterprise bean.
- To a remote client, the location of the enterprise bean is transparent.

To create an enterprise bean with remote access, you must code a remote interface and a home interface. The *remote interface* defines the business methods that are specific to the bean. For example, the remote interface of a bean named `BankAccountEJB` might have business methods named deposit and credit. The *home interface* defines the bean's life cycle methods—`create` and `remove`. For entity beans, the home interface also defines finder methods and home methods.

Finder methods are used to locate entity beans. Home methods are business methods that are invoked on all instances of an entity bean class. Figure 3–2 shows how the interfaces control the client's view of an enterprise bean.

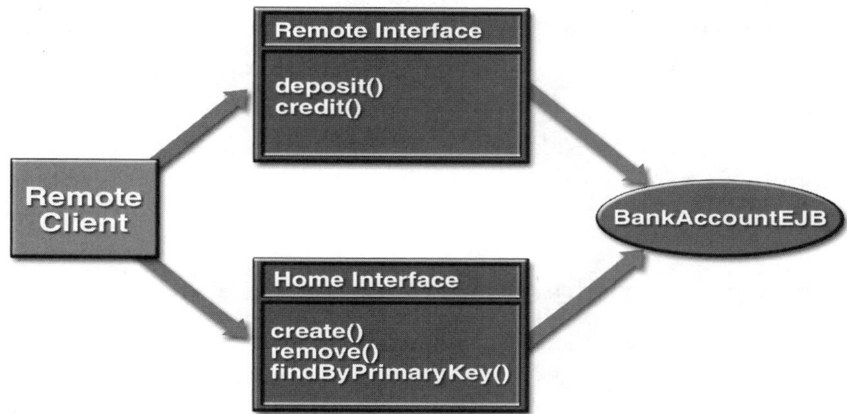

Figure 3–2 Interfaces for an Enterprise Bean With Remote Access

Local Access

A local client has these characteristics:

- It must run in the same JVM as the enterprise bean it accesses.
- It may be a Web component or another enterprise bean.
- To the local client, the location of the enterprise bean it accesses is not transparent.
- It is often an entity bean that has a container-managed relationship with another entity bean.

To build an enterprise bean that allows local access, you must code the local interface and the local home interface. The *local interface* defines the bean's business methods, and the *local home* interface defines its life cycle and finder methods.

Local Interfaces and Container-Managed Relationships

If an entity bean is the target of a container-managed relationship, then it must have local interfaces. The direction of the relationship determines whether or not a bean is the target. In Figure 3–1, for example, `ProductEJB` is the target of a unidirectional relationship with `LineItemEJB`. Because `LineItemEJB` accesses `ProductEJB` locally, `ProductEJB` must have the local interfaces. `LineItemEJB` also needs local interfaces—not because of its relationship with `ProductEJB`—but because it is the target of a relationship with `OrderEJB`. And because the relationship between `LineItemEJB` and `OrderEJB` is bidirectional, both beans must have local interfaces.

Because they require local access, entity beans that participate in a container-managed relationship must reside in the same EJB JAR file. The primary benefit of this locality is increased performance—local calls are usually faster than remote calls.

Deciding on Remote or Local Access

The decision regarding whether to allow local or remote access depends on the following factors.

Container-managed relationships: If an entity bean is the target of a container-managed relationship, it must use local access.

Tight or loose coupling of related beans: Tightly coupled beans depend on one another. For example, a completed sales order must have one or more line items, which cannot exist without the order to which they belong. The `OrderEJB` and `LineItemEJB` entity beans that model this relationship are tightly coupled. Tightly coupled beans are good candidates for local access. Since they fit together as a logical unit, they probably call each other often and would benefit from the increased performance that is possible with local access.

Type of client: If an enterprise bean is accessed by J2EE application clients, then it should allow remote access. In a production environment, these clients almost always run on different machines than the J2EE server. If an enterprise bean's clients are Web components or other enterprise beans, then the type of access depends on how you want to distribute your components.

Component distribution: J2EE applications are scalable because their server-side components can be distributed across multiple machines. In a distributed application, for example, the Web components may run on a different server than the enterprise beans they access. In this distributed scenario, the enterprise beans should allow remote access.

If you aren't sure which type of access an enterprise bean should have, then choose remote access. This decision gives you more flexibility—in the future you can distribute your components to accommodate growing demands on your application.

Although uncommon, it is possible for an enterprise bean to allow both remote and local access. Such a bean would require both remote and local interfaces.

Performance and Access

Because of factors such as network latency, remote calls may be slower than local calls. On the other hand, if you distribute components among different servers, you might improve the application's overall performance. Both of these statements are generalizations; actual performance can vary in different operational environments. Nevertheless, you should keep in mind how your application design might affect performance.

Method Parameters and Access

The type of access affects the parameters of the bean methods that are called by clients. The following topics apply not only to method parameters, but also to method return values.

Isolation

An argument in a remote call is passed by value; it is a copy of an object. But an argument in a local call is passed by reference, just like a normal method call in the Java programming language.

The parameters of remote calls are more isolated than those of local calls. With remote calls, the client and bean operate on different copies of a parameter object. If the client changes the value of the object, the value of the copy in the bean does not change. This layer of isolation can help protect the bean if the client accidentally modifies the data.

In a local call, both the client and the bean may modify the same object. In general, you should not rely on this side effect of local calls. Perhaps someday you will want to distribute your components, replacing the local calls with remote ones.

Granularity of Accessed Data

Because remote calls are likely to be slower than local calls, the parameters in remote methods should be relatively coarse-grained. Since a coarse-grained object contains more data than a fine-grained one, fewer access calls are required.

For example, suppose that a `CustomerEJB` entity bean is accessed remotely. This bean would have a single getter method that returns a `CustomerDetails` object, which encapsulates all of the customer's information. But if `CustomerEJB` is to be accessed locally, it could have a getter method for each instance variable: `getFirstName`, `getLastName`, `getPhoneNumber`, and so forth. Because local calls are fast, the multiple calls to these finer-grained getter methods would not significantly degrade performance.

The Contents of an Enterprise Bean

To develop an enterprise bean, you must provide the following files:

- **Deployment descriptor**: An XML file that specifies information about the bean such as its persistence type and transaction attributes. The `deploytool` utility creates the deployment descriptor when you step through the New Enterprise Bean wizard.
- **Enterprise bean class**: Implements the methods defined in the following interfaces.
- **Interfaces**: The remote and home interfaces are required for remote access. For local access, the local and local home interfaces are required. See the section Defining Client Access with Interfaces (page 58). (Please note that these interfaces are not used by message-driven beans.)
- **Helper classes**: Other classes needed by the enterprise bean class, such as exception and utility classes.

You package the files in the preceding list into an EJB JAR file, the module that stores the enterprise bean. An EJB JAR file is portable and may be used for different applications. To assemble a J2EE application, you package one or more modules—such as EJB JAR files—into an EAR file, the archive file that holds the application. When you deploy the EAR file that contains the bean's EJB JAR file, you also deploy the enterprise bean onto the J2EE server.

Naming Conventions for Enterprise Beans

Because enterprise beans are composed of multiple parts, it's useful to follow a naming convention for your applications. Table 3–2 summarizes the conventions for the example beans of this tutorial.

Table 3–2 Naming Conventions for Enterprise Beans

Item	Syntax	Example
Enterprise bean name (DD)	<*name*>EJB	AccountEJB
EJB JAR display name (DD)	<*name*>JAR	AccountJAR
Enterprise bean class	<*name*>Bean	AccountBean
Home interface	<*name*>Home	AccountHome
Remote interface	<*name*>	Account
Local home interface	Local<*name*>Home	LocalAccountHome
Local interface	Local<*name*>	LocalAccount
Abstract schema (DD)	<*name*>	Account

DD means that the item is an element in the bean's deployment descriptor.

The Life Cycles of Enterprise Beans

An enterprise bean goes through various stages during its lifetime, or life cycle. Each type of enterprise bean—session, entity, or message-driven—has a different life cycle.

The descriptions that follow refer to methods that are explained along with the code examples in the next two chapters. If you are new to enterprise beans, you should skip this section and try out the code examples first.

The Life Cycle of a Stateful Session Bean

Figure 3–3 illustrates the stages that a session bean passes through during its lifetime. The client initiates the life cycle by invoking the `create` method. The EJB container instantiates the bean and then invokes the `setSessionContext` and `ejbCreate` methods in the session bean. The bean is now ready to have its business methods invoked.

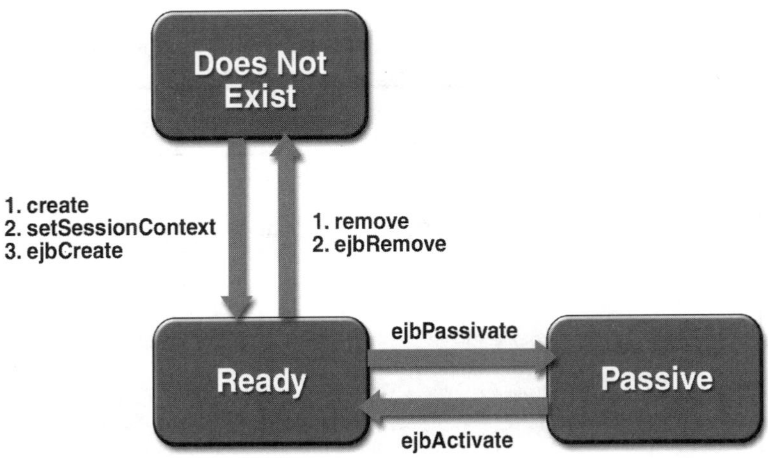

Figure 3–3 Life Cycle of a Stateful Session Bean

While in the ready stage, the EJB container may decide to deactivate, or *passivate*, the bean by moving it from memory to secondary storage. (Typically, the EJB container uses a least-recently-used algorithm to select a bean for passivation.) The EJB container invokes the bean's `ejbPassivate` method immediately before passivating it. If a client invokes a business method on the bean while it is in the passive stage, the EJB container activates the bean, moving it back to the ready stage, and then calls the bean's `ejbActivate` method.

At the end of the life cycle, the client invokes the `remove` method and the EJB container calls the bean's `ejbRemove` method. The bean's instance is ready for garbage collection.

Your code controls the invocation of only two life-cycle methods—the `create` and `remove` methods in the client. All other methods in Figure 3–3 are invoked by the EJB container. The `ejbCreate` method, for example, is inside the bean class, allowing you to perform certain operations right after the bean is instantiated. For instance, you may wish to connect to a database in the `ejbCreate` method. See Chapter 16 for more information.

The Life Cycle of a Stateless Session Bean

Because a stateless session bean is never passivated, its life cycle has just two stages: nonexistent and ready for the invocation of business methods. Figure 3–4 illustrates the stages of a stateless session bean.

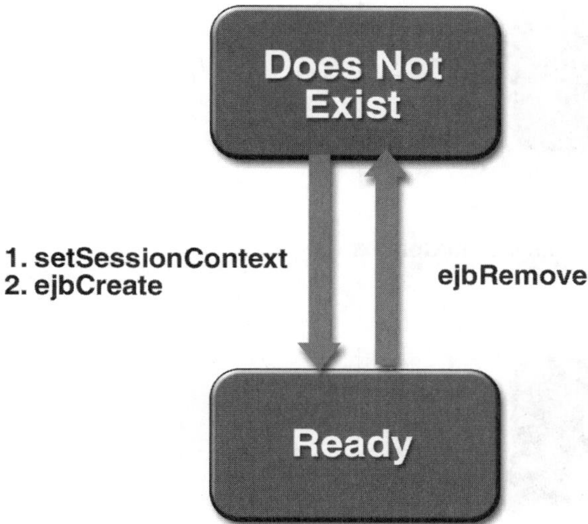

Figure 3–4 Life Cycle of a Stateless Session Bean

The Life Cycle of an Entity Bean

Figure 3–5 shows the stages that an entity bean passes through during its lifetime. After the EJB container creates the instance, it calls the `setEntityContext` method of the entity bean class. The `setEntityContext` method passes the entity context to the bean.

After instantiation, the entity bean moves to a pool of available instances. While in the pooled stage, the instance is not associated with any particular EJB object identity. All instances in the pool are identical. The EJB container assigns an identity to an instance when moving it to the ready stage.

There are two paths from the pooled stage to the ready stage. On the first path, the client invokes the `create` method, causing the EJB container to call the `ejbCreate` and `ejbPostCreate` methods. On the second path, the EJB container invokes the `ejbActivate` method. While in the ready stage, an entity bean's business methods may be invoked.

There are also two paths from the ready stage to the pooled stage. First, a client may invoke the `remove` method, which causes the EJB container to call the `ejbRemove` method. Second, the EJB container may invoke the `ejbPassivate` method.

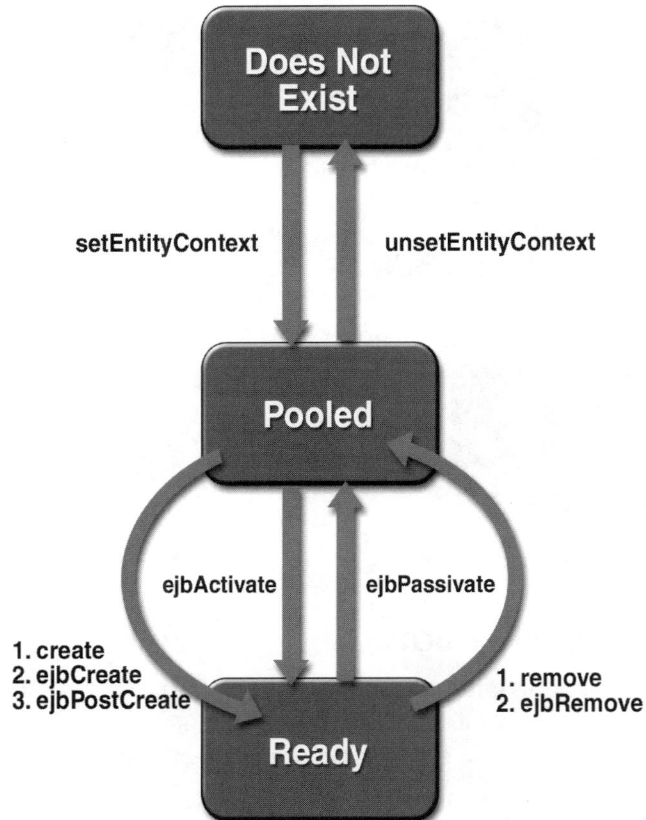

Figure 3–5 Life Cycle of an Entity Bean

At the end of the life cycle, the EJB container removes the instance from the pool and invokes the `unsetEntityContext` method.

In the pooled state, an instance is not associated with any particular EJB object identity. With bean-managed persistence, when the EJB container moves an instance from the pooled state to the ready state, it does not automatically set the primary key. Therefore, the `ejbCreate` and `ejbActivate` methods must assign a value to the primary key. If the primary key is incorrect, the `ejbLoad` and `ejbStore` methods cannot synchronize the instance variables with the database. In the section The SavingsAccountEJB Example (page 84), the `ejbCreate` method assigns the primary key from one of the input parameters. The `ejbActivate` method sets the primary key (`id`) as follows:

```
id = (String)context.getPrimaryKey();
```

In the pooled state, the values of the instance variables are not needed. You can make these instance variables eligible for garbage collection by setting them to `null` in the `ejbPasssivate` method.

The Life Cycle of a Message-Driven Bean

Figure 3–6 illustrates the stages in the life cycle of a message-driven bean.

The EJB container usually creates a pool of message-driven bean instances. For each instance, the EJB container instantiates the bean and performs these tasks:

1. It calls the `setMessageDrivenContext` method to pass the context object to the instance.
2. It calls the instance's `ejbCreate` method.

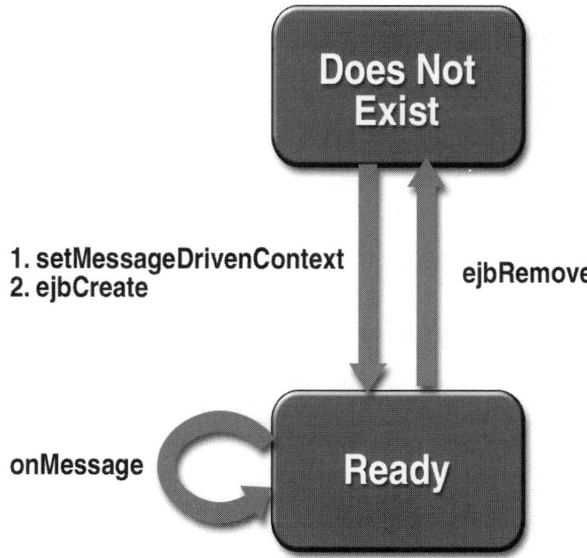

Figure 3–6 Life Cycle of a Message-Driven Bean

Like a stateless session bean, a message-driven bean is never passivated, and it has only two states: nonexistent and ready to receive messages.

At the end of the life cycle, the container calls the `ejbRemove` method. The bean's instance is then ready for garbage collection.

4

A Session Bean Example

Dale Green

SESSION beans are powerful because they extend the reach of your clients into remote servers—yet they're easy to build. In Chapter 2, you built a stateless session bean named `ConverterEJB`. This chapter examines the source code of a stateful session bean called `CartEJB`.

In This Chapter

The CartEJB Example

The CartEJB session bean represents a shopping cart in an online bookstore. The bean's client may add a book to the cart, remove a book, or retrieve the cart's contents. To construct CartEJB, you need the following code:

- Session bean class (CartBean)
- Home interface (CartHome)
- Remote interface (Cart)

All session beans require a session bean class. All enterprise beans that permit remote access must have a home and remote interface. To meet the needs of a specific application, an enterprise bean may also need some helper classes. The CartEJB session bean uses two helper classes, BookException and IdVerifier, which are discussed in the section Helper Classes (page 76).

The source code for this example is in the j2eetutorial/examples/src/ejb/cart directory. To compile the code, go to the j2eetutorial/examples directory and type ant cart. A sample CartApp.ear file is in the j2eetutorial/examples/ears directory.

Session Bean Class

The session bean class for this example is called CartBean. Like any session bean, the CartBean class must meet these requirements:

- It implements the SessionBean interface.
- The class is defined as public.
- The class cannot be defined as abstract or final.
- It implements one or more ejbCreate methods.
- It implements the business methods.
- It contains a public constructor with no parameters.
- It must not define the finalize method.

The source code for the CartBean class follows.

```
import java.util.*;
import javax.ejb.*;

public class CartBean implements SessionBean {

   String customerName;
```

```
String customerId;
Vector contents;

public void ejbCreate(String person)
   throws CreateException {

   if (person == null) {
      throw new CreateException("Null person not allowed.");
   }
   else {
      customerName = person;
   }

   customerId = "0";
   contents = new Vector();
}

public void ejbCreate(String person, String id)
   throws CreateException {

   if (person == null) {
      throw new CreateException("Null person not allowed.");
   }
   else {
      customerName = person;
   }

   IdVerifier idChecker = new IdVerifier();
   if (idChecker.validate(id)) {
      customerId = id;
   }
   else {
      throw new CreateException("Invalid id: "+ id);
   }

   contents = new Vector();
}

public void addBook(String title) {
   contents.addElement(title);
}

public void removeBook(String title) throws BookException {

   boolean result = contents.removeElement(title);
   if (result == false) {
      throw new BookException(title + "not in cart.");
   }
```

```
    }

    public Vector getContents() {
       return contents;
    }

    public CartBean() {}
    public void ejbRemove() {}
    public void ejbActivate() {}
    public void ejbPassivate() {}
    public void setSessionContext(SessionContext sc) {}

}
```

The SessionBean Interface

The `SessionBean` interface extends the `EnterpriseBean` interface, which in turn extends the `Serializable` interface. The `SessionBean` interface declares the `ejbRemove`, `ejbActivate`, `ejbPassivate`, and `setSessionContext` methods. The `CartBean` class doesn't use these methods, but it must implement them because they're declared in the `SessionBean` interface. Consequently, these methods are empty in the `CartBean` class. Later sections explain when you might use these methods.

The ejbCreate Methods

Because an enterprise bean runs inside an EJB container, a client cannot directly instantiate the bean. Only the EJB container can instantiate an enterprise bean. During instantiation, the example program performs the following steps.

1. The client invokes a `create` method on the home object:

   ```
   Cart shoppingCart = home.create("Duke DeEarl","123");
   ```

2. The EJB container instantiates the enterprise bean.
3. The EJB container invokes the appropriate `ejbCreate` method in `CartBean`:

   ```
   public void ejbCreate(String person, String id)
      throws CreateException {

      if (person == null) {
         throw new CreateException("Null person not allowed.");
      }
      else {
         customerName = person;
   ```

```
        }

        IdVerifier idChecker = new IdVerifier();
        if (idChecker.validate(id)) {
           customerId = id;
        }
        else {
           throw new CreateException("Invalid id: "+ id);
        }

        contents = new Vector();
     }
```

Typically, an `ejbCreate` method initializes the state of the enterprise bean. The preceding `ejbCreate` method, for example, initializes the `customerName` and `customerId` variables with the arguments passed by the `create` method.

An enterprise bean must have one or more `ejbCreate` methods. The signatures of the methods must meet the following requirements:

- The access control modifier must be `public`.
- The return type must be `void`.
- If the bean allows remote access, the arguments must be legal types for the Java Remote Method Invocation ("Java RMI") API.
- The modifier cannot be `static` or `final`.

The `throws` clause may include the `javax.ejb.CreateException` and other exceptions that are specific to your application. The `ejbCreate` method usually throws a `CreateException` if an input parameter is invalid.

Business Methods

The primary purpose of a session bean is to run business tasks for the client. The client invokes business methods on the remote object reference that is returned by the `create` method. From the client's perspective, the business methods appear to run locally, but they actually run remotely in the session bean. The following code snippet shows how the `CartClient` program invokes the business methods:

```
Cart shoppingCart = home.create("Duke DeEarl", "123");
...
shoppingCart.addBook("The Martian Chronicles");
shoppingCart.removeBook("Alice In Wonderland");
bookList = shoppingCart.getContents();
```

The CartBean class implements the business methods in the following code:

```
public void addBook(String title) {
   contents.addElement(title);
}

public void removeBook(String title) throws BookException {
   boolean result = contents.removeElement(title);
   if (result == false) {
      throw new BookException(title + "not in cart.");
   }
}

public Vector getContents() {
   return contents;
}
```

The signature of a business method must conform to these rules:

- The method name must not conflict with one defined by the EJB architecture. For example, you cannot call a business method ejbCreate or ejbActivate.
- The access control modifier must be public.
- If the bean allows remote access, the arguments and return types must be legal types for the Java RMI API.
- The modifier must not be static or final.

The throws clause may include exceptions that you define for your application. The removeBook method, for example, throws the BookException if the book is not in the cart.

To indicate a system-level problem, such as the inability to connect to a database, a business method should throw the javax.ejb.EJBException. When a business method throws an EJBException, the container wraps it in a RemoteException, which is caught by the client. The container will not wrap application exceptions such as BookException. Because EJBException is a subclass of RuntimeException, you do not need to include it in the throws clause of the business method.

Home Interface

A home interface extends the javax.ejb.EJBHome interface. For a session bean, the purpose of the home interface is to define the create methods that a remote client may invoke. The `CartClient` program, for example, invokes this `create` method:

```
Cart shoppingCart = home.create("Duke DeEarl", "123");
```

Every `create` method in the home interface corresponds to an `ejbCreate` method in the bean class. The signatures of the `ejbCreate` methods in the `CartBean` class follow:

```
public void ejbCreate(String person) throws CreateException
...
public void ejbCreate(String person, String id)
   throws CreateException
```

Compare the `ejbCreate` signatures with those of the `create` methods in the `CartHome` interface:

```
import java.io.Serializable;
import java.rmi.RemoteException;
import javax.ejb.CreateException;
import javax.ejb.EJBHome;

public interface CartHome extends EJBHome {
   Cart create(String person) throws
                RemoteException, CreateException;
   Cart create(String person, String id) throws
                RemoteException, CreateException;
}
```

The signatures of the `ejbCreate` and `create` methods are similar, but differ in important ways. The rules for defining the signatures of the `create` methods of a home interface follow.

- The number and types of arguments in a `create` method must match those of its corresponding `ejbCreate` method.
- The arguments and return type of the `create` method must be valid RMI types.
- A `create` method returns the remote interface type of the enterprise bean. (But an `ejbCreate` method returns `void`.)
- The `throws` clause of the `create` method must include the `java.rmi.RemoteException` and the `javax.ejb.CreateException`.

Remote Interface

The remote interface, which extends `javax.ejb.EJBObject`, defines the business methods that a remote client may invoke. Here is the source code for the `Cart` remote interface:

```
import java.util.*;
import javax.ejb.EJBObject;
import java.rmi.RemoteException;

public interface Cart extends EJBObject {

   public void addBook(String title) throws RemoteException;
   public void removeBook(String title) throws
                  BookException, RemoteException;
   public Vector getContents() throws RemoteException;
}
```

The method definitions in a remote interface must follow these rules:

- Each method in the remote interface must match a method implemented in the enterprise bean class.
- The signatures of the methods in the remote interface must be identical to the signatures of the corresponding methods in the enterprise bean class.
- The arguments and return values must be valid RMI types.
- The `throws` clause must include the `java.rmi.RemoteException`.

Helper Classes

The `CartEJB` session bean has two helper classes: `BookException` and `IdVerifier`. The `BookException` is thrown by the `removeBook` method and the `IdVerifier` validates the `customerId` in one of the `ejbCreate` methods. Helper classes must reside in the EJB JAR file that contains the enterprise bean class.

Running the CartEJB Example

1. Start the J2EE server and `deploytool`. For instructions, see the section Setting Up (page 22).
2. In `deploytool` open the `j2eetutorial/examples/ears/CartApp.ear` file (File→Open). You should see the application that is displayed in Figure 4–1.

3. Deploy the `CartApp` application (Tools→Deploy). In the Introduction dialog box, make sure that you select the Return Client JAR checkbox. For detailed instructions, see Deploying the J2EE Application (page 37).
4. Run the application.

   a. In a terminal window, go to the `j2eetutorial/examples/ears` directory.

   b. Set the `APPCPATH` environment variable to `CartAppClient.jar`.

   c. Type the following command:

   ```
   runclient -client CartApp.ear -name CartClient -textauth
   ```

   d. At the login prompts, enter `guest` for the user name and `guest123` for the password.

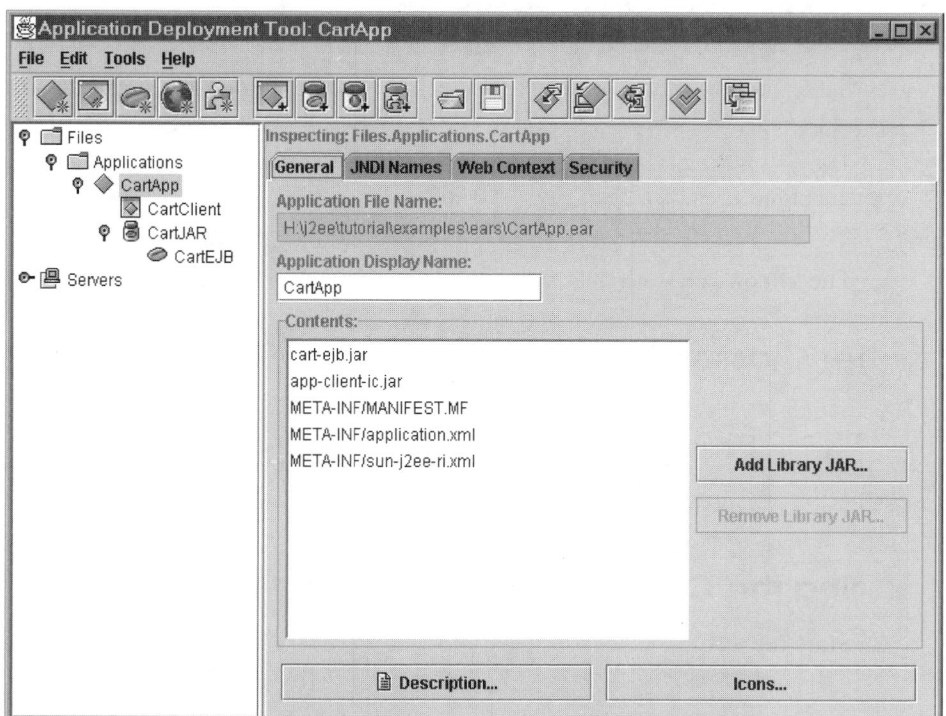

Figure 4–1 General Tabbed Pane of the `CartApp` Application

Other Enterprise Bean Features

The topics that follow apply to both session and entity beans.

Accessing Environment Entries

Stored in an enterprise bean's deployment descriptor, an *environment entry* is a name-value pair that allows you to customize the bean's business logic without changing its source code. An enterprise bean that calculates discounts, for example, might have an environment entry named `Discount Percent`. Before deploying the bean's application, you could run `deploytool` and assign `Discount Percent` a value of .05 on the Env. Entries tab. (See Figure 4–2.) When you run the application, the enterprise bean fetches the .05 value from its environment.

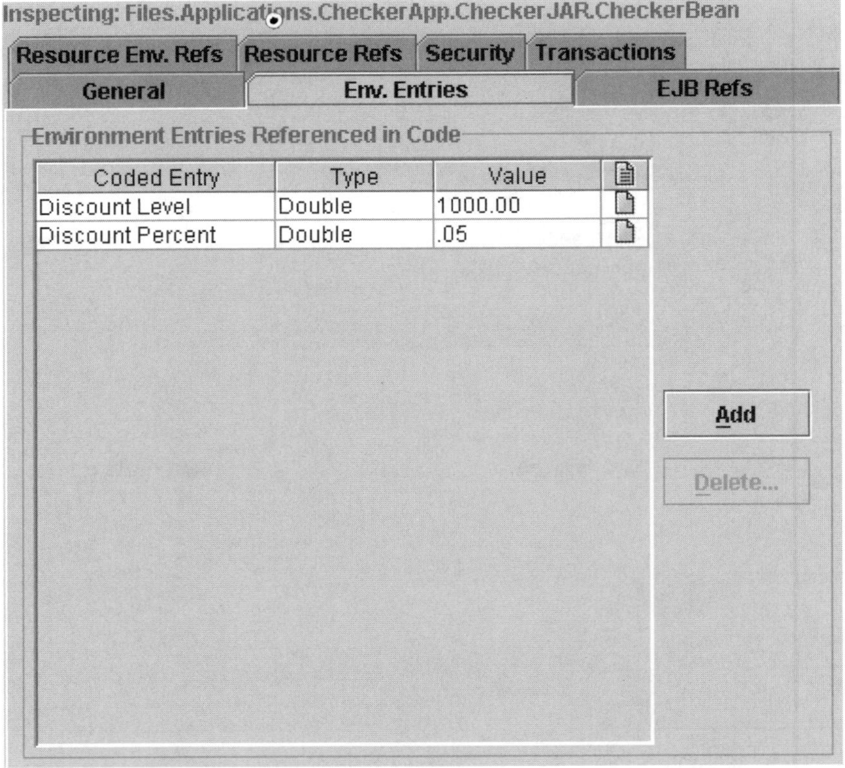

Figure 4–2 Env. Entries Tab of `CheckerBean`

In the following code example, the applyDiscount method uses environment entries to calculate a discount based on the purchase amount. First, the method locates the environment naming context by invoking lookup with the java:comp/env parameter. Then it calls lookup on the environment to get the values for the Discount Level and Discount Percent names. For example, if you assign a value of .05 to the Discount Percent name in deploytool, the code will assign .05 to the discountPercent variable. The applyDiscount method, which follows, is in the CheckerBean class. The source code for this example is in j2eetutorial/examples/src/ejb/checker. A sample CheckerApp.ear file is in the j2eetutorial/examples/ears directory.

```
public double applyDiscount(double amount) {

   try {

      double discount;

      Context initial = new InitialContext();
         Context environment =
            (Context)initial.lookup("java:comp/env");

      Double discountLevel =
         (Double)environment.lookup("Discount Level");
            Double discountPercent =
               (Double)environment.lookup("Discount Percent");

      if (amount >= discountLevel.doubleValue()) {
         discount = discountPercent.doubleValue();
      }
      else {
         discount = 0.00;
      }

      return amount * (1.00 - discount);

   } catch (NamingException ex) {
      throw new EJBException("NamingException: "+
         ex.getMessage());
   }
}
```

Comparing Enterprise Beans

A client can determine if two stateful session beans are identical by invoking the `isIdentical` method:

```
bookCart = home.create("Bill Shakespeare");
videoCart = home.create("Lefty Lee");
...
if (bookCart.isIdentical(bookCart)) {
   // true ... }
if (bookCart.isIdentical(videoCart)) {
   // false ... }
```

Because stateless session beans have the same object identity, the `isIdentical` method always returns `true` when used to compare them.

To determine if two entity beans are identical, the client can invoke the `isIdentical` method, or it can fetch and compare the beans's primary keys:

```
String key1 = (String)accta.getPrimaryKey();
String key2 = (String)acctb.getPrimaryKey();

if (key1.compareTo(key2) == 0)
   System.out.println("equal");
```

Passing an Enterprise Bean's Object Reference

Suppose that your enterprise bean needs to pass a reference to itself to another bean. You might want to pass the reference, for example, so that the second bean can call the first bean's methods. You can't pass the `this` reference because it points to the bean's instance, which is running in the EJB container. Only the container may directly invoke methods on the bean's instance. Clients access the instance indirectly by invoking methods on the object whose type is the bean's remote interface. It is the reference to this object (the bean's remote reference) that the first bean would pass to the second bean.

A session bean obtains its remote reference by calling the `getEJBObject` method of the `SessionContext` interface. An entity bean would call the `getEJBObject` method of the `EntityContext` interface. These interfaces provide beans with access to the instance contexts maintained by the EJB container. Typically, the bean saves the context in the `setSessionContext` method. The following code fragment shows how a session bean might use these methods.

```
public class WagonBean implements SessionBean {

   SessionContext context;
   ...
   public void setSessionContext(SessionContext sc) {
      this.context = sc;
   }
   ...
   public void passItOn(Basket basket) {
   ...
      basket.copyItems(context.getEJBObject());
   }
   ...
```

5

Bean-Managed Persistence Examples

Dale Green

DATA is at the heart of most business applications. In J2EE applications, entity beans represent the business objects that are stored in a database. For entity beans with bean-managed persistence, you must write the code for the database access calls. Although writing this code is an additional responsibility, you will have more control over how the entity bean accesses a database.

This chapter discusses the coding techniques for entity beans with bean-managed persistence. For conceptual information on entity beans, please see What Is an Entity Bean? (page 51).

In This Chapter

The SavingsAccountEJB Example

The entity bean illustrated in this section represents a simple bank account. The state of `SavingsAccountEJB` is stored in the `savingsaccount` table of a relational database. The `savingsaccount` table is created by the following SQL statement:

```
CREATE TABLE savingsaccount
   (id VARCHAR(3)
   CONSTRAINT pk_savingsaccount PRIMARY KEY,
   firstname VARCHAR(24),
   lastname  VARCHAR(24),
   balance   NUMERIC(10,2));
```

The `SavingsAccountEJB` example requires the following code:

- Entity bean class (`SavingsAccountBean`)
- Home interface (`SavingsAccountHome`)
- Remote interface (`SavingsAccount`)

This example also makes use of the following classes:

- A utility class named `InsufficientBalanceException`
- A client class called `SavingsAccountClient`

The source code for this example is in the `j2eetutorial/examples/src/ejb/savingsaccount` directory. To compile the code, go to the `j2eetutorial/examples` directory and type `ant savingsaccount`. A sample `SavingsAccountApp.ear` file is in the `j2eetutorial/examples/ears` directory.

Entity Bean Class

The sample entity bean class is called `SavingsAccountBean`. As you look through its code, note that it meets the requirements of any entity bean with bean-managed persistence. First of all, it implements the following:

- `EntityBean` interface

- Zero or more ejbCreate and ejbPostCreate methods
- Finder methods
- Business methods
- Home methods

In addition, an entity bean class with bean-managed persistence has these requirements:

- The class is defined as public.
- The class cannot be defined as abstract or final.
- It contains an empty constructor.
- It does not implement the finalize method.

The EntityBean Interface

The EntityBean interface extends the EnterpriseBean interface, which extends the Serializable interface. The EntityBean interface declares a number of methods, such as ejbActivate and ejbLoad, which you must implement in your entity bean class. These methods are discussed in later sections.

The ejbCreate Method

When the client invokes a create method, the EJB container invokes the corresponding ejbCreate method. Typically, an ejbCreate method in an entity bean performs the following tasks:

- Inserts the entity state into the database
- Initializes the instance variables
- Returns the primary key

The ejbCreate method of SavingsAccountBean inserts the entity state into the database by invoking the private insertRow method, which issues the SQL INSERT statement. Here is the source code for the ejbCreate method:

```
public String ejbCreate(String id, String firstName,
   String lastName, BigDecimal balance)
   throws CreateException {

   if (balance.signum() == -1)  {
      throw new CreateException
         ("A negative initial balance is not allowed.");
   }

   try {
```

```
            insertRow(id, firstName, lastName, balance);
        } catch (Exception ex) {
            throw new EJBException("ejbCreate: " +
               ex.getMessage());
        }

        this.id = id;
        this.firstName = firstName;
        this.lastName = lastName;
        this.balance = balance;

        return id;
    }
```

Although the SavingsAccountBean class has just one ejbCreate method, an enterprise bean may contain multiple ejbCreate methods. For an example, see the CartEJB.java source code in the j2eetutorial/examples/src/ejb/cart directory.

When writing an ejbCreate method for an entity bean, be sure to follow these rules:

- The access control modifier must be public.
- The return type must be the primary key.
- The arguments must be legal types for the Java RMI API.
- The method modifier cannot be final or static.

The throws clause may include the javax.ejb.CreateException and exceptions that are specific to your application. An ejbCreate method usually throws a CreateException if an input parameter is invalid. If an ejbCreate method cannot create an entity because another entity with the same primary key already exists, it should throw a javax.ejb.DuplicateKeyException (a subclass of CreateException). If a client receives a CreateException or a DuplicateKeyException, it should assume that the entity was not created.

The state of an entity bean may be directly inserted into the database by an application that is unknown to the J2EE server. For example, a SQL script might insert a row into the savingsaccount table. Although the entity bean for this row was not created by an ejbCreate method, the bean can be located by a client program.

The ejbPostCreate Method

For each ejbCreate method, you must write an ejbPostCreate method in the entity bean class. The EJB container invokes ejbPostCreate immediately after it calls `ejbCreate`. Unlike the `ejbCreate` method, the `ejbPostCreate` method can invoke the `getPrimaryKey` and `getEJBObject` methods of the `EntityContext` interface. For more information on the `getEJBObject` method, see the section Passing an Enterprise Bean's Object Reference (page 80). Often, your `ejbPostCreate` methods will be empty.

The signature of an `ejbPostCreate` method must meet the following requirements:

- The number and types of arguments must match a corresponding `ejbCreate` method.
- The access control modifier must be `public`.
- The method modifier cannot be `final` or `static`.
- The return type must be `void`.

The `throws` clause may include the `javax.ejb.CreateException` and exceptions that are specific to your application.

The ejbRemove Method

A client deletes an entity bean by invoking the `remove` method. This invocation causes the EJB container to call the `ejbRemove` method, which deletes the entity state from the database. In the `SavingsAccountBean` class, the `ejbRemove` method invokes a private method named `deleteRow`, which issues a SQL `DELETE` statement. The `ejbRemove` method is short:

```
public void ejbRemove() {
    try {
        deleteRow(id);
    catch (Exception ex) {
        throw new EJBException("ejbRemove: " +
        ex.getMessage());
    }
}
```

If the `ejbRemove` method encounters a system problem, it should throw the `javax.ejb.EJBException`. If it encounters an application error, it should throw a `javax.ejb.RemoveException`. For a comparison of system and application exceptions, see the section Handling Exceptions (page 116).

An entity bean may also be removed directly by a database deletion. For example, if a SQL script deletes a row that contains an entity bean state, then that entity bean is removed.

The ejbLoad and ejbStore Methods

If the EJB container needs to synchronize the instance variables of an entity bean with the corresponding values stored in a database, it invokes the ejbLoad and ejbStore methods. The ejbLoad method refreshes the instance variables from the database, and the ejbStore method writes the variables to the database. The client may not call ejbLoad and ejbStore.

If a business method is associated with a transaction, the container invokes ejbLoad before the business method executes. Immediately after the business method executes, the container calls ejbStore. Because the container invokes ejbLoad and ejbStore, you do not have to refresh and store the instance variables in your business methods. The SavingsAccountBean class relies on the container to synchronize the instance variables with the database. Therefore, the business methods of SavingsAccountBean should be associated with transactions.

If the ejbLoad and ejbStore methods cannot locate an entity in the underlying database, they should throw the javax.ejb.NoSuchEntityException. This exception is a subclass of EJBException. Because EJBException is a subclass of RuntimeException, you do not have to include it in the throws clause. When NoSuchEntityException is thrown, the EJB container wraps it in a RemoteException before returning it to the client.

In the SavingsAccountBean class, ejbLoad invokes the loadRow method, which issues a SQL SELECT statement and assigns the retrieved data to the instance variables. The ejbStore method calls the storeRow method, which stores the instance variables in the database with a SQL UPDATE statement. Here is the code for the ejbLoad and ejbStore methods:

```
public void ejbLoad() {

   try {
      loadRow();
   } catch (Exception ex) {
      throw new EJBException("ejbLoad: " +
         ex.getMessage());
   }
}

public void ejbStore() {

   try {
      storeRow();
   } catch (Exception ex) {
```

```
        throw new EJBException("ejbStore: " +
            ex.getMessage());
    }
}
```

The Finder Methods

The finder methods allow clients to locate entity beans. The SavingsAccount-Client program locates entity beans with three finder methods:

```
SavingsAccount jones = home.findByPrimaryKey("836");
...
Collection c = home.findByLastName("Smith");
...
Collection c = home.findInRange(20.00, 99.00);
```

For every finder method available to a client, the entity bean class must implement a corresponding method that begins with the prefix ejbFind. The SavingsAccountBean class, for example, implements the ejbFindByLastName method as follows:

```
public Collection ejbFindByLastName(String lastName)
    throws FinderException {

    Collection result;

    try {
        result = selectByLastName(lastName);
    } catch (Exception ex) {
        throw new EJBException("ejbFindByLastName " +
            ex.getMessage());
    }
    return result;
}
```

The finder methods that are specific to your application, such as ejbFindByLastName and ejbFindInRange, are optional—but the ejbFindByPrimaryKey method is required. As its name implies, the ejbFindByPrimaryKey method accepts as an argument the primary key, which it uses to locate an entity bean. In the SavingsAccountBean class, the primary key is the id variable. Here is the code for the ejbFindByPrimaryKey method:

```
public String ejbFindByPrimaryKey(String primaryKey)
    throws FinderException {

    boolean result;
```

```
      try {
         result = selectByPrimaryKey(primaryKey);
      } catch (Exception ex) {
         throw new EJBException("ejbFindByPrimaryKey: " +
            ex.getMessage());
      }

      if (result) {
         return primaryKey;
      }
      else {
         throw new ObjectNotFoundException
            ("Row for id " + primaryKey + " not found.");
      }
   }
```

The `ejbFindByPrimaryKey` method may look strange to you, because it uses a primary key for both the method argument and return value. However, remember that the client does not call `ejbFindByPrimaryKey` directly. It is the EJB container that calls the `ejbFindByPrimaryKey` method. The client invokes the `findByPrimaryKey` method, which is defined in the home interface.

The following list summarizes the rules for the finder methods that you implement in an entity bean class with bean-managed persistence:

- The `ejbFindByPrimaryKey` method must be implemented.
- A finder method name must start with the prefix `ejbFind`.
- The access control modifier must be `public`.
- The method modifier cannot be `final` or `static`.
- The arguments and return type must be legal types for the Java RMI API. (This requirement applies only to methods defined in a remote—not local—home interface.)
- The return type must be the primary key or a collection of primary keys.

The `throws` clause may include the `javax.ejb.FinderException` and exceptions that are specific to your application. If a finder method returns a single primary key and the requested entity does not exist, the method should throw the `javax.ejb.ObjectNotFoundException` (a subclass of `FinderException`). If a finder method returns a collection of primary keys and it does not find any objects, it should return an empty collection.

The Business Methods

The business methods contain the business logic that you want to encapsulate within the entity bean. Usually, the business methods do not access the database, allowing you to separate the business logic from the database access code. The SavingsAccountBean class contains the following business methods:

```
public void debit(BigDecimal amount)
   throws InsufficientBalanceException {

   if (balance.compareTo(amount) == -1) {
       throw new InsufficientBalanceException();
   }
   balance = balance.subtract(amount);
}

public void credit(BigDecimal amount) {

   balance = balance.add(amount);
}

public String getFirstName() {

   return firstName;
}

public String getLastName() {

   return lastName;
}

public BigDecimal getBalance() {

   return balance;
}
```

The SavingsAccountClient program invokes the business methods as follows:

```
BigDecimal zeroAmount = new BigDecimal("0.00");
SavingsAccount duke = home.create("123", "Duke", "Earl",
    zeroAmount);
...
duke.credit(new BigDecimal("88.50"));
duke.debit(new BigDecimal("20.25"));
BigDecimal balance = duke.getBalance();
```

The requirements for the signature of a business method are the same for both session and entity beans:

- The method name must not conflict with a method name defined by the EJB architecture. For example, you cannot call a business method `ejbCreate` or `ejbActivate`.
- The access control modifier must be `public`.
- The method modifier cannot be `final` or `static`.
- The arguments and return types must be legal types for the Java RMI API. This requirement applies only to methods defined in a remote—not local—home interface.

The `throws` clause may include the exceptions that you define for your application. The `debit` method, for example, throws the `InsufficientBalanceException`. To indicate a system-level problem, a business method should throw the `javax.ejb.EJBException`.

The Home Methods

A home method contains the business logic that applies to all entity beans of a particular class. In contrast, the logic in a business method applies to a single entity bean, an instance with a unique identity. During a home method invocation, the instance has neither a unique identity nor a state that represents a business object. Consequently, a home method must not access the bean's persistence state (instance variables). (For container-managed persistence, a home method also must not access relationships.)

Typically, a home method locates a collection of bean instances and invokes business methods as it iterates through the collection. This approach is taken by the `ejbHomeChargeForLowBalance` method of the `SavingsAccountBean` class. The `ejbHomeChargeForLowBalance` method applies a service charge to all savings accounts with balances less than a specified amount. The method locates these accounts by invoking the `findInRange` method. As it iterates through the collection of `SavingsAccount` instances, the `ejbHomeChargeForLowBalance` method checks the balance and invokes the `debit` business method. Here is the source code of the `ejbHomeChargeForLowBalance` method:

```
public void ejbHomeChargeForLowBalance(
    BigDecimal minimumBalance, BigDecimal charge)
    throws InsufficientBalanceException {

   try {
       SavingsAccountHome home =
```

```
            (SavingsAccountHome)context.getEJBHome();
            Collection c = home.findInRange(new BigDecimal("0.00"),
                minimumBalance.subtract(new BigDecimal("0.01")));

            Iterator i = c.iterator();

            while (i.hasNext()) {
               SavingsAccount account = (SavingsAccount)i.next();
               if (account.getBalance().compareTo(charge) == 1) {
                  account.debit(charge);
               }
            }

        } catch (Exception ex) {
            throw new EJBException("ejbHomeChargeForLowBalance: "
                + ex.getMessage());
        }
    }
```

The home interface defines a corresponding method named chargeForLowBalance (see Home Method Definitions, page 96). Since the interface provides the client view, the SavingsAccountClient program invokes the home method as follows:

```
SavingsAccountHome home;
...
home.chargeForLowBalance(new BigDecimal("10.00"),
   new BigDecimal("1.00"));
```

In the entity bean class, the implementation of a home method must adhere to these rules:

- A home method name must start with the prefix ejbHome.
- The access control modifier must be public.
- The method modifier cannot be static.

The throws clause may include exceptions that are specific to your application; it must not throw the java.rmi.RemoteException.

Database Calls

Table 5–1 summarizes the database access calls in the SavingsAccountBean class. The business methods of the SavingsAccountBean class are absent from the preceding table because they do not access the database. Instead, these business methods update the instance variables, which are written to the database when the EJB container calls ejbStore. Another developer might have chosen to access the database in the business methods of the SavingsAccountBean class. This choice is one of those design decisions that depend on the specific needs of your application.

Before accessing a database, you must connect to it. For more information, see Chapter 16.

Table 5–1 SQL Statements in SavingsAccountBean

Method	SQL Statement
ejbCreate	INSERT
ejbFindByPrimaryKey	SELECT
ejbFindByLastName	SELECT
ejbFindInRange	SELECT
ejbLoad	SELECT
ejbRemove	DELETE
ejbStore	UPDATE

Home Interface

The home interface defines the create, finder, and home methods. The SavingsAccountHome interface follows:

```
import java.util.Collection;
import java.math.BigDecimal;
import java.rmi.RemoteException;
import javax.ejb.*;

public interface SavingsAccountHome extends EJBHome {

    public SavingsAccount create(String id, String firstName,
        String lastName, BigDecimal balance)
        throws RemoteException, CreateException;

    public SavingsAccount findByPrimaryKey(String id)
        throws FinderException, RemoteException;

    public Collection findByLastName(String lastName)
```

```
            throws FinderException, RemoteException;

        public Collection findInRange(BigDecimal low,
            BigDecimal high)
            throws FinderException, RemoteException;

       public void chargeForLowBalance(BigDecimal minimumBalance,
          BigDecimal charge)
          throws InsufficientBalanceException, RemoteException;
}
```

create Method Definitions

Each `create` method in the home interface must conform to the following requirements:

- It has the same number and types of arguments as its matching `ejbCreate` method in the enterprise bean class.
- It returns the remote interface type of the enterprise bean.
- The `throws` clause includes the exceptions specified by the `throws` clause of the corresponding `ejbCreate` and `ejbPostCreate` methods.
- The `throws` clause includes the `javax.ejb.CreateException`.
- If the method is defined in a remote—not local—home interface, then the `throws` clause includes the `java.rmi.RemoteException`.

Finder Method Definitions

Every finder method in the home interface corresponds to a finder method in the entity bean class. The name of a finder method in the home interface begins with `find`, whereas the corresponding name in the entity bean class begins with `ejbFind`. For example, the `SavingsAccountHome` class defines the `findByLastName` method, and the `SavingsAccountBean` class implements the `ejbFindByLastName` method. The rules for defining the signatures of the finder methods of a home interface follow.

- The number and types of arguments must match those of the corresponding method in the entity bean class.
- The return type is the entity bean's remote interface type, or a collection of those types.

- The exceptions in the `throws` clause include those of the corresponding method in the entity bean class.
- The `throws` clause contains the `javax.ejb.FinderException`.
- If the method is defined in a remote—not local—home interface, then the throws clause includes the `java.rmi.RemoteException`.

Home Method Definitions

Each home method definition in the home interface corresponds to a method in the entity bean class. In the home interface, the method name is arbitrary, provided that it does not begin with `create` or `find`. In the bean class, the matching method name begins with `ejbHome`. For example, in the `SavingsAccountBean` class the name is `ejbHomeChargeForLowBalance`, but in the `SavingsAccountHome` interface the name is `chargeForLowBalance`.

The home method signature must follow the same rules specified for finder methods in the previous section (except that a home method does not throw a `FinderException`).

Remote Interface

The remote interface extends `javax.ejb.EJBObject` and defines the business methods that a remote client may invoke. Here is the `SavingsAccount` remote interface:

```
import javax.ejb.EJBObject;
import java.rmi.RemoteException;
import java.math.BigDecimal;

public interface SavingsAccount extends EJBObject {

    public void debit(BigDecimal amount)
        throws InsufficientBalanceException, RemoteException;

    public void credit(BigDecimal amount)
        throws RemoteException;

    public String getFirstName()
        throws RemoteException;

    public String getLastName()
        throws RemoteException;
```

```
    public BigDecimal getBalance()
        throws RemoteException;
}
```

The requirements for the method definitions in a remote interface are the same for both session and entity beans:

- Each method in the remote interface must match a method in the enterprise bean class.
- The signatures of the methods in the remote interface must be identical to the signatures of the corresponding methods in the enterprise bean class.
- The arguments and return values must be valid RMI types.
- The `throws` clause must include `java.rmi.RemoteException`.

A local interface has the same requirements, with the following exceptions:

- The arguments and return values are not required to be valid RMI types.
- The `throws` clause does not include `java.rmi.RemoteException`.

Running the SavingsAccountEJB Example

Setting Up the Database

The instructions that follow explain how to use the `SavingsAccountEJB` example with a Cloudscape database. The Cloudscape software is included with the J2EE SDK download bundle.

1. From the command-line prompt, run the Cloudscape database server by typing `cloudscape -start`. (When you are ready to shut down the server, type `cloudscape -stop`.)
2. Create the `savingsaccount` database table.
   a. Go to the `j2eetutorial/examples` directory
   b. Type `ant create-savingsaccount-table`.

You may also run this example with databases other than Cloudscape. (See the Release Notes of the J2EE SDK for a list of supported databases.) If you are using one of these other databases, you may run the `j2eetutorial/examples/sql/savingsaccount.sql` script to create the `savingsaccount` table.

Deploying the Application

1. In `deploytool`, open the `j2eetutorial/examples/ears/SavingsAccountApp.ear` file (File→Open).
2. Deploy the `SavingsAccountApp` application (Tools→Deploy). In the Introduction dialog box, make sure that you select the Return Client JAR checkbox. For detailed instructions, see Deploying the J2EE Application (page 37).

Running the Client

1. In a terminal window, go to the `j2eetutorial/examples/ears` directory.
2. Set the `APPCPATH` environment variable to `SavingsAccountAppClient.jar`.
3. Type the following command on a single line:

```
runclient -client SavingsAccountApp.ear -name
   SavingsAccountClient -textauth
```

4. At the login prompts, enter `guest` for the user name and `guest123` for the password.
5. The client should display the following lines:

```
balance = 68.25
balance = 32.55
456: 44.77
730: 19.54
268: 100.07
836: 32.55
456: 44.77
4.00
7.00
```

deploytool Tips for Entity Beans with Bean-Managed Persistence

Chapter 4 gave step-by-step instructions for creating and packaging a session bean. To build an entity bean, you follow the same procedures, but with the following exceptions.

1. In the New Enterprise Bean wizard, specify the bean's type and persistent management.
   a. In the General dialog box, select the Entity radio button.
   b. In the Entity Settings dialog box, select the radio button for Bean-Managed Persistence.
2. In the Resource Refs tab, specify the resource factories referenced by the bean. These settings enable the bean to connect to the database. For instructions, see the section deploytool Tips for Resource References (page 354).
3. Before you deploy the bean, verify that the JNDI names are correct.
   a. Select the application from the tree.
   b. Select the JNDI Names tab.

Mapping Table Relationships for Bean-Managed Persistence

In a relational database, tables can be related by common columns. The relationships between the tables affect the design of their corresponding entity beans. The entity beans discussed in this section are backed up by tables with the following types of relationships:

- One-to-one
- One-to-many
- Many-to-many

One-to-One Relationships

In a one-to-one relationship, each row in a table is related to a single row in another table. For example, in a warehouse application, a `storagebin` table might have a one-to-one relationship with a `widget` table. This application would model a physical warehouse in which each storage bin contains one type of widget and each widget resides in one storage bin.

Figure 5–1 illustrates the `storagebin` and `widget` tables. Because the `storagebinid` uniquely identifies a row in the `storagebin` table, it is that table's primary key. The `widgetid` is the primary key of the `widget` table. The two tables are related because the `widgetid` is also a column in the `storagebin` table. By referring to the primary key of the `widget` table, the `widgetid` in the `storagebin` table identifies which widget resides in a particular storage bin in the warehouse. Because the `widgetid` of the `storagebin` table refers to the primary key of another table, it is called a *foreign key.* (The figures in this chapter denote a primary key with PK and a foreign key with FK.)

Figure 5–1 One-to-One Table Relationship

A dependent (child) table includes a foreign key that matches the primary key of the referenced (parent) table. The values of the foreign keys in the `storagebin` (child) table depend on the primary keys in the `widget` (parent) table. For example, if the `storagebin` table has a row with a `widgetid` of 344, then the widget table should also have a row whose `widgetid` is 344.

When designing a database application, you may choose to enforce the dependency between the parent and child tables. There are two ways to enforce such a dependency: by defining a referential constraint in the database or by performing checks in the application code. The `storagebin` table has a referential constraint named `fk_widgetid`:

```
CREATE TABLE storagebin
   (storagebinid VARCHAR(3)
    CONSTRAINT pk_storagebin PRIMARY KEY,
    widgetid VARCHAR(3),
    quantity INTEGER,
    CONSTRAINT fk_widgetid
    FOREIGN KEY (widgetid)
     REFERENCES widget(widgetid));
```

The source code for the following example is in the j2eetutorial/examples/src/ejb/storagebin directory. To compile the code, go to the j2eetutorial/examples directory and type ant storagebin. A sample StorageBinApp.ear file is in the j2eetutorial/examples/ears directory.

The StorageBinBean and WidgetBean classes illustrate the one-to-one relationship of the storagebin and widget tables. The StorageBinBean class contains variables for each column in the storagebin table, including the foreign key, widgetId:

```
private String storageBinId;
private String widgetId;
private int quantity;
```

The ejbFindByWidgetId method of the StorageBinBean class returns the storageBinId that matches a given widgetId:

```
public String ejbFindByWidgetId(String widgetId)
   throws FinderException {

   String storageBinId;

   try {
      storageBinId = selectByWidgetId(widgetId);
    } catch (Exception ex) {
        throw new EJBException("ejbFindByWidgetId: " +
           ex.getMessage());
    }

   if (storageBinId == null) {
      throw new ObjectNotFoundException
         ("Row for widgetId " + widgetId + " not found.");
   }
   else {
      return storageBinId;
   }
}
```

The ejbFindByWidgetId method locates the widgetId by querying the database in the selectByWidgetId method:

```
private String selectByWidgetId(String widgetId)
   throws SQLException {

   String storageBinId;
```

```
      String selectStatement =
            "select storagebinid " +
            "from storagebin where widgetid = ? ";
      PreparedStatement prepStmt =
            con.prepareStatement(selectStatement);
      prepStmt.setString(1, widgetId);

      ResultSet rs = prepStmt.executeQuery();

      if (rs.next()) {
         storageBinId = rs.getString(1);
      }
      else {
         storageBinId = null;
      }

      prepStmt.close();
      return storageBinId;
   }
```

To find out in which storage bin a widget resides, the `StorageBinClient` program calls the `findByWidgetId` method:

```
String widgetId = "777";
StorageBin storageBin =
   storageBinHome.findByWidgetId(widgetId);
String storageBinId = (String)storageBin.getPrimaryKey();
int quantity = storageBin.getQuantity();
```

Running the StorageBinEJB Example

1. Create the `storagebin` database table.
   a. Go to the `j2eetutorial/examples` directory.
   b. Type `ant create-storagebin-table`.
2. Deploy the `StorageBinApp.ear` file (located in the `j2eetutorial/examples/ears` directory).
3. Run the client.
   a. Go to the `j2eetutorial/examples/ears` directory.
   b. Set the `APPCPATH` environment variable to `StorageBinAppClient.jar`.

c. Type the following command on a single line:

```
runclient -client StorageBinApp.ear -name
   StorageBinClient -textauth
```

d. At the login prompts, enter `guest` for the user name and `guest123` for the password.

One-to-Many Relationships

If the primary key in a parent table matches multiple foreign keys in a child table, then the relationship is one-to-many. This relationship is common in database applications. For example, an application for a sports league might access a `team` table and a `player` table. Each team has multiple players, and each player belongs to a single team. Every row in the child table (`player`) has a foreign key identifying the player's team. This foreign key matches the `team` table's primary key.

The sections that follow describe how you might implement one-to-many relationships in entity beans. When designing such entity beans, you must decide whether both tables are represented by entity beans, or just one.

A Helper Class for the Child Table

Not every database table needs to be mapped to an entity bean. If a database table doesn't represent a business entity, or if it stores information that is contained in another entity, then the table should be represented with a helper class. In an online shopping application, for example, each order submitted by a customer can have multiple line items. The application stores the information in the database tables shown by Figure 5–2.

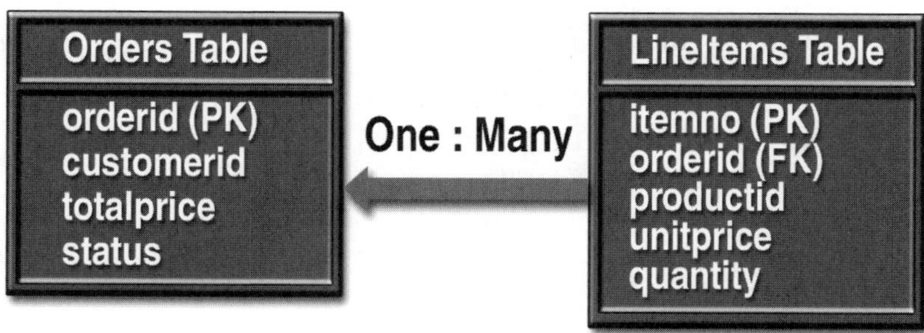

Figure 5–2 One-to-Many Relationship: Order and Line Items

Not only does a line item belong to an order, it also does not exist without the order. Therefore, the `lineitems` table should be represented with a helper class and not with an entity bean. Using a helper class in this case is not required, but doing so might improve performance because a helper class uses fewer system resources than an entity bean.

The source code for the following example is in the `j2eetutorial/examples/src/ejb/order` directory. To compile the code, go to the `j2eetutorial/examples` directory and type `ant order`. A sample `OrderApp.ear` file is in the `j2eetutorial/examples/ears` directory.

The `LineItem` and `OrderBean` classes show how to implement a one-to-many relationship with a helper class (`LineItem`). The instance variables in the `LineItem` class correspond to the columns in the `lineitems` table. The `itemNo` variable matches the primary key for the `lineitems` table, and the `orderId` variable represents the table's foreign key. Here is the source code for the `LineItem` class:

```
public class LineItem implements java.io.Serializable {

   String productId;
   int quantity;
   double unitPrice;
   int itemNo;
   String orderId;


   public LineItem(String productId, int quantity,
     double unitPrice, int itemNo, String orderId) {

      this.productId = productId;
      this.quantity = quantity;
      this.unitPrice = unitPrice;
      this.itemNo = itemNo;
      this.orderId = orderId;
   }

   public String getProductId() {
      return productId;
   }

   public int getQuantity() {
      return quantity;
   }

   public double getUnitPrice() {
```

```
      return unitPrice;
   }

   public int getItemNo() {
      return itemNo;
   }

   public String getOrderId() {
      return orderId;
   }
}
```

The `OrderBean` class contains an `ArrayList` variable named `lineItems`. Each element in the `lineItems` variable is a `LineItem` object. The `lineItems` variable is passed to the `OrderBean` class in the `ejbCreate` method. For every `LineItem` object in the `lineItems` variable, the `ejbCreate` method inserts a row into the `lineitems` table. It also inserts a single row into the `orders` table. The code for the `ejbCreate` method follows:

```
public String ejbCreate(String orderId, String customerId,
    String status, double totalPrice, ArrayList lineItems)
    throws CreateException {

    try {
       insertOrder(orderId, customerId, status, totalPrice);
       for (int i = 0; i < lineItems.size(); i++) {
          LineItem item = (LineItem)lineItems.get(i);
          insertItem(item);
       }
    } catch (Exception ex) {
        throw new EJBException("ejbCreate: " +
           ex.getMessage());
    }

    this.orderId = orderId;
    this.customerId = customerId;
    this.status = status;
    this.totalPrice = totalPrice;
    this.lineItems = lineItems ;

    return orderId;
}
```

The OrderClient program creates and loads an ArrayList of LineItem objects. The program passes this ArrayList to the entity bean when it invokes the create method:

```
ArrayList lineItems = new ArrayList();
lineItems.add(new LineItem("p23", 13, 12.00, 1, "123"));
lineItems.add(new LineItem("p67", 47, 89.00, 2, "123"));
lineItems.add(new LineItem("p11", 28, 41.00, 3, "123"));
...
Order duke = home.create("123", "c44", "open",
   totalItems(lineItems), lineItems);
```

Other methods in the OrderBean class also access both database tables. The ejbRemove method, for example, not only deletes a row from the orders table, but also deletes all corresponding rows in the lineitems table. The ejbLoad and ejbStore methods synchronize the state of an OrderEJB instance, including the lineItems ArrayList, with the orders and lineitems tables.

The ejbFindByProductId method enables clients to locate all orders that have a particular product. This method queries the lineitems table for all rows with a specific productId. The method returns a Collection of Order objects. The OrderClient program iterates through the Collection and prints the primary key of each order:

```
Collection c = home.findByProductId("p67");
Iterator i=c.iterator();
while (i.hasNext()) {
   Order order = (Order)i.next();
   String id = (String)order.getPrimaryKey();
   System.out.println(id);
}
```

Running the OrderEJB Example

1. Create the orders database table:.
   a. Go to the j2eetutorial/examples directory.
   b. Type ant create-order-table.
2. Deploy the OrderApp.ear file (located in the j2eetutorial/examples/ears directory).
3. Run the client.
   a. Go to the j2eetutorial/examples/ears directory.
   b. Set the APPCPATH environment variable to OrderAppClient.jar.

c. Type the following command on a single line:

```
runclient -client OrderApp.ear -name OrderClient
-textauth
```

d. At the login prompts, enter `guest` for the user name and `guest123` for the password.

An Entity Bean for the Child Table

You should consider building an entity bean for a child table under the following conditions:

- The information in the child table is not dependent on the parent table.
- The business entity of the child table could exist without that of the parent table.
- The child table might be accessed by another application that does not access the parent table.

These conditions exist in the following scenario. Suppose that each sales representative in a company has multiple customers and that each customer has only one sales representative. The company tracks its sales force with a database application. In the database, each row in the `salesrep` table (parent) matches multiple rows in the `customer` table (child). Figure 5–3 illustrates this relationship.

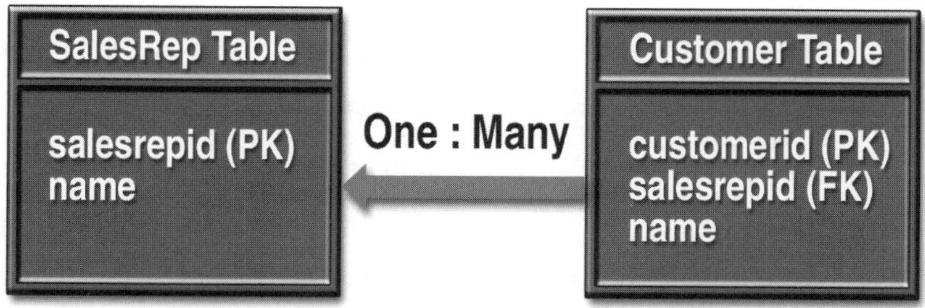

Figure 5–3 One-to-Many Relationship: Sales Representative and Customers

The `SalesRepBean` and `CustomerBean` entity bean classes implement the one-to-many relationship of the `sales` and `customer` tables.

The source code for this example is in the `j2eetutorial/examples/src/ejb/salesrep` directory. To compile the code, go to the j2eetutorial/examples directory and type ant salesrep. A sample SalesRepApp.ear file is in the j2eetutorial/examples/ears directory.

The SalesRepBean class contains a variable named customerIds, which is an ArrayList of String elements. These String elements identify which customers belong to the sales representative. Because the customerIds variable reflects this relationship, the SalesRepBean class must keep the variable up to date.

The SalesRepBean class instantiates the customerIds variable in the setEntityContext method, not in ejbCreate. The container invokes setEntityContext just once—when it creates the bean instance—ensuring that customerIds is instantiated just once. Because the same bean instance can assume different identities during its life cycle, instantiating customerIds in ejbCreate might cause multiple and unnecessary instantiations. Therefore, the SalesRepBean class instantiates the customerIds variable in setEntityContext:

```
public void setEntityContext(EntityContext context) {

   this.context = context;
   customerIds = new ArrayList();

   try {
      makeConnection();
      Context initial = new InitialContext();
      Object objref =
         initial.lookup("java:comp/env/ejb/Customer");

      customerHome =
         (CustomerHome)PortableRemoteObject.narrow(objref,
            CustomerHome.class);
   } catch (Exception ex) {
      throw new EJBException("setEntityContext: " +
         ex.getMessage());
   }
}
```

Invoked by the ejbLoad method, loadCustomerIds is a private method that refreshes the customerIds variable. There are two approaches when coding a method such as loadCustomerIds: fetch the identifiers from the customer database table or get them from the CustomerEJB entity bean. Fetching the identifiers from the database might be faster, but exposes the code in the SalesRepBean class to the CustomerEJB bean's underlying database table. In the future, if you were to change the CustomerEJB bean's table (or move the bean to a different J2EE server), you might need to change the SalesRepBean code. But if the SalesRepBean class gets the identifiers from the CustomerEJB entity bean, no coding changes would be required. The two approaches present a trade-off: performance versus flexibility. The `SalesRepEJB` example opts for flexibility, loading the `customerIds` variable by calling the `findBySalesRep` and `getPrimaryKey` methods of `CustomerEJB`. Here is the code for the `loadCustomerIds` method:

```
private void loadCustomerIds() {

   customerIds.clear();

   try {
      Collection c = customerHome.findBySalesRep(salesRepId);
      Iterator i=c.iterator();

      while (i.hasNext()) {
         Customer customer = (Customer)i.next();
         String id = (String)customer.getPrimaryKey();
         customerIds.add(id);
      }

   } catch (Exception ex) {
      throw new EJBException("Exception in loadCustomerIds: " +
          ex.getMessage());
   }
}
```

If a customer's sales representative changes, the client program updates the database by calling the `setSalesRepId` method of the `CustomerBean` class. The next time a business method of the `SalesRepBean` class is called, the `ejbLoad` method invokes `loadCustomerIds`, which refreshes the `customerIds` variable. (To ensure that `ejbLoad` is invoked before each business method, set the transaction attributes of the business methods to Required.) For example, the `SalesRepClient` program changes the `salesRepId` for a customer named Mary Jackson as follows:

```
Customer mary = customerHome.findByPrimaryKey("987");
mary.setSalesRepId("543");
```

The `salesRepId` value 543 identifies a sales representative named Janice Martin. To list all of Janice's customers, the `SalesRepClient` program invokes the getCustomerIds method, iterates through the ArrayList of identifiers, and locates each CustomerEJB entity bean by calling its findByPrimaryKey method:

```
SalesRep janice = salesHome.findByPrimaryKey("543");
ArrayList a = janice.getCustomerIds();
i = a.iterator();

while (i.hasNext()) {
   String customerId = (String)i.next();
   Customer customer =
customerHome.findByPrimaryKey(customerId);
   String name = customer.getName();
   System.out.println(customerId + ": " + name);
}
```

Running the SalesRepEJB Example

1. Create the database tables.
   a. Go to the j2eetutorial/examples/src directory.
   b. Type ant create-salesrep-table.
2. Deploy the SalesRepApp.ear file (located in the j2eetutorial/examples/ears directory).
3. Run the client.
   a. Go to the j2eetutorial/examples/ears directory.
   b. Set the APPCPATH environment variable to SalesRepAppClient.jar.
   c. Type the following command on a single line:

   ```
   runclient -client SalesRepApp.ear -name SalesRepClient
   -textauth
   ```

   d. At the login prompts, enter guest for the user name and guest123 for the password.

Many-to-Many Relationships

In a many-to-many relationship, each entity may be related to multiple occurrences of the other entity. For example, a college course has many students and each student may take several courses. In a database, this relationship is represented by a cross reference table containing the foreign keys. In Figure 5–4, the cross reference table is the enrollment table. These tables are accessed by the StudentBean, CourseBean, and EnrollerBean classes.

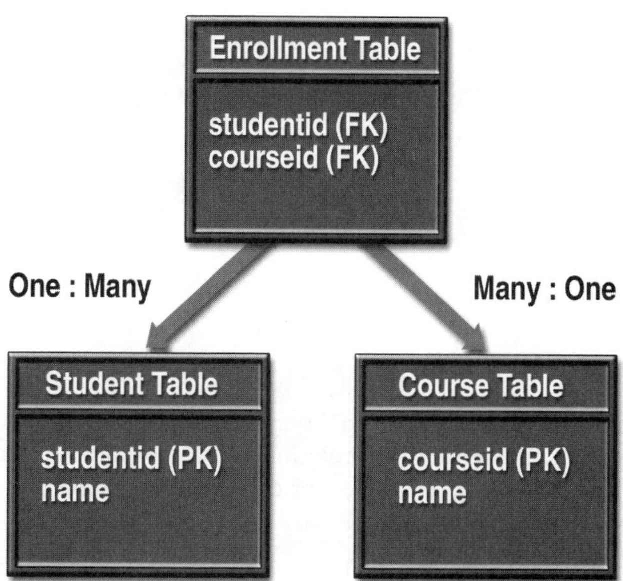

Figure 5–4 Many-to-Many Relationship: Students and Courses

The source code for this example is in the `j2eetutorial/examples/src/ejb/enroller` directory. To compile the code, go to the `j2eetutorial/examples` directory and type `ant enroller`. A sample `EnrollerApp.ear` file is in the `j2eetutorial/examples/ears` directory.

The `StudentBean` and `CourseBean` classes are complementary. Each class contains an `ArrayList` of foreign keys. The `StudentBean` class contains an `ArrayList` named `courseIds`, which identifies the courses the student is enrolled in. Likewise, the `CourseBean` class contains an `ArrayList` named `studentIds`.

The `ejbLoad` method of the `StudentBean` class adds elements to the `courseIds` `ArrayList` by calling `loadCourseIds`, a private method. The `loadCourseIds` method gets the course identifiers from the `EnrollerEJB` session bean. The source code for the `loadCourseIds` method follows:

```
private void loadCourseIds() {

   courseIds.clear();

   try {
      Enroller enroller = enrollerHome.create();
```

```
            ArrayList a = enroller.getCourseIds(studentId);
            courseIds.addAll(a);

        } catch (Exception ex) {
            throw new EJBException("Exception in loadCourseIds: " +
                ex.getMessage());
        }
    }
```

Invoked by the `loadCourseIds` method, the `getCourseIds` method of the `EnrollerBean` class queries the `enrollment` table:

```
select courseid from enrollment
where studentid = ?
```

Only the `EnrollerBean` class accesses the `enrollment` table. Therefore, the `EnrollerBean` class manages the student-course relationship represented in the `enrollment` table. If a student enrolls in a course, for example, the client calls the `enroll` business method, which inserts a row:

```
insert into enrollment
values (studentid, courseid)
```

If a student drops a course, the `unEnroll` method deletes a row:

```
delete from enrollment
where studentid = ? and courseid = ?
```

And if a student leaves the school, the `deleteStudent` method deletes all rows in the table for that student:

```
delete from enrollment
where student = ?
```

The `EnrollerBean` class does not delete the matching row from the `student` table. That action is performed by the `ejbRemove` method of the `StudentBean` class. To ensure that both deletes are executed as a single operation, they should belong to the same transaction. See Chapter 14 for more information.

Running the EnrollerEJB Example

1. Create the database tables.
    a. Go to the `j2eetutorial/examples` directory.
    b. Type `ant create-enroller-table`.

2. Deploy the EnrollerApp.ear file (located in the j2eetutorial/examples/ears directory).
3. Run the client.
   a. Go to the j2eetutorial/examples/ears directory.
   b. Set the APPCPATH environment variable to EnrollerAppClient.jar.
   c. Type the following command on a single line:

   ```
   runclient -client EnrollerApp.ear -name EnrollerClient
   -textauth
   ```

   d. At the login prompts, enter guest for the user name and guest123 for the password.

Primary Keys for Bean-Managed Persistence

You specify the primary key class in the entity bean's deployment descriptor. In most cases, your primary key class will be a String, an Integer, or some other class that belongs to the J2SE or J2EE standard libraries. For some entity beans, you will need to define your own primary key class. For example, if the bean has a composite primary key (that is, one composed of multiple fields), then you must create a primary key class.

The Primary Key Class

The following primary key class is a composite key—the productId and vendorId fields together uniquely identify an entity bean.

```
public class ItemKey implements java.io.Serializable {

   public String productId;
   public String vendorId;

   public ItemKey() { };

   public ItemKey(String productId, String vendorId) {

     this.productId = productId;
     this.vendorId = vendorId;
   }
```

```
    public String getProductId() {

       return productId;
    }

    public String getVendorId() {

       return vendorId;
    }

    public boolean equals(Object other) {

       if (other instanceof ItemKey) {
          return (productId.equals(((ItemKey)other).productId)
                  && vendorId.equals(((ItemKey)other).vendorId));
       }
       return false;
    }

    public int hashCode() {

       return productId.concat(vendorId).hashCode();
    }
}
```

For bean-managed persistence, a primary key class must meet these requirements:

- The access control modifier of the class is `public`.
- All fields are declared as `public`.
- The class has a public default constructor.
- The class implements the `hashCode()` and `equals(Object other)` methods.
- The class is serializable.

Primary Keys in the Entity Bean Class

With bean-managed persistence, the `ejbCreate` method assigns the input parameters to instance variables and then returns the primary key class:

```
public ItemKey ejbCreate(String productId, String vendorId,
   String description) throws CreateException {

   if (productId == null || vendorId == null) {
      throw new CreateException(
```

```
                  "The productId and vendorId are required.");
       }

       this.productId = productId;
       this.vendorId = vendorId;
       this.description = description;

       return new ItemKey(productId, vendorId);
    }
```

The `ejbFindByPrimaryKey` verifies the existence of the database row for the given primary key:

```
public ItemKey ejbFindByPrimaryKey(ItemKey primaryKey)
   throws FinderException {

   try {
      if (selectByPrimaryKey(primaryKey))
         return primaryKey;
   ...
}

private boolean selectByPrimaryKey(ItemKey primaryKey)
   throws SQLException {

   String selectStatement =
         "select productid " +
         "from item where productid = ? and vendorid = ?";
   PreparedStatement prepStmt =
         con.prepareStatement(selectStatement);
   prepStmt.setString(1, primaryKey.getProductId());
   prepStmt.setString(2, primaryKey.getVendorId());
   ResultSet rs = prepStmt.executeQuery();
   boolean result = rs.next();
   prepStmt.close();
   return result;
}
```

Getting the Primary Key

A client can fetch the primary key of an entity bean by invoking the `getPrimaryKey` method of the `EJBObject` class:

```
SavingsAccount account;
...
String id = (String)account.getPrimaryKey();
```

The entity bean retrieves its own primary key by calling the `getPrimaryKey` method of the `EntityContext` class:

```
EntityContext context;
...
String id = (String) context.getPrimaryKey();
```

Handling Exceptions

The exceptions thrown by enterprise beans fall into two categories: system and application.

A *system exception* indicates a problem with the services that support an application. Examples of these problems include the following: a database connection cannot be obtained, a SQL insert fails because the database is full, or a `lookup` method cannot find the desired object. If your enterprise bean encounters a system-level problem, it should throw a `javax.ejb.EJBException`. The container will wrap the `EJBException` in a `RemoteException`, which it passes back to the client. Because the `EJBException` is a subclass of the `RuntimeException`, you do not have to specify it in the `throws` clause of the method declaration. If a system exception is thrown, the EJB container might destroy the bean instance. Therefore, a system exception cannot be handled by the bean's client program; it requires intervention by a system administrator.

An *application exception* signals an error in the business logic of an enterprise bean. There are two types of application exceptions: customized and predefined. A customized exception is one that you've coded yourself, such as the `InsufficentBalanceException` thrown by the `debit` business method of the `SavingsAccountEJB` example. The `javax.ejb` package includes several predefined exceptions that are designed to handle common problems. For example, an `ejbCreate` method should throw a `CreateException` to indicate an invalid input parameter. When an enterprise bean throws an application exception, the container does not wrap it in another exception. The client should be able to handle any application exception it receives.

If a system exception occurs within a transaction, the EJB container rolls back the transaction. However, if an application exception is thrown within a transaction, the container does not roll back the transaction.

Table 5–2 summarizes the exceptions of the `javax.ejb` package. All of these exceptions are application exceptions, except for the `NoSuchEntityException` and the `EJBException`, which are system exceptions.

Table 5–2 Exceptions

Method Name	Exception It Throws	Reason for Throwing
`ejbCreate`	`CreateException`	An input parameter is invalid.
`ejbFindByPrimaryKey` (and other finder methods that return a single object)	`ObjectNotFoundException` (subclass of `FinderException`)	The database row for the requested entity bean cannot be found.
`ejbRemove`	`RemoveException`	The entity bean's row cannot be deleted from the database.
`ejbLoad`	`NoSuchEntityException`	The database row to be loaded cannot be found.
`ejbStore`	`NoSuchEntityException`	The database row to be updated cannot be found.
(all methods)	`EJBException`	A system problem has been encountered.

6

Container-Managed Persistence Examples

Dale Green

AN entity bean with container-managed persistence offers important advantages to the bean developer. First, the EJB container handles all database storage and retrieval calls. Second, the container manages the relationships between the entity beans. Because of these services, you don't have to code the database access calls in the entity bean. Instead, you specify settings in the bean's deployment descriptor. Not only does this approach save you time, but it makes the bean portable across various database servers.

This chapter focuses on the source code and deployment settings for an example called `RosterApp`, an application that features entity beans with container-managed persistence. If you are unfamiliar with the terms and concepts mentioned in this chapter, please consult the section Container-Managed Persistence (page 53).

In This Chapter

Overview of the RosterApp Application

The `RosterApp` application maintains the team rosters for players in sports leagues. The application has five components. The `RosterAppClient` component is a J2EE application client that accesses the `RosterEJB` session bean through the bean's remote interfaces. `RosterEJB` accesses three entity beans—`PlayerEJB`, `TeamEJB`, and `LeagueEJB`—through their local interfaces.

The entity beans use container-managed persistence and relationships. The `TeamEJB` and `PlayerEJB` entity beans have a bidirectional, many-to-many relationship. In a bidirectional relationship, each bean has a relationship field whose value identifies the related bean instance. The multiplicity of the `TeamEJB`-

PlayerEJB relationship is many-to-many: Players who participate in more than one sport belong to multiple teams, and each team has multiple players. The LeagueEJB and TeamEJB entity beans also have a bidirectional relationship, but the multiplicity is one-to-many: A league has many teams, but a team can belong to just one league.

Figure 6–1 shows the components and relationships of the RosterApp application. The dotted lines represent the access gained through invocations of the JNDI lookup method. The solid lines represent the container-managed relationships.

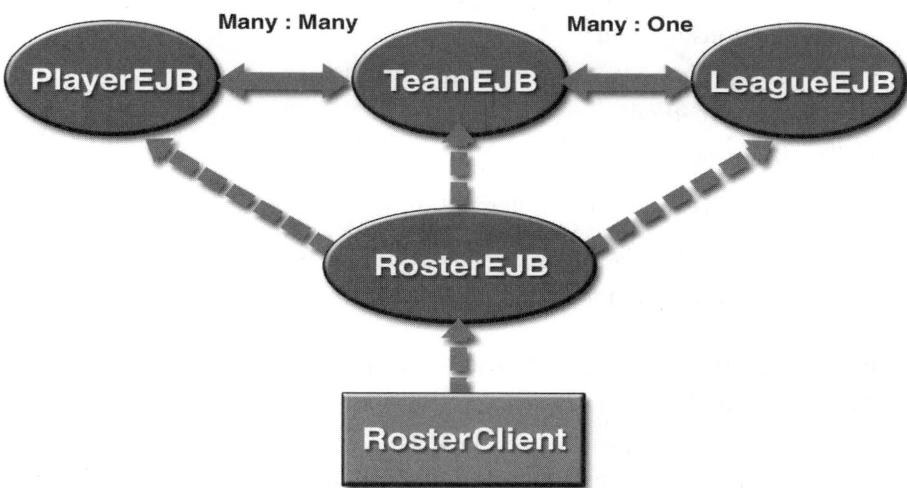

Figure 6–1 RosterApp J2EE Application

The PlayerEJB Code

The PlayerEJB entity bean represents a player in a sports league. Like any entity bean with container-managed persistence, PlayerEJB needs the following code:

- Entity bean class (PlayerBean)
- Local home interface (LocalPlayerHome)
- Local interface (LocalPlayer)

The source code for this example is in the j2eetutorial/examples/src/ejb/cmproster directory. To compile the code, go to the j2eetutorial/examples directory and type ant cmproster. A sample Roster-App.ear file is in the j2eetutorial/examples/ears directory.

Entity Bean Class

For container-managed persistence, the code of the entity bean class must meet the syntax requirements. First, the class must be defined as public and abstract. Also, the class must implement the following:

- The EntityBean interface
- Zero or more ejbCreate and ejbPostCreate methods
- The get and set access methods, defined as abstract, for the persistent and relationship fields
- Any select methods, defining them as abstract
- The home methods
- The business methods

The entity bean class must not implement these methods:

- The finder methods
- The finalize method

Differences between Container-Managed and Bean-Managed Code

Because it contains no calls to access the database, an entity bean with container-managed persistence requires a lot less code than one with bean-managed persistence. For example, the PlayerBean.java source file discussed in this chapter is much smaller than the SavingsAccountBean.java code documented in Chapter 5. Table 6–1 compares the code of the two types of entity beans.

Table 6–1 Coding Differences between Persistent Types

Difference	Container-Managed	Bean-Managed
Class definition	Abstract	Not abstract
Database access calls	Generated by tools	Coded by developers
Persistent state	Represented by virtual persistent fields	Coded as instance variables

Table 6–1 Coding Differences between Persistent Types (Continued)

Difference	Container-Managed	Bean-Managed
Access methods for persistent and relationship fields	Required	None
`findByPrimaryKey` method	Handled by container	Coded by developers
Customized finder methods	Handled by container, but the developer must define the EJB QL) queries	Coded by developers
Select methods	Handled by container	None
Return value of `ejbCreate`	Should be null	Must be the primary key

Note that for both types of persistence, the rules for implementing business and home methods are the same. See the sections The Business Methods (page 91) and The Home Methods (page 92) in Chapter 5.

Access Methods

An entity bean with container-managed persistence has persistent and relationship fields. These fields are virtual, so you do not code them in the class as instance variables. Instead, you specify them in the bean's deployment descriptor. To permit access to the fields, you define abstract `get` and `set` methods in the entity bean class.

Access Methods for Persistent Fields

The EJB container automatically performs the database storage and retrieval of the bean's persistent fields. The deployment descriptor of `PlayerEJB` specifies the following persistent fields:

- `playerId` (primary key)
- `name`
- `position`
- `salary`

The PlayerBean class defines the access methods for the persistent fields as follows:

```
public abstract String getPlayerId();
public abstract void setPlayerId(String id);

public abstract String getName();
public abstract void setName(String name);

public abstract String getPosition();
public abstract void setPosition(String position);

public abstract double getSalary();
public abstract void setSalary(double salary);
```

The name of an access method begins with get or set, followed by the capitalized name of the persistent or relationship field. For example, the accessor methods for the salary field are getSalary and setSalary. This naming convention is similar to that of JavaBeans components.

Access Methods for Relationship Fields

In the RosterApp application, since a player can belong to multiple teams, a PlayerEJB instance may be related to many TeamEJB instances. To specify this relationship, the deployment descriptor of PlayerEJB defines a relationship field named teams. In the PlayerBean class, the access methods for the teams relationship field are as follows:

```
public abstract Collection getTeams();
public abstract void setTeams(Collection teams);
```

Select Methods

A select method is similar to a finder method in the following ways:

- A select method can return a local or remote interface (or a collection of interfaces).
- A select method queries a database.
- The deployment descriptor specifies an EJB QL query for a select method.
- The entity bean class does not implement the select method.

However, a select method differs significantly from a finder method:

- A select method can return a persistent field (or a collection thereof) of a related entity bean. A finder method can return only a local or remote interface (or a collection of interfaces).
- Since it is not exposed in any of the local or remote interfaces, a select method cannot be invoked by a client. It can be invoked only by the methods implemented within the entity bean class. A select method is usually invoked by a business method.
- A select method is defined in the entity bean class. For bean-managed persistence, a finder method is defined in the entity bean class, but for container-managed persistence it is not.

The `PlayerBean` class defines these select methods:

```
public abstract Collection ejbSelectLeagues(LocalPlayer player)
   throws FinderException;
public abstract Collection ejbSelectSports(LocalPlayer player)
   throws FinderException;
```

The signature for a select method must follow these rules:

- The prefix of the method name must be `ejbSelect`.
- The access control modifier must be `public`.
- The method must be declared as `abstract`.
- The `throws` clause must include the `javax.ejb.FinderException`.

Business Methods

Since clients cannot invoke select methods, the `PlayerBean` class wraps them in the `getLeagues` and `getSports` business methods:

```
public Collection getLeagues() throws FinderException {

   LocalPlayer player =
      (team.LocalPlayer)context.getEJBLocalObject();
   return ejbSelectLeagues(player);
}

public Collection getSports() throws FinderException {

   LocalPlayer player =
      (team.LocalPlayer)context.getEJBLocalObject();
   return ejbSelectSports(player);
}
```

Entity Bean Methods

Because the container handles persistence, the life-cycle methods in the PlayerBean class are nearly empty.

The ejbCreate method initializes the bean instance by assigning the input arguments to the persistent fields. After the ejbCreate method completes, the container inserts a row into the database. Here is the source code for the ejbCreate method:

```
public String ejbCreate (String id, String name,
    String position, double salary) throws CreateException {

    setPlayerId(id);
    setName(name);
    setPosition(position);
    setSalary(salary);
    return null;
}
```

Except for a debug statement, the ejbRemove method in the PlayerBean class is empty. The container invokes ejbRemove right before it deletes the database row.

The ejbPostCreate method returns void and it has the same input parameters as the ejbCreate method. If you want to set a relationship field to initialize the bean instance, you should do so in the ejbPostCreate method. You may not set a relationship field in the ejbCreate method.

The container automatically synchronizes the state of the entity bean with the database. After the container loads the bean's state from the database, it invokes the ejbLoad method. In like manner, before storing the state in the database, the container invokes the ejbStore method.

Local Home Interface

The local home interface defines the create, finder, and home methods that may be invoked by local clients.

The syntax rules for a create method follow:

- The name begins with create.
- It has the same number and types of arguments as its matching ejbCreate method in the entity bean class.
- It returns the local interface type of the entity bean.

- The throws clause includes the exceptions specified by the throws clause of the corresponding ejbCreate method.
- The throws clause contains the javax.ejb.CreateException.

These rules apply for a finder method:

- The name begins with find.
- The return type is the entity bean's local interface type, or a collection of those types.
- The throws clause contains the javax.ejb.FinderException.
- The findByPrimaryKey method must be defined.

An excerpt of the LocalPlayerHome interface follows.

```
package team;

import java.util.*;
import javax.ejb.*;

public interface LocalPlayerHome extends EJBLocalHome {

    public LocalPlayer create (String id, String name,
        String position, double salary)
        throws CreateException;

    public LocalPlayer findByPrimaryKey (String id)
        throws FinderException;

    public Collection findByPosition(String position)
        throws FinderException;
     ...
    public Collection findByLeague(LocalLeague league)
        throws FinderException;
    ...
  }
```

Local Interface

This interface defines the business and access methods that a local client may invoke. The PlayerBean class implements two business methods: getLeagues and getSports. It also defines several get and set access methods for the persistent and relationship fields. The set methods are hidden from the bean's clients because they are not defined in the `LocalPlayer` interface. However, the `get` methods are exposed to the clients by the interface:

```
package team;

import java.util.*;
import javax.ejb.*;

public interface LocalPlayer extends EJBLocalObject {

    public String getPlayerId();
    public String getName();
    public String getPosition();
    public double getSalary();
    public Collection getTeams();

    public Collection getLeagues() throws FinderException;
    public Collection getSports() throws FinderException;
}
```

A Guided Tour of the RosterApp Settings

This section introduces you to the settings of the deployment descriptors for entity beans with container-managed persistence and relationships. As this tour guides you through the `deploytool` screens, it discusses the highlights of the tabs and dialog boxes that appear.

To begin our tour, please run `deploytool` and open the `RosterApp.ear` file, which is in the `j2eetutorial/examples/ears` directory.

RosterApp

To view the deployment settings for the application, select the `RosterApp` node in the tree view.

General Tab (RosterApp)

The Contents field displays the files contained in the `RosterApp.ear` file, including the two EJB JAR files (`team-ejb.jar`, `roster-ejb.jar`) and the J2EE application client JAR file (`roster-ac.jar`). See Figure 6–2.

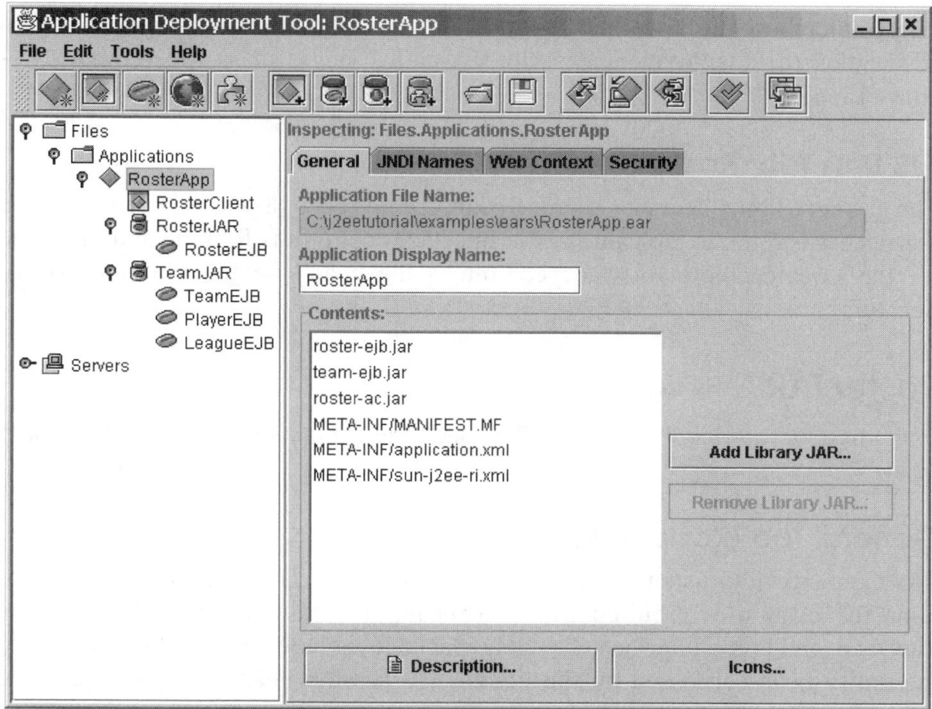

Figure 6–2 General Tab of `RosterApp`

JNDI Names Tab (RosterApp)

The Application table lists the JNDI names for the enterprise beans in the `RosterApp` application.

The References table has two entries. The EJB Ref entry maps the coded name (`ejb/SimpleRoster`) in the `RosterClient` to the JNDI name of the `RosterEJB` session bean. The Resource entry specifies the JNDI name for the database that is accessed by the entity beans contained in the `TeamJAR` module.

RosterClient

To view this client, expand the `RosterApp` node by clicking its adjacent key icon in the tree view. Next, select `RosterClient`.

JAR File Tab (RosterClient)

The Contents field shows the files contained by the roster-ac.jar file: two XML files (the deployment descriptors) and a single class file (RosterClient.class).

EJB Refs Tab (RosterClient)

The RosterClient accesses a single bean, the RosterEJB session bean. Because this access is remote, the value in the Interfaces column is Remote and the value for the Local/Remote Interface column is the bean's remote interface (roster.Roster).

RosterJAR

In the tree view, select RosterJAR. This JAR file contains the RosterEJB session bean.

General Tab (RosterJAR)

The Contents field lists three packages of class files. The roster package contains the class files required for RosterEJB—the session bean class, remote interface, and home interface. The team package includes the local interfaces for the entity beans accessed by the RosterEJB session bean. The util package holds the utility classes for this application.

RosterEJB

In the tree view, expand the RosterJAR node and select RosterEJB.

General Tab (RosterEJB)

This tab shows that RosterEJB is a stateful session bean with remote access. Because it allows no local access, the Local Interfaces fields are empty.

EJB Refs Tab (RosterEJB)

The RosterEJB session bean accesses three entity beans: PlayerEJB, TeamEJB, and LeagueEJB. Because this access is local, the entries in the Interfaces columns are defined as Local. The Home Interface column lists the local home interfaces of the entity beans. The Local/Remote Interfaces column displays the local interfaces of the entity beans.

To view the runtime deployment settings, select a row in the table. For example, when you select the row with the Coded Name of ejb/SimpleLeague, the

LeagueEJB name appears in the Enterprise Bean Name field. If a component references a local entity bean, then you must enter the name of the referenced bean in the Enterprise Bean Name field.

TeamJAR

In the tree view, select the TeamJAR node. This JAR file contains the three related entity beans: LeagueEJB, TeamEJB, and PlayerEJB.

General Tab (TeamJAR)

The Contents field shows two packages of class files: team and util. The team package has the entity bean classes, local interfaces, and local home interfaces for all three entity beans. The util package contains utility classes.

Relationships Tab (TeamJAR)

On this tab (Figure 6–3) you define the relationships between entity beans with container-managed persistence.

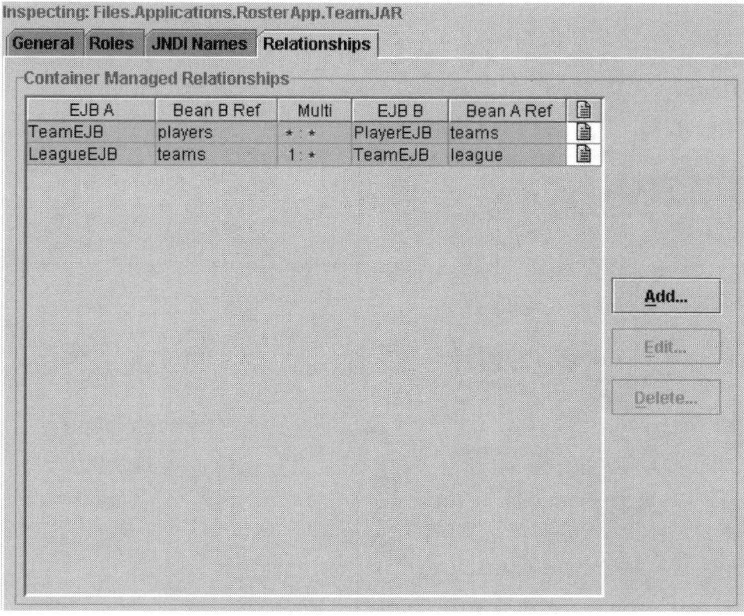

Figure 6–3 Relationships Tab of TeamJAR

The Container Managed Relationships table summarizes two relationships: `TeamEJB-PlayerEJB` and `LeagueEJB-TeamEJB`. In the `TeamEJB-PlayerEJB` relationship, `TeamEJB` is designated as EJB A and `PlayerEJB` as EJB B. (This designation is arbitrary—we could have assigned `PlayerEJB` to EJB A and `TeamEJB` to EJB B.)

Edit Relationship Dialog Box (TeamJAR)

To view the Edit Relationship dialog box (Figure 6–4), on the Relationships tab select a row and click Edit. For example, to view the `TeamEJB-PlayerEJB` relationship, select the row in which the EJB A value is `Team` and then click Edit.

TeamEJB-PlayerEJB Relationship

The Multiplicity combo box offers four choices. For this relationship, the Many To Many choice should be selected because a team has many players and a player can belong to more than one team.

The information in the Enterprise Bean A box defines `TeamEJB` side of the relationship. The Field Referencing Bean B combo box displays the relationship field (`players`) in `TeamEJB`. This field corresponds to the relationship access methods in the `TeamBean.java` source code:

```
public abstract Collection getPlayers();
public abstract void setPlayers(Collection players);
```

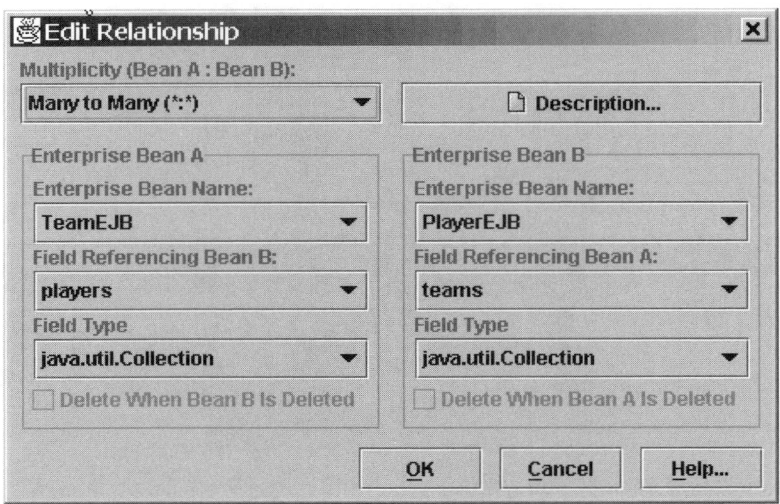

Figure 6–4 Edit Relationship Dialog Box of `TeamJAR`

The selection of the Field Type combo box is `java.util.Collection`, which matches the `players` type in the access methods. The `players` type is a multi-valued object (`Collection`) because on the `TeamEJB` side of the relationship the multiplicity is many.

The `TeamEJB-PlayerEJB` relationship is bidirectional—each bean has a relationship field that identifies the related bean. If this relationship were unidirectional, then one of the beans would not have a relationship field identifying the other bean. For the bean without the relationship field, the value of the Field Referencing combo box would be `<none>`.

LeagueEJB-TeamEJB Relationship

In the Edit Relationship dialog box, the Multiplicity choice should be One to Many. This choice indicates that a single league has multiple teams.

For `LeagueEJB`, the relationship field is `teams` and for `TeamEJB` it is `league`. Because `TeamEJB` is on the multiple side of the relationship, the `teams` field is a `Collection`. In contrast, since `LeagueEJB` is on the single side of the relationship, the `league` field is a single-valued object, a `LocalLeague`. The `TeamBean.java` code defines the league relationship field with these access methods:

```
public abstract LocalLeague getLeague();
public abstract void setLeague(LocalLeague players);
```

For `TeamEJB` (Enterprise Bean B), the Delete When Bean A Is Deleted checkbox is selected. Because of this selection, when a `LeagueEJB` instance is deleted the related `TeamEJB` instances are automatically deleted. This type of deletion, in which one deletion triggers another, is called a *cascade delete*. For `LeagueEJB`, the corresponding checkbox is disabled: If you delete a team, you don't want to automatically delete the league, because there may be other teams in that league. In general, if a bean is on the multiple side of a relationship, the other bean cannot be automatically deleted.

PlayerEJB

In the tree view, expand the `TeamJAR` node and select the `PlayerEJB` entity bean.

General Tab (PlayerEJB)

This tab shows the enterprise bean class and interfaces. Since the `PlayerEJB` entity bean uses container-managed persistence, it has local interfaces. It does not have remote interfaces because it does not allow remote access.

Entity Tab (PlayerEJB)

The radio buttons at the top of the tabbed page define the bean's persistence type (Figure 6–5). For `PlayerEJB`, this type is container-managed persistence, version 2.0. (Because version 1.0 did not support relationships, it is not recommended. These version numbers identify a particular release of the Enterprise JavaBeans Specification, not the J2EE SDK software.)

The Fields To Be Persisted box lists the persistent and relationship fields defined by the access methods in the `PlayerBean.java` code. The checkboxes for the persistent fields must be selected, but those for the relationship fields must not be selected. The `PlayerEJB` entity bean has one relationship field: `teams`.

The abstract schema name is `Player`, a name that represents the relationships and persistent fields of the `PlayerEJB` entity bean. This abstract name is referenced in the `PlayerEJB` EJB QL queries. For more information on EJB QL, see Chapter 8.

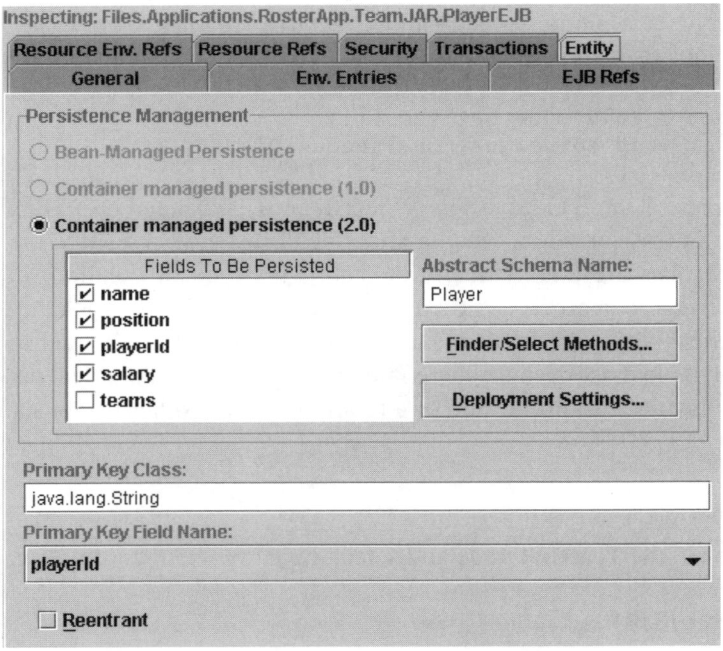

Figure 6–5 Entity Tab of `PlayerEJB`

Finder/Select Methods Dialog Box (PlayerEJB)

To open this dialog box, click Finder/Select Methods on the Entity tab. This dialog box (Figure 6–6) enables you to view and edit the EJB QL queries for a bean's finder and select methods. For example, to list the finder methods defined in the `LocalPlayerHome` interface, select the Local Finders radio button. When you select the finder method, its EJB QL query appears in an editable text field.

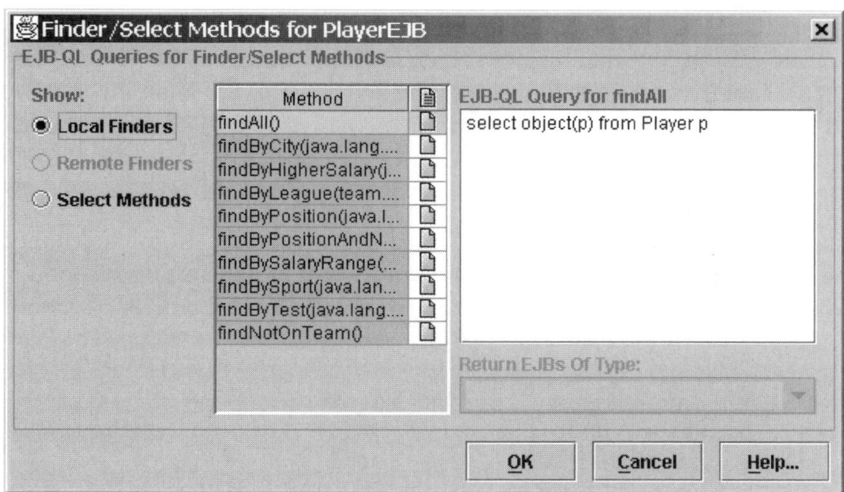

Figure 6–6 Finder/Select Methods Dialog Box of `PlayerEJB`

Entity Deployment Settings Dialog Box (PlayerEJB)

To view this dialog box, click Deployment Settings in the Entity tab. In this dialog box, you define the runtime settings of an entity bean with container-managed persistence. These runtime settings are specific to the J2EE SDK; other implementations of the J2EE platform may take a different approach.

In the J2EE SDK, the bean's persistent fields are stored in a relational database table. In the checkboxes of the Database Table box, you specify whether or not the server automatically creates or drops the table. If you want to save the data in your table between deployments, then make sure that the Delete Table checkbox is not selected. Otherwise, every time you undeploy the bean, the table will be deleted.

The J2EE server accesses the database by issuing SQL calls. In an entity bean with container-managed persistence, you do not code these calls. The `deploytool` utility creates the SQL calls automatically when you click the Generate

Default SQL button. To view the SQL statement for a finder method, for example, select the Local Finder radio button and then select an entry in the Method list. You may modify a SQL statement by editing the text in the SQL Query field.

For the finder and select methods, the corresponding EJB QL query is also displayed. When you click Generate Default SQL, `deploytool` translates the EJB QL queries into SQL calls. If you change an EJB QL query, you should click the Generate Default SQL button again.

To view the SQL `CREATE TABLE` statement, for example, click the Container Methods radio button and then select the createTable entry in the Method list. The `CREATE TABLE` statement defines column names for the bean's persistent fields and specifies a primary key constraint for `playerId`, the bean's primary key field.

When the EJB container creates a new `PlayerEJB` instance, it issues a SQL `INSERT` statement. To examine this statement, select createRow from the Method list. In the `INSERT` statement, the parameters in the `VALUES` clause correspond to the arguments of the `create` method that is defined in the `LocalPlayerHome` interface:

```
public LocalPlayer create (String id, String name,
   String position, double salary) throws CreateException;
```

Database Deployment Settings Dialog Box (PlayerEJB)

To access this dialog box, click Deployment Settings on the Entity tab. Next, in the Deployment Settings dialog box that appears, click Database Settings. The Deployment Settings dialog box with the Database Settings label should appear.

It is important that you set the JNDI name of the database. (If it is not set, the bean cannot connect to the database.) For this example, the Database JNDI Name field should be `jdbc/Cloudscape`. The User Name and Password fields are blank because they are not required for Cloudscape.

Method Invocations in RosterApp

To show how the various components interact, this section describes the sequence of method invocations that occur for particular functions. The source code for the components is in the `j2eetutorial/examples/src/ejb/cmproster` directory.

Creating a Player

1. RosterClient

The RosterClient invokes the createPlayer business method of the RosterEJB session bean. In the following line of code, the type of the myRoster object is Roster, the remote interface of RosterEJB. The argument of the createPlayer method is a PlayerDetails object, which encapsulates information about a particular player.

```
myRoster.createPlayer(new PlayerDetails("P1", "Phil Jones",
   "goalkeeper", 100.00));
```

2. RosterEJB

The createPlayer method of the RosterEJB session bean creates a new instance of the PlayerEJB entity bean. Because the access of PlayerEJB is local, the create method is defined in the local home interface, LocalPlayerHome. The type of the playerHome object is LocalPlayerHome. Here is the source code for the createPlayer method:

```
public void createPlayer(PlayerDetails details) {

try {
   LocalPlayer player = playerHome.create(details.getId(),
      details.getName(), details.getPosition(),
         details.getSalary());
} catch (Exception ex) {
      throw new EJBException(ex.getMessage());
   }
}
```

3. PlayerEJB

The ejbCreate method assigns the input arguments to the bean's persistent fields by calling the set access methods. After invoking the ejbCreate method, the container saves the persistent fields in the database by issuing a SQL INSERT statement. The code for the ejbCreate method follows.

```
public String ejbCreate (String id, String name,
   String position, double salary) throws CreateException {

   setPlayerId(id);
   setName(name);
```

```
        setPosition(position);
        setSalary(salary);
        return null;
    }
```

Adding a Player to a Team

1. RosterClient

The RosterClient calls the addPlayer business method of the RosterEJB session bean. The P1 and T1 parameters are the primary keys of the PlayerEJB and TeamEJB instances, respectively.

```
myRoster.addPlayer("P1", "T1");
```

2. RosterEJB

The addPlayer method performs two steps. First, it calls findByPrimaryKey to locate the PlayerEJB and TeamEJB instances. Second, it invokes the addPlayer business method of the TeamEJB entity bean. Here is the source code for the addPlayer method of the RosterEJB session bean:

```
public void addPlayer(String playerId, String teamId) {

   try {
      LocalTeam team = teamHome.findByPrimaryKey(teamId);
      LocalPlayer player =
         playerHome.findByPrimaryKey(playerId);
      team.addPlayer(player);
   } catch (Exception ex) {
      throw new EJBException(ex.getMessage());
   }
}
```

3. TeamEJB

The TeamEJB entity bean has a relationship field named players, a Collection that represents the players that belong to the team. The access methods for the players relationship field are as follows:

```
public abstract Collection getPlayers();
public abstract void setPlayers(Collection players);
```

The addPlayer method of TeamEJB invokes the getPlayers access method to fetch the Collection of related LocalPlayer objects. Next, the addPlayer method invokes the add method of the Collection interface. Here is the source code for the addPlayer method:

```
public void addPlayer(LocalPlayer player) {
   try {
      Collection players = getPlayers();
      players.add(player);
   } catch (Exception ex) {
      throw new EJBException(ex.getMessage());
   }
}
```

Removing a Player

1. RosterClient

To remove player P4, the client would invoke the removePlayer method of the RosterEJB session bean:

```
myRoster.removePlayer("P4");
```

2. RosterEJB

The removePlayer method locates the PlayerEJB instance by calling findByPrimaryKey and then invokes the remove method on the instance. This invocation signals the container to delete the row in the database that corresponds to the PlayerEJB instance. The container also removes the item for this instance from the players relationship field in the TeamEJB entity bean. By this removal, the container automatically updates the TeamEJB-PlayerEJB relationship. Here is the removePlayer method of the RosterEJB session bean:

```
public void removePlayer(String playerId) {
   try {
      LocalPlayer player =
         playerHome.findByPrimaryKey(playerId);
      player.remove();
   } catch (Exception ex) {
      throw new EJBException(ex.getMessage());
   }
}
```

Dropping a Player from a Team

1. RosterClient

To drop player P2 from team T1, the client would call the dropPlayer method of the RosterEJB session bean:

```
myRoster.dropPlayer("P2", "T1");
```

2. RosterEJB

The dropPlayer method retrieves the PlayerEJB and TeamEJB instances by calling their findByPrimaryKey methods. Next, it invokes the dropPlayer business method of the TeamEJB entity bean. The dropPlayer method of the RosterEJB session bean follows:

```
public void dropPlayer(String playerId, String teamId) {

   try {
      LocalPlayer player =
         playerHome.findByPrimaryKey(playerId);
      LocalTeam team = teamHome.findByPrimaryKey(teamId);
      team.dropPlayer(player);
   } catch (Exception ex) {
      throw new EJBException(ex.getMessage());
   }
}
```

3. TeamEJB

The dropPlayer method updates the TeamEJB-PlayerEJB relationship. First, the method retrieves the Collection of LocalPlayer objects that correspond to the players relationship field. Next, it drops the target player by calling the remove method of the Collection interface. Here is the dropPlayer method of the TeamEJB entity bean:

```
public void dropPlayer(LocalPlayer player) {

   try {
      Collection players = getPlayers();
      players.remove(player);
   } catch (Exception ex) {
      throw new EJBException(ex.getMessage());
   }
}
```

Getting the Players of a Team

1. RosterClient

The client can fetch a team's players by calling the `getPlayersOfTeam` method of the `RosterEJB` session bean. This method returns an `ArrayList` of `PlayerDetails` objects. A `PlayerDetail` object contains four variables—`playerId`, `name`, `position`, and `salary`—which are copies of the `PlayerEJB` persistent fields. The `RosterClient` calls the `getPlayersOfTeam` method as follows:

```
playerList = myRoster.getPlayersOfTeam("T2");
```

2. RosterEJB

The `getPlayersOfTeam` method of the `RosterEJB` session bean locates the `LocalTeam` object of the target team by invoking the `findByPrimaryKey` method. Next, the `getPlayersOfTeam` method calls the `getPlayers` method of the `TeamEJB` entity bean. Here is the source code for the `getPlayersOfTeam` method:

```
public ArrayList getPlayersOfTeam(String teamId) {

   Collection players = null;

   try {
      LocalTeam team = teamHome.findByPrimaryKey(teamId);
      players = team.getPlayers();
   } catch (Exception ex) {
      throw new EJBException(ex.getMessage());
   }

   return copyPlayersToDetails(players);
}
```

The `getPlayersOfTeam` method returns the `ArrayList` of `PlayerDetails` objects that is generated by the `copyPlayersToDetails` method:

```
private ArrayList copyPlayersToDetails(Collection players) {

   ArrayList detailsList = new ArrayList();
   Iterator i = players.iterator();

   while (i.hasNext()) {
      LocalPlayer player = (LocalPlayer) i.next();
      PlayerDetails details =
         new PlayerDetails(player.getPlayerId(),
```

```
            player.getName(), player.getPosition(),
            player.getSalary());
        detailsList.add(details);
    }

    return detailsList;
}
```

3. TeamEJB

The `getPlayers` method of the `TeamEJB` entity bean is an access method of the `players` relationship field:

```
public abstract Collection getPlayers();
```

This method is exposed to local clients because it is defined in the local interface, `LocalTeam`:

```
public Collection getPlayers();
```

When invoked by a local client, a `get` access method returns a reference to the relationship field. If the local client alters the object returned by a `get` access method, it also alters the value of the relationship field inside the entity bean. For example, a local client of the `TeamEJB` entity bean could drop a player from a team as follows:

```
LocalTeam team = teamHome.findByPrimaryKey(teamId);
Collection players = team.getPlayers();
players.remove(player);
```

If you want to prevent a local client from modifying a relationship field in this manner, you should take the approach described in the next section.

Getting a Copy of a Team's Players

In contrast to the methods discussed in the preceding section, the methods in this section demonstrate the following techniques:

- Filtering the information passed back to the remote client
- Preventing the local client from directly modifying a relationship field

1. RosterClient

If you wanted to hide the salary of a player from a remote client, you would require the client to call the `getPlayersOfTeamCopy` method of the `RosterEJB` session bean. Like the `getPlayersOfTeam` method, the `getPlayersOfTeamCopy` method returns an `ArrayList` of `PlayerDetails` objects. However, the objects returned by `getPlayersOfTeamCopy` are different—their `salary` variables have been set to zero. The `RosterClient` calls the `getPlayersOfTeamCopy` method as follows:

```
playerList = myRoster.getPlayersOfTeamCopy("T5");
```

2. RosterEJB

Unlike the `getPlayersOfTeam` method, the `getPlayersOfTeamCopy` method does not invoke the `getPlayers` access method that is exposed in the `LocalTeam` interface. Instead, the `getPlayersOfTeamCopy` method retrieves a copy of the player information by invoking the `getCopyOfPlayers` business method that is defined in the `LocalTeam` interface. As a result, the `getPlayersOfTeamCopy` method cannot modify the `players` relationship field of `TeamEJB`. Here is the source code for the `getPlayersOfTeamCopy` method of `RosterEJB`:

```
public ArrayList getPlayersOfTeamCopy(String teamId) {

   ArrayList playersList = null;

   try {
      LocalTeam team = teamHome.findByPrimaryKey(teamId);
      playersList = team.getCopyOfPlayers();
   } catch (Exception ex) {
      throw new EJBException(ex.getMessage());
   }

   return playersList;
}
```

3. TeamEJB

The `getCopyOfPlayers` method of `TeamEJB` returns an `ArrayList` of `PlayerDetails` objects. To create this `ArrayList`, the method iterates through the `Collection` of related `LocalPlayer` objects and copies information to the variables of the `PlayerDetails` objects. The method copies the values of `PlayerEJB` persistent fields—except for the `salary` field, which it sets to zero. As a result, a player's salary is hidden from a client that invokes the `getPlayersOfTeamCopy` method. The source code for the getCopyOfPlayers method of TeamEJB follows.

```
public ArrayList getCopyOfPlayers() {

   ArrayList playerList = new ArrayList();
   Collection players = getPlayers();

   Iterator i = players.iterator();
   while (i.hasNext()) {
      LocalPlayer player = (LocalPlayer) i.next();
      PlayerDetails details =
         new PlayerDetails(player.getPlayerId(),
            player.getName(), player.getPosition(), 0.00);
         playerList.add(details);
   }

   return playerList;
}
```

Finding the Players by Position

1. RosterClient

The client starts the procedure by invoking the getPlayersByPosition method of the RosterEJB session bean:

```
playerList = myRoster.getPlayersByPosition("defender");
```

2. RosterEJB

The getPlayersByPosition method retrieves the players list by invoking the findByPosition method of the PlayerEJB entity bean:

```
public ArrayList getPlayersByPosition(String position) {

   Collection players = null;

   try {
      players = playerHome.findByPosition(position);
   } catch (Exception ex) {
      throw new EJBException(ex.getMessage());
   }

   return copyPlayersToDetails(players);
}
```

3. PlayerEJB

The LocalPlayerHome interface defines the findByPosition method:

```
public Collection findByPosition(String position)
   throws FinderException;
```

Because the PlayerEJB entity bean uses container-managed persistence, the entity bean class (PlayerBean) does not implement its finder methods. To specify the queries associated with the finder methods, EJB QL queries must be defined in the bean's deployment descriptor. For example, the findByPosition method has this EJB QL query:

```
SELECT DISTINCT OBJECT(p) FROM Player p
WHERE p.position = ?1
```

The deploytool utility translates the EJB QL query into a SQL SELECT statement. At runtime, when the container invokes the findByPosition method, it will execute the SQL SELECT statement.

For details about EJB QL, please refer to Chapter 8. To learn how to view and edit an EJB QL query in deploytool, see the section Finder/Select Methods Dialog Box (PlayerEJB) (page 135).

Getting the Sports of a Player

1. RosterClient

The client invokes the getSportsOfPlayer method of the RosterEJB session bean:

```
sportList = myRoster.getSportsOfPlayer("P28");
```

2. RosterEJB

The getSportsOfPlayer method returns an ArrayList of String objects that represent the sports of the specified player. It constructs the ArrayList from a Collection returned by the getSports business method of the PlayerEJB entity bean. Here is the source code for the getSportsOfPlayer method of the RosterEJB session bean:

```
public ArrayList getSportsOfPlayer(String playerId) {

   ArrayList sportsList = new ArrayList();
   Collection sports = null;
```

```
        try {
            LocalPlayer player =
                playerHome.findByPrimaryKey(playerId);
            sports = player.getSports();
        } catch (Exception ex) {
            throw new EJBException(ex.getMessage());
        }

        Iterator i = sports.iterator();
        while (i.hasNext()) {
            String sport = (String) i.next();
            sportsList.add(sport);
        }
        return sportsList;
    }
```

3. PlayerEJB

The `getSports` method is a wrapper for the `ejbSelectSports` method. Since the parameter of the `ejbSelectSports` method is of type `LocalPlayer`, the `getSports` method passes along a reference to the entity bean instance. The `PlayerBean` class implements the `getSports` method as follows:

```
public Collection getSports() throws FinderException {

    LocalPlayer player =
        (team.LocalPlayer)context.getEJBLocalObject();
    return ejbSelectSports(player);
}
```

The `PlayerBean` class defines the `ejbSelectSports` method:

```
public abstract Collection ejbSelectSports(LocalPlayer player)
    throws FinderException;
```

The bean's deployment descriptor specifies the following EJB QL query for the `ejbSelectSports` method:

```
SELECT DISTINCT t.league.sport
FROM Player p, IN (p.teams) AS t
WHERE p = ?1
```

Before deploying `PlayerEJB`, you run `deploytool` to generate SQL `SELECT` statements for the bean's EJB QL queries. Because `PlayerEJB` uses container-managed persistence, when the `ejbSelectSports` method is invoked the EJB container will execute its corresponding SQL `SELECT` statement.

Running the RosterApp Example

Setting Up

1. In a terminal window, start the Cloudscape database server.

   ```
   cloudscape -start
   ```

2. In another terminal window, start the J2EE server.

   ```
   j2ee -verbose
   ```

3. Run the `deploytool` utility.

   ```
   deploytool
   ```

Deploying the Application

1. In `deploytool`, open the `RosterApp.ear` file.
   a. Choose File→Open from the main menu.
   b. In the Open Object dialog box, navigate to the `j2eetutorial/examples/ears` directory.
   c. Select the `RosterApp.ear` file.
   d. Click Open Object.
2. Deploy the application.
   a. In deploytool, select `RosterApp` from the tree view.
   b. Choose Tools→Deploy from the main menu.
   c. In the Introduction dialog box, select the Return Client JAR checkbox.
   d. In the Client JAR File Name field, make sure that the file is called `RosterAppClient.jar` and that its path refers to the `j2eetutorial/examples/ears` directory.
   e. Click Next until the Review dialog box appears.
   f. Click Finish.

Running the Client

1. In a terminal window, go to the `j2eetutorial/examples/ears` directory.
2. Set the `APPCPATH` environment variable to `RosterAppClient.jar`.
3. Type the following command:

```
runclient -client RosterApp.ear -name RosterClient -textauth
```

4. At the login prompts, enter `guest` for the user name and `guest123` for the password.

deploytool Tips for Entity Beans with Container-Managed Persistence

Chapter 2 covered the basic steps for building and packaging enterprise beans. This section highlights the tasks in `deploytool` that are needed for entity beans with container-managed persistence. The examples referenced in this section are from A Guided Tour of the RosterApp Settings (page 128).

Specifying the Bean's Type

In the New Enterprise Bean wizard, specify the bean's type and persistent management.

1. In the Edit Contents dialog box, add all of the classes required by the entity bean and by its related beans.
2. In the General dialog box, select the Entity radio button.
3. In the General dialog box, specify the local interfaces of the entity bean. (If the bean also has remote interfaces, specify them as well.)
4. In the Entity Settings dialog box, select the radio button for Container-Managed Persistence (2.0). You may skip the other settings in this dialog box and enter them later in the Entity tab.

Selecting the Persistent Fields and Abstract Schema Name

In the Entity tab, enter the field information and the abstract schema name.

1. In the Fields To Be Persisted list, select the fields that will be saved in the database. The names of the persistent fields are determined by the access methods defined in the entity bean code.
2. Enter values in the Primary Key Class and Primary Key Field Name fields. The primary key uniquely identifies the entity bean.
3. In the Abstract Schema Name field, enter a name that represents the entity bean. This name will be referenced in the EJB QL queries.

An example is shown in the section Entity Tab (PlayerEJB) (page 134).

Defining EJB QL Queries for Finder and Select Methods

You specify these settings in the Finder/Select Methods dialog box.

1. To open the Finder/Select Methods dialog box, go to the Entity tab and click Finder/Select Methods.
2. To display a set of finder or select methods, click one of the radio buttons under the Show label.
3. To specify an EJB QL query, choose the name of the finder or select method from the Method list and then enter the query in the field labeled EJB QL Query.

An example is shown in the section Finder/Select Methods Dialog Box (PlayerEJB) (page 135).

Generating SQL and Specifying Table Creation

In `deploytool`, the various Deployment Settings dialog boxes enable you to enter information needed by the server at runtime. These settings are specific to the J2EE SDK implementation.

1. To open the Deployment Settings dialog box, go to the Entity tab and click Deployment Settings.
2. With container-managed persistence, the container can automatically create or delete the database table used by the entity bean. If you've loaded test data into the table, you may want to deselect the checkboxes in the Database Table box.

3. To translate the EJB QL queries into SQL `SELECT` statements, click Generate Default SQL. If this button is disabled, you must first specify the database settings.

An example is shown in the section Entity Deployment Settings Dialog Box (PlayerEJB) (page 135).

Specifying the Database JNDI Name, User Name, and Password

You specify these settings in the Database Settings dialog box.

1. To open the Database Settings dialog box, go to the Entity tab and click Deployment Settings. In the Deployment Settings dialog box, click Database Settings.
2. Enter a value in the Database JNDI Name field. The examples in this book use the `jdbc/Cloudscape` JNDI name.
3. The Cloudscape database shipped with the J2EE SDK does not require a user name or password. So, if your bean connects to the Cloudscape database, you may leave the User Name and Password fields blank. To connect to other types of databases, you may need to enter values into these fields.

An example is shown in the section Database Deployment Settings Dialog Box (PlayerEJB) (page 136).

Defining Relationships

The Relationships tab enables you to define relationships between entity beans that reside in the same EJB JAR file.

1. Before you create a relationship between two entity beans, you must first create both beans with the New Enterprise Bean wizard.
2. To display the Relationships tab, select the EJB JAR in the tree view and then select the Relationships tab.
3. To add or edit a relationship, go the Relationships tab and click the appropriate button.
4. The Add (or Edit) Relationship dialog box appears. (The Add Relationship and Edit Relationship dialog boxes are identical.)

An example is shown in the section Edit Relationship Dialog Box (TeamJAR) (page 132).

Primary Keys for Container-Managed Persistence

If the primary key class does not belong to the J2SE or J2EE standard libraries, then you must implement the class and package it along with the entity bean. For example, if your entity bean requires a composite primary key (which is made up of multiple fields), then you need to provide a customized primary key class.

The Primary Key Class

In the following example, the `PurchaseOrderKey` class implements a composite key for the `PurchaseOrderEJB` entity bean. The key is composed of two fields, `productModel` and `vendorId`, whose names must match two of the persistent fields in the entity bean class.

```
public class PurchaseOrderKey implements java.io.Serializable {

    public String productModel;
    public String vendorId;

    public PurchaseOrderKey() { };

    public String getProductModel() {

        return productModel;
    }

    public String getVendorId() {

        return vendorId;
    }

    public boolean equals(Object other) {

        if (other instanceof PurchaseOrderKey) {
           return (productModel.equals(
               ((PurchaseOrderKey)other).productModel) &&
               vendorId.equals(
               ((PurchaseOrderKey)other).vendorId));
        }
        return false;
    }

    public int hashCode() {
```

```
            return productModel.concat(vendorId).hashCode();
        }

    }
```

For container-managed persistence, a primary key class must meet the following requirements:

- The access control modifier of the class is `public`.
- All fields are declared as `public`.
- The fields are a subset of the bean's persistent fields.
- The class has a public default constructor.
- The class implements the `hashCode()` and `equals(Object other)` methods.
- The class is serializable.

Primary Keys in the Entity Bean Class

In the `PurchaseOrderBean` class, the following access methods define the persistent fields (`vendorId` and `productModel`) that make up the primary key:

```
public abstract String getVendorId();
public abstract void setVendorId(String id);

public abstract String getProductModel();
public abstract void setProductModel(String name);
```

The next code sample shows the `ejbCreate` method of the `PurchaseOrderBean` class. The return type of the `ejbCreate` method is the primary key, but the return value is `null`. Although not required, the `null` return value is recommended for container-managed persistence. This approach saves overhead because the bean does not have to instantiate the primary key class for the return value.

```
public PurchaseOrderKey ejbCreate (String vendorId,
    String productModel, String productName)
    throws CreateException {

setVendorId(vendorId);
    setProductModel(productModel);
    setProductName(productName);

    return null;
}
```

Generating Primary Key Values

For some entity beans, the value of a primary key has a meaning for the business entity. For example, in an entity bean that represents a phone call to a support center, the primary key might include a time stamp that indicates when the call was received. But for other beans, the key's value is arbitrary—provided that it's unique. With container-managed persistence, these key values can be generated automatically by the EJB container. To take advantage of this feature, an entity bean must meet these requirements:

- In the deployment descriptor, the primary key class is defined as a `java.lang.Object`. The primary key field is not specified.
- In the home interface, the argument of the `findByPrimaryKey` method must be a `java.lang.Object`.
- In the entity bean class, the return type of the `ejbCreate` method must be a `java.lang.Object`.

In these entity beans, the primary key values are in an internal field that only the EJB container can access. You cannot associate the primary key with a persistent field or any other instance variable. However, you can fetch the bean's primary key by invoking the `getPrimaryKey` method, and you can locate the bean by invoking its `findByPrimaryKey` method.

7

A Message-Driven Bean Example

Dale Green and Kim Haase

SINCE message-driven beans are based on the Java Message Service (JMS) technology, to understand the example in this chapter you should already be familiar with basic JMS concepts such as queues and messages. The best place to learn about these concepts is the Java Message Service Tutorial:

```
http://java.sun.com/products/jms/tutorial/index.html
```

This chapter describes the source code of a simple message-driven bean example. Before proceeding, you should read the basic conceptual information in the section What Is a Message-Driven Bean? (page 56).

In This Chapter

Example Application Overview

This application has the following components:

- `SimpleMessageClient`: A J2EE application client that sends several messages to a queue.
- `SimpleMessageEJB`: A message-driven bean that asynchronously receives and processes the messages that are sent to the queue.

Figure 7–1 illustrates the structure of this application. The application client sends messages to the queue, which was created administratively using the `j2eeadmin` command. The JMS provider (in this, case the J2EE server) delivers the messages to the instances of the message-driven bean, which then processes the messages.

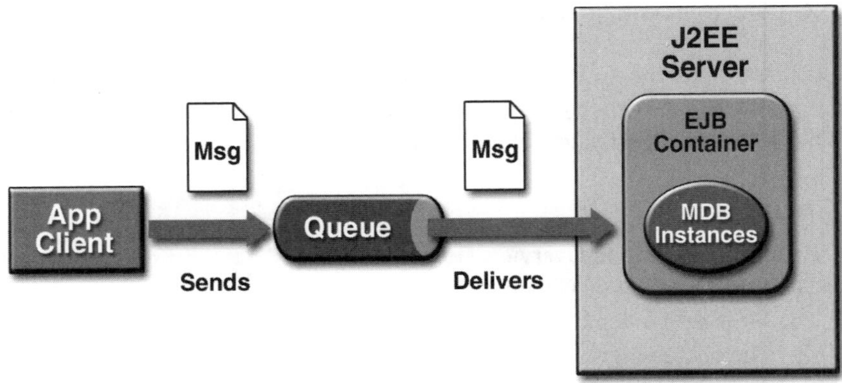

Figure 7–1 The `SimpleMessageApp` Application

The source code for this application is in the `j2eetutorial/examples/src/ejb/simplemessage` directory. To compile the code, go to the `j2eetutorial/examples` directory and type `ant simplemessage`. A sample `SimpleMessageApp.ear` file is in the `j2eetutorial/examples/ears` directory.

The J2EE Application Client

The `SimpleMessageClient` sends messages to the queue that the `SimpleMessageBean` listens to. The client starts out by locating the connection factory and queue:

```
queueConnectionFactory = (QueueConnectionFactory)
    jndiContext.lookup
    ("java:comp/env/jms/MyQueueConnectionFactory");
queue = (Queue)
     jndiContext.lookup("java:comp/env/jms/QueueName");
```

Next, the client creates the queue connection, session, and sender:

```
queueConnection =
    queueConnectionFactory.createQueueConnection();
queueSession =
    queueConnection.createQueueSession(false,
    Session.AUTO_ACKNOWLEDGE);
queueSender = queueSession.createSender(queue);
```

Finally, the client sends several messages to the queue:

```
message = queueSession.createTextMessage();

for (int i = 0; i < NUM_MSGS; i++) {
     message.setText("This is message " + (i + 1));
     System.out.println("Sending message: " +
         message.getText());
     queueSender.send(message);
}
```

The Message-Driven Bean Class

The code for the `SimpleMessageEJB` class illustrates the requirements of a message-driven bean class:

- It implements the `MessageDrivenBean` and `MessageListener` interfaces.

- The class is defined as `public`.
- The class cannot be defined as `abstract` or `final`.
- It implements one `onMessage` method.
- It implements one `ejbCreate` method and one `ejbRemove` method.
- It contains a public constructor with no arguments.
- It must not define the `finalize` method.

Unlike session and entity beans, message-driven beans do not have the remote or local interfaces that define client access. Client components do not locate message-driven beans and invoke methods on them. Although message-driven beans do not have business methods, they may contain helper methods that are invoked internally by the `onMessage` method.

The onMessage Method

When the queue receives a message, the EJB container invokes the `onMessage` method of the message-driven bean. In the `SimpleMessageBean` class, the `onMessage` method casts the incoming message to a `TextMessage` and displays the text:

```
public void onMessage(Message inMessage) {
    TextMessage msg = null;

    try {
        if (inMessage instanceof TextMessage) {
            msg = (TextMessage) inMessage;
            System.out.println
                ("MESSAGE BEAN: Message received: "
                + msg.getText());
        } else {
            System.out.println
                ("Message of wrong type: "
                + inMessage.getClass().getName());
        }
    } catch (JMSException e) {
        e.printStackTrace();
        mdc.setRollbackOnly();
    } catch (Throwable te) {
        te.printStackTrace();
    }
}
```

The ejbCreate and ejbRemove Methods

The signatures of these methods have the following requirements:

- The access control modifier must be `public`.
- The return type must be `void`.
- The modifier cannot be `static` or `final`.
- The `throws` clause must not define any application exceptions.
- The method has no arguments.

In the `SimpleMessageBean` class, the `ejbCreate` and `ejbRemove` methods are empty.

Running the SimpleMessageEJB Example

Starting the J2EE Server

To view the output of the message-driven bean, you must start the server in verbose mode:

```
j2ee -verbose
```

Creating the Queue

1. Create the queue with the `j2eeadmin` command:

   ```
   j2eeadmin -addJmsDestination jms/MyQueue queue
   ```

2. Verify that the queue was created:

   ```
   j2eeadmin -listJmsDestination
   ```

Deploying the Application

1. In `deploytool`, open the `j2eetutorial/examples/ears/SimpleMessageApp.ear` file (File→Open).
2. Deploy the `SimpleMessageApp` application (Tools→Deploy). In the Introduction dialog box, make sure that you select the Return Client JAR checkbox. For detailed instructions, see Deploying the J2EE Application (page 37).

Running the Client

1. In a terminal window, go to the `j2eetutorial/examples/ears` directory.
2. Set the `APPCPATH` environment variable to `SimpleMessageAppClient.jar`.
3. Type the following command on a single line:

```
runclient -client SimpleMessageApp.ear -name
   SimpleMessageClient -textauth
```

4. At the login prompts, enter `j2ee` for the user name and `j2ee` for the password.
5. The client displays these lines:

```
Sending message: This is message 1
Sending message: This is message 2
Sending message: This is message 3
```

6. In the terminal window in which you've started the J2EE server (in verbose mode), the following lines should be displayed:

```
MESSAGE BEAN: Message received: This is message 1
MESSAGE BEAN: Message received: This is message 2
MESSAGE BEAN: Message received: This is message 3
```

deploytool Tips for Message-Driven Beans

Chapter 2 covered the basic steps for building and packaging enterprise beans. This section describes the tasks in `deploytool` that are necessary for message-driven beans. To view an example in `deploytool`, open the `j2eetutorial/examples/ears/SimpleMessageApp.ear` file and select `SimpleMessageEJB` from the tree view.

Specifying the Bean's Type and Transaction Management

You specify the type when you create the bean with the New Enterprise Bean wizard.

1. To start the wizard, select File→New→Enterprise Bean.
2. In the General dialog box of the wizard, select the Message-Driven radio button.
3. In the Transaction Management dialog box, you may select either the Container-Managed or Bean-Managed radio button. If you select the Bean-Managed button, then in step 4 of the next section, you may select the acknowledgment type.

Setting the Message-Driven Bean's Characteristics

You may specify these settings in two places:

- The Message-Driven Bean Settings dialog box of the New Enterprise Bean wizard
- The Message tab of the bean (see Figure 7–2)

These settings are as follows:

1. For the Destination Type, select either the Queue or Topic radio button. A queue uses the point-to-point messaging domain and may have at most one consumer. A topic uses the publish-subscribe messaging domain; it may have zero, one, or many consumers.
2. In the Destination combo box, select the JNDI name of the destination that you have created administratively. For an example, see the section Creating the Queue (page 159). The destination is either a `Queue` or a `Topic` object; it represents the source of incoming messages and the target of outgoing messages.
3. In the Connection Factory combo box, select the appropriate object, either a `QueueConnectionFactory` or a `TopicConnectionFactory`. These objects produce the connections through which J2EE components access the messaging service.
4. If you've specified bean-managed transactions, then you may select the acknowledgment type—either Auto-Acknowledge or Duplicates-OK—from the Acknowledgement combo box. The Auto-Acknowledge type instructs the session to automatically acknowledge that the bean has consumed the message. The Duplicates-OK type instructs the session to lazily

acknowledge the delivery of messages; this type may result in duplicate messages, but it reduces session overhead.

5. In the JMS Message Selector field, you may enter a statement that filters the messages received by the bean.

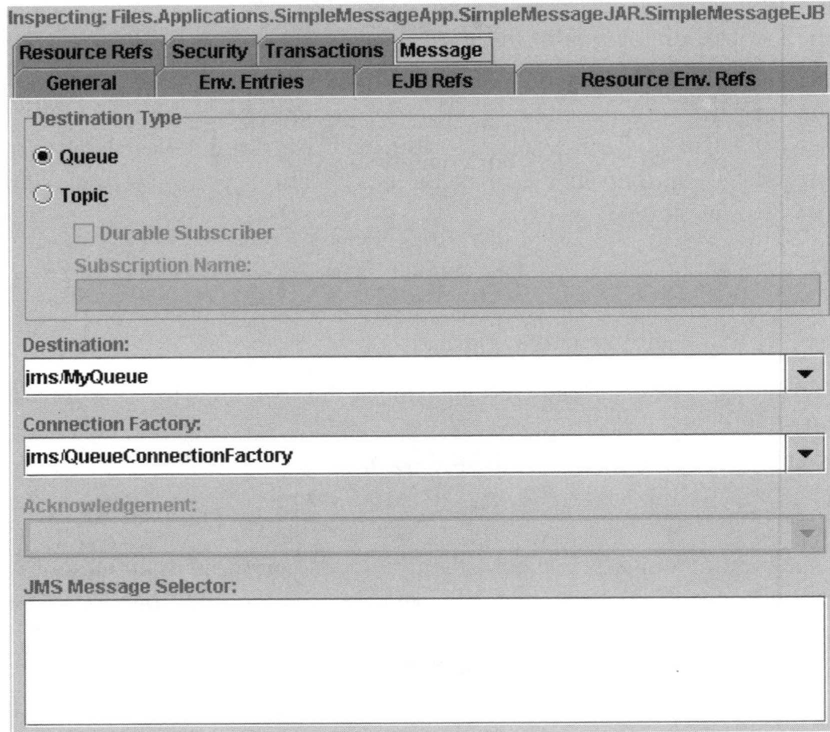

Figure 7–2 Message Tab of `SimpleMessageEJB`

deploytool Tips for JMS Clients

For more information on JMS clients, please see the Java Message Service Tutorial:

```
http://java.sun.com/products/jms/tutorial/index.html
```

Setting the Resource References

1. In the tree view, select the client's node.

2. Select the Resource Refs tab.
3. Click Add.
4. In the Coded Name field, enter the name that matches the parameter of the `lookup` method in the client's code. For example, if the `lookup` parameter is `java:comp/env/jms/MyQueueConnectionFactory`, the Coded Name should be `jms/QueueConnectionFactory`.
5. In the Type field, select the connection factory class that matches the destination type.
6. In the Authentication field, in most cases you will select Container. You would select Application if your code explicitly logs on to the messaging service.
7. In the Sharable field, make sure the checkbox is selected. This choice allows the container to optimize connections.
8. Enter strings in the User Name and Password fields. The authentication service of the J2EE SDK will prompt you for these fields when you run the client.

Setting the Resource Environment References

1. Select the Resource Env. Refs tab.
2. Click Add.
3. In the Coded Name field, enter a name that matches the parameter of the `lookup` call that locates the queue or topic. For example, if the `lookup` parameter is `java:comp/env/jms/QueueName`, the Coded Name should be `jms/QueueName`.
4. In the Type field, select the class that matches the destination type.

Specifying the JNDI Names

1. In the tree view, select the application's node.

2. Select the JNDI Names tab and enter the appropriate names. For example, the `SimpleMessageApp` discussed in this chapter uses the JNDI names shown in Table 7–1.

Table 7–1 JNDI Names for the `SimpleMessageApp` Application

Component or Reference Name	JNDI Name
`SimpleMessageEJB`	`jms/MyQueue`
`jms/MyQueueConnectionFactory`	`jms/QueueConnectionFactory`
`jms/QueueName`	`jms/MyQueue`

8

Enterprise JavaBeans Query Language

Dale Green

THE Enterprise JavaBeans Query Language ("EJB QL") defines the queries for the finder and select methods of an entity bean with container-managed persistence. A subset of SQL92, EJB QL has extensions that allow navigation over the relationships defined in an entity bean's abstract schema. The scope of an EJB QL query spans the abstract schemas of related entity beans that are packaged in the same EJB JAR file.

You define EJB QL queries in the deployment descriptor of the entity bean. Typically, a tool will translate these queries into the target language of the underlying data store. Because of this translation, entity beans with container-managed persistence are portable—their code is not tied to a specific type of data store.

This chapter relies on the material presented in earlier chapters. For conceptual information, see the section Container-Managed Persistence (page 53). For code examples, see Chapter 6.

In This Chapter

Terminology

The following list defines some of the terms referred to in this chapter.

- **Abstract schema**: The part of an entity bean's deployment descriptor that defines the bean's persistent fields and relationships.
- **Abstract schema name**: A logical name that is referenced in EJB QL queries. You specify an abstract schema name for each entity bean with container-managed persistence.
- **Abstract schema type**: All EJB QL expressions evaluate to a type. If the expression is an abstract schema name, by default its type is the local interface of the entity bean for which the abstract schema name is defined.
- **Backus-Naur Form (BNF)**: A notation that describes the syntax of high-level languages. The syntax diagrams in this chapter are in BNF notation.
- **Navigation**: The traversal of relationships in an EJB QL expression. The navigation operator is a period.
- **Path expression**: An expression that navigates to a related entity bean.
- **Persistent field**: A virtual field of an entity bean with container-managed persistence; it is stored in a database.
- **Relationship field**: A virtual field of an entity bean with container-managed persistence; it identifies a related entity bean.

Simplified Syntax

This section briefly describes the syntax of EJB QL so that you can quickly move on to the next section, Example Queries. When you are ready to learn about the syntax in more detail, see the section Full Syntax (page 173).

An EJB QL query has three clauses: `SELECT`, `FROM`, and `WHERE`. The `SELECT` and `FROM` clauses are required, but the `WHERE` clause is optional. Here is the high-level BNF syntax of an EJB QL query:

```
EJB QL ::= select_clause from_clause [where_clause]
```

The `SELECT` clause defines the types of the objects or values returned by the query. A return type is either a local interface, a remote interface, or a persistent field.

The `FROM` clause defines the scope of the query by declaring one or more identification variables, which may be referenced in the `SELECT` and `WHERE` clauses. An identification variable represents one of the following elements:

- The abstract schema name of an entity bean
- A member of a collection that is the multiple side of a one-to-many relationship

The `WHERE` clause is a conditional expression that restricts the objects or values retrieved by the query. Although optional, most queries have a `WHERE` clause.

Example Queries

The following queries are from the `PlayerEJB` entity bean of the `RosterApp` J2EE application, which is documented in Chapter 6. To see the relationships between the beans of the `RosterApp`, see Figure 6–1 (page 121).

Simple Finder Queries

If you are unfamiliar with EJB QL, these simple queries are a good place to start.

Example 1

```
SELECT OBJECT(p)
FROM Player p
```

Data retrieved: All players.

Finder method: `findall()`

Description: The `FROM` clause declares an identification variable named `p`, omitting the optional keyword `AS`. If the `AS` keyword were included, the clause would be written as follows:

```
FROM Player AS p
```

The `Player` element is the abstract schema name of the `PlayerEJB` entity bean. Because the bean defines the `findall` method in the `LocalPlayerHome` interface, the objects returned by the query have the `LocalPlayer` type.

See also: Identification Variables (page 177)

Example 2

```
SELECT DISTINCT OBJECT(p)
FROM Player p
WHERE p.position = ?1
```

Data retrieved: The players with the position specified by the finder method's parameter.

Finder method: `findByPosition(String position)`

Description: In a `SELECT` clause, the `OBJECT` keyword must precede a stand-alone identification variable such as `p`. The `DISTINCT` keyword eliminates duplicate values.

The `WHERE` clause restricts the players retrieved by checking their `position`, a persistent field of the `PlayerEJB` entity bean. The `?1` element denotes the input parameter of the `findByPosition` method.

See also: Input Parameters (page 183), DISTINCT and OBJECT Keywords (page 191)

Example 3

```
SELECT DISTINCT OBJECT(p)
FROM Player p
WHERE p.position = ?1 AND p.name = ?2
```

Data retrieved: The players with the specified position and name.

Finder method: `findByPositionAndName(String position, String name)`

Description: The `position` and `name` elements are persistent fields of the `PlayerEJB` entity bean. The `WHERE` clause compares the values of these fields with the parameters of the `findByPositionAndName` method. EJB QL denotes an input parameter with a question mark followed by an integer. The first input parameter is `?1`, the second is `?2`, and so forth.

Finder Queries That Navigate to Related Beans

In EJB QL, an expression can traverse—or navigate—to related beans. These expressions are the primary difference between EJB QL and SQL. EJB QL navigates to related beans, whereas SQL joins tables.

Example 4

```
SELECT DISTINCT OBJECT(p)
FROM Player p, IN (p.teams) AS t
WHERE t.city = ?1
```

Data retrieved: The players whose teams belong to the specified city.

Finder method: `findByCity(String city)`

Description: The `FROM` clause declares two identification variables: `p` and `t`. The `p` variable represents the `PlayerEJB` entity bean, and the `t` variable represents the related `TeamEJB` beans. The declaration for `t` references the previously declared `p` variable. The `IN` keyword signifies that `teams` is a collection of related beans. The `p.teams` expression navigates from a `PlayerEJB` bean to its related `TeamEJB` beans. The period in the `p.teams` expression is the navigation operator.

In the `WHERE` clause, the period preceding the persistent variable `city` is a delimiter, not a navigation operator. Strictly speaking, expressions can navigate to relationship fields (related beans), but not to persistent fields. To access a persistent field, an expression uses the period as a delimiter.

Expressions may not navigate beyond (or further qualify) relationship fields that are collections. In the syntax of an expression, a collection-valued field is a terminal symbol. Because the `teams` field is a collection, the `WHERE` clause cannot specify `p.teams.city`—an illegal expression.

See also: Path Expressions (page 179)

Example 5

```
SELECT DISTINCT OBJECT(p)
FROM Player p, IN (p.teams) AS t
WHERE t.league = ?1
```

Data retrieved: The players that belong to the specified league.

Finder method: `findByLeague(LocalLeague league)`

Description: The expressions in this query navigate over two relationships. The `p.teams` expression navigates the `PlayerEJB-TeamEJB` relationship, and the `t.league` expression navigates the `TeamEJB-LeagueEJB` relationship.

In the other examples, the input parameters are `String` objects, but in this example the parameter is an object whose type is a `LocalLeague` interface. This type matches the `league` relationship field in the comparison expression of the `WHERE` clause.

Example 6

```
SELECT DISTINCT OBJECT(p)
FROM Player p, IN (p.teams) AS t
WHERE t.league.sport = ?1
```

Data retrieved: The players who participate in the specified sport.

Finder method: `findBySport(String sport)`

Description: The `sport` persistent field belongs to the `LeagueEJB` bean. To reach the `sport` field, the query must first navigate from the `PlayerEJB` bean to the `TeamEJB` bean (`p.teams`) and then from the `TeamEJB` bean to the `LeagueEJB` bean (`t.league`). Because the `league` relationship field is not a collection, it may be followed by the `sport` persistent field.

Finder Queries with Other Conditional Expressions

Every `WHERE` clause must specify a conditional expression, of which there are several kinds. In the previous examples, the conditional expressions are comparison expressions that test for equality. The following examples demonstrate some of the other kinds of conditional expressions. For descriptions of all conditional expressions, see the section WHERE Clause (page 182).

Example 7

```
SELECT OBJECT(p)
FROM Player p
WHERE p.teams IS EMPTY
```

Data retrieved: All players who do not belong to a team.

Finder method: `findNotOnTeam()`

Description: The `teams` relationship field of the `PlayerEJB` bean is a collection. If a player does not belong to a team, then the `teams` collection is empty and the conditional expression is `TRUE`.

See also: Empty Collection Comparison Expressions (page 186)

Example 8

```
SELECT DISTINCT OBJECT(p)
FROM Player p
WHERE p.salary BETWEEN ?1 AND ?2
```

Data retrieved: The players whose salaries fall within the range of the specified salaries.

Finder method: `findBySalaryRange(double low, double high)`

Description: This `BETWEEN` expression has three arithmetic expressions: a persistent field (`p.salary`) and the two input parameters (`?1` and `?2`). The following expression is equivalent to the `BETWEEN` expression:

```
p.salary >= ?1 AND p.salary <= ?2
```

See also: BETWEEN Expressions (page 184)

Example 9

```
SELECT DISTINCT OBJECT(p1)
FROM Player p1, Player p2
WHERE p1.salary > p2.salary AND p2.name = ?1
```

Data retrieved: All players whose salaries are higher than the salary of the player with the specified name.

Finder method: `findByHigherSalary(String name)`

Description: The `FROM` clause declares two identification variables (`p1` and `p2`) of the same type (`Player`). Two identification variables are needed because the `WHERE` clause compares the salary of one player (`p2`) with that of the other players (`p1`).

See also: Identification Variables (page 177)

Select Queries

The queries in this section are for select methods. Unlike finder methods, a select method may return persistent fields or other entity beans.

Example 10

```
SELECT DISTINCT t.league
FROM Player p, IN (p.teams) AS t
WHERE p = ?1
```

Data retrieved: The leagues to which the specified player belongs.

Select Method: `ejbSelectLeagues(LocalPlayer player)`

Description: The return type of this query is the abstract schema type of the `LeagueEJB` entity bean. This abstract schema type maps to the `LocalLeague-Home` interface. Because the expression `t.league` is not a stand-alone identification variable, the `OBJECT` keyword is omitted.

See also: SELECT Clause (page 190)

Example 11

```
SELECT DISTINCT t.league.sport
FROM Player p, IN (p.teams) AS t
WHERE p = ?1
```

Data retrieved: The sports that the specified player participates in.

Select Method: `ejbSelectSports(LocalPlayer player)`

Description: This query returns a `String` named `sport`, which is a persistent field of the `LeagueEJB` entity bean.

Full Syntax

This section discusses the EJB QL syntax, as defined in the Enterprise JavaBeans Specification. Much of the following material paraphrases or directly quotes the specification.

BNF Symbols

Table 8–1 describes the BNF symbols used in this chapter.

Table 8–1 BNF Symbol Summary

Symbol	Description
::=	The element to the left of the symbol is defined by the constructs on the right.
*	The preceding construct may occur zero or more times.
{...}	The constructs within the curly braces are grouped together.
[...]	The constructs within the square brackets are optional.
|	An exclusive OR.
BOLDFACE	A keyword (although capitalized in the BNF diagram, keywords are not case sensitive).
Whitespace	A whitespace character can be a space, horizontal tab, or line feed.

BNF Grammar of EJB QL

Here is the entire BNF diagram for EJB QL:

```
EJB QL ::= select_clause from_clause [where_clause]

from_clause ::= FROM identification_variable_declaration
    [, identification_variable_declaration]*

identification_variable_declaration ::=
    collection_member_declaration |
    range_variable_declaration
```

```
collection_member_declaration ::=
    IN (collection_valued_path_expression) [AS] identifier

range_variable_declaration ::=
    abstract_schema_name [AS] identifier

single_valued_path_expression ::=
    {single_valued_navigation |
    identification_variable}.cmp_field |
    single_valued_navigation

single_valued_navigation ::=
    identification_variable.[single_valued_cmr_field.]*
    single_valued_cmr_field

collection_valued_path_expression ::=
    identification_variable.[single_valued_cmr_field.]*
    collection_valued_cmr_field

select_clause ::= SELECT [DISTINCT]
    {single_valued_path_expression |
    OBJECT(identification_variable)}

where_clause ::= WHERE conditional_expression

conditional_expression ::= conditional_term |
    conditional_expression OR conditional_term

conditional_term ::= conditional_factor |
    conditional_term AND conditional_factor

conditional_factor ::= [ NOT ] conditional_test

conditional_test ::= conditional_primary

conditional_primary ::=
    simple_cond_expression | (conditional_expression)

simple_cond_expression ::=
    comparison_expression |
    between_expression |
    like_expression |
    in_expression |
    null_comparison_expression |
    empty_collection_comparison_expression |
    collection_member_expression
```

```
between_expression ::=
    arithmetic_expression [NOT] BETWEEN
    arithmetic_expression AND arithmetic_expression

in_expression ::=
    single_valued_path_expression
    [NOT] IN (string_literal [, string_literal]* )

like_expression ::=
    single_valued_path_expression
    [NOT] LIKE pattern_value [ESCAPE escape-character]

null_comparison_expression ::=
    single_valued_path_expression IS [NOT] NULL

empty_collection_comparison_expression ::=
    collection_valued_path_expression IS [NOT] EMPTY

collection_member_expression ::=
    {single_valued_navigation | identification_variable |
    input_parameter}
    [NOT] MEMBER [OF] collection_valued_path_expression

comparison_expression ::=
    string_value { =|<>} string_expression |
    boolean_value { =|<>} boolean_expression} |
    datetime_value { = | <> | > | < } datetime_expression |
    entity_bean_value { = | <> } entity_bean_expression |
    arithmetic_value comparison_operator
    single_value_designator

arithmetic_value ::= single_valued_path_expression |
    functions_returning_numerics

single_value_designator ::= scalar_expression

comparison_operator ::=
    = | > | >= | < | <= | <>

scalar_expression ::= arithmetic_expression

arithmetic_expression ::= arithmetic_term |
    arithmetic_expression { + | - } arithmetic_term

arithmetic_term ::= arithmetic_factor |
    arithmetic_term { * | / } arithmetic_factor

arithmetic_factor ::= { + |- } arithmetic_primary
```

```
arithmetic_primary ::= single_valued_path_expression |
    literal | (arithmetic_expression) |
    input_parameter | functions_returning_numerics

string_value ::= single_valued_path_expression |
    functions_returning_strings

string_expression ::= string_primary | input_expression

string_primary ::= single_valued_path_expression | literal |
    (string_expression) | functions_returning_strings

datetime_value ::= single_valued_path_expression

datetime_expression ::= datetime_value | input_parameter

boolean_value ::= single_valued_path_expression

boolean_expression ::= single_valued_path_expression |
   literal | input_parameter

entity_bean_value ::=
    single_valued_navigation | identification_variable

entity_bean_expression ::= entity_bean_value | input_parameter

functions_returning_strings ::=
    CONCAT(string_expression, string_expression) |
    SUBSTRING(string_expression, arithmetic_expression,
    arithmetic_expression)

functions_returning_numerics::=
    LENGTH(string_expression) |
    LOCATE(string_expression,
    string_expression[, arithmetic_expression]) |
    ABS(arithmetic_expression) |
    SQRT(arithmetic_expression)
```

FROM Clause

The FROM clause defines the domain of the query by declaring identification variables. Here is the syntax of the FROM clause:

```
from_clause ::= FROM identification_variable_declaration
    [, identification_variable_declaration]*
```

```
identification_variable_declaration ::=
    collection_member_declaration |
    range_variable_declaration

collection_member_declaration ::=
    IN (collection_valued_path_expression) [AS] identifier

range_variable_declaration ::=
    abstract_schema_name [AS] identifier
```

Identifiers

An identifier is a sequence of one or more characters. The first character must be a valid first character (letter, $, _) in an identifier of the Java programming language (hereafter in this chapter called simply "Java"). Each subsequent character in the sequence must be a valid non-first character (letter, digit, $, _) in a Java identifier. (For details, see the J2SE API documentation of the isJavaIdentifierStart and isJavaIdentifierPart methods of the Character class.) The question mark (?) is a reserved character in EJB QL and cannot be used in an identifier. Unlike a Java variable, an EJB QL identifier is not case sensitive.

An identifier cannot be the same as an EJB QL keyword:

```
AND       MEMBER
AS        NOT
BETWEEN   NULL
DISTINCT  OBJECT
EMPTY     OF
FALSE     OR
FROM      SELECT
IN        TRUE
IS        UNKNOWN
LIKE      WHERE
```

EJB QL keywords are also reserved words in SQL. In the future, the list of EJB QL keywords may expand to include other reserved SQL words. The Enterprise JavaBeans Specification recommends that you not use other reserved SQL words for EJB QL identifiers.

Identification Variables

An *identification variable* is an identifier declared in the FROM clause. Although the SELECT and WHERE clauses may reference identification variables, they cannot declare them. All identification variables must be declared in the FROM clause.

Since an identification variable is an identifier, it has the same naming conventions and restrictions as an identifier. For example, an identification variable is not case sensitive and it cannot be the same as an EJB QL keyword. (See the previous section for more naming rules.) Also, within a given EJB JAR file, an identifier name must not match the name of any entity bean or abstract schema.

The `FROM` clause may contain multiple declarations, separated by commas. A declaration may reference another identification variable that has been previously declared (to the left). In the following `FROM` clause, the variable `t` references the previously declared variable `p`:

```
FROM Player p, IN (p.teams) AS t
```

Even if an identification variable is not used in the `WHERE` clause, its declaration can affect the results of the query. For an example, compare the next two queries. The following query returns all players, whether or not they belong to a team:

```
SELECT OBJECT(p)
FROM Player p
```

In contrast, because the next query declares the `t` identification variable, it fetches all players that belong to a team:

```
SELECT OBJECT(p)
FROM Player p, IN (p.teams) AS t
```

The following query returns the same results as the preceding query, but the `WHERE` clause makes it easier to read:

```
SELECT OBJECT(p)
FROM Player p
WHERE p.teams IS NOT EMPTY
```

An identification variable always designates a reference to a single value, whose type is that of the expression used in the declaration. There are two kinds of declarations: range variable and collection member.

Range Variable Declarations

To declare an identification variable as an abstract schema type, you specify a range variable declaration. In other words, an identification variable can range over the abstract schema type of an entity bean. In the following example, an identification variable named `p` represents the abstract schema named `Player`:

```
FROM Player p
```

A range variable declaration may include the optional AS operator:

```
FROM Player AS p
```

In most cases, to obtain objects a query navigates through the relationships with path expressions. But for those objects that cannot be obtained by navigation, you can use a range variable declaration to designate a starting point (or *root*).

If the query compares multiple values of the same abstract schema type, then the FROM clause must declare multiple identification variables for the abstract schema:

```
FROM Player p1, Player p2
```

For a sample of such a query, see Example 9 (page 171).

Collection Member Declarations

In a one-to-many relationship, the multiple side consists of a collection of entity beans. An identification variable may represent a member of this collection. To access a collection member, the path expression in the variable's declaration navigates through the relationships in the abstract schema. (For more information on path expressions, see the following section.) Because a path expression may be based on another path expression, the navigation can traverse several relationships. See Example 6 (page 170).

A collection member declaration must include the IN operator, but it may omit the optional AS operator.

In the following example, the entity bean represented by the abstract schema named Player has a relationship field called teams. The identification variable called t represents a single member of the teams collection.

```
FROM Player p, IN (p.teams) AS t
```

Path Expressions

Path expressions are important constructs in the syntax of EJB QL, for several reasons. First, they define navigation paths through the relationships in the abstract schema. These path definitions affect both the scope and the results of a query. Second, they may appear in any of the three main clauses of an EJB QL query (SELECT, WHERE, FROM). Finally, although much of EJB QL is a subset of SQL, path expressions are extensions not found in SQL.

Syntax

There are two types of path expressions: single-valued and collection-valued. Here is the syntax for path expressions:

```
single_valued_path_expression ::=
   {single_valued_navigation |
   identification_variable}.cmp_field |
   single_valued_navigation

single_valued_navigation ::=
   identification_variable.[single_valued_cmr_field.]*
   single_valued_cmr_field

collection_valued_path_expression ::=
   identification_variable.[single_valued_cmr_field.]*
   collection_valued_cmr_field
```

In the preceding diagram, the `cmp_field` element represents a persistent field, and the `cmr_field` element designates a relationship field. The term `single_valued` qualifies the relationship field as the single side of a one-to-one or one-to-many relationship; the term `collection_valued` designates it as the multiple (collection) side of a relationship.

The period (.) in a path expression serves two functions. If a period precedes a persistent field, it is a delimiter between the field and the identification variable. If a period precedes a relationship field, it is a navigation operator.

Examples

In the following query, the `WHERE` clause contains a single-valued expression. The `p` is an identification variable, and `salary` is a persistent field of `Player`.

```
SELECT DISTINCT OBJECT(p)
FROM Player p
WHERE p.salary BETWEEN ?1 AND ?2
```

The `WHERE` clause of the next example also contains a single-valued expression. The `t` is an identification variable, `league` is a single-valued relationship field, and `sport` is a persistent field of `league`.

```
SELECT DISTINCT OBJECT(p)
FROM Player p, IN (p.teams) AS t
WHERE t.league.sport = ?1
```

In the next query, the `WHERE` clause contains a collection-valued expression. The `p` is an identification variable, and `teams` designates a collection-valued relationship field.

```
SELECT DISTINCT OBJECT(p)
FROM Player p
WHERE p.teams IS EMPTY
```

Expression Types

The type of an expression is the type of the object represented by the ending element, which can be one of the following:

- Persistent field
- Single-valued relationship field
- Collection-valued relationship field

For example, the type of the expression `p.salary` is `double` because the terminating persistent field (`salary`) is a `double`.

In the expression `p.teams`, the terminating element is a collection-valued relationship field (`teams`). This expression's type is a collection of the abstract schema type named `Team`. Because `Team` is the abstract schema name for the `TeamEJB` entity bean, this type maps to the bean's local interface, `LocalTeam`. For more information on the type mapping of abstract schemas, see the section Return Types (page 190).

Navigation

A path expression enables the query to navigate to related entity beans. The terminating elements of an expression determine whether navigation is allowed. If an expression contains a single-valued relationship field, the navigation may continue to an object that is related to the field. However, an expression cannot navigate beyond a persistent field or a collection-valued relationship field. For example, the expression `p.teams.league.sport` is illegal, since `teams` is a collection-valued relationship field. To reach the `sport` field, the `FROM` clause could define an identification variable named `t` for the `teams` field:

```
FROM Player AS p, IN (p.teams) t
WHERE t.league.sport = 'soccer'
```

WHERE Clause

The `WHERE` clause specifies a conditional expression that limits the values returned by the query. The query returns all corresponding values in the data store for which the conditional expression is `TRUE`. Although usually specified, the `WHERE` clause is optional. If the `WHERE` clause is omitted, then the query returns all values. The high-level syntax for the `WHERE` clause follows:

```
where_clause ::= WHERE conditional_expression
```

Literals

There are three kinds of literals: string, numeric, and boolean.

String Literals

A string literal is enclosed in single quotes:

```
'Duke'
```

If a string literal contains a single quote, you indicate the quote with two single quotes:

```
'Duke''s'
```

Like a Java `String`, a string literal in EJB QL uses the Unicode character encoding.

Numeric Literals

There are two types of numeric literals: exact and approximate.

An exact numeric literal is a numeric value without a decimal point, such as 65, –233, +12. Using the Java integer syntax, exact numeric literals support numbers in the range of a Java `long`.

An approximate numeric literal is a numeric value in scientific notation, such as 57., –85.7, +2.1. Using the syntax of the Java floating point literal, approximate numeric literals support numbers in the range of a Java `double`.

Boolean Literals

A boolean literal is either `TRUE` or `FALSE`. These keywords are not case sensitive.

Input Parameters

An input parameter is designated by a question mark (?) followed by an integer. For example, the first input parameter is ?1, the second is ?2, and so forth.

The following rules apply to input parameters:

- They can be used only in a WHERE clause.
- Their use is restricted to a single-valued path expression within a conditional expression.
- They must be numbered, starting with the integer 1.
- The number of input parameters in the WHERE clause must not exceed the number of input parameters in the corresponding finder or select method.
- The type of an input parameter in the WHERE clause must match the type of the corresponding argument in the finder or select method.

Conditional Expressions

A WHERE clause consists of a conditional expression, which is evaluated from left to right within a precedence level. You may change the order of evaluation with parentheses.

Here is the syntax of a conditional expression:

```
conditional_expression ::= conditional_term |
   conditional_expression OR conditional_term

conditional_term ::= conditional_factor |
   conditional_term AND conditional_factor

conditional_factor ::= [ NOT ] conditional_test

conditional_test ::= conditional_primary

conditional_primary ::=
   simple_cond_expression | (conditional_expression)

simple_cond_expression ::=
   comparison_expression |
   between_expression |
   like_expression |
   in_expression |
   null_comparison_expression |
   empty_collection_comparison_expression |
   collection_member_expression
```

Operators and Their Precedence

Table 8–2 lists the EJB QL operators in order of decreasing precedence.

Table 8–2 EJB QL Operator Precedence

Type	Precedence Order
Navigation	`.` (a period)
Arithmetic	`+ -` (unary) `* /` (multiplication and division) `+ -` (addition and subtraction)

Comparison	`=`
	`>`
	`>=`
	`<`
	`<=`
	`<>` (not equal)

Logical	`NOT`
	`AND`
	`OR`

BETWEEN Expressions

A `BETWEEN` expression determines whether an arithmetic expression falls within a range of values. The syntax of the `BETWEEN` expression follows:

```
between_expression ::=
  arithmetic_expression [NOT] BETWEEN
  arithmetic_expression AND arithmetic_expression
```

These two expressions are equivalent:

```
p.age BETWEEN 15 AND 19
p.age >= 15 AND p.age <= 19
```

The following two expressions are also equivalent:

```
p.age NOT BETWEEN 15 AND 19
p.age < 15 OR p.age > 19
```

If an arithmetic expression has a NULL value, then the value of the BETWEEN expression is unknown.

IN Expressions

An IN expression determines whether or not a string belongs to a set of string literals. Here is the syntax of the IN expression:

```
in_expression ::=
   single_valued_path_expression
   [NOT] IN (string_literal [, string_literal]* )
```

The single-valued path expression must have a String value. If the single-valued path expression has a NULL value, then the value of the IN expression is unknown.

In the following example, if the country is UK the expression is TRUE. If the country is Peru it is FALSE.

```
o.country IN ('UK', 'US', 'France')
```

LIKE Expressions

A LIKE expression determines whether a wildcard pattern matches a string. Here is the syntax:

```
like_expression ::=
   single_valued_path_expression
   [NOT] LIKE pattern_value [ESCAPE escape-character]
```

The single-valued path expression must have a String value. If this value is NULL, then the value of the LIKE expression is unknown. The pattern value is a string literal that may contain wildcard characters. The underscore (_) wildcard character represents any single character. The percent (%) wildcard character represents zero or more characters. The ESCAPE clause specifies an escape character for the wildcard characters in the pattern value.

Table 8–3 shows some sample LIKE expressions. The TRUE and FALSE columns indicate the value of the LIKE expression for a single-valued path expression.

Table 8–3 `LIKE` Expression Examples

Expression	TRUE	FALSE
`address.phone LIKE '12%3'`	'123' '12993'	'1234'
`asentence.word LIKE 'l_se'`	'lose'	'loose'
`aword.underscored LIKE '\_%' ESCAPE '\'`	'_foo'	'bar'
`address.phone NOT LIKE '12%3'`	1234	'123' '12993'

NULL Comparison Expressions

A `NULL` comparison expression tests whether a single-valued path expression has a `NULL` value. Usually, this expression is used to test whether or not a single-valued relationship has been set. If a path expression contains a `NULL` value during evaluation, it returns a `NULL` value. Here is the syntax of a `NULL` comparison expression:

```
null_comparison_expression ::=
   single_valued_path_expression IS [NOT] NULL
```

Empty Collection Comparison Expressions

An empty collection comparison expression tests whether a collection-valued path expression has no elements. In other words, it tests whether or not a collection-valued relationship has been set. Here is the syntax:

```
empty_collection_comparison_expression ::=
   collection_valued_path_expression IS [NOT] EMPTY
```

If the collection-valued path expression is `NULL`, then the empty collection comparison expression has a `NULL` value.

Collection Member Expressions

The collection member expression determines whether a value is a member of a collection. The value and the collection members must have the same type. The expression syntax follows:

```
collection_member_expression ::=
   {single_valued_navigation | identification_variable |
   input_parameter}
   [NOT] MEMBER [OF] collection_valued_path_expression
```

If the collection-valued path expression is unknown, then the collection member expression is unknown. If the collection-valued path expression designates an empty collection, then the collection member expression is `FALSE`.

Functional Expressions

EJB QL includes several string and arithmetic functions, which are listed in the following tables. In Table 8–4, the `start` and `length` arguments are of type `int`. They designate positions in the `String` argument. In Table 8–5, the `number` argument may be either an `int`, a `float`, or a `double`.

Table 8–4 String Expressions

Function Syntax	Return Type
`CONCAT(String, String)`	`String`
`SUBSTRING(String, start, length)`	`String`
`LOCATE(String, String [, start])`	`int`
`LENGTH(String)`	`int`

Table 8–5 Arithmetic Expressions

Function Syntax	Return Type
`ABS(number)`	`int`, `float`, or `double`
`SQRT(double)`	`double`

NULL Values

If the target of a reference is not in the persistent store, then the target is `NULL`. For conditional expressions containing `NULL`, EJB QL uses the semantics defined by SQL92. Briefly, these semantics are as follows:

- If a comparison or arithmetic operation has an unknown value, it yields a `NULL` value.
- If a path expression contains a `NULL` value during evaluation, it returns a `NULL` value.
- The `IS NULL` test converts a `NULL` persistent field or a single-valued relationship field to `TRUE`. The `IS NOT NULL` test converts them to `FALSE`.
- Boolean operators and conditional tests use the three-valued logic defined by the following tables. (In these tables, T stands for `TRUE`, F for `FALSE`, and U for unknown.)

Table 8–6 `AND` Operator Logic

AND	T	F	U
T	T	F	U
F	F	F	F
U	U	F	U

Table 8–7 `OR` Operator Logic

OR	T	F	U
T	T	T	T
F	T	F	U
U	T	U	U

Equality Semantics

In EJB QL, only values of the same type can be compared. However, this rule has one exception: Exact and approximate numeric values can be compared. In such a comparison, the required type conversion adheres to the rules of Java numeric promotion.

EJB QL treats compared values as if they were Java types, not as if they represented types in the underlying data store. For example, if a persistent field could be either an integer or a `NULL`, then it must be designated as an `Integer` object, not as an `int` primitive. This designation is required because a Java object can be `NULL` but a primitive cannot.

Two strings are equal only if they contain the same sequence of characters. Trailing blanks are significant; for example, the strings `'abc'` and `'abc  '` are not equal.

Two entity beans of the same abstract schema type are equal only if their primary keys have the same value.

Table 8–8 `NOT` Operator Logic

NOT	
T	F
F	T
U	U

Table 8–9 Conditional Test

Conditional Test	T	F	U
Expression `IS TRUE`	T	F	F
Expression `IS FALSE`	F	T	F
Expression is unknown	F	F	T

SELECT Clause

The SELECT clause defines the types of the objects or values returned by the query. The SELECT clause has the following syntax:

```
select_clause ::= SELECT [DISTINCT]
   {single_valued_path_expression |
   OBJECT(identification_variable)}
```

Return Types

The return type defined by the SELECT clause must match that of the finder or select method for which the query is defined.

For finder method queries, the return type of the SELECT clause is the abstract schema type of the entity bean that defines the finder method. This abstract schema type maps to either a remote or local interface. If the bean's remote home interface defines the finder method, then the return type is the remote interface (or a collection of remote interfaces). Likewise, if the local home interface defines the finder method, the return type is the local interface (or a collection). For example, the LocalPlayerHome interface of the PlayerEJB entity bean defines the findall method:

```
public Collection findAll() throws FinderException;
```

The EJB QL query of the findall method returns a collection of LocalPlayer interface types:

```
SELECT OBJECT(p)
FROM Player p
```

For select method queries, the return type of the SELECT clause may be one of the following:

- The abstract schema of the entity bean that contains the select method
- The abstract schema of a related entity bean

  (By default, each of these abstract schema types maps to the local interface of the entity bean. Although uncommon, in the deployment descriptor you may override the default mapping by specifying a remote interface.)

- A persistent field

The `PlayerEJB` entity bean, for example, implements the `ejbSelectSports` method, which returns a collection of `String` objects for `sport`. The `sport` is a persistent field of the `LeagueEJB` entity bean. See Example 11 (page 172).

A `SELECT` clause cannot specify a collection-valued expression. For example, the `SELECT` clause `p.teams` is invalid because `teams` is a collection. However, the clause in the following query is valid because the `t` is a single element of the `teams` collection:

```
SELECT t
FROM Player p, IN (p.teams) AS t
```

DISTINCT and OBJECT Keywords

The `DISTINCT` keyword eliminates duplicate return values. If the method of the query returns a `java.util.Collection`—which allows duplicates—then you must specify the `DISTINCT` keyword to eliminate duplicates. However, if the method returns a `java.util.Set`, the `DISTINCT` keyword is redundant because a `java.util.Set` may not contain duplicates.

The `OBJECT` keyword must precede a stand-alone identification variable, but it must not precede a single-valued path expression. If an identification variable is part of a single-valued path expression, it is not stand-alone.

EJB QL Restrictions

EJB QL has a few restrictions:

- Comments are not allowed.
- Date and time values are in milliseconds and use a Java `long`. A date or time literal should be an integer literal. To generate a millisecond value, you may use the `java.util.Calendar` class.
- Currently, container-managed persistence does not support inheritance. For this reason, two entity beans of different types cannot be compared.

9

Web Clients and Components

Stephanie Bodoff

WHEN a Web client such as a browser communicates with a J2EE application, it does so through server-side objects called *Web components*. There are two types of Web components: Java Servlets and JavaServer Pages (JSP) pages. Servlets are Java programming language classes that dynamically process requests and construct responses. JSP pages are text-based documents that execute as servlets but allow a more natural approach to creating static content. Although servlets and JSP pages can be used interchangeably, each has its own strengths. Servlets are best suited to managing the control functions of an application, such as dispatching requests and handling nontextual data. JSP pages are more appropriate for generating text-based markup such as HTML, SVG, WML, and XML.

This chapter describes the packaging, configuration, and deployment procedures for Web clients. Chapters 10 and 11 cover how to develop the Web components. Many features of JSP technology are determined by Java Servlet technology, so you should familiarize yourself with that material even if you do not intend to write servlets.

Most J2EE Web clients use the HTTP protocol, and support for HTTP is a major aspect of Web components. For a brief summary of HTTP protocol features, see Appendix A.

In This Chapter

Web Client Life Cycle

The server-side portion of a Web client consists of Web components, static resource files such as images, and helper classes and libraries. The J2EE platform provides many supporting services that enhance the capabilities of Web components and make them easier to develop. However, because it must take these services into account, the process for creating and running a Web client is different from that of traditional stand-alone Java classes.

Web components run within an environment called a *Web container*. The Web container provides services such as request dispatching, security, concurrency, and life-cycle management. It also gives Web components access to the J2EE platform APIs such as naming, transactions, and e-mail.

Before it can be executed, a Web client must be packaged into a *Web application archive* (WAR), which is a JAR similar to the package used for Java class libraries, and installed (or *deployed)* into a Web container.

Certain aspects of Web client behavior can be configured when it is deployed. The configuration information is maintained in a text file in XML format called a *Web application deployment descriptor*. When you create Web clients and components using the J2EE SDK `deploytool` utility, it automatically generates or updates the deployment descriptor based on data that you enter in `deploytool` wizards and inspectors. You can also manually create a deployment descriptor according to the schema described in the Java Servlet specification.

The process for creating, deploying, and executing a Web client can be summarized as follows:

1. Develop the Web component code (including possibly a deployment descriptor).
2. Package the Web client components along with any static resources (for example, images) and helper classes referenced by the component.
3. Deploy the application.
4. Access a URL that references the Web client.

Developing Web component code is covered in chapters 10 and 11. Steps 2 through 4 are expanded on in the following sections, illustrated with a Hello, World-style application. This application allows a user to enter a name into an HTML form (Figure 9–1) and then displays a greeting after the name is submitted (Figure 9–2).

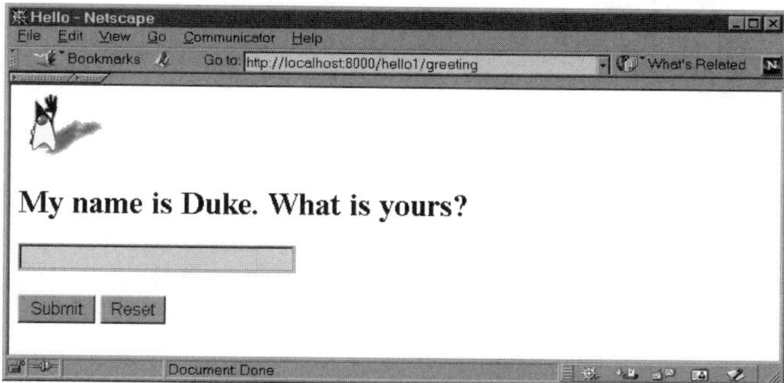

Figure 9–1 Greeting

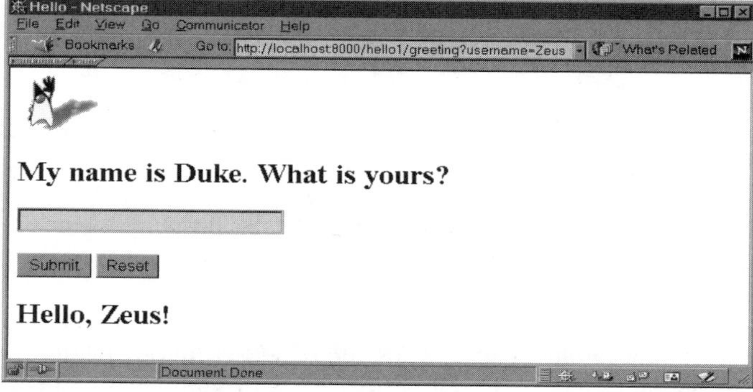

Figure 9–2 Response

The Hello application contains two Web components that generate the greeting and the response. This tutorial has two versions of this application: a servlet version called `Hello1App` in which the components are implemented by two servlet classes, `GreetingServlet.java` and `ResponseServlet.java`, and a JSP version called `Hello2App` in which the components are implemented by two JSP pages, `greeting.jsp` and `response.jsp`. The two versions are used to illustrate the tasks involved in packaging, deploying, and running a J2EE application that contains Web components.

Web Application Archives

Web clients are packaged in Web application archives. In addition to Web components, a Web application archive usually contains other files, including the following:

- Server-side utility classes (database beans, shopping carts, and so on). Often these classes conform to the JavaBeans component architecture.
- Static Web content (HTML, image, and sound files, and so on).
- Client-side classes (applets and utility classes).

Web components and static Web content files are called *Web resources*.

A WAR has a specific directory structure. The top-level directory of a WAR is the *document root* of the application. The document root is where JSP pages, client-side classes and archives, and static Web resources are stored.

The document root contains a subdirectory called `WEB-INF`, which contains the following files and directories:

- `web.xml`: The Web application deployment descriptor
- Tag library descriptor files (see Tag Library Descriptors, page 290)
- `classes`: A directory that contains server-side classes: servlets, utility classes, and JavaBeans components
- `lib`: A directory that contains JAR archives of libraries (tag libraries and any utility libraries called by server-side classes).

You can also create application-specific subdirectories (that is, package directories) in either the document root or the `WEB-INF/classes` directory.

Note: When you add classes and archives to a WAR, `deploytool` automatically packages them in the `WEB-INF` subdirectory. This is correct for Web components and server-side utility classes, but incorrect for client-side classes such as applets and any archives accessed by applets. To put client-side classes and archives in the correct location, you must drag them to the document root after you have added them to the archive.

Creating a WAR File

When you add the first Web component to a J2EE application, `deploytool` automatically creates a new WAR file to contain the component. A later section describes how to add a Web component.

You can also manually create a WAR in three ways:

- With the `packager` tool distributed with the J2EE SDK. This tool is described in the section Packager Tool (page 436).
- With the `war` task of the `ant` portable build tool. `Ant` is used to build the J2EE Tutorial examples. The example application described in the section The Example JSP Pages (page 249) uses `ant` to create the WAR.
- With the JAR tool distributed with the J2SE. If you arrange your application development directory in the structure required by the WAR format, it is straightforward to create a Web application archive file in the required format. You simply execute the following command in the top-level directory of the application:

```
jar cvf archiveName.war .
```

Note that to use any of these methods, you must also manually create a deployment descriptor in the correct format.

Adding a WAR File to an EAR File

If you manually create a WAR file or obtain a WAR file from another party, you can add it to an existing EAR file as follows:

1. Select a J2EE application.
2. Select File→Add→Web WAR.
3. Navigate to the directory containing the WAR file, select the WAR file, and click Add Web WAR.

See The Example JSP Pages (page 249) for an example.

You can also add a WAR file to a J2EE application using the `packager` tool. The Duke's Bank application described in Building, Packaging, Deploying, and Running the Application (page 416) uses `packager`.

Adding a Web Component to a WAR File

The following procedure describes how to create and add the Web component in the `Hello1App` application to a WAR. Although the Web component wizard solicits WAR and component-level configuration information when you add the component, this chapter describes how to add the component and provide configuration information at a later time using application, WAR, and Web component inspectors:

1. Go to `j2eetutorial/examples` and build the example by running `ant hello1`. For detailed instructions, see About the Examples (page xxi).
2. Create a J2EE application called `Hello1App`.
   a. Select File→New→Application.
   b. Click Browse.
   c. In the file chooser, navigate to `j2eetutorial/examples/src/web/hello1`.
   d. In the File Name field, enter `Hello1App`.
   e. Click New Application.
   f. Click OK.
3. Create the WAR file and add the `GreetingServlet` Web component and all of the `Hello1App` application content.
   a. Invoke the Web component wizard by selecting File→New→Web Component.
   b. In the combo box labelled Create New WAR File in Application select Hello1App. Enter `Hello1WAR` in the field labeled WAR Display Name.
   c. Click Edit to add the content files.
   d. In the Edit Contents dialog box, navigate to `j2eetutorial/examples/build/web/hello1`. Select `GreetingServlet.class`, `ResponseServlet.class`, and `duke.waving.gif`, and click Add. Click OK.
   e. Click Next.
   f. Select the Servlet radio button.
   g. Click Next.

h. Select `GreetingServlet` from the Servlet Class combo box.
i. Click Finish.

4. Add the `ResponseServlet` Web component.
   a. Invoke the Web component wizard by selecting File→New→Web Component.
   b. In the combo box labeled Add To Existing WAR File, select `Hello1WAR`.
   c. Click Next.
   d. Select the Servlet radio button.
   e. Click Next.
   f. Select `ResponseServlet` from the Servlet Class combo box.
   g. Click Finish.

Note: You can add JSP pages to a WAR file without creating a new Web component for each page. You simply select the WAR file, click Edit to edit the contents of the WAR, and add the pages. The JSP version of the Hello, World application, described in Updating Web Clients (page 204), shows how to do this. If you choose this method, you will not be able to specify alias paths (described in Specifying an Alias Path, page 202) for the pages.

Configuring Web Clients

The following sections describe the Web client configuration parameters that you will usually want to specify. Configuration parameters are specified at three levels: application, WAR, and component. A number of security parameters can be applied at the WAR and component levels. For information on these security parameters, see Web-Tier Security (page 337).

Application-Level Configuration

Context Root

A *context root* is a name that gets mapped to the document root of a Web client. If your client's context root is `catalog`, then the request URL

```
http://<host>:8000/catalog/index.html
```

will retrieve the file `index.html` from the document root.

To specify the context root for `Hello1App` in `deploytool`,

1. Select `Hello1App`.
2. Select the Web Context tab
3. Enter `hello1` in the Context Root field.

WAR-Level Configuration

The following sections give generic procedures for specifying WAR-level configuration information. For some specific examples, see The Example Servlets (page 211).

Context Parameters

The Web components in a WAR share an object that represents their Web context (see Accessing the Web Context, page 237). To specify initialization parameters that are passed to the context,

1. Select the WAR.
2. Select the Context tab.
3. Click Add.

References to Environment Entries, Enterprise Beans, Resource Environment Entries, or Resources

If your Web components reference environment entries, enterprise beans, resource environment entries, or resources such as databases, you must declare the references as follows:

1. Select the WAR.
2. Select the Environment, Enterprise Bean Refs, Resource Env. Refs or Resource Refs tab.
3. Click Add in the pane to add a new reference.

Event Listeners

To add an event listener class (described in Handling Servlet Life-Cycle Events, page 216),

1. Select the WAR.
2. Select the Event Listeners tab.

3. Click Add.
4. Select the listener class from the new field in the Event Listener Classes pane.

Error Mapping

You can specify a mapping between the status code returned in an HTTP response or a Java programming language exception returned by any Web component and a Web resource (see Handling Errors, page 218). To set up the mapping,

1. Select the WAR.
2. Select the File Refs tab.
3. Click Add in the Error Mapping pane.
4. Enter the HTTP status code (see HTTP Responses, page 428) or fully-qualified class name of an exception in the Error/Exception field.
5. Enter the name of a resource to be invoked when the status code or exception is returned. The name should have a leading forward slash `/`.

Note: You can also define error pages for a JSP page contained in a WAR. If error pages are defined for both the WAR and a JSP page, the JSP page's error page takes precedence.

Filter Mapping

A Web container uses filter mapping declarations to decide which filters to apply to a request, and in what order (see Filtering Requests and Responses, page 227). The container matches the request Uniform Resource Identifier (URI) to a servlet as described in Specifying an Alias Path (page 202). To determine which filters to apply, it matches filter mapping declarations by servlet name or URL pattern. The order in which filters are invoked is the order in which filter mapping declarations that match a request URI for a servlet appear in the filter mapping list.

You specify a filter mapping in `deploytool` as follows:

1. Select the WAR.
2. Select the Filter Mapping tab.
3. Add a filter.
   a. Click Edit Filter List.

   b. Click Add.
   c. Select the filter class.
   d. Enter a filter name.
   e. Add any filter initialization parameters.
   f. Click OK.
4. Map the filter.
   a. Click Add.
   b. Select the filter name.
   c. Select the target type. A filter can be mapped to a specific servlet or to all servlets that match a given URL pattern.
   d. Specify the target. If the target is a servlet, select the servlet from the drop-down list. If the target is a URL pattern, enter the pattern.

Component-Level Configuration

Initialization Parameters

To specify parameters that are passed to the Web component when it is initialized,

1. Select the Web component.
2. Select the Init. Parameters tab.
3. Click Add to add a new parameter and value.

Specifying an Alias Path

When a request is received by a Web container, it must determine which Web component should handle the request. It does so by mapping the URL path contained in the request to a Web component. A URL path contains the context root (described in the section Context Root, page 199) and an *alias* path:

```
http://<host>:8000/context root/alias path
```

Before a servlet can be accessed, the Web container must have at least one alias path for the component. The alias path must start with a / and end with a string or a wildcard expression with an extension (`*.jsp`, for example). Since Web containers automatically map an alias path that ends with `*.jsp`, you do not have to specify an alias path for a JSP page unless you wish to refer to the page by a name other than its file name. In the example discussed in the section Updating

Web Clients (page 204), the page `greeting.jsp` has an alias, `/greeting`, but the page `response.jsp` is referenced by its file name within `greeting.jsp`.

You set up the mappings for the servlet version of the Hello application using the Web component inspector as follows:

1. Select the `GreetingServlet` Web component.
2. Select the Aliases tab.
3. Click Add to add a new mapping.
4. Type `/greeting` in the aliases list.
5. Select the `ResponseServlet` Web component.
6. Click Add.
7. Type `/response` in the aliases list.

Deploying Web Clients

The next step after you have created, packaged, and configured a Web client is to deploy the EAR file that contains the client. To deploy the `Hello1App` application,

1. Select `Hello1App`.
2. Select Tools→Deploy.
3. Select a target server.
4. Click Finish.

Running Web Clients

A Web client is executed when a Web browser references a URL that is mapped to a component contained in the client. Once you have deployed the `Hello1App` application, you can run the Web client by pointing a browser at

```
http://<host>:8000/hello1/greeting
```

Replace *<host>* with the name of the host running the J2EE server. If your browser is running on the same host as the J2EE server, you may replace *<host>* with `localhost`.

Updating Web Clients

During development, you will often need to make changes to Web clients. To update a servlet you modify the source file, recompile the servlet class, update the component in the WAR, and redeploy the application. Except for the compilation step, you update a JSP page in the same way.

To try this feature, first build, package, and deploy the JSP version of the Hello application:

1. Go to `j2eetutorial/examples/src` and build the example by running `ant hello2`.
2. Create a J2EE application called `Hello2App`.
   a. Select File→New→Application.
   b. In the file chooser, navigate to `j2eetutorial/examples/src/web/hello2`.
   c. In the File Name field, enter `Hello2App`.
   d. Click New Application.
   e. Click OK.
3. Create the WAR and add the `greeting` Web component and all of the `Hello2App` application content.
   a. Invoke the Web component wizard by selecting File→New→Web Component.
   b. In the combo box labeled Create New WAR File in Application select `Hello2App`. Enter `Hello2WAR` in the field labeled WAR Display Name.
   c. Click Edit to add the content files.
   d. In the Edit Contents dialog box, navigate to `examples/build/web/hello2`. Select `greeting.jsp`, `response.jsp`, and `duke.waving.gif`, and click Add. Click OK.
   e. Click Next.
   f. Select the JSP radio button.
   g. Click Next.
   h. Select `greeting.jsp` from the JSP Filename combo box.
   i. Click Finish.
4. Add the alias `/greeting` for the `greeting` Web component.
5. Specify the context root `hello2`.
6. Deploy `Hello2App`.

7. Execute the application by pointing a Web browser at `http://<host>:8000/hello2/greeting`. Replace *<host>* with the name of the host running the J2EE server.

Now modify one of the JSP files. For example, you could replace the contents of `response.jsp` with the following:

```
<h2>Hi, <%=username%>!</h2>
```

To update the file in the WAR and redeploy the application:

1. Edit `response.jsp`.
2. Execute `ant hello2` to copy the modified file to the build directory.
3. Select `Hello2App`.
4. In `deploytool`, select Tools→Update Files.
5. A dialog box appears reporting the changed file.Verify that `response.jsp` has been changed and dismiss the dialog box.
6. Select Tools→Deploy. Make sure the checkbox labeled Save Object Before Deploying is checked.

You can also perform steps 4 through 6 by selecting Tools→Update And Redeploy. The `deploytool` utility replaces the old JSP file in `Hello2App.ear` with the new one and then redeploys the application.

When you execute the application, the response should be changed (Figure 9–3)

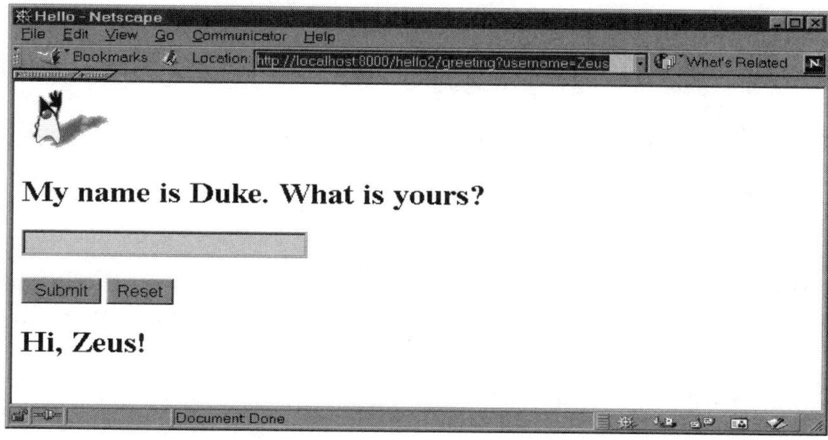

Figure 9–3 New Response

Internationalizing Web Clients

Internationalization is the process of preparing an application to support various languages. *Localization* is the process of adapting an internationalized application to support a specific language or locale. Although all client user interfaces should be internationalized and localized, it is particularly important for Web clients because of the far-reaching nature of the Web. For a good overview of internationalization and localization, see

```
http://java.sun.com/docs/books/tutorial/i18n/index.html
```

In the simplest internationalized program, strings are read from a resource bundle that contains translations for the language in use. The resource bundle maps keys used by a program to the strings displayed to the user. Thus, instead of creating strings directly in your code, you create a resource bundle that contains translations and read the translations from that bundle using the corresponding key. A resource bundle can be backed by a text file (properties resource bundle) or a class (list resource bundle) containing the mappings.

In the following chapters on Web technology, the Duke's Bookstore example is internationalized and localized into English and Spanish. The key and value pairs are contained in list resource bundles named `messages.BookMessage_*.class`. To give you an idea of what the key and string pairs in a resource bundle look like, here are a few lines from the file `messages.BookMessages.java`.

```
{"TitleCashier", "Cashier"},
{"TitleBookDescription", "Book Description"},
{"Visitor", "You are visitor number "},
{"What", "What We"re Reading"},
{"Talk", " talks about how Web components can transform the way
you develop applications for the Web. This is a must read for
any self respecting Web developer!"},
{"Start", "Start Shopping"},
```

To get the correct strings for a given user, a Web component retrieves the locale (set by a browser language preference) from the request, opens the resource bundle for that locale, and then saves the bundle as a session attribute (see Associating Attributes with a Session, page 238):

```
ResourceBundle messages = (ResourceBundle)session.
  getAttribute("messages");
  if (messages == null) {
    Locale locale=request.getLocale();
    messages = ResourceBundle.getBundle("WebMessages",
      locale);
    session.setAttribute("messages", messages);
  }
```

A Web component retrieves the resource bundle from the session:

```
ResourceBundle messages =
  (ResourceBundle)session.getAttribute("messages");
```

and looks up the string associated with the key `TitleCashier` as follows:

```
messages.getString("TitleCashier");
```

In addition to Duke's Bookstore, both the Web client and the J2EE application client distributed with this tutorial's case study application, Duke's Bank, are internationalized; see the section Internationalization (page 414) in Chapter 18.

This has been a very brief introduction to internationalizing Web clients. For more information on this subject, see the Java Blueprints:

```
http://java.sun.com/blueprints
```

10

Java Servlet Technology

Stephanie Bodoff

As soon as the Web began to be used for delivering services, service providers recognized the need for dynamic content. Applets, one of the earliest attempts towards this goal, focused on using the client platform to deliver dynamic user experiences. At the same time, developers also investigated using the server platform for this purpose. Initially, Common Gateway Interface (CGI) scripts were the main technology used to generate dynamic content. Though widely used, CGI scripting technology has a number of shortcomings, including platform dependence and lack of scalability. To address these limitations, Java Servlet technology was created as a portable way to provide dynamic, user-oriented content.

In This Chapter

What Is a Servlet?

A *servlet* is a Java programming language class used to extend the capabilities of servers that host applications accessed via a request-response programming model. Although servlets can respond to any type of request, they are commonly used to extend the applications hosted by Web servers. For such applications, Java Servlet technology defines HTTP-specific servlet classes.

The `javax.servlet` and `javax.servlet.http` packages provide interfaces and classes for writing servlets. All servlets must implement the `Servlet` interface, which defines life-cycle methods.

When implementing a generic service, you can use or extend the `GenericServlet` class provided with the Java Servlet API. The `HttpServlet` class provides methods, such as `doGet` and `doPost`, for handling HTTP-specific services.

This chapter focuses on writing servlets that generate responses to HTTP requests. Some knowledge of the HTTP protocol is assumed; if you are unfamiliar with this protocol, you can get a brief introduction to HTTP in Appendix A.

The Example Servlets

This chapter uses the Duke's Bookstore application to illustrate the tasks involved in programming servlets. Table 10–1 lists the servlets that handle each bookstore function. Each programming task is illustrated by one or more servlets. For example, `BookDetailsServlet` illustrates how to handle HTTP `GET` requests, `BookDetailsServlet` and `CatalogServlet` show how to construct responses, and `CatalogServlet` illustrates how to track session information.

Table 10–1 Duke's Bookstore Example Servlets

Function	Servlet
Enter the bookstore	`BookStoreServlet`
Create the bookstore banner	`BannerServlet`
Browse the bookstore catalog	`CatalogServlet`
Put a book in a shopping cart	`CatalogServlet`, `BookDetailsServlet`
Get detailed information on a specific book	`BookDetailsServlet`
Display the shopping cart	`ShowCartServlet`
Remove one or more books from the shopping cart	`ShowCartServlet`
Buy the books in the shopping cart	`CashierServlet`
Receive an acknowledgement for the purchase	`ReceiptServlet`

The data for the bookstore application is maintained in a database and accessed through the helper class `database.BookDB`. The `database` package also contains the class `BookDetails`, which represents a book. The shopping cart and shopping cart items are represented by the classes `cart.ShoppingCart` and `cart.ShoppingCartItem`, respectively.

The source code for the bookstore application is located in the `j2eetutorial/examples/src/web/bookstore1` directory created when you unzip the tutorial bundle (see Downloading the Examples, page xxii). To build, deploy, and run the example, follow these steps.

1. Go to `j2eetutorial/examples` and build the example by running `ant bookstore1` (see How to Build and Run the Examples, page xxii).
2. Start the `j2ee` server.
3. Start `deploytool`.
4. Start the Cloudscape database server by running `cloudscape -start`.
5. Load the bookstore data into the database by running `ant create-web-db`.
6. Create a J2EE application called `Bookstore1App`.
   a. Select File→New→Application.
   b. In the file chooser, navigate to `j2eetutorial/examples/src/web/bookstore1`.
   c. In the File Name field, enter `Bookstore1App`.
   d. Click New Application.
   e. Click OK.
7. Create the WAR and add the `BannerServlet` Web component and all of the Duke's Bookstore content to the `Bookstore1App` application.
   a. Select File→New→Web Component.
   b. Click the Create New WAR File In Application radio button and select `Bookstore1App` from the combo box. Enter `Bookstore1WAR` in the field labeled WAR Display Name.
   c. Click Edit to add the content files.
   d. In the Edit Archive Contents dialog box, navigate to `j2eetutorial/examples/build/web/bookstore1`. Select `BannerServlet.class`, `BookStoreServlet.class`, `BookDetailsServlet.class`, `CatalogServlet.class`, `ShowCartServlet.class`, `CashierServlet.class`, and `ReceiptServlet.class`. Click Add. Add `errorpage.html` and `duke.books.gif`. Add the `cart`, `database`, `exception`, `filters`, `listeners`, `messages`, and `util` packages. Click OK.
   e. Click Next.
   f. Select the Servlet radio button.
   g. Click Next.
   h. Select `BannerServlet` from the Servlet Class combo box.

i. Click Next twice.

j. In the Component Aliases pane, click Add and then type `/banner` in the Alias field.

k. Click Finish.

8. Add each of the Web components listed in Table 10–2. For each servlet, click the Add to Existing WAR File radio button and select `Bookstore1WAR` from the combo box. Since the WAR contains all of the servlet classes, you do not have to add any more content.

Table 10–2 Duke's Bookstore Web Components

Web Component Name	Servlet Class	Component Alias
`BookStoreServlet`	`BookStoreServlet`	`/enter`
`CatalogServlet`	`CatalogServlet`	`/catalog`
`BookDetailsServlet`	`BookDetailsServlet`	`/bookdetails`
`ShowCartServlet`	`ShowCartServlet`	`/showcart`
`CashierServlet`	`CashierServlet`	`/cashier`
`ReceiptServlet`	`ReceiptServlet`	`/receipt`

9. Add a resource reference for the Cloudscape database.

   a. Select `Bookstore1WAR`.

   b. Select the Resource Refs tab.

   c. Click Add.

   d. Select `javax.sql.DataSource` from the Type column

   e. Enter `jdbc/BookDB` in the Coded Name field.

   f. Enter `jdbc/Cloudscape` in the JNDI Name field.

10. Add the listener class `listeners.ContextListener` (described in Handling Servlet Life-Cycle Events, page 216).

   a. Select the Event Listeners tab.

   b. Click Add.

   c. Select the `listeners.ContextListener` class from the drop-down field in the Event Listener Classes pane.

11. Add an error page (described in Handling Errors, page 218).
    a. Select the File Refs tab.
    b. In the Error Mapping panel, click Add.
    c. Enter `exception.BookNotFoundException` in the Error/Exception field.
    d. Enter `/errorpage.html` in the Resource To Be Called field.
    e. Repeat for `exception.BooksNotFoundException` and `javax.servlet.UnavailableException`.
12. Add the filters `filters.HitCounterFilter` and `filters.OrderFilter` (described in Filtering Requests and Responses, page 227).
    a. Select the Filter Mapping tab.
    b. Click Edit Filter List.
    c. Click Add.
    d. Select `filters.HitCounterFilter` from the Filter Class column. The `deploytool` utility will automatically enter `HitCounterFilter` in the Display Name column.
    e. Click Add.
    f. Select `filters.OrderFilter` from the Filter Class column. The `deploytool` utility will automatically enter `OrderFilter` in the Display Name column.
    g. Click OK.
    h. Click Add.
    i. Select `HitCounterFilter` from the Filter Name column.
    j. Select Servlet from the Target Type column.
    k. Select `BookStoreServlet` from the Target column.
    l. Repeat for `OrderFilter`. The target type is Servlet and the target is `ReceiptServlet`.
13. Enter the context root.
    a. Select `Bookstore1App`.
    b. Select the Web Context tab.
    c. Enter `bookstore1`.
14. Deploy the application.
    a. Select Tools→Deploy.
    b. Click Finish.

15. Open the bookstore URL `http://<host>:8000/bookstore1/enter`.

Troubleshooting

The section Common Problems and Their Solutions (page 40) (in particular, Web Client Runtime Errors, page 44) lists some reasons why a Web client can fail. In addition, Duke's Bookstore returns the following exceptions:

- `BookNotFoundException`: Returned if a book can't be located in the bookstore database. This will occur if you haven't loaded the bookstore database with data by running `ant create-web-db` or if the Cloudscape server hasn't been started or it has crashed.
- `BooksNotFoundException`: Returned if the bookstore data can't be retrieved. This will occur if you haven't loaded the bookstore database with data by running `ant create-web-db` or if the Cloudscape server hasn't been started or has crashed.
- `UnavailableException`: Returned if a servlet can't retrieve the Web context attribute representing the bookstore. This will occur if you haven't added the listener class to the application.

Since we have specified an error page, you will see the message `The application is unavailable. Please try later`. If you don't specify an error page, the Web container generates a default page containing the message `A Servlet Exception Has Occurred` and a stack trace that can help diagnose the cause of the exception. If you use `errorpage.html`, you will have to look in the Web container's log to determine the cause of the exception. Web log files reside in the directory

```
$J2EE_HOME/logs/<host>/web
```

and are named `catalina.<date>.log`.

The `<logs>` element is the directory specified by the `log.directory` entry in the `default.properties` file. The default value is `logs`. The *<host>* element is the name of the computer. See the *Configuration Guide* provided with the J2EE SDK for more information about J2EE SDK log files.

Servlet Life Cycle

The life cycle of a servlet is controlled by the container in which the servlet has been deployed. When a request is mapped to a servlet, the container performs the following steps.

1. If an instance of the servlet does not exist, the Web container
   a. Loads the servlet class.
   b. Creates an instance of the servlet class.
   c. Initializes the servlet instance by calling the `init` method. Initialization is covered in Initializing a Servlet (page 222).
2. Invokes the `service` method, passing a request and response object. Service methods are discussed in the section Writing Service Methods (page 222).

If the container needs to remove the servlet, it finalizes the servlet by calling the servlet's `destroy` method. Finalization is discussed in Finalizing a Servlet (page 241).

Handling Servlet Life-Cycle Events

You can monitor and react to events in a servlet's life cycle by defining listener objects whose methods get invoked when life cycle events occur. To use these listener objects, you must define the listener class and specify the listener class.

Defining The Listener Class

You define a listener class as an implementation of a listener interface. Table 10–3 lists the events that can be monitored and the corresponding interface that must be implemented. When a listener method is invoked, it is passed an event that contains information appropriate to the event. For example, the methods in the `HttpSessionListener` interface are passed an `HttpSessionEvent`, which contains an `HttpSession`.

Table 10–3 Servlet Life-Cycle Events

Object	Event	Listener Interface and Event Class
Web context (See Accessing the Web Context, page 237)	Initialization and destruction	`javax.servlet.ServletContextListener` and `ServletContextEvent`
	Attribute added, removed, or replaced	`javax.servlet.ServletContextAttributeListener` and `ServletContextAttributeEvent`
Session (See Maintaining Client State, page 238)	Creation, invalidation, and timeout	`javax.servlet.http.HttpSessionListener` and `HttpSessionEvent`
	Attribute added, removed, or replaced	`javax.servlet.http.HttpSessionAttributeListener` and `HttpSessionBindingEvent`

The `listeners.ContextListener` class creates and removes the database helper and counter objects used in the Duke's Bookstore application. The methods retrieve the Web context object from `ServletContextEvent` and then store (and remove) the objects as servlet context attributes.

```
import database.BookDB;
import javax.servlet.*;
import util.Counter;

public final class ContextListener
   implements ServletContextListener {
   private ServletContext context = null;
   public void contextInitialized(ServletContextEvent event) {
      context = event.getServletContext();
      try {
         BookDB bookDB = new BookDB();
         context.setAttribute("bookDB", bookDB);
      } catch (Exception ex) {
         System.out.println(
            "Couldn't create database: " + ex.getMessage());
      }
      Counter counter = new Counter();
      context.setAttribute("hitCounter", counter);
```

```
            context.log("Created hitCounter" +
               counter.getCounter());
            counter = new Counter();
            context.setAttribute("orderCounter", counter);
            context.log("Created orderCounter" +
               counter.getCounter());
         }

         public void contextDestroyed(ServletContextEvent event) {
            context = event.getServletContext();
            BookDB bookDB = context.getAttribute(
               "bookDB");
            bookDB.remove();
            context.removeAttribute("bookDB");
            context.removeAttribute("hitCounter");
            context.removeAttribute("orderCounter");
         }
      }
```

Specifying Event Listener Classes

You specify a listener class for a WAR in the `deploytool` Event Listeners inspector (see Event Listeners, page 200).

Handling Errors

Any number of exceptions can occur when a servlet is executed. The Web container will generate a default page containing the message `A Servlet Exception Has Occurred` when an exception occurs, but you can also specify that the container should return a specific error page for a given exception. You specify error pages for a WAR in the `deploytool` File Refs inspector (see Error Mapping, page 201).

Sharing Information

Web components, like most objects, usually work with other objects to accomplish their tasks. There are several ways they can do this. They can use private helper objects (for example, JavaBeans components), they can share objects that are attributes of a public scope, they can use a database, and they can invoke other Web resources. The Java Servlet technology mechanisms that allow a Web component to invoke other Web resources are described in the section Invoking Other Web Resources (page 234).

Using Scope Objects

Collaborating Web components share information via objects maintained as attributes of four scope objects. These attributes are accessed with the `[get|set]Attribute` methods of the class representing the scope. Table 10–4 lists the scope objects. Figure 10–1 shows the scoped attributes maintained by the Duke's Bookstore application.

Table 10–4 Scope Objects

Scope Object	Class	Accessible From
Web context	`javax.servlet. ServletContext`	Web components within a Web context (see Accessing the Web Context, page 237)
session	`javax.servlet. http.HttpSession`	Web components handling a request that belongs to the session (see Maintaining Client State, page 238)
request	Subtype of `javax.servlet. ServletRequest`	Web components handling the request
page	`javax.servlet. jsp.PageContext`	The JSP page that creates the object (see Chapter 11)

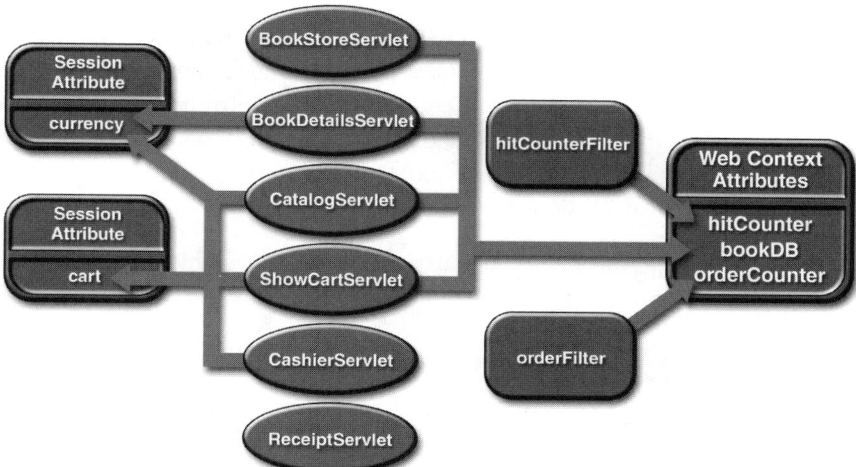

Figure 10–1 Duke's Bookstore Scoped Attributes

Controlling Concurrent Access to Shared Resources

In a multithreaded server, it is possible for shared resources to be accessed concurrently. Besides scope object attributes, shared resources include in-memory data such as instance or class variables, and external objects such as files, database connections, and network connections. Concurrent access can arise in several situations:

- Multiple Web components accessing objects stored in the Web context
- Multiple Web components accessing objects stored in a session
- Multiple threads within a Web component accessing instance variables. A Web container will typically create a thread to handle each request. If you want to ensure that a servlet instance handles only one request at a time, a servlet can implement the `SingleThreadModel` interface. If a servlet implements this interface, you are guaranteed that no two threads will execute concurrently in the servlet's service method. A Web container can implement this guarantee by synchronizing access to a single instance of the servlet, or by maintaining a pool of Web component instances and dispatching each new request to a free instance. This interface does not prevent synchronization problems that result from Web components accessing shared resources such as static class variables or external objects.

When resources can be accessed concurrently, they can be used in an inconsistent fashion. To prevent this, you must control the access using the synchronization techniques described in the Threads lesson in *The Java™ Tutorial.*

In the previous section we showed five scoped attributes shared by more than one servlet: `bookDB`, `cart`, `currency`, `hitCounter`, and `orderCounter`. The `bookDB` attribute is discussed in the next section. The cart, currency, and counters can be set and read by multiple multithreaded servlets. To prevent these objects from being used inconsistently, access is controlled by synchronized methods. For example, here is the `util.Counter` class:

```
public class Counter {
   private int counter;
   public Counter() {
      counter = 0;
   }
   public synchronized int getCounter() {
      return counter;
   }
   public synchronized int setCounter(int c) {
      counter = c;
```

```
        return counter;
    }
    public synchronized int incCounter() {
        return(++counter);
    }
}
```

Accessing Databases

Data that is shared between Web components and is persistent between invocations of a J2EE application is usually maintained by a database. Web components use the JDBC 2.0 API to access relational databases. The data for the bookstore application is maintained in a database and accessed through the helper class `database.BookDB`. For example, `ReceiptServlet` invokes the `BookDB.buyBooks` method to update the book inventory when a user makes a purchase. The `buyBooks` method invokes `buyBook` for each book contained in the shopping cart. To ensure the order is processed in its entirety, the calls to `buyBook` are wrapped in a single JDBC transaction. The use of the shared database connection is synchronized via the `[get|release]Connection` methods.

```
public void buyBooks(ShoppingCart cart) throws OrderException{
    Collection items = cart.getItems();
    Iterator i = items.iterator();
    try {
        getConnection();
        con.setAutoCommit(false);
        while (i.hasNext()) {
            ShoppingCartItem sci = (ShoppingCartItem)i.next();
            BookDetails bd = (BookDetails)sci.getItem();
            String id = bd.getBookId();
            int quantity = sci.getQuantity();
            buyBook(id, quantity);
        }
        con.commit();
        con.setAutoCommit(true);
        releaseConnection();
    } catch (Exception ex) {
        try {
        con.rollback();
        releaseConnection();
        throw new OrderException("Transaction failed: " +
            ex.getMessage());
        } catch (SQLException sqx) {
            releaseConnection();
            throw new OrderException("Rollback failed: " +
```

```
                  sqx.getMessage());
            }
        }
    }
```

Initializing a Servlet

After the Web container loads and instantiates the servlet class and before it delivers requests from clients, the Web container initializes the servlet. You can customize this process to allow the servlet to read persistent configuration data, initialize resources, and perform any other one-time activities by overriding the `init` method of the `Servlet` interface. A servlet that cannot complete its initialization process should throw `UnavailableException`.

All the servlets that access the bookstore database (`BookStoreServlet`, `CatalogServlet`, `BookDetailsServlet`, and `ShowCartServlet`) initialize a variable in their `init` method that points to the database helper object created by the Web context listener:

```
public class CatalogServlet extends HttpServlet {
   private BookDB bookDB;
   public void init() throws ServletException {
      bookDB = (BookDB)getServletContext().
         getAttribute("bookDB");
      if (bookDB == null) throw new
         UnavailableException("Couldn't get database.");
   }
}
```

Writing Service Methods

The service provided by a servlet is implemented in the `service` method of a `GenericServlet`, the do*Method* methods (where *Method* can take the value `Get`, `Delete`, `Options`, `Post`, `Put`, `Trace`) of an `HttpServlet`, or any other protocol-specific methods defined by a class that implements the `Servlet` interface. In the rest of this chapter, the term *service method* will be used for any method in a servlet class that provides a service to a client.

The general pattern for a service method is to extract information from the request, access external resources, and then populate the response based on that information.

For HTTP servlets, the correct procedure for populating the response is to first fill in the response headers, then retrieve an output stream from the response, and finally write any body content to the output stream. Response headers must always be set before a `PrintWriter` or `ServletOutputStream` is retrieved because the HTTP protocol expects to receive all headers before body content. The next two sections describe how to get information from requests and generate responses.

Getting Information from Requests

A request contains data passed between a client and the servlet. All requests implement the `ServletRequest` interface. This interface defines methods for accessing the following information:

- Parameters, which are typically used to convey information between clients and servlets
- Object-valued attributes, which are typically used to pass information between the servlet container and a servlet or between collaborating servlets
- Information about the protocol used to communicate the request and the client and server involved in the request
- Information relevant to localization

For example, in `CatalogServlet` the identifier of the book that a customer wishes to purchase is included as a parameter to the request. The following code fragment illustrates how to use the `getParameter` method to extract the identifier:

```
String bookId = request.getParameter("Add");
if (bookId != null) {
  BookDetails book = bookDB.getBookDetails(bookId);
```

You can also retrieve an input stream from the request and manually parse the data. To read character data, use the `BufferedReader` object returned by the request's `getReader` method. To read binary data, use the `ServletInputStream` object returned by `getInputStream`.

HTTP servlets are passed an HTTP request object, `HttpServletRequest`, which contains the request URL, HTTP headers, query string, and so on.

An HTTP request URL contains the following parts:

```
http://<host>:<port><request path>?<query string>
```

The request path is further composed of the following elements:

- **Context path:** A concatenation of a forward slash (`/`) with the context root of the servlet's J2EE application.
- **Servlet path:** The path section that corresponds to the component alias that activated this request. This path starts with a forward slash (`/`).
- **Path info:** The part of the request path that is not part of the context path or the servlet path.

If the context path is `/catalog`, and the aliases are as listed in Table 10–5, then Table 10–6 gives some examples of how the URL will be broken down:

Table 10–5 Aliases

Pattern	Servlet
`/lawn/*`	`LawnServlet`
`/*.jsp`	`JSPServlet`

Table 10–6 Request Path Elements

Request Path	Servlet Path	Path Info
`/catalog/lawn/index.html`	`/lawn`	`/index.html`
`/catalog/help/feedback.jsp`	`/help/feedback.jsp`	`null`

Query strings are composed of a set of parameters and values. Individual parameters are retrieved from a request with the `getParameter` method. There are two ways to generate query strings:

- A query string can explicitly appear in a Web page. For example, an HTML page generated by `CatalogServlet` could contain the link

```
<a href="/bookstore1/catalog?Add=101">Add To Cart</a>
```

CatalogServlet extracts the parameter named Add as follows:

```
String bookId = request.getParameter("Add");
```

- A query string is appended to a URL when a form with a GET HTTP method is submitted. In the Duke's Bookstore application, CashierServlet generates a form, then a user name input to the form is appended to the URL that maps to ReceiptServlet, and finally ReceiptServlet extracts the user name using the getParameter method.

Constructing Responses

A response contains data passed between a server and the client. All responses implement the ServletResponse interface. This interface defines methods that allow you to do the following:

- Retrieve an output stream to use to send data to the client. To send character data, use the PrintWriter returned by the response's getWriter method. To send binary data in a MIME body response, use the ServletOutputStream returned by getOutputStream. To mix binary and text data, for example, to create a multipart response, use a ServletOutputStream and manage the character sections manually.
- Indicate the content type (for example, text/html), being returned by the response. A registry of content type names is kept by the Internet Assigned Numbers Authority (IANA) at:

  ftp://ftp.isi.edu/in-notes/iana/assignments/media-types

- Indicate whether to buffer output. By default, any content written to the output stream is immediately sent to the client. Buffering allows content to be written before anything is actually sent back to the client, thus providing the servlet with more time to set appropriate status codes and headers or forward to another Web resource.
- Set localization information.

HTTP response objects, `HttpServletResponse`, have fields representing HTTP headers such as

- Status codes, which are used to indicate the reason a request is not satisfied.
- Cookies, which are used to store application-specific information at the client. Sometimes cookies are used to maintain an identifier for tracking a user's session (see Maintaining Client State, page 238).

In Duke's Bookstore, `BookDetailsServlet` generates an HTML page that displays information about a book that the servlet retrieves from a database. The servlet first sets response headers: the content type of the response and the buffer size. The servlet buffers the page content because the database access can generate an exception that would cause forwarding to an error page. By buffering the response, the client will not see a concatenation of part of a Duke's Bookstore page with the error page should an error occur. The `doGet` method then retrieves a `PrintWriter` from the response.

For filling in the response, the servlet first dispatches the request to `BannerServlet`, which generates a common banner for all the servlets in the application. This process is discussed in the section Including Other Resources in the Response (page 234). Then the servlet retrieves the book identifier from a request parameter and uses the identifier to retrieve information about the book from the bookstore database. Finally, the servlet generates HTML markup that describes the book information and commits the response to the client by calling the `close` method on the `PrintWriter`.

```
public class BookDetailsServlet extends HttpServlet {
   public void doGet (HttpServletRequest request,
      HttpServletResponse response)
      throws ServletException, IOException {
     // set headers before accessing the Writer
     response.setContentType("text/html");
     response.setBufferSize(8192);
     PrintWriter out = response.getWriter();

     // then write the response
     out.println("<html>" +
     "<head><title>+
     messages.getString("TitleBookDescription")
     +</title></head>");

     // Get the dispatcher; it gets the banner to the user
     RequestDispatcher dispatcher =
       getServletContext().
```

```
            getRequestDispatcher("/banner");
        if (dispatcher != null)
            dispatcher.include(request, response);

        //Get the identifier of the book to display
        String bookId = request.getParameter("bookId");
        if (bookId != null) {
            // and the information about the book
            try {
                BookDetails bd =
                    bookDB.getBookDetails(bookId);
                ...
                //Print out the information obtained
                out.println("<h2>" + bd.getTitle() + "</h2>" +
                ...
            } catch (BookNotFoundException ex) {
                response.resetBuffer();
                throw new ServletException(ex);
            }
        }
        out.println("</body></html>");
        out.close();
    }
}
```

BookDetailsServlet generates a page that looks like Figure 10–2.

Filtering Requests and Responses

A *filter* is an object that can transform the header or content or both of a request or response. Filters differ from Web components in that they usually do not themselves create a response. Instead, a filter provides functionality that can be "attached" to any kind of Web resource. As a consequence, a filter should not have any dependencies on a Web resource for which it is acting as a filter, so that it can be composable with more than one type of Web resource. The main tasks that a filter can perform are as follows:

- Query the request and act accordingly.
- Block the request-and-response pair from passing any further.
- Modify the request headers and data. You do this by providing a customized version of the request.

- Modify the response headers and data. You do this by providing a customized version of the response.
- Interact with external resources.

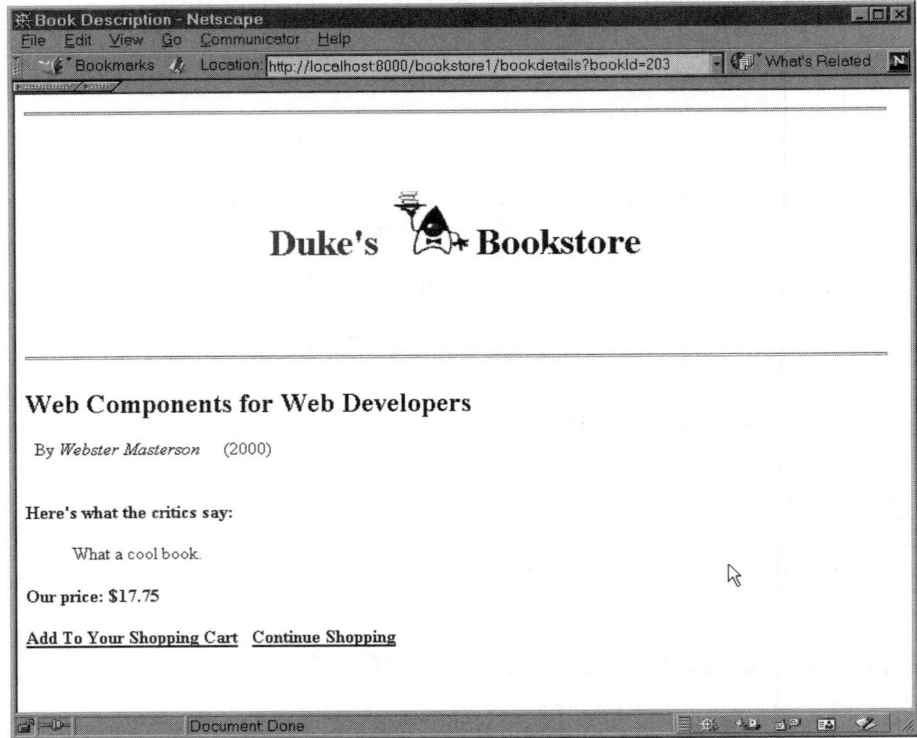

Figure 10–2 Book Details

Applications of filters include authentication, logging, image conversion, data compression, encryption, tokenizing streams, and XML transformations.

You can configure a Web resource to be filtered by a chain of zero, one, or more filters in a specific order. This chain is specified when the Web application containing the component is deployed and is instantiated when a Web container loads the component.

In summary, the tasks involved in using filters include

- Programming the filter

- Programming customized requests and responses
- Specifying the filter chain for each Web resource

Programming Filters

The filtering API is defined by the `Filter`, `FilterChain`, and `FilterConfig` interfaces in the `javax.servlet` package. You define a filter by implementing the `Filter` interface. The most important method in this interface is the `doFilter` method, which is passed request, response, and filter chain objects. This method can perform the following actions:

- Examine the request headers.
- Customize the request object if it wishes to modify request headers or data.
- Customize the response object if it wishes to modify response headers or data.
- Invoke the next entity in the filter chain. If the current filter is the last filter in the chain that ends with the target Web component or static resource, the next entity is the resource at the end of the chain; otherwise, it is the next filter that was configured in the WAR. It invokes the next entity by calling the `doFilter` method on the chain object (passing in the request and response it was called with, or the wrapped versions it may have created). Alternatively, it can choose to block the request by not making the call to invoke the next entity. In the latter case, the filter is responsible for filling out the response.
- Examine response headers after it has invoked the next filter in the chain.
- Throw an exception to indicate an error in processing.

In addition to `doFilter`, you must implement the `init` and `destroy` methods. The `init` method is called by the container when the filter is instantiated. If you wish to pass initialization parameters to the filter, you retrieve them from the `FilterConfig` object passed to `init`.

The Duke's Bookstore application uses the filters `HitCounterFilter` and `OrderFilter` to increment and log the value of a counter when the entry and receipt servlets are accessed.

In the `doFilter` method, both filters retrieve the servlet context from the filter configuration object so that they can access the counters stored as context attributes. After the filters have completed application-specific processing, they invoke `doFilter` on the filter chain object passed into the original `doFilter` method. The elided code is discussed in the next section.

```
public final class HitCounterFilter implements Filter {
   private FilterConfig filterConfig = null;

   public void init(FilterConfig filterConfig)
      throws ServletException {
      this.filterConfig = filterConfig;
   }
   public void destroy() {
      this.filterConfig = null;
   }
   public void doFilter(ServletRequest request,
      ServletResponse response, FilterChain chain)
      throws IOException, ServletException {
      if (filterConfig == null)
         return;
      StringWriter sw = new StringWriter();
      PrintWriter writer = new PrintWriter(sw);
      Counter counter = (Counter)filterConfig.
         getServletContext().
         getAttribute("hitCounter");
      writer.println();
      writer.println("===============");
      writer.println("The number of hits is: " +
         counter.incCounter());
      writer.println("===============");
      // Log the resulting string
      writer.flush();
      filterConfig.getServletContext().
         log(sw.getBuffer().toString());
      ...
      chain.doFilter(request, wrapper);
      ...
   }
}
```

Programming Customized Requests and Responses

There are many ways for a filter to modify a request or response. For example, a filter could add an attribute to the request or insert data in the response. In the Duke's Bookstore example, `HitCounterFilter` inserts the value of the counter into the response.

A filter that modifies a response must usually capture the response before it is returned to the client. The way to do this is to pass a stand-in stream to the servlet that generates the response. The stand-in stream prevents the servlet from closing the original response stream when it completes and allows the filter to modify the servlet's response.

To pass this stand-in stream to the servlet, the filter creates a response wrapper that overrides the `getWriter` or `getOutputStream` method to return this stand-in stream. The wrapper is passed to the `doFilter` method of the filter chain. Wrapper methods default to calling through to the wrapped request or response object. This approach follows the well-known Wrapper or Decorator pattern described in *Design Patterns: Elements of Reusable Object-Oriented Software* (Addison-Wesley, 1995). The following sections describe how the hit counter filter described earlier and other types of filters use wrappers.

To override request methods, you wrap the request in an object that extends `ServletRequestWrapper` or `HttpServletRequestWrapper`. To override response methods, you wrap the response in an object that extends `ServletResponseWrapper` or `HttpServletResponseWrapper`.

`HitCounterFilter` wraps the response in a `CharResponseWrapper`. The wrapped response is passed to the next object in the filter chain, which is `BookStoreServlet`. `BookStoreServlet` writes its response into the stream created by `CharResponseWrapper`. When `chain.doFilter` returns, `HitCounterFilter` retrieves the servlet's response from `PrintWriter` and writes it to a buffer. The filter inserts the value of the counter into the buffer, resets the content length header of the response, and finally writes the contents of the buffer to the response stream.

```
PrintWriter out = response.getWriter();
CharResponseWrapper wrapper = new CharResponseWrapper(
   (HttpServletResponse)response);
chain.doFilter(request, wrapper);
CharArrayWriter caw = new CharArrayWriter();
caw.write(wrapper.toString().substring(0,
   wrapper.toString().indexOf("</body>")-1));
caw.write("<p>\n<center><center>" +
   messages.getString("Visitor") + "<font color='red'>" +
   counter.getCounter() + "</font><center>");
caw.write("\n</body></html>");
response.setContentLength(caw.toString().length());
out.write(caw.toString());
out.close();

public class CharResponseWrapper extends
   HttpServletResponseWrapper {
   private CharArrayWriter output;
   public String toString() {
      return output.toString();
   }
   public CharResponseWrapper(HttpServletResponse response){
```

```
         super(response);
         output = new CharArrayWriter();
      }
      public PrintWriter getWriter(){
         return new PrintWriter(output);
      }
   }
```

Figure 10–3 shows the entry page for Duke's Bookstore with the hit counter.

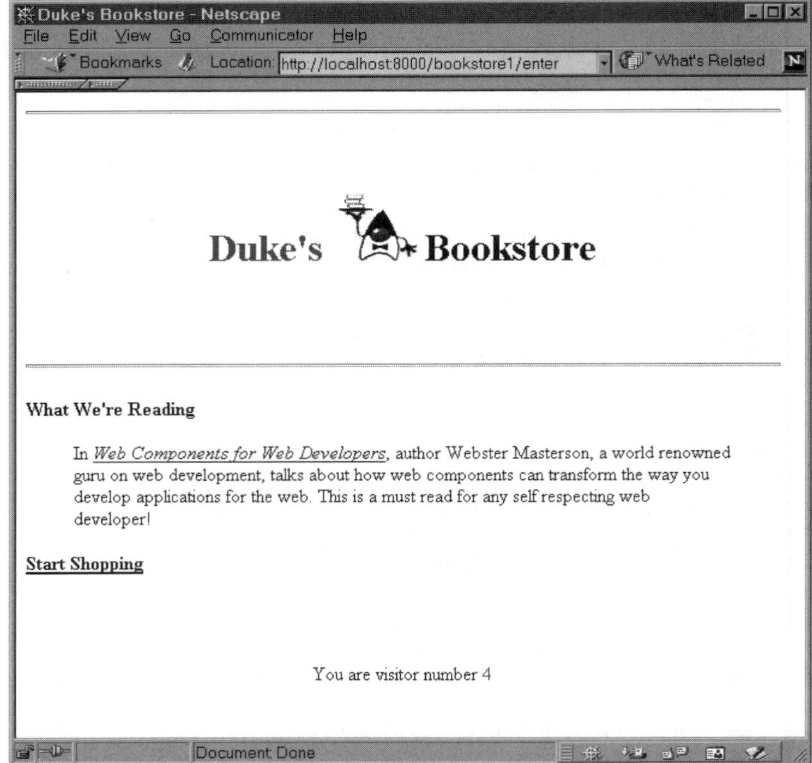

Figure 10–3 Duke's Bookstore Entry Page

Specifying Filter Mappings

A Web container uses filter mappings to decide how to apply filters to Web resources. A filter mapping matches a filter to a Web component by name or to Web resources by URL pattern. The filters are invoked in the order in which filter mappings appear in the filter mapping list of a WAR. You specify a filter mapping list for a WAR in the `deploytool` Filter Mapping inspector (see Filter Mapping, page 201).

Table 10–7 contains the filter mapping list for the Duke's Bookstore application. The filters are matched by servlet name and each filter chain contains only one filter.

Table 10–7 Duke's Bookstore Filter Mapping List

Servlet Name	Filter
`BookStoreServlet`	`HitCounterFilter`
`ReceiptServlet`	`OrderFilter`

You can map a filter to one or more Web resources, and you can map more than one filter to a Web resource. This is illustrated in Figure 10–4, where filter F1 is mapped to servlets S1, S2, and S3, filter F2 is mapped to servlet S2, and filter F3 is mapped to servlets S1 and S2.

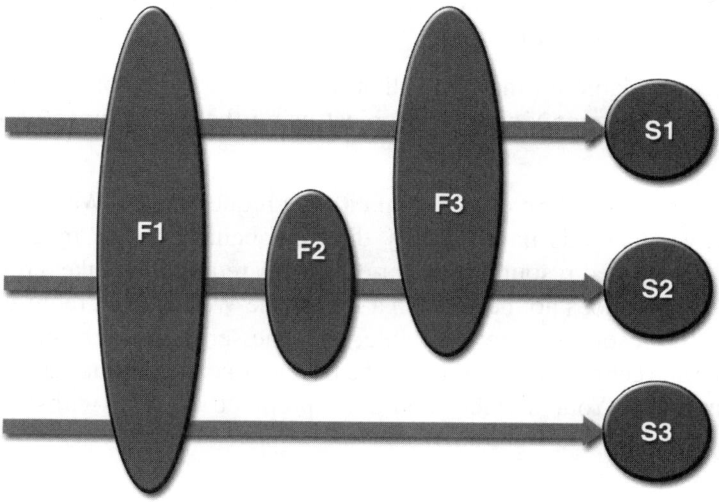

Figure 10–4 Filter to Servlet Mapping

Recall that a filter chain is one of the objects passed to the `doFilter` method of a filter. This chain is formed indirectly via filter mappings. The order of the filters in the chain is the same as the order in which filter mappings appear in the Web application deployment descriptor.

When a filter is mapped to servlet S1, the Web container invokes the `doFilter` method of F1. The `doFilter` method of each filter in S1's filter chain is invoked by the preceding filter in the chain via the `chain.doFilter` method. Since S1's filter chain contains filters F1 and F3, F1's call to `chain.doFilter` invokes the `doFilter` method of filter F3. When F3's `doFilter` method completes, control returns to F1's `doFilter` method.

Invoking Other Web Resources

Web components can invoke other Web resources in two ways: indirect and direct. A Web component indirectly invokes another Web resource when it embeds in content returned to a client a URL that points to another Web component. In the Duke's Bookstore application, most Web components contain embedded URLs that point to other Web components. For example, `ReceiptServlet` indirectly invokes the `CatalogServlet` through the embedded URL `/bookstore1/catalog`.

A Web component can also directly invoke another resource while it is executing. There are two possibilities: it can include the content of another resource, or it can forward a request to another resource.

To invoke a resource available on the server that is running a Web component, you must first obtain a `RequestDispatcher` object using the `getRequestDispatcher("URL")` method.

You can get a `RequestDispatcher` object from either a request or the Web context; however, the two methods have slightly different behavior. The method takes the path to the requested resource as an argument. A request can take a relative path (that is, one that does not begin with a `/`), but the Web context requires an absolute path. If the resource is not available, or if the server has not implemented a `RequestDispatcher` object for that type of resource, `getRequestDispatcher` will return null. Your servlet should be prepared to deal with this condition.

Including Other Resources in the Response

It is often useful to include another Web resource, for example, banner content or copyright information, in the response returned from a Web component. To include another resource, invoke the `include` method of a `RequestDispatcher` object:

```
include(request, response);
```

If the resource is static, the `include` method enables programmatic server-side includes. If the resource is a Web component, the effect of the method is to send the request to the included Web component, execute the Web component, and then include the result of the execution in the response from the containing servlet. An included Web component has access to the request object, but it is limited in what it can do with the response object:

- It can write to the body of the response and commit a response.
- It cannot set headers or call any method (for example, `setCookie`) that affects the headers of the response.

The banner for the Duke's Bookstore application is generated by `BannerServlet`. Note that both the `doGet` and `doPost` methods are implemented because `BannerServlet` can be dispatched from either method in a calling servlet.

```
public class BannerServlet extends HttpServlet {
   public void doGet (HttpServletRequest request,
      HttpServletResponse response)
      throws ServletException, IOException {

      PrintWriter out = response.getWriter();
      out.println("<body bgcolor=\"#ffffff\">" +
      "<center>" + "<hr> <br>  " + "<h1>" +
      "<font size=\"+3\" color=\"#CC0066\">Duke's </font>" +
      <img src=\"" + request.getContextPath() +
      "/duke.books.gif\">" +
      "<font size=\"+3\" color=\"black\">Bookstore</font>" +
      "</h1>" + "</center>" + "<br>   <hr> <br> ");
   }
   public void doPost (HttpServletRequest request,
      HttpServletResponse response)
      throws ServletException, IOException {

      PrintWriter out = response.getWriter();
      out.println("<body bgcolor=\"#ffffff\">" +
      "<center>" + "<hr> <br>  " + "<h1>" +
      "<font size=\"+3\" color=\"#CC0066\">Duke's </font>" +
      <img src=\"" + request.getContextPath() +
      "/duke.books.gif\">" +
```

```
         "<font size=\"+3\" color=\"black\">Bookstore</font>" +
         "</h1>" + "</center>" + "<br>   <hr> <br> ");
      }
   }
```

Each servlet in the Duke's Bookstore application includes the result from `BannerServlet` with the following code:

```
   RequestDispatcher dispatcher =
      getServletContext().getRequestDispatcher("/banner");
   if (dispatcher != null)
      dispatcher.include(request, response);
   }
```

Transferring Control to Another Web Component

In some applications, you might want to have one Web component do preliminary processing of a request and have another component generate the response. For example, you might want to partially process a request and then transfer to another component depending on the nature of the request.

To transfer control to another Web component, you invoke the `forward` method of a `RequestDispatcher`. When a request is forwarded, the request URL is set to the path of the forwarded page. If the original URL is required for any processing, you can save it as a request attribute. The `Dispatcher` servlet, used by a version of the Duke's Bookstore application described in the section A Template Tag Library (page 308), saves the path information from the original URL, retrieves a `RequestDispatcher` from the request, and then forwards to the JSP page `template.jsp`.

```
   public class Dispatcher extends HttpServlet {
      public void doGet(HttpServletRequest request,
         HttpServletResponse response) {
         request.setAttribute("selectedScreen",
            request.getServletPath());
         RequestDispatcher dispatcher = request.
            getRequestDispatcher("/template.jsp");
         if (dispatcher != null)
            dispatcher.forward(request, response);
      }
      public void doPost(HttpServletRequest request,
      ...
   }
```

The `forward` method should be used to give another resource responsibility for replying to the user. If you have already accessed a `ServletOutputStream` or `PrintWriter` object within the servlet, you cannot use this method; it throws an `IllegalStateException`.

Accessing the Web Context

The context in which Web components execute is an object that implements the `ServletContext` interface. You retrieve the Web context with the `getServletContext` method. The Web context provides methods for accessing:

- Initialization parameters
- Resources associated with the Web context
- Object-valued attributes
- Logging capabilities

The Web context is used by the Duke's Bookstore filters `filters.HitCounterFilter` and `OrderFilter`, discussed in the section Filtering Requests and Responses (page 227). The filters store a counter as a context attribute. Recall from Controlling Concurrent Access to Shared Resources (page 220) that the counter's access methods are synchronized to prevent incompatible operations by servlets that are running concurrently. A filter retrieves the counter object with the context's `getAttribute` method. The incremented value of the counter is recorded with the context's `log` method.

```
public final class HitCounterFilter implements Filter {
  private FilterConfig filterConfig = null;
  public void doFilter(ServletRequest request,
    ServletResponse response, FilterChain chain)
    throws IOException, ServletException {
    ...
    StringWriter sw = new StringWriter();
    PrintWriter writer = new PrintWriter(sw);
    ServletContext context = filterConfig.
      getServletContext();
    Counter counter = (Counter)context.
      getAttribute("hitCounter");
    ...
    writer.println("The number of hits is: " +
      counter.incCounter());
    ...
```

```
            context.log(sw.getBuffer().toString());
            ...
        }
    }
```

Maintaining Client State

Many applications require a series of requests from a client to be associated with one another. For example, the Duke's Bookstore application saves the state of a user's shopping cart across requests. Web-based applications are responsible for maintaining such state, called a *session*, because the HTTP protocol is stateless. To support applications that need to maintain state, Java Servlet technology provides an API for managing sessions and allows several mechanisms for implementing sessions.

Accessing a Session

Sessions are represented by an `HttpSession` object. You access a session by calling the `getSession` method of a request object. This method returns the current session associated with this request, or, if the request does not have a session, it creates one. Since `getSession` may modify the response header (if cookies are the session tracking mechanism), it needs to be called before you retrieve a `PrintWriter` or `ServletOutputStream`.

Associating Attributes with a Session

You can associate object-valued attributes with a session by name. Such attributes are accessible by any Web component that belongs to the same Web context *and* is handling a request that is part of the same session.

The Duke's Bookstore application stores a customer's shopping cart as a session attribute. This allows the shopping cart to be saved between requests and also allows cooperating servlets to access the cart. `CatalogServlet` adds items to the cart; `ShowCartServlet` displays, deletes items from, and clears the cart; and `CashierServlet` retrieves the total cost of the books in the cart.

```
public class CashierServlet extends HttpServlet {
    public void doGet (HttpServletRequest request,
        HttpServletResponse response)
        throws ServletException, IOException {

        // Get the user's session and shopping cart
```

```
HttpSession session = request.getSession();
ShoppingCart cart =
   (ShoppingCart)session.
      getAttribute("cart");
...
// Determine the total price of the user's books
double total = cart.getTotal();
```

Notifying Objects That Are Associated with a Session

Recall that your application can notify Web context and session listener objects of servlet life-cycle events (see Handling Servlet Life-Cycle Events, page 216). You can also notify objects of certain events related to their association with a session, such as the following:

- When the object is added to or removed from a session. To receive this notification, your object must implement the `javax.http.HttpSessionBindingListener` interface.
- When the session to which the object is attached will be passivated or activated. A session will be passivated or activated when it is moved between virtual machines or saved to and restored from persistent storage. To receive this notification, your object must implement the `javax.http.HttpSessionActivationListener` interface.

Session Management

Since there is no way for an HTTP client to signal that it no longer needs a session, each session has an associated timeout so that its resources can be reclaimed. The timeout period can be accessed with a session's `[get|set]MaxInactiveInterval` methods. You can also set the timeout period in `deploytool`:

1. Select the WAR.
2. Select the General tab.
3. Enter the timeout period in the Advanced box.

To ensure that an active session is not timed out, you should periodically access the session via service methods because this resets the session's time-to-live counter.

When a particular client interaction is finished, you use the session's `invalidate` method to invalidate a session on the server side and remove any session data.

The bookstore application's `ReceiptServlet` is the last servlet to access a client's session, so it has responsibility for invalidating the session:

```
public class ReceiptServlet extends HttpServlet {
  public void doPost(HttpServletRequest request,
          HttpServletResponse response)
          throws ServletException, IOException {
    // Get the user's session and shopping cart
    HttpSession session = request.getSession();
    // Payment received -- invalidate the session
    session.invalidate();
    ...
```

Session Tracking

A Web container can use several methods to associate a session with a user, all of which involve passing an identifier between the client and server. The identifier can be maintained on the client as a cookie or the Web component can include the identifier in every URL that is returned to the client.

If your application makes use of session objects, you must ensure that session tracking is enabled by having the application rewrite URLs whenever the client turns off cookies. You do this by calling the response's `encodeURL(URL)` method on all URLs returned by a servlet. This method includes the session ID in the URL only if cookies are disabled; otherwise, it returns the URL unchanged.

The `doGet` method of `ShowCartServlet` encodes the three URLs at the bottom of the shopping cart display page as follows:

```
out.println("<p>   <p><strong><a href=\"" +
  response.encodeURL(request.getContextPath() + "/catalog") +
    "\">" + messages.getString("ContinueShopping") +
    "</a>      " +
    "<a href=\"" +
  response.encodeURL(request.getContextPath() + "/cashier") +
    "\">" + messages.getString("Checkout") +
    "</a>      " +
    "<a href=\"" +
  response.encodeURL(request.getContextPath() +
    "/showcart?Clear=clear") +
    "\">" + messages.getString("ClearCart") +
    "</a></strong>");
```

If cookies are turned off, the session is encoded in the Check Out URL as follows:

```
http://localhost:8080/bookstore1/cashier;
   jsessionid=c0o7fszeb1
```

If cookies are turned on, the URL is simply

```
http://localhost:8080/bookstore1/cashier
```

Finalizing a Servlet

When a servlet container determines that a servlet should be removed from service (for example, when a container wants to reclaim memory resources, or when it is being shut down), it calls the `destroy` method of the `Servlet` interface. In this method, you release any resources the servlet is using and save any persistent state. The following `destroy` method releases the database object created in the `init` method described in Initializing a Servlet (page 222):

```
public void destroy() {
   bookDB = null;
}
```

All of a servlet's `service` methods should be complete when a servlet is removed. The server tries to ensure this completion by calling the `destroy` method only after all service requests have returned or after a server-specific grace period, whichever comes first.

If your servlet has potentially long-running service requests, use the techniques described below to do the following:

- Keep track of how many threads are currently running the `service` method.
- Provide a clean shutdown by having the `destroy` method notify long-running threads of the shutdown and wait for them to complete.
- Have the long-running methods poll periodically to check for shutdown and, if necessary, stop working, clean up, and return.

Tracking Service Requests

To track service requests, include in your servlet class a field that counts the number of service methods that are running. The field should have synchronized access methods to increment, decrement, and return its value.

```
public class ShutdownExample extends HttpServlet {
   private int serviceCounter = 0;
   ...
   //Access methods for serviceCounter
   protected synchronized void enteringServiceMethod() {
      serviceCounter++;
   }
   protected synchronized void leavingServiceMethod() {
      serviceCounter--;
   }
   protected synchronized int numServices() {
      return serviceCounter;
   }
}
```

The `service` method should increment the service counter each time the method is entered and should decrement the counter each time the method returns. This is one of the few times that your `HttpServlet` subclass should override the `service` method. The new method should call `super.service` to preserve all of the original `service` method's functionality:

```
protected void service(HttpServletRequest req,
             HttpServletResponse resp)
             throws ServletException,IOException {
   enteringServiceMethod();
   try {
      super.service(req, resp);
   } finally {
      leavingServiceMethod();
   }
}
```

Notifying Methods to Shut Down

To ensure a clean shutdown, your `destroy` method should not release any shared resources until all of the service requests have completed. One part of doing this is to check the service counter. Another part is to notify the long-running methods that it is time to shut down. For this notification, another field is required. The field should have the usual access methods:

```
public class ShutdownExample extends HttpServlet {
   private boolean shuttingDown;
   ...
   //Access methods for shuttingDown
   protected synchronized void setShuttingDown(boolean flag) {
      shuttingDown = flag;
   }
   protected synchronized boolean isShuttingDown() {
      return shuttingDown;
   }
}
```

An example of the `destroy` method using these fields to provide a clean shutdown follows:

```
public void destroy() {
   /* Check to see whether there are still service methods /*
   /* running, and if there are, tell them to stop. */
   if (numServices() > 0) {
      setShuttingDown(true);
   }

   /* Wait for the service methods to stop. */
   while(numServices() > 0) {
      try {
         Thread.sleep(interval);
      } catch (InterruptedException e) {
      }
   }
}
```

Creating Polite Long-Running Methods

The final step in providing a clean shutdown is to make any long-running methods behave politely. Methods that might run for a long time should check the value of the field that notifies them of shutdowns and should interrupt their work, if necessary.

```
public void doPost(...) {
   ...
   for(i = 0; ((i < lotsOfStuffToDo) &&
      !isShuttingDown()); i++) {
      try {
```

```
            partOfLongRunningOperation(i);
        } catch (InterruptedException e) {
            ...
        }
    }
}
```

11

JavaServer Pages Technology

Stephanie Bodoff

JAVASERVER Pages (JSP) technology allows you to easily create Web content that has both static and dynamic components. JSP technology projects all the dynamic capabilities of Java Servlet technology but provides a more natural approach to creating static content. The main features of JSP technology are

- A language for developing JSP pages, which are text-based documents that describe how to process a request and construct a response
- Constructs for accessing server-side objects
- Mechanisms for defining extensions to the JSP language

JSP technology also contains an API that is used by developers of Web containers, but this API is not covered in this chapter.

In This Chapter

What Is a JSP Page?

A *JSP page* is a text-based document that contains two types of text: static template data, which can be expressed in any text-based format, such as HTML, SVG, WML, and XML; and JSP elements, which construct dynamic content. A syntax card and reference for the JSP elements are available at:

```
http://java.sun.com/products/jsp/technical.html#syntax
```

The Web page in Figure 11–1 is a form that allows you to select a locale and displays the date in a manner appropriate to the locale.

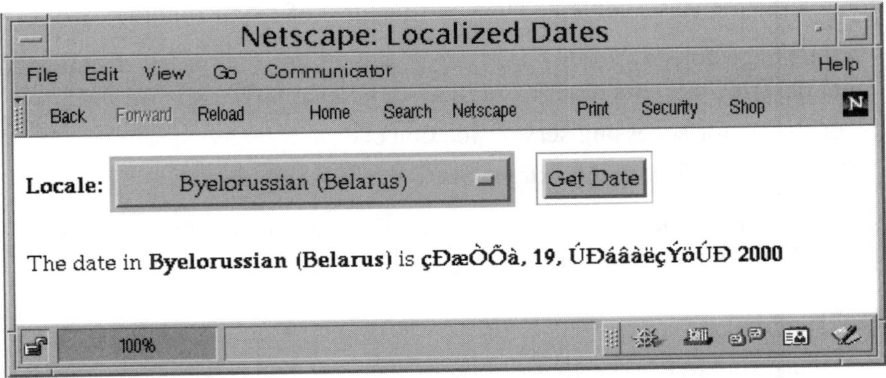

Figure 11–1 Localized Date Form

The source code for this example is in the `j2eetutorial/examples/src/web/date` directory created when you unzip the tutorial bundle. The JSP page `index.jsp` used to create the form appears below; it is a typical mixture of static HTML markup and JSP elements. If you have developed Web pages, you are probably familiar with the HTML document structure statements

(<head>, <body>, and so on) and the HTML statements that create a form (<form>) and a menu (<select>). The lines in bold in the example code contain the following types of JSP constructs:

- Directives (**<%@ page ... %>**) import classes in the `java.util` package and the `MyLocales` class, and set the content type returned by the page.
- The **`jsp:useBean`** element creates an object containing a collection of locales and initializes a variable that points to that object.
- Scriptlets (**`<% ... %>`**) retrieve the value of the `locale` request parameter, iterate over a collection of locale names, and conditionally insert HTML text into the output.
- Expressions (**`<%= ... %>`**) insert the value of the locale name into the response.
- The **`jsp:include`** element sends a request to another page (`date.jsp`) and includes the response in the response from the calling page.

```
<%@ page import="java.util.*,MyLocales" %>
<%@ page contentType="text/html; charset=ISO-8859-5" %>
<html>
<head><title>Localized Dates</title></head>
<body bgcolor="white">
<jsp:useBean id="locales" scope="application"
  class="MyLocales"/>
<form name="localeForm" action="index.jsp" method="post">
<b>Locale:</b>
<select name=locale>
<%
  String selectedLocale = request.getParameter("locale");
  Iterator i = locales.getLocaleNames().iterator();
  while (i.hasNext()) {
     String locale = (String)i.next();
     if (selectedLocale != null &&
        selectedLocale.equals(locale)) {
%>
        <option selected><%=locale%></option>
<%
     } else {
%>
        <option><%=locale%></option>
<%
     }
  }
%>
</select>
<input type="submit" name="Submit" value="Get Date">
```

```
</form>
<jsp:include page="date.jsp"/>
</body>
</html>
```

To build, deploy, and execute this JSP page:

1. Go to `j2eetutorial/examples` and build the example by executing `ant date` (see How to Build and Run the Examples, page xxii).
2. Create a J2EE application called `DateApp`.
   a. Select File→New→Application.
   b. In the file chooser, navigate to `j2eetutorial/examples/src/web/date`.
   c. In the File Name field, enter `DateApp`.
   d. Click New Application.
   e. Click OK.
3. Create the WAR and add the Web components to the `DateApp` application.
   a. Select File→New→Web Component.
   b. Select `DateApp` from the Create New WAR File In Application combo box.
   c. Enter `DateWAR` in the WAR Display Name field.
   d. Click Edit.
   e. Navigate to `j2eetutorial/examples/build/web/date`. Select `index.jsp`, `date.jsp`, `MyDate.class`, and `MyLocales.class` and click Add. Then click Finish.
   f. Click Next.
   g. Click JSP In The Web Component radio button, and then click Next.
   h. Select `index.jsp` from the JSP Filename combo box. Click Finish.
4. Enter the context root.
   a. Select `DateApp`.
   b. Select the Web Context tab.
   c. Enter `date`.
5. Deploy the application.
   a. Select Tools→Deploy.
   b. Click Finish.
6. Invoke the URL `http://<host>:8000/date` in a browser.

You will see a combo box whose entries are locales. Select a locale and click Get Date. You will see the date expressed in a manner appropriate for that locale.

The Example JSP Pages

To illustrate JSP technology, this chapter rewrites each servlet in the Duke's Bookstore application introduced in The Example Servlets (page 211) in as a JSP page. Table 11–1 lists the functions and their corresponding JSP pages.

Table 11–1 Duke's Bookstore Example JSP Pages

Function	JSP Pages
Enter the bookstore	`bookstore.jsp`
Create the bookstore banner	`banner.jsp`
Browse the books offered for sale	`catalog.jsp`
Put a book in a shopping cart	`catalog.jsp` and `bookdetails.jsp`
Get detailed information on a specific book	`bookdetails.jsp`
Display the shopping cart	`showcart.jsp`
Remove one or more books from the shopping cart	`showcart.jsp`
Buy the books in the shopping cart	`cashier.jsp`
Receive an acknowledgement for the purchase	`receipt.jsp`

The data for the bookstore application is still maintained in a database. However, two changes are made to the database helper object `database.BookDB`.

- The database helper object is rewritten to conform to JavaBeans component design patterns as described in JavaBeans Component Design Conventions (page 270). This change is made so that JSP pages can access the helper object using JSP language elements specific to JavaBeans components.
- Instead of accessing the bookstore database directly, the helper object goes through an enterprise bean. The advantage of using an enterprise

bean is that the helper object is no longer responsible for connecting to the database; this job is taken over by the enterprise bean. Furthermore, because the EJB container maintains the pool of database connections, an enterprise bean can get a connection quicker than the helper object can. The relevant interfaces and classes for the enterprise bean are the `database.BookDBEJBHome` home interface, `database.BookDBEJB` remote interface, and the `database.BookDBEJBImpl` implementation class, which contains all the JDBC calls to the database.

The implementation of the database helper object follows. The bean has two instance variables: the current book and a reference to the database enterprise bean.

```
public class BookDB {
   private String bookId = "0";
   private BookDBEJB database = null;

   public BookDB () throws Exception {
   }
   public void setBookId(String bookId) {
      this.bookId = bookId;
   }
   public void setDatabase(BookDBEJB database) {
      this.database = database;
   }
   public BookDetails getBookDetails()
      throws Exception {
      try {
         return (BookDetails)database.
            getBookDetails(bookId);
      } catch (BookNotFoundException ex) {
         throw ex;
      }
   }
   ...
}
```

Finally, this version of the example contains an applet to generate a dynamic digital clock in the banner. See Including an Applet (page 265) for a description of the JSP element that generates HTML for downloading the applet.

The source code for the application is located in the `j2eetutorial/examples/src/web/bookstore2` directory created when you unzip the tutorial bundle (see Downloading the Examples, page xxii). To build, deploy, and run the example:

1. Go to `j2eetutorial/examples` and build the example by running `ant bookstore2`.
2. Start the `j2ee` server.
3. Start `deploytool`.
4. Start the Cloudscape database by executing `cloudscape -start`.
5. If you have not already created the bookstore database, run `ant create-web-db`.
6. Create a J2EE application called `Bookstore2App`.
   a. Select File→New→Application.
   b. In the file chooser, navigate to `j2eetutorial/examples/src/web/bookstore2`.
   c. In the File Name field, enter `Bookstore2App`.
   d. Click New Application.
   e. Click OK.
7. Add the `Bookstore2WAR` WAR to the `Bookstore2App` application.
   a. Select File→Add→Web WAR.
   b. In the Add Web WAR dialog box, navigate to `j2eetutorial/examples/build/web/bookstore2`. Select `bookstore2.war`. Click Add Web WAR.
8. Add the `BookDBEJB` enterprise bean to the application.
   a. Select File→New Enterprise Bean.
   b. Select Bookstore2App from the Create New JAR File In Application combo box.
   c. Type `BookDBJAR` in the JAR Display Name field.
   d. Click Edit to add the content files.
   e. In the Edit Archive Contents dialog box, navigate to the `j2eetutorial/examples/build/web/ejb` directory and add the `database` and `exception` packages. Click Next.
   f. Choose Session and Stateless for the Bean Type.
   g. Select `database.BookDBEJBImpl` for Enterprise Bean Class.
   h. In the Remote Interfaces box, select `database.BookDBEJBHome` for Remote Home Interface and `database.BookDBEJB` for Remote Interface.

   i. Enter `BookDBEJB` for Enterprise Bean Name.
   j. Click Next and then click Finish.

9. Add a resource reference for the Cloudscape database to the `BookDBEJB` bean.
   a. Select the `BookDBEJB` enterprise bean.
   b. Select the Resource Refs tab.
   c. Click Add.
   d. Select `javax.sql.DataSource` from the Type column.
   e. Enter `jdbc/BookDB` in the Coded Name field.
10. Save `BookDBJAR`.
   a. Select `BookDBJAR`.
   b. Select File→Save As.
   c. Navigate to the directory `examples/build/web/ejb`.
   d. Enter `bookDB.jar` in the File Name field.
   e. Click Save EJB JAR As.
11. Add a reference to the enterprise bean `BookDBEJB`.
   a. Select `Bookstore2WAR`.
   b. Select the EJB Refs tab.
   c. Click Add.
   d. Enter `ejb/BookDBEJB` in the Coded Name column.
   e. Select Session in the Type column.
   f. Select Remote in the Interfaces column.
   g. Enter `database.BookDBEJBHome` in the Home Interface column.
   h. Enter `database.BookDBEJB` in the Local/Remote Interface column.
12. Specify the JNDI Names.
   a. Select `Bookstore2App`.
   b. In the Application table, locate the EJB component and enter `BookDBEJB` in the JNDI Name column.
   c. In the References table, locate the EJB Ref and enter `BookDBEJB` in the JNDI Name column.
   d. In the References table, locate the Resource component and enter `jdbc/Cloudscape` in the JNDI Name column.

13. Enter the context root.
    a. Select the Web Context tab.
    b. Enter `bookstore2`.
14. Deploy the application.
    a. Select Tools→Deploy.
    b. Click Finish.
15. Open the bookstore URL `http://<host>:8000/bookstore2/enter`.

See Troubleshooting (page 215) for help with diagnosing common problems.

The Life Cycle of a JSP Page

A JSP page services requests as a servlet. Thus, the life cycle and many of the capabilities of JSP pages (in particular the dynamic aspects) are determined by Java Servlet technology and much of the discussion in this chapter refers to functions described in chapter 10.

When a request is mapped to a JSP page, it is handled by a special servlet that first checks whether the JSP page's servlet is older than the JSP page. If it is, it translates the JSP page into a servlet class and compiles the class. During development, one of the advantages of JSP pages over servlets is that the build process is performed automatically.

Translation and Compilation

During the translation phase, each type of data in a JSP page is treated differently. Template data is transformed into code that will emit the data into the stream that returns data to the client. JSP elements are treated as follows:

- Directives are used to control how the Web container translates and executes the JSP page.
- Scripting elements are inserted into the JSP page's servlet class. See JSP Scripting Elements (page 260) for details.
- Elements of the form `<jsp:XXX ... />` are converted into method calls to JavaBeans components or invocations of the Java Servlet API.

For a JSP page named *pageName*, the source for a JSP page's servlet is kept in the file

```
J2EE_HOME/repository/host/web/
  context_root/_0002fpageName_jsp.java
```

For example, the source for the index page (named `index.jsp`) for the `date` localization example discussed at the beginning of the chapter would be named

```
J2EE_HOME/repository/host/web/date/_0002findex_jsp.java
```

Both the translation and compilation phases can yield errors that are only observed when the page is requested for the first time. If an error occurs while the page is being translated (for example, if the translator encounters a malformed JSP element), the server will return a `ParseException`, and the servlet class source file will be empty or incomplete. The last incomplete line will give a pointer to the incorrect JSP element.

If an error occurs while the JSP page is being compiled (for example, there is a syntax error in a scriptlet), the server will return a `JasperException` and a message that includes the name of the JSP page's servlet and the line where the error occurred.

Once the page has been translated and compiled, the JSP page's servlet for the most part follows the servlet life cycle described in the section Servlet Life Cycle (page 216):

1. If an instance of the JSP page's servlet does not exist, the container:
   a. Loads the JSP page's servlet class
   b. Instantiates an instance of the servlet class
   c. Initializes the servlet instance by calling the `jspInit` method
2. Invokes the `_jspService` method, passing a request and response object.

If the container needs to remove the JSP page's servlet, it calls the `jspDestroy` method.

Execution

You can control various JSP page execution parameters using by `page` directives. The directives that pertain to buffering output and handling errors are discussed here. Other directives are covered in the context of specific page authoring tasks throughout the chapter.

Buffering

When a JSP page is executed, output written to the response object is automatically buffered. You can set the size of the buffer with the following `page` directive:

```
<%@ page buffer="none|xxxkb" %>
```

A larger buffer allows more content to be written before anything is actually sent back to the client, thus providing the JSP page with more time to set appropriate status codes and headers or to forward to another Web resource. A smaller buffer decreases server memory load and allows the client to start receiving data more quickly.

Handling Errors

Any number of exceptions can arise when a JSP page is executed. To specify that the Web container should forward control to an error page if an exception occurs, include the following `page` directive at the beginning of your JSP page:

```
<%@ page errorPage="file_name" %>
```

The Duke's Bookstore application page `initdestroy.jsp` contains the directive

```
<%@ page errorPage="errorpage.jsp"%>
```

The beginning of `errorpage.jsp` indicates that it is serving as an error page with the following `page` directive:

```
<%@ page isErrorPage="true|false" %>
```

This directive makes the exception object (of type `javax.servlet.jsp.JspException`) available to the error page, so that you can retrieve, interpret, and possibly display information about the cause of the exception in the error page.

Note: You can also define error pages for the WAR that contains a JSP page. If error pages are defined for both the WAR and a JSP page, the JSP page's error page takes precedence.

Initializing and Finalizing a JSP Page

You can customize the initialization process to allow the JSP page to read persistent configuration data, initialize resources, and perform any other one-time activities by overriding the `jspInit` method of the `JspPage` interface. You release resources using the `jspDestroy` method. The methods are defined using JSP declarations, discussed in Declarations (page 261).

The bookstore example page `initdestroy.jsp` defines the `jspInit` method to retrieve or create an enterprise bean `database.BookDBEJB` that accesses the bookstore database; `initdestroy.jsp` stores a reference to the bean in `bookDBEJB`. The enterprise bean is created using the techniques described in Chapter 2.

```
private BookDBEJB bookDBEJB;
public void jspInit() {
   bookDBEJB =
      (BookDB)getServletContext().getAttribute("bookDBEJB");
   if (bookDBEJB == null) {
      try {

         InitialContext ic = new InitialContext();
         Object objRef = ic.lookup(
            "java:comp/env/ejb/BookDBEJB");
         BookDBEJBHome home =
            (BookDBEJBHome)PortableRemoteObject.narrow(objRef,
               database.BookDBEJBHome.class);
         bookDBEJB = home.create();
         getServletContext().setAttribute("bookDBEJB",
            bookDBEJB);

      } catch (RemoteException ex) {
         System.out.println(
            "Couldn't create database bean." + ex.getMessage());
      } catch (CreateException ex) {
         System.out.println(
            "Couldn't create database bean." + ex.getMessage());
      } catch (NamingException ex) {
         System.out.println("Unable to lookup home: " +
            "java:comp/env/ejb/BookDBEJB."+ ex.getMessage());
      }
   }
}
```

When the JSP page is removed from service, the jspDestroy method releases the BookDBEJB variable:

```
public void jspDestroy() {
   bookDBEJB = null;
}
```

Since the enterprise bean is shared between all the JSP pages, it should be initialized when the application is started, instead of in each JSP page. Java Servlet technology provides application life cycle events and listener classes for this purpose. As an exercise, you can move the code that manages the creation of the enterprise bean to a context listener class. See Handling Servlet Life-Cycle Events (page 216) for the context listener that initializes the Java Servlet version of the bookstore application.

Creating Static Content

You create static content in a JSP page by simply writing it as if you were creating a page that consisted only of that content. Static content can be expressed in any text-based format, such as HTML, WML, and XML. The default format is HTML. If you want to use a format other than HTML, you include a page directive with the contentType attribute set to the format type at the beginning of your JSP page. For example, if you want a page to contain data expressed in the wireless markup language (WML), you need to include the following directive:

```
<%@ page contentType="text/vnd.wap.wml"%>
```

A registry of content type names is kept by the IANA at

```
ftp://ftp.isi.edu/in-notes/iana/assignments/media-types
```

Creating Dynamic Content

You create dynamic content by accessing Java programming language objects from within scripting elements.

Using Objects within JSP Pages

You can access a variety of objects, including enterprise beans and JavaBeans components, within a JSP page. JSP technology automatically makes some objects available, and you can also create and access application-specific objects.

Implicit Objects

Implicit objects are created by the Web container and contain information related to a particular request, page, or application. Many of the objects are defined by the Java Servlet technology underlying JSP technology and are discussed at length in Chapter 10. Table 11–2 summarizes the implicit objects.

Table 11–2 Implicit Objects

Variable	Class	Description
`application`	`javax.servlet.ServletContext`	The context for the JSP page's servlet and any Web components contained in the same application. See Accessing the Web Context (page 237).
`config`	`javax.servlet.ServletConfig`	Initialization information for the JSP page's servlet.
`exception`	`java.lang.Throwable`	Accessible only from an error page. See Handling Errors (page 255).
`out`	`javax.servlet.jsp.JspWriter`	The output stream.
`page`	`java.lang.Object`	The instance of the JSP page's servlet processing the current request. Not typically used by JSP page authors.
`pageContext`	`javax.servlet.jsp.PageContext`	The context for the JSP page. Provides a single API to manage the various scoped attributes described in Sharing Information (page 218). This API is used extensively when implementing tag handlers. See Tag Handlers (page 289).
`request`	Subtype of `javax.servlet.ServletRequest`	The request triggering the execution of the JSP page. See Getting Information from Requests (page 223).

Table 11–2 Implicit Objects (Continued)

Variable	Class	Description
`response`	Subtype of `javax.servlet.ServletResponse`	The response to be returned to the client. Not typically used by JSP page authors.
`session`	`javax.servlet.http.HttpSession`	The session object for the client. See Accessing the Web Context (page 237).

Application-Specific Objects

When possible, application behavior should be encapsulated in objects so that page designers can focus on presentation issues. Objects can be created by developers who are proficient in the Java programming language and in accessing databases and other services. There are four ways to create and use objects within a JSP page:

- Instance and class variables of the JSP page's servlet class are created in *declarations* and accessed in *scriptlets* and *expressions*.
- Local variables of the JSP page's servlet class are created and used in *scriptlets* and *expressions*.
- Attributes of scope objects (see Using Scope Objects, page 219) are created and used in *scriptlets* and *expressions*.
- JavaBeans components can be created and accessed using streamlined JSP elements. These elements are discussed in Chapter 12. You can also create a JavaBeans component in a declaration or scriptlet and invoke the methods of a JavaBeans component in a scriptlet or expression.

Declarations, scriptlets, and expressions are described in JSP Scripting Elements (page 260).

Shared Objects

The conditions affecting concurrent access to shared objects described in Sharing Information (page 218) apply to objects accessed from JSP pages that run as multithreaded servlets. You can indicate how a Web container should dispatch multiple client requests with the following `page` directive:

```
<%@ page isThreadSafe="true|false" %>
```

When isThreadSafe is set to true, the Web container may choose to dispatch multiple concurrent client requests to the JSP page. This is the *default* setting. If using true, you must ensure that you properly synchronize access to any shared objects defined at the page level. This includes objects created within declarations, JavaBeans components with page scope, and attributes of the page scope object.

If isThreadSafe is set to false, requests are dispatched one at a time, in the order they were received, and access to page-level objects does not have to be controlled. However, you still must ensure that access to attributes of the application or session scope objects and to JavaBeans components with application or session scope is properly synchronized.

JSP Scripting Elements

JSP scripting elements are used to create and access objects, define methods, and manage the flow of control. Since one of the goals of JSP technology is to separate static template data from the code needed to dynamically generate content, very sparing use of JSP scripting is recommended. Much of the work that requires the use of scripts can be eliminated by using custom tags, described in Extending the JSP Language (page 267).

JSP technology allows a container to support any scripting language that can call Java objects. If you wish to use a scripting language other than the default, java, you must specify it in a page directive at the beginning of a JSP page:

```
<%@ page language="scripting language" %>
```

Since scripting elements are converted to programming language statements in the JSP page's servlet class, you must import any classes and packages used by a JSP page. If the page language is java, you import a class or package with the page directive:

```
<%@ page import="packagename.*, fully_qualified_classname" %>
```

For example, the bookstore example page showcart.jsp imports the classes needed to implement the shopping cart with the following directive:

```
<%@ page import="java.util.*, cart.*" %>
```

Declarations

A *JSP declaration* is used to declare variables and methods in a page's scripting language. The syntax for a declaration is as follows:

```
<%! scripting language declaration %>
```

When the scripting language is the Java programming language, variables and methods in JSP declarations become declarations in the JSP page's servlet class.

The bookstore example page `initdestroy.jsp` defines an instance variable named `bookDBEJB` and the initialization and finalization methods `jspInit` and `jspDestroy` discussed earlier in a declaration:

```
<%!
  private BookDBEJB bookDBEJB;

  public void jspInit() {
    ...
  }
  public void jspDestroy() {
    ...
  }
%>
```

Scriptlets

A *JSP scriptlet* is used to contain any code fragment that is valid for the scripting language used in a page. The syntax for a scriptlet is as follows:

```
<%
  scripting language statements
%>
```

When the scripting language is set to `java`, a scriptlet is transformed into a Java programming language statement fragment and is inserted into the service method of the JSP page's servlet. A programming language variable created within a scriptlet is accessible from anywhere within the JSP page.

The JSP page `showcart.jsp` contains a scriptlet that retrieves an iterator from the collection of items maintained by a shopping cart and sets up a construct to loop through all the items in the cart. Inside the loop, the JSP page extracts properties of the book objects and formats them using HTML markup. Since the `while` loop opens a block, the HTML markup is followed by a scriptlet that closes the block.

```
<%
   Iterator i = cart.getItems().iterator();
   while (i.hasNext()) {
      ShoppingCartItem item =
         (ShoppingCartItem)i.next();
      BookDetails bd = (BookDetails)item.getItem();
%>

      <tr>
      <td align="right" bgcolor="#ffffff">
      <%=item.getQuantity()%>
      </td>
      <td bgcolor="#ffffaa">
      <strong><a href="
      <%=request.getContextPath()%>/bookdetails?bookId=
      <%=bd.getBookId()%>"><%=bd.getTitle()%></a></strong>
      </td>
      ...
<%
   // End of while
   }
%>
```

The output appears in Figure 11–2.

Expressions

A *JSP expression* is used to insert the value of a scripting language expression, converted into a string, into the data stream returned to the client. When the scripting language is the Java programming language, an expression is transformed into a statement that converts the value of the expression into a `String` object and inserts it into the implicit `out` object.

The syntax for an expression is as follows:

```
<%= scripting language expression %>
```

Note that a semicolon is not allowed within a JSP expression, even if the same expression has a semicolon when you use it within a scriptlet.

The following scriptlet retrieves the number of items in a shopping cart:

```
<%
   // Print a summary of the shopping cart
   int num = cart.getNumberOfItems();
   if (num > 0) {
%>
```

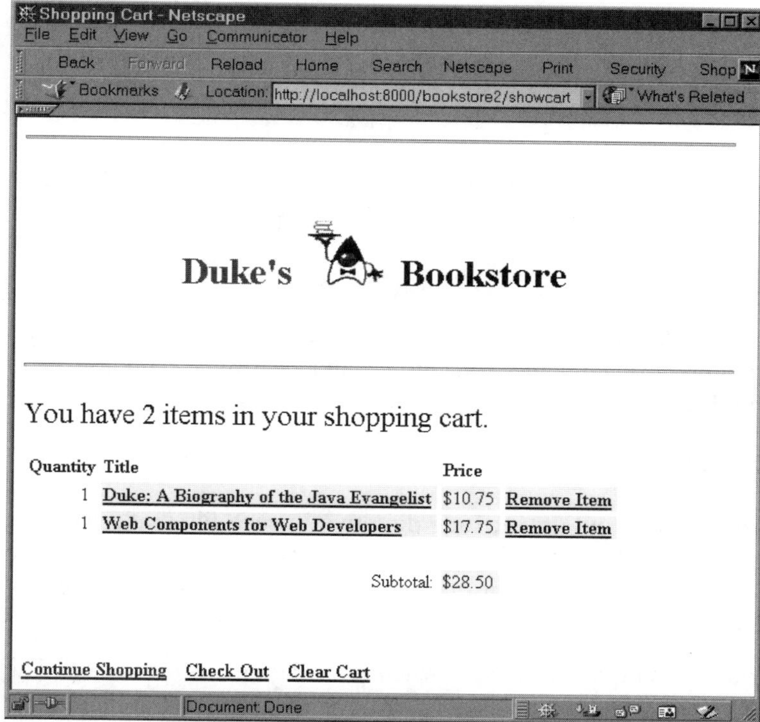

Figure 11–2 Duke's Bookstore Shopping Cart

Expressions are then used to insert the value of `num` into the output stream and determine the appropriate string to include after the number:

```
<font size="+2">
<%=messages.getString("CartContents")%> <%=num%>
   <%=(num==1 ? <%=messages.getString("CartItem")%> :
   <%=messages.getString("CartItems"))%></font>
```

Including Content in a JSP Page

There are two mechanisms for including another Web resource in a JSP page: the `include` directive and the `jsp:include` element.

The `include` directive is processed when the JSP page is *translated* into a servlet class. The effect of the directive is to insert the text contained in another file—either static content or another JSP page—in the including JSP page. You would probably use the `include` directive to include banner content, copyright information, or any chunk of content that you might want to reuse in another page. The syntax for the `include` directive is as follows:

```
<%@ include file="filename" %>
```

For example, all the bookstore application pages include the file `banner.jsp` containing the banner content with the following directive:

```
<%@ include file="banner.jsp" %>
```

In addition, the pages `bookstore.jsp`, `bookdetails.jsp`, `catalog.jsp`, and `showcart.jsp` include JSP elements that create and destroy a database bean with the following directive:

```
<%@ include file="initdestroy.jsp" %>
```

Because you must statically put an `include` directive in each file that reuses the resource referenced by the directive, this approach has its limitations. For a more flexible approach to building pages out of content chunks, see A Template Tag Library (page 308).

The `jsp:include` element is processed when a JSP page is *executed.* The `include` action allows you to include either a static or dynamic resource in a JSP file. The results of including static and dynamic resources are quite different. If the resource is static, its content is inserted into the calling JSP file. If the resource is dynamic, the request is sent to the included resource, the included page is executed, and then the result is included in the response from the calling JSP page. The syntax for the `jsp:include` element is as follows:

```
<jsp:include page="includedPage" />
```

The `date` application introduced at the beginning of this chapter includes the page that generates the display of the localized date with the following statement:

```
<jsp:include page="date.jsp"/>
```

Transferring Control to Another Web Component

The mechanism for transferring control to another Web component from a JSP page uses the functionality provided by the Java Servlet API as described in Transferring Control to Another Web Component (page 236) in Chapter 10. You access this functionality from a JSP page with the `jsp:forward` element:

```
<jsp:forward page="/main.jsp" />
```

Note that if any data has already been returned to a client, the `jsp:forward` element will fail with an `IllegalStateException`.

Param Element

When an `include` or `forward` element is invoked, the original request object is provided to the target page. If you wish to provide additional data to that page, you can append parameters to the request object with the `jsp:param` element:

```
<jsp:include page="..." >
   <jsp:param name="param1" value="value1"/>
</jsp:include>
```

Including an Applet

You can include an applet or JavaBeans component in a JSP page by using the `jsp:plugin` element. This element generates HTML that contains the appropriate client-browser-dependent constructs (`<object>` or `<embed>`) that will result in the download of the Java Plug-in software (if required) and client-side component and subsequent execution of any client-side component. The syntax for the `jsp:plugin` element is as follows:

```
<jsp:plugin
   type="bean|applet"
   code="objectCode"
   codebase="objectCodebase"
   { align="alignment" }
   { archive="archiveList" }
   { height="height" }
   { hspace="hspace" }
   { jreversion="jreversion" }
   { name="componentName" }
```

```
    { vspace="vspace" }
    { width="width" }
    { nspluginurl="url" }
    { iepluginurl="url" } >
    { <jsp:params>
      { <jsp:param name="paramName" value="paramValue" /> }+
    </jsp:params> }
    { <jsp:fallback> arbitrary_text </jsp:fallback> }
</jsp:plugin>
```

The `jsp:plugin` tag is replaced by either an `<object>` or `<embed>` tag as appropriate for the requesting client. The attributes of the `jsp:plugin` tag provide configuration data for the presentation of the element as well as the version of the plug-in required. The `nspluginurl` and `iepluginurl` attributes specify the URL where the plug-in can be downloaded.

The `jsp:param` elements specify parameters to the applet or JavaBeans component. The `jsp:fallback` element indicates the content to be used by the client browser if the plug-in cannot be started (either because `<object>` or `<embed>` is not supported by the client or because of some other problem).

If the plug-in can start but the applet or JavaBeans component cannot be found or started, a plug-in-specific message will be presented to the user, most likely a pop-up window reporting a `ClassNotFoundException`.

The Duke's Bookstore page `banner.jsp` that creates the banner displays a dynamic digital clock generated by `DigitalClock` (Figure 11–3).

The `jsp:plugin` element used to download the applet follows:

```
<jsp:plugin
  type="applet"
  code="DigitalClock.class"
  codebase="/bookstore2"
  jreversion="1.3"
  align="center" height="25" width="300"
  nspluginurl="http://java.sun.com/products/plugin/1.3.0_01
    /plugin-install.html"
  iepluginurl="http://java.sun.com/products/plugin/1.3.0_01
    /jinstall-130_01-win32.cab#Version=1,3,0,1" >
  <jsp:params>
    <jsp:param name="language"
      value="<%=request.getLocale().getLanguage()%>" />
    <jsp:param name="country"
      value="<%=request.getLocale().getCountry()%>" />
    <jsp:param name="bgcolor" value="FFFFFF" />
    <jsp:param name="fgcolor" value="CC0066" />
```

```
    </jsp:params>
      <jsp:fallback>
      <p>Unable to start plugin.</p>
    </jsp:fallback>
  </jsp:plugin>
```

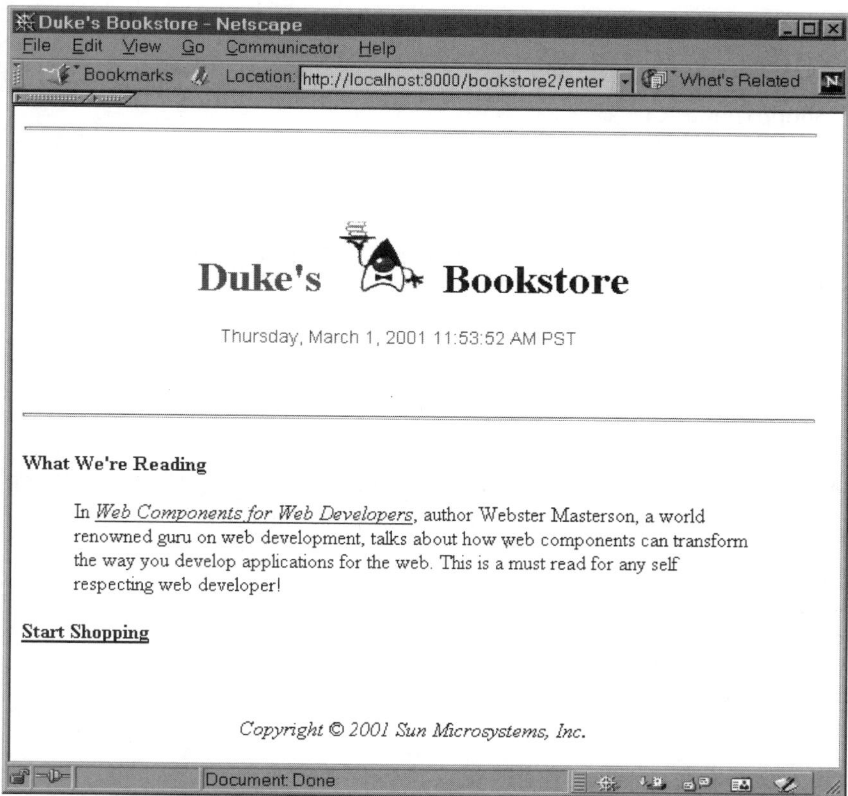

Figure 11–3 Duke's Bookstore with Applet

Extending the JSP Language

You can perform a wide variety of dynamic processing tasks including accessing databases, using enterprise services such as e-mail and directories, and managing flow control with JavaBeans components in conjunction with scriptlets. One of the drawbacks of scriptlets, however, is that they tend to make JSP pages more difficult to maintain. Alternatively, JSP technology provides a mechanism, called *custom tags*, that allows you to encapsulate dynamic functionality in objects that are accessed through extensions to the JSP language. Custom tags bring the benefits of another level of componentization to JSP pages.

For example, recall the scriptlet used to loop through and display the contents of the Duke's Bookstore shopping cart:

```
<%
   Iterator i = cart.getItems().iterator();
   while (i.hasNext()) {
      ShoppingCartItem item =
         (ShoppingCartItem)i.next();
      ...
%>
      <tr>
      <td align="right" bgcolor="#ffffff">
      <%=item.getQuantity()%>
      </td>
      ...
<%
   }
%>
```

An `iterate` custom tag eliminates the code logic and manages the scripting variable `item` that references elements in the shopping cart:

```
<logic:iterate id="item"
   collection="<%=cart.getItems()%>">
   <tr>
   <td align="right" bgcolor="#ffffff">
   <%=item.getQuantity()%>
   </td>
   ...
</logic:iterate>
```

Custom tags are packaged and distributed in a unit called a *tag library*. The syntax of custom tags is the same as that used for the JSP elements, namely, `<prefix:tag>`; however, for custom tags, `prefix` is defined by the *user* of the tag library and `tag` is defined by the *tag developer*. Chapter 13 explains how to use and develop custom tags.

12

JavaBeans Components in JSP Pages

Stephanie Bodoff

JAVABEANS components are Java classes that can be easily reused and composed together into applications. Any Java class that follows certain design conventions can be a JavaBeans component.

JavaServer Pages technology directly supports using JavaBeans components with JSP language elements. You can easily create and initialize beans and get and set the values of their properties. This chapter provides basic information about JavaBeans components and the JSP language elements for accessing beans in your JSP pages. For further information about the JavaBeans component model, see `http://java.sun.com/products/javabeans`.

In This Chapter

JavaBeans Component Design Conventions

JavaBeans component design conventions govern the properties of the class, and govern the public methods that give access to the properties.

A JavaBeans component property can be

- Read/write, read-only, or write-only
- Simple, which means it contains a single value, or indexed, which means it represents an array of values

There is no requirement that a property be implemented by an instance variable; the property must simply be accessible using public methods that conform to certain conventions:

- For each readable property, the bean must have a method of the form `PropertyClass getProperty() { ... }`
- For each writable property, the bean must have a method of the form `setProperty(PropertyClass pc) { ... }`

In addition to the property methods, a JavaBeans component must define a constructor that takes no parameters.

The Duke's Bookstore application JSP pages `enter.jsp`, `bookdetails.jsp`, `catalog.jsp`, and `showcart.jsp` use the `database.BookDB` and `database.BookDetails` JavaBeans components. `BookDB` provides a JavaBeans component front end to the enterprise bean `BookDBEJB`. Both beans are used extensively by bean-oriented custom tags (see Tags That Define Scripting Variables, page 298). The JSP pages `showcart.jsp` and `cashier.jsp` use `cart.ShoppingCart` to represent a user's shopping cart.

The JSP pages `catalog.jsp`, `showcart.jsp`, and `cashier.jsp` use the `util.Currency` JavaBeans component to format currency in a locale-sensitive manner. The bean has two writable properties, `locale` and `amount`, and one readable property, `format`. The `format` property does not correspond to any instance variable, but returns a function of the `locale` and `amount` properties.

```
public class Currency {
   private Locale locale;
   private double amount;
   public Currency() {
      locale = null;
      amount = 0.0;
```

```
    }
    public void setLocale(Locale l) {
        locale = l;
    }
    public void setAmount(double a) {
        amount = a;
    }
    public String getFormat() {
        NumberFormat nf =
            NumberFormat.getCurrencyInstance(locale);
        return nf.format(amount);
    }
}
```

Why Use a JavaBeans Component?

A JSP page can create and use any type of Java programming language object within a declaration or scriptlet. The following scriptlet creates the bookstore shopping cart and stores it as a session attribute:

```
<%
    ShoppingCart cart = (ShoppingCart)session.
        getAttribute("cart");
    // If the user has no cart, create a new one
    if (cart == null) {
        cart = new ShoppingCart();
        session.setAttribute("cart", cart);
    }
%>
```

If the shopping cart object conforms to JavaBeans conventions, JSP pages can use JSP elements to create and access the object. For example, the Duke's Bookstore pages `bookdetails.jsp`, `catalog.jsp`, and `showcart.jsp` replace the scriptlet with the much more concise JSP `useBean` element:

```
<jsp:useBean id="cart" class="cart.ShoppingCart"
    scope="session"/>
```

Creating and Using a JavaBeans Component

You declare that your JSP page will use a JavaBeans component using either one of the following formats:

```
<jsp:useBean id="beanName"
  class="fully_qualified_classname" scope="scope"/>
```

or

```
<jsp:useBean id="beanName"
  class="fully_qualified_classname" scope="scope">
  <jsp:setProperty .../>
</jsp:useBean>
```

The second format is used when you want to include `jsp:setProperty` statements, described in the next section, for initializing bean properties.

The `jsp:useBean` element declares that the page will use a bean that is stored within and accessible from the specified scope, which can be `application`, `session`, `request`, or `page`. If no such bean exists, the statement creates the bean and stores it as an attribute of the scope object (see Using Scope Objects, page 219). The value of the `id` attribute determines the *name* of the bean in the scope and the *identifier* used to reference the bean in other JSP elements and scriptlets.

Note: In the section JSP Scripting Elements (page 260) we mentioned that you must import any classes and packages used by a JSP page. This rule is slightly altered if the class is only referenced by `useBean` elements. In these cases, you must only import the class if the class is in the unnamed package. For example, in What Is a JSP Page? (page 246), the page `index.jsp` imports the `MyLocales` class. However, in the Duke's Bookstore example, all classes are contained in packages and thus are not explicitly imported.

The following element creates an instance of `Currency` if none exists, stores it as an attribute of the `session` object, and makes the bean available throughout the session by the identifier `currency`:

```
<jsp:useBean id="currency" class="util.Currency"
  scope="session"/>
```

Setting JavaBeans Component Properties

There are two ways to set JavaBeans component properties in a JSP page: with the `jsp:setProperty` element or with a scriptlet

```
<% beanName.setPropName(value); %>
```

The syntax of the `jsp:setProperty` element depends on the source of the property value. Table 12–1 summarizes the various ways to set a property of a JavaBeans component using the `jsp:setProperty` element.

Table 12–1 Setting JavaBeans Component Properties

Value Source	Element Syntax
String constant	`<jsp:setProperty name="beanName" property="propName" value="string constant"/>`
Request parameter	`<jsp:setProperty name="beanName" property="propName" param="paramName"/>`
Request parameter name matches bean property	`<jsp:setProperty name="beanName" property="propName"/>` `<jsp:setProperty name="beanName" property="*"/>`
Expression	`<jsp:setProperty name="beanName" property="propName" value="<%= expression %>"/>`

1. *beanName* must be the same as that specified for the `id` attribute in a `useBean` element.
2. There must be a *setPropName* method in the JavaBeans component.
3. *paramName* must be a request parameter name.

A property set from a constant string or request parameter must have a type listed in Table 12–2. Since both a constant and request parameter are strings, the Web container automatically converts the value to the property's type; the conversion applied is shown in the table. `String` values can be used to assign values to a property that has a `PropertyEditor` class. When that is the case, the `setAsText(String)` method is used. A conversion failure arises if the method throws an `IllegalArgumentException`. The value assigned to an indexed property must be an array, and the rules just described apply to the elements.

Table 12–2 Valid Value Assignments

Property Type	Conversion on String Value
Bean property	Uses `setAsText(`*`string-literal`*`)`
`boolean` or `Boolean`	As indicated in `java.lang.Boolean.valueOf(String)`
`byte` or `Byte`	As indicated in `java.lang.Byte.valueOf(String)`
`char` or `Character`	As indicated in `java.lang.String.charAt(0)`
`double` or `Double`	As indicated in `java.lang.Double.valueOf(String)`
`int` or `Integer`	As indicated in `java.lang.Integer.valueOf(String)`
`float` or `Float`	As indicated in `java.lang.Float.valueOf(String)`
`long` or `Long`	As indicated in `java.lang.Long.valueOf(String)`
`short` or `Short`	As indicated in `java.lang.Short.valueOf(String)`
`Object`	`new String(`*`string-literal`*`)`

You would use a runtime expression to set the value of a property whose type is a compound Java programming language type. Recall from the section Expressions (page 262) that a JSP expression is used to insert the value of a scripting language expression, converted into a `String`, into the stream returned to the client. When used within a `setProperty` element, an expression simply returns its value; *no* automatic conversion is performed. As a consequence, the type returned from an expression must match or be castable to the type of the property.

The Duke's Bookstore application demonstrates how to use the `setProperty` element and a scriptlet to set the current book for the database helper bean. For example, `bookstore3/bookdetails.jsp` uses the form

```
<jsp:setProperty name="bookDB" property="bookId"/>
```

whereas `bookstore2/bookdetails.jsp` uses the form

```
<% bookDB.setBookId(bookId); %>
```

The following fragments from the page `bookstore3/showcart.jsp` illustrate how to initialize a currency bean with a `Locale` object and amount determined by evaluating request-time expressions. Because the first initialization is nested in a `useBean` element, it is only executed when the bean is created.

```
<jsp:useBean id="currency" class="util.Currency"
  scope="session">
  <jsp:setProperty name="currency" property="locale"
    value="<%= request.getLocale() %>"/>
</jsp:useBean>

<jsp:setProperty name="currency" property="amount"
  value="<%=cart.getTotal()%>"/>
```

Retrieving JavaBeans Component Properties

There are several ways to retrieve JavaBeans component properties. Two of the methods (the `jsp:getProperty` element and an expression) convert the value of the property into a `String` and insert the value into the current implicit `out` object:

- `<jsp:getProperty name="`*`beanName`*`" property="`*`propName`*`"/>`
- `<%= `*`beanName.getPropName`*`() %>`

For both methods, *`beanName`* must be the same as that specified for the `id` attribute in a `useBean` element, and there must be a `get`*`PropName`* method in the JavaBeans component.

If you need to retrieve the value of a property without converting it and inserting it into the `out` object, you must use a scriptlet:

```
<% Object o = beanName.getPropName(); %>
```

Note the differences between the expression and the scriptlet: the expression has an = after the opening `%` and does not terminate with a semicolon, as does the scriptlet.

The Duke's Bookstore application demonstrates how to use both forms to retrieve the formatted currency from the currency bean and insert it into the page. For example, `bookstore3/showcart.jsp` uses the form

```
<jsp:getProperty name="currency" property="format"/>
```

whereas `bookstore2/showcart.jsp` uses the form

```
<%= currency.getFormat() %>
```

The Duke's Bookstore application page `bookstore2/showcart.jsp` uses the following scriptlet to retrieve the number of books from the shopping cart bean and open a conditional insertion of text into the output stream:

```
<%
  // Print a summary of the shopping cart
  int num = cart.getNumberOfItems();
  if (num > 0) {
%>
```

Although scriptlets are very useful for dynamic processing, using custom tags (see Chapter 13) to access object properties and perform flow control is considered to be a better approach. For example, `bookstore3/showcart.jsp` replaces the scriptlet with the following custom tags:

```
<bean:define id="num" name="cart" property="numberOfItems" />
<logic:greaterThan name="num" value="0" >
```

Figure 12–1 summarizes where various types of objects are stored and how those objects can be accessed from a JSP page. Objects created by the `jsp:useBean` tag are stored as attributes of the scope objects and can be accessed by `jsp:[get|set]Property` tags and in scriptlets and expressions. Objects created in declarations and scriptlets are stored as variables of the JSP page's servlet class and can be accessed in scriptlets and expressions.

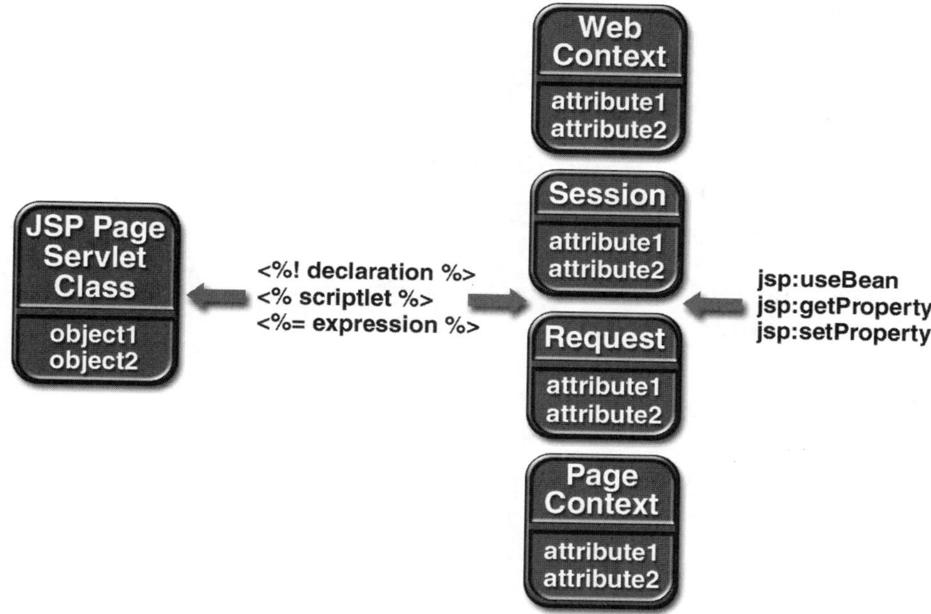

Figure 12–1 Accessing Objects from a JSP Page

13

Custom Tags in JSP Pages

Stephanie Bodoff

THE standard JSP tags for invoking operations on JavaBeans components and performing request dispatching simplify JSP page development and maintenance. JSP technology also provides a mechanism for encapsulating other types of dynamic functionality in *custom tags*, which are extensions to the JSP language. Custom tags are usually distributed in the form of a *tag library*, which defines a set of related custom tags and contains the objects that implement the tags.

Some examples of tasks that can be performed by custom tags include operations on implicit objects, processing forms, accessing databases and other enterprise services such as e-mail and directories, and performing flow control. JSP tag libraries are created by developers who are proficient at the Java programming language and expert in accessing data and other services, and are used by Web application designers who can focus on presentation issues rather than being concerned with how to access enterprise services. As well as encouraging division of labor between library developers and library users, custom tags increase productivity by encapsulating recurring tasks so that they can be reused across more than one application.

Tag libraries are receiving a great deal of attention in the JSP technology community. For more information about tag libraries and for pointers to some freely-available libraries see

```
http://java.sun.com/products/jsp/taglibraries.html
```

In This Chapter

What Is a Custom Tag?

A custom tag is a user-defined JSP language element. When a JSP page containing a custom tag is translated into a servlet, the tag is converted to operations on an object called a *tag handler*. The Web container then invokes those operations when the JSP page's servlet is executed.

Custom tags have a rich set of features. They can

- Be customized via attributes passed from the calling page.
- Access all the objects available to JSP pages.
- Modify the response generated by the calling page.

- Communicate with each other. You can create and initialize a JavaBeans component, create a variable that refers to that bean in one tag, and then use the bean in another tag.
- Be nested within one another, allowing for complex interactions within a JSP page.

The Example JSP Pages

This chapter describes the tasks involved in using and defining tags. The chapter illustrates the tasks with excerpts from the JSP version of the Duke's Bookstore application discussed in Chapter 11 rewritten to take advantage of two tag libraries: Struts and tutorial-template. The section in this chapter entitled Examples (page 304) describes some tags in detail: the `iterate` tag from Struts and the set of tags in the tutorial-template tag library.

The Struts tag library provides a framework for building internationalized Web applications that implement the Model-View-Controller design pattern. Struts includes a comprehensive set of utility custom tags for handling

- HTML forms
- Templates
- JavaBeans components
- Logic processing

The Duke's Bookstore application uses tags from the Struts `bean` and `logic` sublibraries.

The tutorial-template tag library defines a set of tags for creating an application template. The template is a JSP page with placeholders for the parts that need to change with each screen. Each of these placeholders is referred to as a *parameter* of the template. For example, a simple template could include a title parameter and a body parameter that refers to a JSP page for the custom content of the screen. The template is created with a set of nested tags—`definition`, `screen`, and `parameter`—that are used to build a table of screen definitions for Duke's Bookstore and with an `insert` tag to insert parameters from the table into the screen.

Figure 13–1 shows the flow of a request through the following Duke's Bookstore Web components:

- `template.jsp`, which determines the structure of each screen. It uses the `insert` tag to compose a screen from subcomponents.

- `screendefinitions.jsp`, which defines the subcomponents used by each screen. All screens have the same banner, but different title and body content (specified by the JSP Pages column in Table 11–1).
- `Dispatcher`, a servlet, which processes requests and forwards to `template.jsp`.

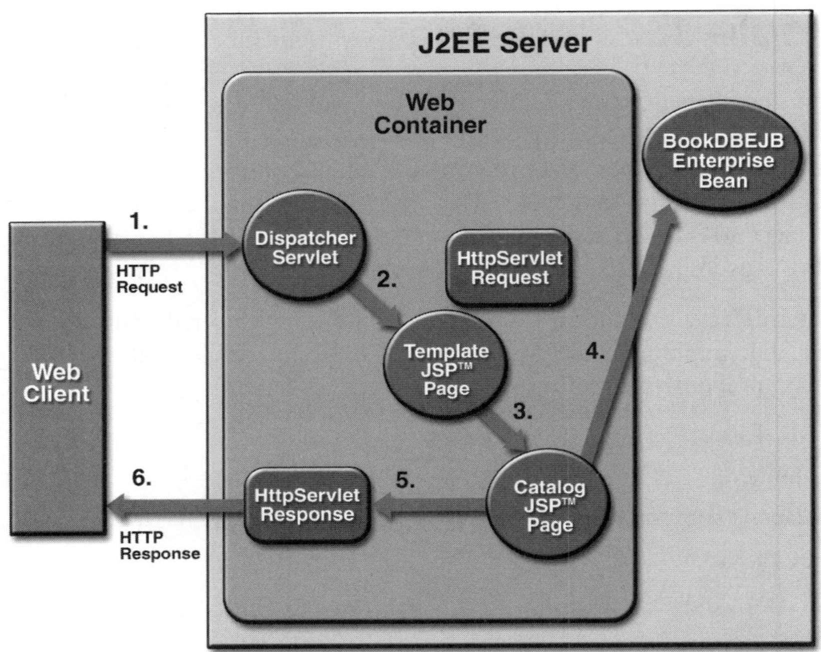

Figure 13–1 Request Flow through Duke's Bookstore Components

The source for the Duke's Bookstore application is located in the `j2eetutorial/examples/src/web/bookstore3` directory created when you unzip the tutorial bundle (see Downloading the Examples, page xxii). To build, deploy, and run the example:

1. Go to `j2eetutorial/examples` and build the application by executing `ant bookstore3` (see How to Build and Run the Examples, page xxii).
2. Download and unpack Struts version 1.0 from

```
http://jakarta.apache.org/builds/jakarta-struts/
   release/v1.0/
```

Copy `struts-bean.tld`, `struts-logic.tld`, and `struts.jar` from `jakarta-struts-1.0/lib` to `examples/build/web/bookstore3`

3. Start the `j2ee` server.
4. Start `deploytool`.
5. Start the Cloudscape database by executing `cloudscape -start`.
6. If you have not already created the bookstore database, run `ant create-web-db`.
7. Create a J2EE application called `Bookstore3App`.
   a. Select File→New Application.
   b. In the file chooser, navigate to `j2eetutorial/examples/src/web/bookstore3`.
   c. In the File Name field, enter `Bookstore3App`.
   d. Click New Application.
   e. Click OK.
8. Create the WAR and add the `DispatcherServlet` Web component and all of the Duke's Bookstore content to `Bookstore3App`.
   a. Select File→New→Web Component.
   b. Click the Create New WAR File in Application radio button and select `Bookstore3App` from the combo box. Enter `Bookstore3WAR` in the field labeled WAR Display Name.
   c. Click Edit to add the content files. In the Edit Contents dialog box, navigate to `j2eetutorial/examples/build/web/bookstore3`. Select Dispatcher.class and click Add. Add the JSP pages `banner.jsp`, `bookstore.jsp`, `bookdetails.jsp`, `catalog.jsp`, `showcart.jsp`, `cashier.jsp`, `receipt.jsp`, `initdestroy.jsp`, `template.jsp`, `screendefinitions.jsp`, and `errorpage.jsp`. Add `duke.books.gif`, `struts-bean.tld`, `struts-logic.tld`, `tutorial-template.tld`, and `struts.jar`. Add the `cart`, `database`, `messages`, `taglib`, and `util` packages. Click OK.
   d. Click Next.
   e. Select the Servlet radio button.
   f. Click Next.
   g. Select `Dispatcher` from the Servlet Class combo box.
   h. Click Next twice.

   i. In the Component Aliases pane, click Add and then type `/enter` in the Alias field. Repeat to add the aliases `/catalog`, `/bookdetails`, `/showcart`, `/cashier`, and `/receipt`.
   j. Click Finish.

9. Add the `BookDBEJB` enterprise bean that you created in the section The Example JSP Pages (page 249).
   a. Select File→Add→EJB JAR.
   b. Navigate to the directory `examples/build/web/ejb`.
   c. Select `bookDB.jar`.
   d. Click Add EJB JAR.

10. Add a reference to the enterprise bean `BookDBEJB`.
   a. Select `Bookstore3WAR`.
   b. Select the EJB Refs tab.
   c. Click Add.
   d. Enter `ejb/BookDBEJB` in the Coded Name column.
   e. Enter Session in the Type column.
   f. Select Remote in the Interfaces column.
   g. Enter `database.BookDBEJBHome` in the Home Interface column.
   h. Enter `database.BookDBEJB` in the Local/Remote Interface column.

11. Add the tag library URI to location mappings (see Declaring Tag Libraries, page 285):
   a. Select the File Refs tab.
   b. Click the Add button in the JSP Tag Libraries subpane.
   c. Enter the relative URI `/tutorial-template` in the Coded Reference field.
   d. Enter the absolute location `/WEB-INF/tutorial-template.tld` in the Tag Library field.
   e. Repeat for `/struts-bean` to `/WEB-INF/struts-bean.tld` and `/struts-logic` to `/WEB-INF/struts-logic.tld`.

12. Specify the JNDI names.
   a. Select `Bookstore3App`.
   b. In the Application table, locate the EJB component and enter `BookDBEJB` in the JNDI Name column.

   c. In the References table, locate the EJB Ref and enter `BookDBEJB` in the JNDI Name column.
   d. In the References table, locate the Resource component and enter `jdbc/Cloudscape` in the JNDI Name column.
13. Enter the context root.
   a. Select the Web Context tab.
   b. Enter `bookstore3`.
14. Deploy the application.
   a. Select Tools→Deploy.
   b. Click Finish.
15. Open the bookstore URL `http://<host>:8000/bookstore3/enter`.

See Troubleshooting (page 215) for help with diagnosing common problems.

Using Tags

This section describes how a page author specifies that a JSP page is using a tag library and introduces the different types of tags.

Declaring Tag Libraries

You declare that a JSP page will use tags defined in a tag library by including a `taglib` directive in the page before any custom tag is used:

```
<%@ taglib uri="/WEB-INF/tutorial-template.tld" prefix="tt" %>
```

The `uri` attribute refers to a URI that uniquely identifies the tag library descriptor (TLD), described in the section Tag Library Descriptors (page 290). This URI can be direct or indirect. The `prefix` attribute defines the prefix that distinguishes tags defined by a given tag library from those provided by other tag libraries.

Tag library descriptor file names must have the extension `.tld`. TLD files are stored in the `WEB-INF` directory of the WAR or in a subdirectory of `WEB-INF`. You can reference a TLD directly and indirectly.

The following `taglib` directive directly references a TLD filename:

```
<%@ taglib uri="/WEB-INF/tutorial-template.tld" prefix="tt" %>
```

This taglib directive uses a short logical name to indirectly reference the TLD:

```
<%@ taglib uri="/tutorial-template" prefix="tt" %>
```

A logical name must be mapped to an absolute location in the Web application deployment descriptor. To map the logical name /tutorial-template to the absolute location /WEB-INF/tutorial-template.tld:

1. Select Bookstore3WAR.
2. Select the File Refs tab.
3. Click the Add button in the JSP Tag Libraries subpane.
4. Enter the relative URI /tutorial-template in the Coded Reference field.
5. Enter the absolute location /WEB-INF/tutorial-template.tld in the Tag Library field.

Types of Tags

JSP custom tags are written using XML syntax. They have a start tag and end tag, and possibly a body:

```
<tt:tag>
   body
</tt:tag>
```

A custom tag with no body is expressed as follows:

```
<tt:tag />
```

Simple Tags

A simple tag contains no body and no attributes:

```
<tt:simple />
```

Tags With Attributes

A custom tag can have attributes. Attributes are listed in the start tag and have the syntax attr="value". Attribute values serve to customize the behavior of a custom tag just as parameters are used to customize the behavior of a method.

You specify the types of a tag's attributes in a tag library descriptor (see Tag Library Descriptors, page 290).

You can set an attribute value from a `String` constant or a runtime expression. The conversion process between the constants and runtime expressions and attribute types follows the rules described for JavaBeans component properties in Setting JavaBeans Component Properties (page 273).

The attributes of the Struts `logic:present` tag determine whether the body of the tag is evaluated. In the following example, an attribute specifies a request parameter named `Clear`:

```
<logic:present parameter="Clear">
```

The Duke's Bookstore application page `catalog.jsp` uses a runtime expression to set the value of the attribute that determines the collection of books over which the Struts `logic:iterate` tag iterates:

```
<logic:iterate collection="<%=bookDB.getBooks()%>"
   id="book" type="database.BookDetails">
```

Tags with Bodies

A custom tag can contain custom and core tags, scripting elements, HTML text, and tag-dependent body content between the start and end tag.

In the following example, the Duke's Bookstore application page `showcart.jsp` uses the Struts `logic:present` tag to clear the shopping cart and print a message if the request contains a parameter named `Clear`:

```
<logic:present parameter="Clear">
   <% cart.clear(); %>
   <font color="#ff0000" size="+2"><strong>
   You just cleared your shopping cart!
   </strong><br> <br></font>
</logic:present>
```

Choosing between Passing Information as Attributes or Body

As shown in the last two sections, it is possible to pass a given piece of data as an attribute of the tag or as the tag's body. Generally speaking, any data that is a simple string or can be generated by evaluating a simple expression is best passed as an attribute.

Tags That Define Scripting Variables

A custom tag can define a variable that can be used in scripts within a page. The following example illustrates how to define and use a scripting variable that contains an object returned from a JNDI lookup. Examples of such objects include enterprise beans, transactions, databases, environment entries, and so on:

```
<tt:lookup id="tx" type="UserTransaction"
  name="java:comp/UserTransaction" />
<% tx.begin(); %>
```

In the Duke's Bookstore application, several pages use bean-oriented tags from Struts to define scripting variables. For example, `bookdetails.jsp` uses the `bean:parameter` tag to create the `bookId` scripting variable and set it to the value of the `bookId` request parameter. The `jsp:setProperty` statement also sets the `bookId` property of the `bookDB` object to the value of the `bookId` request parameter. The `bean:define` tag retrieves the value of the bookstore database property `bookDetails` and defines the result as the scripting variable `book`:

```
<bean:parameter id="bookId" name="bookId" />
<jsp:setProperty name="bookDB" property="bookId"/>
<bean:define id="book" name="bookDB" property="bookDetails"
  type="database.BookDetails"/>
<h2><jsp:getProperty name="book" property="title"></h2>
```

Cooperating Tags

Customer tags can cooperate with each other through shared objects. In the following example, `tag1` creates an object called `obj1`, which is then reused by `tag2`.

```
<tt:tag1 attr1="obj1" value1="value" />
<tt:tag2 attr1="obj1" />
```

In the next example, an object created by the enclosing tag of a group of nested tags is available to all inner tags. Since the object is not named, the potential for naming conflicts is reduced. This example illustrates how a set of cooperating nested tags would appear in a JSP page.

```
<tt:outerTag>
  <tt:innerTag />
</tt:outerTag>
```

The Duke's Bookstore page `template.jsp` uses a set of cooperating tags to define the screens of the application. These tags are described in the section A Template Tag Library (page 308).

Defining Tags

To define a tag, you need to:

- Develop a tag handler and helper classes for the tag
- Declare the tag in a tag library descriptor

This section describes the properties of tag handlers and TLDs and explains how to develop tag handlers and library descriptor elements for each type of tag introduced in the previous section.

Tag Handlers

A *tag handler* is an object invoked by a Web container to evaluate a custom tag during the execution of the JSP page that references the tag. Tag handlers must implement either the `Tag` or `BodyTag` interface. Interfaces can be used to take an existing Java object and make it a tag handler. For newly created handlers, you can use the `TagSupport` and `BodyTagSupport` classes as base classes. These classes and interfaces are contained in the `javax.servlet.jsp.tagext` package.

Tag handler methods defined by the `Tag` and `BodyTag` interfaces are called by the JSP page's servlet at various points during the evaluation of the tag. When the start tag of a custom tag is encountered, the JSP page's servlet calls methods to initialize the appropriate handler and then invokes the handler's `doStartTag` method. When the end tag of a custom tag is encountered, the handler's `doEndTag` method is invoked. Additional methods are invoked in between when a tag handler needs to interact with the body of the tag. For further information, see How Is a Tag Handler Invoked? (page 313). In order to provide a tag handler implementation, you must implement the methods, summarized in Table 13–1, that are invoked at various stages of processing the tag.

A tag handler has access to an API that allows it to communicate with the JSP page. The entry point to the API is the page context object (`javax.servlet.jsp.PageContext`), through which a tag handler can retrieve all the other implicit objects (request, session, and application) accessible from a JSP page.

Implicit objects can have named attributes associated with them. Such attributes are accessed using `[set|get]Attribute` methods.

If the tag is nested, a tag handler also has access to the handler (called the *parent*) associated with the enclosing tag.

Table 13–1 Tag Handler Methods

Tag Handler Type	Methods
Simple	`doStartTag, doEndTag, release`
Attributes	`doStartTag, doEndTag, set/getAttribute1...N, release`
Body, evaluation and no interaction	`doStartTag, doEndTag, release`
Body, iterative evaluation	`doStartTag, doAfterBody, doEndTag, release`
Body, interaction	`doStartTag, doEndTag, release, doInitBody, doAfterBody, release`

A set of related tag handler classes (a tag library) is usually packaged and deployed as a JAR archive.

Tag Library Descriptors

A *tag library descriptor* (TLD) is an XML document that describes a tag library. A TLD contains information about a library as a whole and about each tag contained in the library. TLDs are used by a Web container to validate the tags and by JSP page development tools.

TLD file names must have the extension `.tld`. TLD files are stored in the `WEB-INF` directory of the WAR file or in a subdirectory of `WEB-INF`. When you add a TLD to a WAR using `deploytool`, it automatically puts it into `WEB-INF`.

A TLD must begin with an XML document prolog that specifies the version of XML and the document type definition (DTD):

```
<?xml version="1.0" encoding="ISO-8859-1" ?>
<!DOCTYPE taglib PUBLIC "-//Sun Microsystems, Inc.//DTD JSP Tag
Library 1.2//EN"
"http://java.sun.com/dtd/web-jsptaglibrary_1_2.dtd">
```

The J2EE SDK version 1.3 can understand version 1.1 and 1.2 DTDs. However, this chapter documents the 1.2 version because you should use the newer version in any tag libraries that you develop. The template library TLD, `tutorial-tem-`

`plate.tld`, conforms to the 1.2 version. The Struts library TLDs conform to the 1.1 version of the DTD, which has fewer elements and uses slightly different names for some of the elements.

The root of a TLD is the `taglib` element. The subelements of `taglib` are listed in Table 13–2:

Table 13–2 `taglib` Subelements

Element	Description
`tlib-version`	The tag library's version
`jsp-version`	The JSP specification version that the tag library requires
`short-name`	Optional name that could be used by a JSP page authoring tool to create names with a mnemonic value
`uri`	A URI that uniquely identifies the tag library
`display-name`	Optional name intended to be displayed by tools
`small-icon`	Optional small icon that can be used by tools
`large-icon`	Optional large icon that can be used by tools
`description`	Optional tag-specific information
`listener`	See listener Element (page 291)
`tag`	See tag Element (page 292)

listener Element

A tag library can specify some classes that are event listeners (see Handling Servlet Life-Cycle Events, page 216). The listeners are listed in the TLD as `listener` elements, and the Web container will instantiate the listener classes and register them in a way analogous to listeners defined at the WAR level. Unlike WAR-level listeners, the order in which the tag library listeners are registered is undefined. The only subelement of the `listener` element is the `listener-class` element, which must contain the fully qualified name of the listener class.

tag Element

Each tag in the library is described by giving its name and the class of its tag handler, information on the scripting variables created by the tag, and information on the tag's attributes. Scripting variable information can be given directly in the TLD or through a tag extra info class (see Tags That Define Scripting Variables, page 298). Each attribute declaration contains an indication of whether the attribute is required, whether its value can be determined by request-time expressions, and the type of the attribute (see Tags with Attributes, page 294).

A tag is specified in a TLD in a `tag` element. The subelements of `tag` are listed in Table 13–3:

Table 13–3 `tag` Subelements

Element	Description
`name`	The unique tag name.
`tag-class`	The fully-qualified name of the tag handler class.
`tei-class`	Optional subclass of `javax.servlet.jsp.tagext.TagExtraInfo`. See TagExtraInfo Class (page 301).
`body-content`	The body content type. See body-content Element (page 293) and body-content Element (page 298).
`display-name`	Optional name intended to be displayed by tools.
`small-icon`	Optional small-icon that can be used by tools.
`large-icon`	Optional large-icon that can be used by tools.
`description`	Optional tag-specific information.
`variable`	Optional scripting variable information. See variable Element (page 300).
`attribute`	Tag attribute information. See attribute Element (page 294).

The following sections describe the methods and TLD elements that you need to develop for each type of tag introduced in Using Tags (page 285).

Simple Tags

Tag Handlers

The handler for a simple tag must implement the doStartTag and doEndTag methods of the Tag interface. The doStartTag method is invoked when the start tag is encountered. This method returns SKIP_BODY because a simple tag has no body. The doEndTag method is invoked when the end tag is encountered. The doEndTag method needs to return EVAL_PAGE if the rest of the page needs to be evaluated; otherwise, it should return SKIP_PAGE.

The simple tag discussed in the first section,

```
<tt:simple />
```

would be implemented by the following tag handler:

```
public SimpleTag extends TagSupport {
   public int doStartTag() throws JspException {
      try {
         pageContext.getOut().print("Hello.");
      } catch (Exception ex) {
         throw new JspTagException("SimpleTag: " +
            ex.getMessage());
      }
      return SKIP_BODY;
   }
   public int doEndTag() {
      return EVAL_PAGE;
   }
}
```

body-content Element

Tags without bodies must declare that their body content is empty using the body-content element:

```
<body-content>empty</body-content>
```

Tags with Attributes

Defining Attributes in a Tag Handler

For each tag attribute, you must define a property and `get` and `set` methods that conform to the JavaBeans architecture conventions in the tag handler. For example, the tag handler for the Struts `logic:present` tag,

```
<logic:present parameter="Clear">
```

contains the following declaration and methods:

```
protected String parameter = null;
public String getParameter() {
   return (this.parameter);
}
public void setParameter(String parameter) {
   this.parameter = parameter;
}
```

Note that if your attribute is named `id` and your tag handler inherits from the `TagSupport` class, you do not need to define the property and set and get methods because these are already defined by `TagSupport`.

A tag attribute whose value is a `String` can name an attribute of one of the implicit objects available to tag handlers. An implicit object attribute would be accessed by passing the tag attribute value to the `[set|get]Attribute` method of the implicit object. This is a good way to pass scripting variable names to a tag handler where they are associated with objects stored in the page context (see Tags That Define Scripting Variables, page 298).

attribute Element

For each tag attribute, you must specify whether the attribute is required, whether the value can be determined by an expression, and, optionally, the type of the attribute in an `attribute` element. For static values the type is always `java.lang.String`. If the `rtexprvalue` element is `true` or `yes`, then the `type` element defines the return type expected from any expression specified as the value of the attribute.

```
<attribute>
   <name>attr1</name>
   <required>true|false|yes|no</required>
   <rtexprvalue>true|false|yes|no</rtexprvalue>
   <type>fully_qualified_type</type>
</attribute>
```

If a tag attribute is not required, a tag handler should provide a default value.

The `tag` element for the `logic:present` tag declares that the `parameter` attribute is not required (because the tag can also test for the presence of other entities such as bean properties) and that its value can be set by a runtime expression.

```
<tag>
   <name>present</name>
   <tag-class>org.apache.struts.taglib.
      logic.PresentTag</tag-class>
   <body-content>JSP</body-content>
   ...
   <attribute>
      <name>parameter</name>
      <required>false</required>
      <rtexprvalue>true</rtexprvalue>
   </attribute>
   ...
</tag>
```

Attribute Validation

The documentation for a tag library should describe valid values for tag attributes. When a JSP page is translated, a Web container will enforce any constraints contained in the TLD element for each attribute.

The attributes passed to a tag can also be validated at translation time with the `isValid` method of a class derived from `TagExtraInfo`. This class is also used to provide information about scripting variables defined by the tag (see Tags That Define Scripting Variables, page 298).

The `isValid` method is passed the attribute information in a `TagData` object, which contains attribute-value tuples for each of the tag's attributes. Since the validation occurs at translation time, the value of an attribute that is computed at request time will be set to `TagData.REQUEST_TIME_VALUE`.

The tag `<tt:twa attr1="value1"/>` has the following TLD `attribute` element:

```
<attribute>
   <name>attr1</name>
   <required>true</required>
   <rtexprvalue>true</a>
</attribute>
```

This declaration indicates that the value of `attr1` can be determined at runtime.

The following `isValid` method checks that the value of `attr1` is a valid Boolean value. Note that since the value of `attr1` can be computed at runtime, `isValid` must check whether the tag user has chosen to provide a runtime value.

```
public class TwaTEI extends TagExtraInfo {
   public boolean isValid(Tagdata data) {
      Object o = data.getAttribute("attr1");
      if (o != null && o != TagData.REQUEST_TIME_VALUE) {
         if (o.toLowerCase().equals("true") ||
            o.toLowerCase().equals("false") )
            return true;
         else
            return false;
      }
      else
         return true;
   }
}
```

Tags With Bodies

Tag Handlers

A tag handler for a tag with a body is implemented differently depending on whether the tag handler needs to interact with the body or not. By *interact*, we mean that the tag handler reads or modifies the contents of the body.

Tag Handler Does Not Interact with the Body

If the tag handler does not need to interact with the body, the tag handler should implement the `Tag` interface (or be derived from `TagSupport`). If the body of the tag needs to be evaluated, the `doStartTag` method needs to return `EVAL_BODY_INCLUDE`; otherwise, it should return `SKIP_BODY`.

If a tag handler needs to iteratively evaluate the body, it should implement the `IterationTag` interface or be derived from `TagSupport`. It should return `EVAL_BODY_AGAIN` from the `doStartTag` and `doAfterBody` methods if it determines that the body needs to be evaluated again.

Tag Handler Interacts with the Body

If the tag handler needs to interact with the body, the tag handler must implement `BodyTag` (or be derived from `BodyTagSupport`). Such handlers typically implement the `doInitBody` and the `doAfterBody` methods. These methods interact with body content passed to the tag handler by the JSP page's servlet.

Body content supports several methods to read and write its contents. A tag handler can use the body content's `getString` or `getReader` methods to extract information from the body, and the `writeOut(out)` method to write the body contents to an out stream. The writer supplied to the `writeOut` method is obtained using the tag handler's `getPreviousOut` method. This method is used to ensure that a tag handler's results are available to an enclosing tag handler.

If the body of the tag needs to be evaluated, the `doStartTag` method needs to return `EVAL_BODY_BUFFERED`; otherwise, it should return `SKIP_BODY`.

`doInitBody` Method

The `doInitBody` method is called after the body content is set but before it is evaluated. You generally use this method to perform any initialization that depends on the body content.

`doAfterBody` Method

The `doAfterBody` method is called *after* the body content is evaluated. Like the `doStartTag` method, `doAfterBody` must return an indication of whether to continue evaluating the body. Thus, if the body should be evaluated again, as would be the case if you were implementing an iteration tag, `doAfterBody` should return `EVAL_BODY_BUFFERED`; otherwise `doAfterBody` should return `SKIP_BODY`.

`release` Method

A tag handler should reset its state and release any private resources in the `release` method.

The following example reads the content of the body (which contains a SQL query) and passes it to an object that executes the query. Since the body does not need to be reevaluated, `doAfterBody` returns `SKIP_BODY`.

```
public class QueryTag extends BodyTagSupport {
   public int doAfterBody() throws JspTagException {
      BodyContent bc = getBodyContent();
      // get the bc as string
      String query = bc.getString();
      // clean up
      bc.clearBody();
      try {
         Statement stmt = connection.createStatement();
         result = stmt.executeQuery(query);
      } catch (SQLException e) {
         throw new JspTagException("QueryTag: " +
            e.getMessage());
      }
      return SKIP_BODY;
   }
}
```

body-content Element

For tags that have a body, you must specify the type of the body content using the `body-content` element:

```
<body-content>JSP|tagdependent</body-content>
```

Body content containing custom and core tags, scripting elements, and HTML text is categorized as `JSP`. This is the value declared for the Struts `logic:present` tag. All other types of body content—for example, SQL statements passed to the query tag—would be labeled `tagdependent`.

Note that the value of the `body-content` element does not affect the interpretation of the body by the tag handler; the element is only intended to be used by an authoring tool for rendering the body content.

Tags That Define Scripting Variables

Tag Handlers

A tag handler is responsible for creating and setting the object referred to by the scripting variable into a context accessible from the page. It does this by using the `pageContext.setAttribute(name, value, scope)` or `pageContext.setAttribute(name, value)` methods. Typically, an attribute passed to the custom tag specifies the name of the scripting variable object; this name can be retrieved by invoking the attribute's `get` method described in Defining Attributes in a Tag Handler (page 294).

If the value of the scripting variable is dependent on an object present in the tag handler's context, it can retrieve the object using the `pageContext.getAttribute(name, scope)` method.

The usual procedure is that the tag handler retrieves a scripting variable, performs some processing on the object, and then sets the scripting variable's value using the `pageContext.setAttribute(name, object)` method.

The scope that an object can have is summarized in Table 13–4. The scope constrains the accessibility and lifetime of the object.

Table 13–4 Scope of Objects

Name	Accessible From	Lifetime
`page`	Current page	Until the response has been sent back to the user or the request is passed to a new page
`request`	Current page and any included or forwarded pages	Until the response has been sent back to the user
`session`	Current request and any subsequent request from the same browser (subject to session lifetime)	The life of the user's session
`application`	Current and any future request from the same Web application	The life of the application

Providing Information about the Scripting Variable

The example described in Tags That Define Scripting Variables (page 287) defines a scripting variable `book` that is used for accessing book information:

```
<bean:define id="book" name="bookDB" property="bookDetails"
   type="database.BookDetails"/>
<font color="red" size="+2">
   <%=messages.getString("CartRemoved")%>
   <strong><jsp:getProperty name="book"
         property="title"/></strong>
<br> <br>
</font>
```

When the JSP page containing this tag is translated, the Web container generates code to synchronize the scripting variable with the object referenced by the variable. To generate the code, the Web container requires certain information about the scripting variable:

- Variable name
- Variable class
- Whether the variable refers to a new or existing object
- The availability of the variable

There are two ways to provide this information: by specifying the `variable` TLD subelement or by defining a tag extra info class and including the `tei-class` element in the TLD. Using the `variable` element is simpler, but slightly less flexible.

variable Element

The `variable` element has the following subelements:

- `name-given`: The variable name as a constant.
- `name-from-attribute`: The name of an attribute whose translation-time value will give the name of the variable.

One of `name-given` or `name-from-attribute` is required. The following subelements are optional:

- `variable-class`: The fully qualified name of the class of the variable. `java.lang.String` is the default.
- `declare`: Whether the variable refers to a new object. `True` is the default.
- `scope`: The scope of the scripting variable defined. `NESTED` is default. Table 13–5 describes the availability of the scripting variable and the methods in which the value of the variable must be set or reset.

The implementation of the Struts `bean:define` tag conforms to the JSP specification version 1.1, which requires you to define a tag extra info class. The JSP specification version 1.2 adds the `variable` element. You could define the following `variable` element for the `bean:define` tag:

```
<tag>
   <variable>
      <name-from-attribute>id</name-from-attribute>
      <variable-class>database.BookDetails</variable-class>
```

```
      <declare>true</declare>
      <scope>AT_BEGIN</scope>
    </variable>
  </tag>
```

Table 13–5 Scripting Variable Availability

Value	Availability	Methods
NESTED	Between the start tag and the end tag	In doInitBody and doAfterBody for a tag handler implementing BodyTag; otherwise, in doStartTag
AT_BEGIN	From the start tag until the end of the page	In doInitBody, doAfterBody, and doEndTag for a tag handler implementing BodyTag; otherwise, in doStartTag and doEndTag
AT_END	After the end tag until the end of the page	In doEndTag

TagExtraInfo Class

You define a tag extra info class by extending the class javax.servlet.jsp.TagExtraInfo. A TagExtraInfo must implement the getVariableInfo method to return an array of VariableInfo objects containing the following information:

- Variable name
- Variable class
- Whether the variable refers to a new object
- The availability of the variable

The Web container passes a parameter called data to the getVariableInfo method that contains attribute-value tuples for each of the tag's attributes. These attributes can be used to provide the VariableInfo object with a scripting variable's name and class.

The Struts tag library provides information about the scripting variable created by the bean:define tag in the DefineTei tag extra info class. Since the name (book) and class (database.BookDetails) of the scripting variable are passed in as tag attributes, they can be retrieved with the data.getAttributeString method and used to fill in the VariableInfo constructor. To allow the scripting variable book to be used in the rest of the page, the scope of book is set to be AT_BEGIN.

```
public class DefineTei extends TagExtraInfo {
   public VariableInfo[] getVariableInfo(TagData data) {
   String type = data.getAttributeString("type");
      if (type == null)
         type = "java.lang.Object";
      return new VariableInfo[] {
         new VariableInfo(data.getAttributeString("id"),
            type,
            true,
            VariableInfo.AT_BEGIN)
      };
   }
}
```

The fully qualified name of the tag extra info class defined for a scripting variable must be declared in the TLD in the tei-class subelement of the tag element. Thus, the tei-class element for DefineTei would be as follows:

```
<tei-class>org.apache.struts.taglib.bean.DefineTagTei
</tei-class>
```

Cooperating Tags

Tags cooperate by sharing objects. JSP technology supports two styles of object sharing. The first style requires that a shared object be named and stored in the page context (one of the implicit objects accessible to both JSP pages and tag handlers). To access objects created and named by another tag, a tag handler uses the pageContext.getAttribute(name, scope) method.

In the second style of object sharing, an object created by the enclosing tag handler of a group of nested tags is available to all inner tag handlers. This form of object sharing has the advantage that it uses a private namespace for the objects, thus reducing the potential for naming conflicts.

To access an object created by an enclosing tag, a tag handler must first obtain its enclosing tag with the static method TagSupport.findAncestorWithClass(from, class) or the TagSupport.getParent method. The former method should be used when a specific nesting of tag handlers cannot be guaranteed. Once the ancestor has been retrieved, a tag handler can access any statically or dynamically created objects. Statically created objects are members of the parent. Private objects can also be created dynamically. Such objects can be stored in a tag handler with the `setValue` method and retrieved with the `getValue` method.

The following example illustrates a tag handler that supports both the named and private object approaches to sharing objects. In the example, the handler for a query tag checks whether an attribute named `connection` has been set in the `doStartTag` method. If the `connection` attribute has been set, the handler retrieves the connection object from the page context. Otherwise, the tag handler first retrieves the tag handler for the enclosing tag and then retrieves the connection object from that handler.

```
public class QueryTag extends BodyTagSupport {
   private String connectionId;
   public int doStartTag() throws JspException {
      String cid = getConnection();
      if (cid != null) {
      // there is a connection id, use it
         connection =(Connection)pageContext.
            getAttribute(cid);
      } else {
         ConnectionTag ancestorTag =
            (ConnectionTag)findAncestorWithClass(this,
               ConnectionTag.class);
         if (ancestorTag == null) {
            throw new JspTagException("A query without
               a connection attribute must be nested
               within a connection tag.");
         }
         connection = ancestorTag.getConnection();
      }
   }
}
```

The query tag implemented by this tag handler could be used in either of the following ways:

```
<tt:connection id="con01" ....> ... </tt:connection>
<tt:query id="balances" connection="con01">
   SELECT account, balance FROM acct_table
      where customer_number = <%= request.getCustno()%>
</tt:query>

<tt:connection ...>
   <x:query id="balances">
```

```
      SELECT account, balance FROM acct_table
         where customer_number = <%= request.getCustno()%>
   </x:query>
</tt:connection>
```

The TLD for the tag handler must indicate that the `connection` attribute is optional with the following declaration:

```
<tag>
   ...
   <attribute>
      <name>connection</name>
      <required>false</required>
   </attribute>
</tag>
```

Examples

The custom tags described in this section demonstrate solutions to two recurring problems in developing JSP applications: minimizing the amount of Java programming in JSP pages and ensuring a common look and feel across applications. In doing so, they illustrate many of the styles of tags discussed in the first part of the chapter.

An Iteration Tag

Constructing page content that is dependent on dynamically generated data often requires the use of flow control scripting statements. By moving the flow control logic to tag handlers, flow control tags reduce the amount of scripting needed in JSP pages.

The Struts `logic:iterate` tag retrieves objects from a collection stored in a JavaBeans component and assigns them to a scripting variable. The body of the tag retrieves information from the scripting variable. While elements remain in the collection, the `iterate` tag causes the body to be reevaluated.

JSP Page

Two Duke's Bookstore application pages, `catalog.jsp` and `showcart.jsp`, use the `logic:iterate` tag to iterate over collections of objects. An excerpt from `catalog.jsp` is shown below. The JSP page initializes the `iterate` tag with a collection (named by the `property` attribute) of the `bookDB` bean. The `iterate` tag sets the `book` scripting variable on each iteration over the collection. The bookId property of the book variable is exposed as another scripting variable. Properties of both variables are used to dynamically generate a table containing links to other pages and book catalog information.

```
<logic:iterate name="bookDB" property="books"
   id="book" type="database.BookDetails">
   <bean:define id="bookId" name="book" property="bookId"
      type="java.lang.String"/>

   <tr>
   <td bgcolor="#ffffaa">
   <a href="<%=request.getContextPath()%>
      /bookdetails?bookId=<%=bookId%>">
      <strong><jsp:getProperty name="book"
      property="title"/> </strong></a></td>

   <td bgcolor="#ffffaa" rowspan=2>
   <jsp:setProperty name="currency" property="amount"
      value="<%=book.getPrice()%>"/>
   <jsp:getProperty name="currency" property="format"/>
    </td>

   <td bgcolor="#ffffaa" rowspan=2>
   <a href="<%=request.getContextPath()%>
      /catalog?Add=<%=bookId%>">
       <%=messages.getString("CartAdd")%>
       </a></td></tr>

   <tr>
   <td bgcolor="#ffffff">
     <%=messages.getString("By")%> <em>
      <jsp:getProperty name="book"
         property="firstName"/> 
      <jsp:getProperty name="book"
         property="surname"/></em></td></tr>
</logic:iterate>
```

Tag Handler

The implementation of the Struts logic:iterate tag conforms to the capabilities of the JSP version 1.1 specification, which requires you to extend the BodyTagSupport class. The JSP version 1.2 specification adds features (described in the section Tag Handler Does Not Interact with the Body, page 296) that simplify programming tags that iteratively evaluate their body. The following discussion is based on an implementation that uses these features.

The `logic:iterate` tag supports initializing the collection in several ways: from a collection provided as a tag attribute or from a collection that is a bean or a property of a bean. Our example uses the latter method. Most of the code in `doStartTag` is concerned with constructing an iterator over the collection object. The method first checks if the handler's `collection` property is set and, if not, proceeds to check the `bean` and `property` attributes. If the `bean` and `property` attributes are both set, `doStartTag` calls a utility method that uses JavaBeans introspection methods to retrieve the collection. Once the collection object is determined, the method constructs the iterator.

If the iterator contains more elements, `doStartTag` sets the value of the scripting variable to the next element and then indicates that the body should be evaluated; otherwise, it ends the iteration by returning `SKIP_BODY`.

After the body has been evaluated, the `doAfterBody` method retrieves the body content and writes it to the out stream. The body content object is then cleared in preparation for another body evaluation. If the iterator contains more elements, `doAfterBody` again sets the value of the scripting variable to the next element and returns `EVAL_BODY_AGAIN` to indicate that the body should be evaluated again. This causes the reexecution of `doAfterBody`. When there are no remaining elements, `doAfterBody` terminates the process by returning `SKIP_BODY`.

```
public class IterateTag extends TagSupport {
  protected Iterator iterator = null;
  protected Object collection = null;
  protected String id = null;
  protected String name = null;
  protected String property = null;
  protected String type = null;
  public int doStartTag() throws JspException {
    Object collection = this.collection;
    if (collection == null) {
      try {
        Object bean = pageContext.findAttribute(name);
        if (bean == null) {
          ... throw an exception
        }
        if (property == null)
          collection = bean;
        else
          collection =
            PropertyUtils.
              getProperty(bean, property);
        if (collection == null) {
          ... throw an exception
        }
```

```
            } catch
               ... catch exceptions thrown
                  by PropertyUtils.getProperty
            }
         }
         // Construct an iterator for this collection
         if (collection instanceof Collection)
            iterator = ((Collection) collection).iterator();
         else if (collection instanceof Iterator)
            iterator = (Iterator) collection;
            ...
         }
         // Store the first value and evaluate,
         // or skip the body if none
         if (iterator.hasNext()) {
            Object element = iterator.next();
            pageContext.setAttribute(id, element);
            return (EVAL_BODY_AGAIN);
         } else
            return (SKIP_BODY);
   }
      public int doAfterBody() throws JspException {
         if (bodyContent != null) {
            try {
               JspWriter out = getPreviousOut();
               out.print(bodyContent.getString());
               bodyContent.clearBody();
            } catch (IOException e) {
               ...
            }
         }
         if (iterator.hasNext()) {
            Object element = iterator.next();
            pageContext.setAttribute(id, element);
            return (EVAL_BODY_AGAIN);
         } else
            return (SKIP_BODY);
         }
      }
   }
```

Tag Extra Info Class

Information about the scripting variable is provided in the `IterateTei` tag extra info class. The name and class of the scripting variable are passed in as tag attributes and used to fill in the `VariableInfo` constructor.

```
public class IterateTei extends TagExtraInfo {
   public VariableInfo[] getVariableInfo(TagData data) {
   String type = data.getAttributeString("type");
   if (type == null)
      type = "java.lang.Object";

   return new VariableInfo[] {
      new VariableInfo(data.getAttributeString("id"),
         type,
         true,
         VariableInfo.AT_BEGIN)
      };
   }
}
```

A Template Tag Library

A template provides a way to separate the common elements that are part of each screen from the elements that change with each screen of an application. Putting all the common elements together into one file makes it easier to maintain and enforce a consistent look and feel in all the screens. It also makes development of individual screens easier because the designer can focus on portions of a screen that are specific to that screen while the template takes care of the common portions.

The template is a JSP page with placeholders for the parts that need to change with each screen. Each of these placeholders is referred to as a parameter of the template. For example, a simple template could include a title parameter for the top of the generated screen and a body parameter to refer to a JSP page for the custom content of the screen.

The template uses a set of nested tags—`definition`, `screen`, and `parameter`—to define a table of screen definition for an application screen and uses an `insert` tag to insert parameters from a screen definition into the application screen.

JSP Page

The template for the Duke's Bookstore example, `template.jsp`, is shown on the next page. This page includes a JSP page that creates the screen definition and then uses the `insert` tag to insert parameters from the definition into the application screen.

```
<%@ taglib uri="/tutorial-template.tld" prefix="tt" %>
<%@ page errorPage="errorpage.jsp" %>
<%@ include file="screendefinitions.jsp" %><html>
  <head>
    <title>
      <tt:insert definition="bookstore"
        parameter="title"/>
    </title>
  </head>
    <tt:insert definition="bookstore"
      parameter="banner"/>
    <tt:insert definition="bookstore"
      parameter="body"/>
  </body>
</html>
```

`screendefinitions.jsp` creates a screen definition based on a request attribute `selectedScreen`:

```
<tt:definition name="bookstore"
  screen="<%= (String)request.
    getAttribute(\"selectedScreen\") %>">
  <tt:screen id="/enter">
    <tt:parameter name="title"
      value="Duke's Bookstore" direct="true"/>
    <tt:parameter name="banner"
      value="/banner.jsp" direct="false"/>
    <tt:parameter name="body"
      value="/bookstore.jsp" direct="false"/>
  </tt:screen>
  <tt:screen id="/catalog">
    <tt:parameter name="title"
    value="<%=messages.getString("TitleBookCatalog")%>"
    direct="true"/>
    ...
</tt:definition>
```

The template is instantiated by the `Dispatcher` servlet. `Dispatcher` first gets the requested screen and stores it as an attribute of the request. This is necessary because when the request is forwarded to `template.jsp`, the request URL doesn't contain the original request (for example, `/bookstore3/catalog`) but instead reflects the path (/bookstore3/template.jsp) of the forwarded page. Finally, the servlet dispatches the request to template.jsp:

```
public class Dispatcher extends HttpServlet {
  public void doGet(HttpServletRequest request,
      HttpServletResponse response) {
    request.setAttribute("selectedScreen",
      request.getServletPath());
    RequestDispatcher dispatcher =
      request.getRequestDispatcher("/template.jsp");
    if (dispatcher != null)
      dispatcher.forward(request, response);
  }
  public void doPost(HttpServletRequest request,
      HttpServletResponse response) {
    request.setAttribute("selectedScreen",
      request.getServletPath());
    RequestDispatcher dispatcher =
      request.getRequestDispatcher("/template.jsp");
    if (dispatcher != null)
      dispatcher.forward(request, response);
  }
}
```

Tag Handlers

The template tag library contains four tag handlers—DefinitionTag, ScreenTag, ParameterTag, and InsertTag—that demonstrate the use of cooperating tags. DefinitionTag, ScreenTag, and ParameterTag comprise a set of nested tag handlers that share public and private objects. DefinitionTag creates a public named object called definition that is used by InsertTag.

In doStartTag, DefinitionTag creates a public object named screens that contains a hash table of screen definitions. A screen definition consists of a screen identifier and a set of parameters associated with the screen.

```
public int doStartTag() {
  HashMap screens = null;
  screens = (HashMap) pageContext.getAttribute("screens",
    pageContext.APPLICATION_SCOPE);
  if (screens == null)
    pageContext.setAttribute("screens", new HashMap(),
      pageContext.APPLICATION_SCOPE);
  return EVAL_BODY_INCLUDE;
}
```

The table of screen definitions is filled in by `ScreenTag` and `ParameterTag` from text provided as attributes to these tags. Table 13–6 shows the contents of the screen definitions hash table for the Duke's Bookstore application.

Table 13–6 Screen Definitions

Screen Id	Title	Banner	Body
/enter	Duke's Bookstore	/banner.jsp	/bookstore.jsp
/catalog	Book Catalog	/banner.jsp	/catalog.jsp
/bookdetails	Book Description	/banner.jsp	/bookdetails.jsp
/showcart	Your Shopping Cart	/banner.jsp	/showcart.jsp
/cashier	Cashier	/banner.jsp	/cashier.jsp
/receipt	Receipt	/banner.jsp	/receipt.jsp

In `doEndTag`, `DefinitionTag` creates a public object of class `Definition`, selects a screen definition from the `screens` object based on the URL passed in the request, and uses it to initialize the `Definition` object.

```
public int doEndTag()throws JspTagException {
   try {
      Definition definition = new Definition();
      Hashtable screens = null;
      ArrayList params = null;
      TagSupport screen = null;
      screens = (HashMap)
         pageContext.getAttribute("screens",
            pageContext.APPLICATION_SCOPE);
      if (screens != null)
         params = (ArrayList) screens.get(screenId);
      else
         ...
      if (params == null)
         ...
      Iterator ir = null;
      if (params != null)
         ir = params.iterator();
      while ((ir != null) && ir.hasNext())
         definition.setParam((Parameter) ir.next());
         // put the definition in the page context
```

```
      pageContext.setAttribute(
         definitionName, definition);
   } catch (Exception ex) {
      ex.printStackTrace();
   }
   return EVAL_PAGE;
}
```

If the URL passed in the request is `/enter`, the `Definition` contains the items from the first row of Table 13–6:

Title	Banner	Body
`Duke's Bookstore`	`/banner.jsp`	`/bookstore.jsp`

The definition for the URL `/enter` is shown in Table 13–7. The definition specifies that the value of the `Title` parameter, Duke's Bookstore, should be inserted directly into the output stream, but the values of `Banner` and `Body` should be dynamically included.

Table 13–7 Screen Definition for the URL `/enter`

Parameter Name	Parameter Value	isDirect
`title`	`Duke's Bookstore`	`true`
`banner`	`/banner.jsp`	`false`
`body`	`/bookstore.jsp`	`false`

`InsertTag` uses `Definition` to insert parameters of the screen definition into the response. In the `doStartTag` method, it retrieves the definition object from the page context.

```
public int doStartTag() {
   // get the definition from the page context
   definition = (Definition) pageContext.
      getAttribute(definitionName);
```

```
      // get the parameter
      if (parameterName != null && definition != null)
         parameter = (Parameter)definition.
            getParam(parameterName);
      if (parameter != null)
         directInclude = parameter.isDirect();
      return SKIP_BODY;
   }
```

The doEndTag method inserts the parameter value. If the parameter is direct, it is directly inserted into the response; otherwise, the request is sent to the parameter and the response is dynamically included into the overall response.

```
   public int doEndTag()throws JspTagException {
      try {
         if (directInclude && parameter != null)
            pageContext.getOut().print(parameter.getValue());
         else {
            if ((parameter != null) &&
               (parameter.getValue() != null))
               pageContext.include(parameter.getValue());
         }
      } catch (Exception ex) {
         throw new JspTagException(ex.getMessage());
      }
      return EVAL_PAGE;
   }
```

How Is a Tag Handler Invoked?

The Tag interface defines the basic protocol between a tag handler and a JSP page's servlet. It defines the life cycle and the methods to be invoked when the start and end tags are encountered.

The JSP page's servlet invokes the setPageContext, setParent, and attribute setting methods before calling doStartTag. The JSP page's servlet also guarantees that release will be invoked on the tag handler before the end of the page.

Here is a typical tag handler method invocation sequence:

```
ATag t = new ATag();
t.setPageContext(...);
t.setParent(...);
t.setAttribute1(value1);
```

```
t.setAttribute2(value2);
t.doStartTag();
t.doEndTag();
t.release();
```

The BodyTag interface extends Tag by defining additional methods that let a tag handler access its body. The interface provides three new methods:

- setBodyContent: Creates body content and adds to the tag handler
- doInitBody: Called before evaluation of the tag body
- doAfterBody: Called after evaluation of the tag body

A typical invocation sequence is as follows:

```
t.doStartTag();
out = pageContext.pushBody();
t.setBodyContent(out);
// perform any initialization needed after body content is set
t.doInitBody();
t.doAfterBody();
// while doAfterBody returns EVAL_BODY_BUFFERED we
// iterate body evaluation
...
t.doAfterBody();
t.doEndTag();
t.pageContext.popBody();
t.release();
```

14

Transactions

Dale Green

A typical enterprise application accesses and stores information in one or more databases. Because this information is critical for business operations, it must be accurate, current, and reliable. Data integrity would be lost if multiple programs were allowed to update the same information simultaneously. It would also be lost if a system that failed while processing a business transaction were to leave the affected data only partially updated. By preventing both of these scenarios, software transactions ensure data integrity. Transactions control the concurrent access of data by multiple programs. In the event of a system failure, transactions make sure that after recovery the data will be in a consistent state.

In This Chapter

What Is a Transaction?

To emulate a business transaction, a program may need to perform several steps. A financial program, for example, might transfer funds from a checking account to a savings account with the steps listed in the following pseudocode:

```
begin transaction
   debit checking account
   credit savings account
   update history log
commit transaction
```

Either all three of these steps must complete, or none of them at all. Otherwise, data integrity is lost. Because the steps within a transaction are a unified whole, a *transaction* is often defined as an indivisible unit of work.

A transaction can end in two ways: with a commit or a rollback. When a transaction commits, the data modifications made by its statements are saved. If a statement within a transaction fails, the transaction rolls back, undoing the effects of all statements in the transaction. In the pseudocode, for example, if a disk drive crashed during the `credit` step, the transaction would roll back and undo the data modifications made by the `debit` statement. Although the transaction failed, data integrity would be intact because the accounts still balance.

In the preceding pseudocode, the `begin` and `commit` statements mark the boundaries of the transaction. When designing an enterprise bean, you determine how the boundaries are set by specifying either container-managed or bean-managed transactions.

Container-Managed Transactions

In an enterprise bean with container-managed transactions, the EJB container sets the boundaries of the transactions. You can use container-managed transactions with any type of enterprise bean: session, entity, or message-driven. Container-managed transactions simplify development because the enterprise bean code does not explicitly mark the transaction's boundaries. The code does not include statements that begin and end the transaction.

Typically, the container begins a transaction immediately before an enterprise bean method starts. It commits the transaction just before the method exits. Each method can be associated with a single transaction. Nested or multiple transactions are not allowed within a method.

Container-managed transactions do not require all methods to be associated with transactions. When deploying a bean, you specify which of the bean's methods are associated with transactions by setting the transaction attributes.

Transaction Attributes

A transaction attribute controls the scope of a transaction. Figure 14–1 illustrates why controlling the scope is important. In the diagram, `method-A` begins a transaction and then invokes `method-B` of `Bean-2`. When `method-B` executes, does it run within the scope of the transaction started by method-A or does it execute with a new transaction? The answer depends on the transaction attribute of `method-B`.

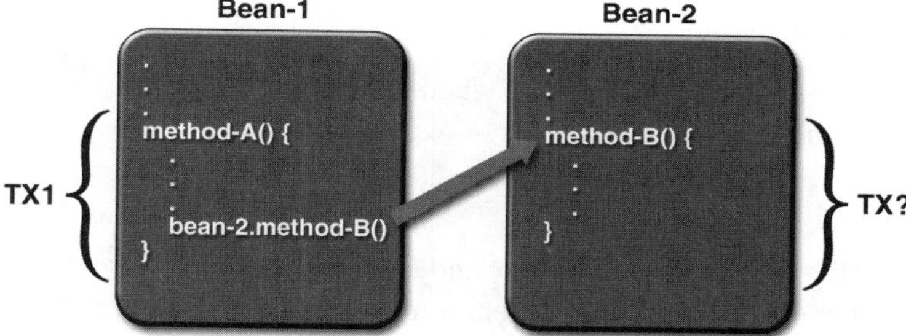

Figure 14–1 Transaction Scope

A transaction attribute may have one of the following values:

- `Required`
- `RequiresNew`
- `Mandatory`
- `NotSupported`
- `Supports`
- `Never`

Required

If the client is running within a transaction and invokes the enterprise bean's method, the method executes within the client's transaction. If the client is not associated with a transaction, the container starts a new transaction before running the method.

The `Required` attribute will work for most transactions. Therefore, you may want to use it as a default, at least in the early phases of development. Because transaction attributes are declarative, you can easily change them at a later time.

RequiresNew

If the client is running within a transaction and invokes the enterprise bean's method, the container takes the following steps:

1. Suspends the client's transaction
2. Starts a new transaction
3. Delegates the call to the method
4. Resumes the client's transaction after the method completes

If the client is not associated with a transaction, the container starts a new transaction before running the method.

You should use the `RequiresNew` attribute when you want to ensure that the method always runs within a new transaction.

Mandatory

If the client is running within a transaction and invokes the enterprise bean's method, the method executes within the client's transaction. If the client is not associated with a transaction, the container throws the `TransactionRequiredException`.

Use the `Mandatory` attribute if the enterprise bean's method must use the transaction of the client.

NotSupported

If the client is running within a transaction and invokes the enterprise bean's method, the container suspends the client's transaction before invoking the method. After the method has completed, the container resumes the client's transaction.

If the client is not associated with a transaction, the container does not start a new transaction before running the method.

Use the `NotSupported` attribute for methods that don't need transactions. Because transactions involve overhead, this attribute may improve performance.

Supports

If the client is running within a transaction and invokes the enterprise bean's method, the method executes within the client's transaction. If the client is not associated with a transaction, the container does not start a new transaction before running the method.

Because the transactional behavior of the method may vary, you should use the `Supports` attribute with caution.

Never

If the client is running within a transaction and invokes the enterprise bean's method, the container throws a `RemoteException`. If the client is not associated with a transaction, the container does not start a new transaction before running the method.

Summary of Transaction Attributes

Table 14–1 summarizes the effects of the transaction attributes. Both the T1 and T2 transactions are controlled by the container. A T1 transaction is associated with the client that calls a method in the enterprise bean. In most cases, the client is another enterprise bean. A T2 transaction is started by the container just before the method executes.

In the last column of Table 14–1, the word "None" means that the business method does not execute within a transaction controlled by the container. However, the database calls in such a business method might be controlled by the transaction manager of the DBMS.

Setting Transaction Attributes

Because transaction attributes are stored in the deployment descriptor, they can be changed during several phases of J2EE application development: enterprise bean creation, application assembly, and deployment. However, it is the responsibility of an enterprise bean developer to specify the attributes when creating the bean. The attributes should be modified only by an application developer who is assembling components into larger applications. Do not expect the person deploying the J2EE application to specify the transaction attributes.

Table 14–1 Transaction Attributes and Scope

Transaction Attribute	Client's Transaction	Business Method's Transaction
`Required`	None	T2
	T1	T1
`RequiresNew`	None	T2
	T1	T2
`Mandatory`	None	error
	T1	T1
`NotSupported`	None	None
	T1	None
`Supports`	None	None
	T1	T1
`Never`	None	None
	T1	Error

You can specify the transaction attributes for the entire enterprise bean or for individual methods. If you've specified one attribute for a method and another for the bean, the attribute for the method takes precedence. When specifying attributes for individual methods, the requirements differ with the type of bean. Session beans need the attributes defined for business methods, but do not allow them for the `create` methods. Entity beans require transaction attributes for the business, `create`, `remove`, and finder methods. Message-driven beans require transaction attributes (either `Required` or `NotSupported`) for the `onMessage` method.

Rolling Back a Container-Managed Transaction

There are two ways to roll back a container-managed transaction. First, if a system exception is thrown, the container will automatically roll back the transaction. Second, by invoking the `setRollbackOnly` method of the `EJBContext` interface, the bean method instructs the container to roll back the transaction. If the bean throws an application exception, the rollback is not automatic, but may be initiated by a call to `setRollbackOnly`. For a description of system and application exceptions, see Handling Exceptions (page 116).

The source code for the following example is in the `j2eetutorial/examples/src/ejb/bank` directory. To compile the code, go to the `j2eetutorial/examples` directory and type `ant bank`. To create the database tables, type `ant create-bank-table`. A sample `BankApp.ear` file is in the `j2eetutorial/examples/ears` directory.

The `transferToSaving` method of the `BankEJB` example illustrates the `setRollbackOnly` method. If a negative checking balance occurs, `transferToSaving` invokes `setRollBackOnly` and throws an application exception (`InsufficientBalanceException`). The `updateChecking` and `updateSaving` methods update database tables. If the updates fail, these methods throw a `SQLException` and the `transferToSaving` method throws an `EJBException`. Because the `EJBException` is a system exception, it causes the container to automatically roll back the transaction. Here is the code for the `transferToSaving` method:

```
public void transferToSaving(double amount) throws
   InsufficientBalanceException  {

   checkingBalance -= amount;
   savingBalance += amount;

   try {
      updateChecking(checkingBalance);
      if (checkingBalance < 0.00) {
         context.setRollbackOnly();
         throw new InsufficientBalanceException();
      }
      updateSaving(savingBalance);
   } catch (SQLException ex) {
       throw new EJBException
          ("Transaction failed due to SQLException: "
          + ex.getMessage());
   }
}
```

When the container rolls back a transaction, it always undoes the changes to data made by SQL calls within the transaction. However, only in entity beans will the container undo changes made to instance variables. (It does so by automatically invoking the entity bean's `ejbLoad` method, which loads the instance variables from the database.) When a rollback occurs, a session bean must explicitly reset any instance variables changed within the transaction. The easiest way to reset a session bean's instance variables is by implementing the `SessionSynchronization` interface.

Synchronizing a Session Bean's Instance Variables

The `SessionSynchronization` interface, which is optional, allows you to synchronize the instance variables with their corresponding values in the database. The container invokes the `SessionSynchronization` methods—`afterBegin`, `beforeCompletion`, and `afterCompletion`—at each of the main stages of a transaction.

The `afterBegin` method informs the instance that a new transaction has begun. The container invokes `afterBegin` immediately before it invokes the business method. The `afterBegin` method is a good place to load the instance variables from the database. The `BankBean` class, for example, loads the `checkingBalance` and `savingBalance` variables in the `afterBegin` method:

```
public void afterBegin() {

   System.out.println("afterBegin()");
   try {
      checkingBalance = selectChecking();
      savingBalance = selectSaving();
   } catch (SQLException ex) {
       throw new EJBException("afterBegin Exception: " +
           ex.getMessage());
   }
}
```

The container invokes the `beforeCompletion` method after the business method has finished, but just before the transaction commits. The `beforeCompletion` method is the last opportunity for the session bean to roll back the transaction (by calling `setRollbackOnly`). If it hasn't already updated the database with the values of the instance variables, the session bean may do so in the `beforeCompletion` method.

The `afterCompletion` method indicates that the transaction has completed. It has a single `boolean` parameter, whose value is `true` if the transaction was committed and `false` if it was rolled back. If a rollback occurred, the session bean can refresh its instance variables from the database in the `afterCompletion` method:

```
public void afterCompletion(boolean committed) {

   System.out.println("afterCompletion: " + committed);
   if (committed == false) {
      try {
         checkingBalance = selectChecking();
         savingBalance = selectSaving();
      } catch (SQLException ex) {
         throw new EJBException("afterCompletion SQLException:
       " + ex.getMessage());
      }
   }
}
```

Methods Not Allowed in Container-Managed Transactions

You should not invoke any method that might interfere with the transaction boundaries set by the container. The list of prohibited methods follows:

- The `commit`, `setAutoCommit`, and `rollback` methods of `java.sql.Connection`
- The `getUserTransaction` method of `javax.ejb.EJBContext`
- Any method of `javax.transaction.UserTransaction`

You may, however, use these methods to set boundaries in bean-managed transactions.

Bean-Managed Transactions

In a bean-managed transaction, the code in the session or message-driven bean explicitly marks the boundaries of the transaction. An entity bean cannot have bean-managed transactions; it must use container-managed transactions instead. Although beans with container-managed transactions require less coding, they have one limitation: When a method is executing, it can be associated with either a single transaction or no transaction at all. If this limitation will make coding your bean difficult, you should consider using bean-managed transactions.

The following pseudocode illustrates the kind of fine-grained control you can obtain with bean-managed transactions. By checking various conditions, the pseudocode decides whether to start or stop different transactions within the business method.

```
begin transaction
...
update table-a
...
if (condition-x)
   commit transaction
else if (condition-y)
   update table-b
   commit transaction
else
   rollback transaction
   begin transaction
   update table-c
   commit transaction
```

When coding a bean-managed transaction for session or message-driven beans, you must decide whether to use JDBC or JTA transactions. The sections that follow discuss both types of transactions.

JDBC Transactions

A *JDBC transaction* is controlled by the transaction manager of the DBMS. You may want to use JDBC transactions when wrapping legacy code inside a session bean. To code a JDBC transaction, you invoke the `commit` and `rollback` methods of the `java.sql.Connection` interface. The beginning of a transaction is implicit. A transaction begins with the first SQL statement that follows the most recent `commit`, `rollback`, or `connect` statement. (This rule is generally true, but may vary with DBMS vendor.)

Source Code

The source code for the following example is in the `j2eetutorial/examples/src/ejb/warehouse` directory. To compile the code, go to the `j2eetutorial/examples` directory and type `ant bank`. To create the database tables, type `ant create-warehouse-table`. A sample `WarehouseApp.ear` file is in the `j2eetutorial/examples/ears` directory.

The following code is from the `WarehouseEJB` example, a session bean that uses the `Connection` interface's methods to delimit bean-managed transactions. The ship method starts by invoking setAutoCommit on the Connection object named con. This invocation tells the DBMS not to automatically commit every SQL statement. Next, the ship method calls routines that update the order_item and inventory database tables. If the updates succeed, the transaction is committed. If an exception is thrown, however, the transaction is rolled back.

```
public void ship (String productId, String orderId, int
quantity) {

   try {
      con.setAutoCommit(false);
      updateOrderItem(productId, orderId);
      updateInventory(productId, quantity);
      con.commit();
   } catch (Exception ex) {
       try {
          con.rollback();
          throw new EJBException("Transaction failed: " +
             ex.getMessage());
       } catch (SQLException sqx) {
           throw new EJBException("Rollback failed: " +
              sqx.getMessage());
       }
   }
}
```

JTA Transactions

JTA is the abbreviation for the Java Transaction API. This API allows you to demarcate transactions in a manner that is independent of the transaction manager implementation. The J2EE SDK implements the transaction manager with the Java Transaction Service ("JTS"). But your code doesn't call the JTS methods directly. Instead, it invokes the JTA methods, which then call the lower-level JTS routines.

A *JTA transaction* is controlled by the J2EE transaction manager. You may want to use a JTA transaction because it can span updates to multiple databases from different vendors. A particular DBMS's transaction manager may not work with heterogeneous databases. However, the J2EE transaction manager does have one limitation—it does not support nested transactions. In other words, it cannot start a transaction for an instance until the previous transaction has ended.

The source code for the following example is in the j2eetutorial/examples/src/ejb/teller directory. To compile the code, go to the `j2eetutorial/examples` directory and type `ant teller`. To create the database tables, type `ant create-bank-teller`. A sample `TellerApp.ear` file is in the `j2eetutorial/examples/ears` directory.

To demarcate a JTA transaction, you invoke the `begin`, `commit`, and `rollback` methods of the `javax.transaction.UserTransaction` interface. The following code, taken from the `TellerBean` class, demonstrates the `UserTransaction` methods. The `begin` and `commit` invocations delimit the updates to the database. If the updates fail, the code invokes the `rollback` method and throws an `EJBException`.

```
public void withdrawCash(double amount) {

   UserTransaction ut = context.getUserTransaction();

   try {
      ut.begin();
      updateChecking(amount);
      machineBalance -= amount;
      insertMachine(machineBalance);
      ut.commit();
   } catch (Exception ex) {
       try {
          ut.rollback();
       } catch (SystemException syex) {
           throw new EJBException
              ("Rollback failed: " + syex.getMessage());
       }
       throw new EJBException
          ("Transaction failed: " + ex.getMessage());
    }
}
```

Returning without Committing

In a stateless session bean with bean-managed transactions, a business method must commit or roll back a transaction before returning. However, a stateful session bean does not have this restriction.

In a stateful session bean with a JTA transaction, the association between the bean instance and the transaction is retained across multiple client calls. Even if each business method called by the client opens and closes the database connection, the association is retained until the instance completes the transaction.

In a stateful session bean with a JDBC transaction, the JDBC connection retains the association between the bean instance and the transaction across multiple calls. If the connection is closed, the association is not retained.

Methods Not Allowed in Bean-Managed Transactions

Do not invoke the `getRollbackOnly` and `setRollbackOnly` methods of the `EJBContext` interface in bean-managed transactions. These methods should be used only in container-managed transactions. For bean-managed transactions, invoke the `getStatus` and `rollback` methods of the `UserTransaction` interface.

Summary of Transaction Options for Enterprise Beans

If you're unsure about how to set up transactions in an enterprise bean, here's a tip: In the bean's deployment descriptor, specify container-managed transactions. Then, set the `Required` transaction attribute for the entire bean. This approach will work most of the time.

Table 14–2 lists the types of transactions that are allowed for the different types of enterprise beans. An entity bean must use container-managed transactions. With container-managed transactions, you specify the transaction attributes in the deployment descriptor and you roll back a transaction with the `setRollbackOnly` method of the `EJBContext` interface.

Table 14–2 Allowed Transaction Types for Enterprise Beans

Bean Type	Container-Managed	Bean-Managed	
		JTA	JDBC
Entity	Y	N	N
Session	Y	Y	Y
Message-driven	Y	Y	Y

A session bean may have either container-managed or bean-managed transactions. There are two types of bean-managed transactions: JDBC and JTA transactions. You delimit JDBC transactions with the `commit` and `rollback` methods of the `Connection` interface. To demarcate JTA transactions, you invoke the `begin`, `commit`, and `rollback` methods of the `UserTransaction` interface.

In a session bean with bean-managed transactions, it is possible to mix JDBC and JTA transactions. This practice is not recommended, however, because it could make your code difficult to debug and maintain.

Like a session bean, a message-driven bean may have either container-managed or bean-managed transactions.

Transaction Timeouts

For container-managed transactions, you control the transaction timeout interval by setting the value of the `transaction.timeout` property in the `default.properties` file, which is in the `config` directory of your J2EE SDK installation. For example, you would set the timeout value to 5 seconds as follows:

```
transaction.timeout=5
```

With this setting, if the transaction has not completed within 5 seconds, the EJB container rolls it back.

When the J2EE SDK is first installed, the timeout value is set to 0:

```
transaction.timeout=0
```

If the value is 0, the transaction will not time out.

Only enterprise beans with container-managed transactions are affected by the `transaction.timeout` property. For enterprise beans with bean-managed JTA transactions, you invoke the `setTransactionTimeout` method of the `UserTransaction` interface.

Isolation Levels

Transactions not only ensure the full completion (or rollback) of the statements that they enclose but also isolate the data modified by the statements. The *isolation level* describes the degree to which the data being updated is visible to other transactions.

Suppose that a transaction in one program updates a customer's phone number, but before the transaction commits another program reads the same phone number. Will the second program read the updated and uncommitted phone number or will it read the old one? The answer depends on the isolation level of the transaction. If the transaction allows other programs to read uncommitted data, performance may improve because the other programs don't have to wait until the transaction ends. But there's a trade-off—if the transaction rolls back, another program might read the wrong data.

You cannot modify the isolation level of entity beans with container-managed persistence. These beans use the default isolation level of the DBMS, which is usually `READ_COMMITTED`.

For entity beans with bean-managed persistence and for all session beans, you can set the isolation level programmatically with the API provided by the underlying DBMS. A DBMS, for example, might allow you to permit uncommitted reads by invoking the `setTransactionIsolation` method:

```
Connection con;
...
con.setTransactionIsolation(TRANSACTION_READ_UNCOMMITTED);
```

Do not change the isolation level in the middle of a transaction. Usually, such a change causes the DBMS software to issue an implicit commit. Because the isolation levels offered by DBMS vendors may vary, you should check the DBMS documentation for more information. Isolation levels are not standardized for the J2EE platform.

Updating Multiple Databases

The J2EE transaction manager controls all enterprise bean transactions except for bean-managed JDBC transactions. The J2EE transaction manager allows an enterprise bean to update multiple databases within a transaction. The figures that follow show two scenarios for updating multiple databases in a single transaction.

In Figure 14–2, the client invokes a business method in `Bean-A`. The business method begins a transaction, updates Database X, updates Database Y, and invokes a business method in `Bean-B`. The second business method updates

Database Z and returns control to the business method in `Bean-A`, which commits the transaction. All three database updates occur in the same transaction.

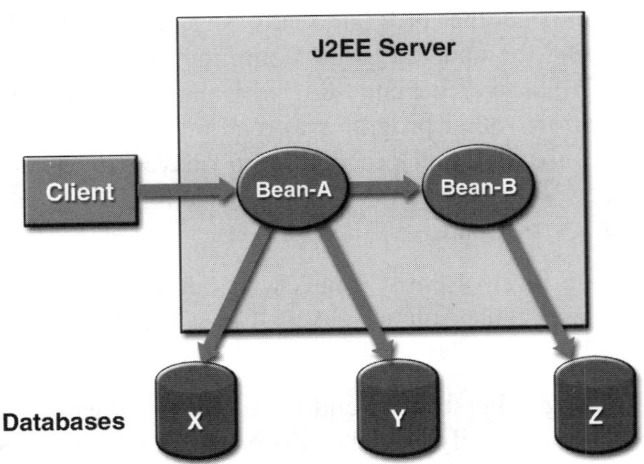

Figure 14–2 Updating Multiple Databases

In Figure 14–3, the client calls a business method in `Bean-A`, which begins a transaction and updates Database X. Then, `Bean-A` invokes a method in `Bean-B`, which resides in a remote J2EE server. The method in `Bean-B` updates Database Y. The transaction managers of the J2EE servers ensure that both databases are updated in the same transaction.

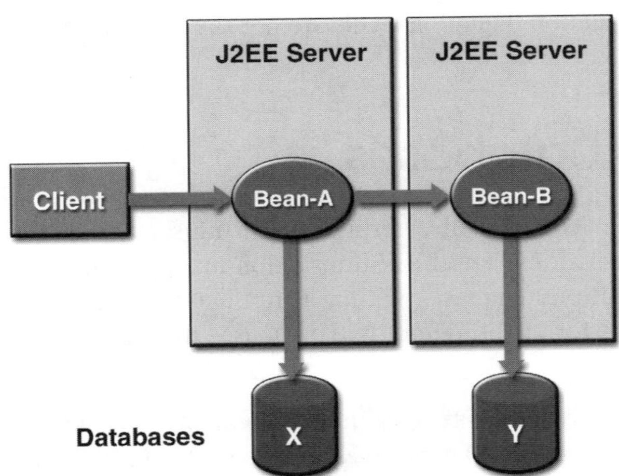

Figure 14–3 Updating Multiple Databases across J2EE Servers

Transactions in Web Components

You may demarcate a transaction in a Web component with either the `java.sql.Connection` or `javax.transaction.UserTransaction` interface. These are the same interfaces that a session bean with bean-managed transactions may use. Transactions demarcated with the `Connection` interface are discussed in the section JDBC Transactions (page 324) and those with the `UserTransaction` interface are discussed in the section JTA Transactions (page 325). For an example of a Web component using transactions, see Accessing Databases (page 221).

15

Security

Eric Jendrock

THE J2EE application programming model insulates developers from mechanism-specific implementation details of application security. J2EE provides this insulation in a way that enhances the portability of applications, allowing them to be deployed in diverse security environments.

Some of the material in this chapter assumes that you have an understanding of basic security concepts. To learn more about these concepts, we highly recommend that you explore the Security trail in *The Java™ Tutorial* (see `http://java.sun.com/docs/books/tutorial/security1.2/index.html`) before you begin this chapter.

In This Chapter

Overview

The J2EE platform defines declarative contracts between those who develop and assemble application components and those who configure applications in operational environments. In the context of application security, application providers are required to declare the security requirements of their applications in such a way that these requirements can be satisfied during application configuration. The *declarative security* mechanisms used in an application are expressed in a declarative syntax in a document called a *deployment descriptor*. An application deployer then employs container-specific tools to map the application requirements that are in a deployment descriptor to security mechanisms that are implemented by J2EE containers. The J2EE SDK provides this functionality with `deploytool`.

Programmatic security refers to security decisions that are made by security-aware applications. Programmatic security is useful when declarative security alone is not sufficient to express the security model of an application. For example, an application might make authorization decisions based on the time of day, the parameters of a call, or the internal state of an enterprise bean or Web component. Another application might restrict access based on user information stored in a database.

J2EE applications are made up of components that can be deployed into different containers. These components are used to build a multitier enterprise application. The goal of the J2EE security architecture is to achieve end-to-end security by securing each tier.

The tiers can contain both protected and unprotected resources. Often, you need to protect resources to ensure that only authorized users have access. *Authorization* provides controlled access to protected resources. Authorization is based on identification and authentication. *Identification* is a process that enables recognition of an entity by a system, and *authentication* is a process that verifies the identity of a user, device, or other entity in a computer system, usually as a prerequisite to allowing access to resources in a system.

Authorization is not required to access unprotected resources. Because authorization is built upon authentication, authentication is also not needed to access unprotected resources. Accessing a resource without authentication is referred to as *unauthenticated* or *anonymous* access.

Security Roles

When you design an enterprise bean or Web component, you should always think about the kinds of users who will access the component. For example, an `Account` enterprise bean might be accessed by customers, bank tellers, and branch managers. Each of these user categories is called a *security role*, an abstract logical grouping of users that is defined by the person who assembles the application. When an application is deployed, the deployer will map the roles to security identities in the operational environment.

A J2EE group also represents a category of users, but it has a different scope from a role. A J2EE group is designated for the entire J2EE server, whereas a role covers only a specific application in a J2EE server.

To create a role for a J2EE application, you declare it for the EJB JAR file or for the WAR file that is contained in the application. For example, you could use the following procedure to create a role in `deploytool`.

1. Select the enterprise bean's EJB JAR file or the Web component's WAR file.
2. In the Roles tab, click Add.
3. In the table, enter values for the Name and Description fields.

Declaring and Linking Role References

A *security role reference* allows an enterprise bean or Web component to reference an existing security role. A security role is an application-specific logical grouping of users, classified by common traits such as customer profile or job title. When an application is deployed, roles are mapped to security identities, such as *principals* (identities assigned to users as a result of authentication) or groups, in the operational environment. Based on this, a user with a certain security role has associated access rights to a J2EE application. The link is the actual name of the security role that is being referenced.

During application assembly, the assembler creates security roles for the application and associates these roles with available security mechanisms. The assembler then resolves the security role references in individual servlets and JSPs by linking them to roles defined for the application.

The security role reference defines a mapping between the name of a role that is called from a Web component using `isUserInRole(String name)` (see Using Programmatic Security in the Web Tier, page 340) or from an enterprise bean using `isCallerInRole(String name)` (see Using Programmatic Security in the EJB Tier, page 341) and the name of a security role that has been defined for the application. For example, to map the security role reference `cust` to the security role with role name `bankCustomer`, you would do the following:

1. Select the Web component or enterprise bean.
2. Select the Security tab.
3. If the `cust` entry does not appear in the Role Names Referenced In Code pane, click the Add button.
4. Enter the name of the security role reference `cust` in the Coded Name column.
5. From the drop-down menu in the Role Name column, select the security role name `bankCustomer` that maps to the coded name.

   If the security role name to which you want to map the security role reference is not listed in the Role Name column, click Edit Roles and add the role (see Security Roles, page 335).
6. Click on the folded paper icon to add a description for the `cust` role reference.
7. In the Description dialog box, enter a description.
8. Click OK to accept the description, or Cancel to cancel it.

In this example, `isUserInRole("bankCustomer")` and `isUserInRole("cust")` will both return `true` for the methods indicated in the Method Permissions pane.

Because a coded name is linked to a role name, you can change the role name at a later time without having to change the coded name. For example, if you were to change the role name from `bankCustomer` to something else, you wouldn't need to change the `cust` name in the code. However, you would need to relink the `cust` coded name to the new role name.

Mapping Roles to J2EE Users and Groups

When you are developing a J2EE application, you should know the roles of your users, but you probably won't know exactly who the users will be. That's taken care of in the J2EE security architecture, because after your component has been deployed, the administrator of the J2EE server will map the roles to the J2EE users (or groups) of the default realm. In the `Account` bean example, the administrator might assign the user Sally to the `Manager` role, and the users Bob, Ted, and Clara to the `Teller` role.

An administrator can map roles to J2EE users and groups by using the following procedure in `deploytool`:

1. Select the J2EE application.
2. In the Security tab, select the appropriate role from the Role Name list.
3. Click Add.
4. In the Users dialog box, select the users and groups that should belong to the role. (See Managing J2EE Users and Groups, page 349 for information about creating users and groups with `deploytool`.)

Web-Tier Security

The following sections address protecting resources and authenticating users in the Web tier.

Protecting Web Resources

You can protect Web resources by specifying a security constraint. A *security constraint* determines who is authorized to access a *Web resource collection*, which is a list of URL patterns and HTTP methods that describe a set of resources to be protected. Security constraints can be defined using `deploytool`, as described in Controlling Access to Web Resources (page 338).

If you try to access a protected Web resource as an unauthenticated user, the Web container will try to authenticate you. The container will only accept the request after you have proven your identity to the container and have been granted permission to access the resource.

Controlling Access to Web Resources

Use the following procedure in `deploytool` to specify a security constraint to control access to a Web resource.

1. Select the WAR containing the Web resource.
2. Select the Security tab.
3. Click the Add button in the Security Constraints section of the screen.
4. Click the Edit button adjacent to the Web Resource Collection field to add a Web resource collection to the security constraint. The Web resource collection describes a URL pattern and HTTP method pair that refer to the resources that need to be protected.
5. Click the Edit button adjacent to the Authorized Roles field to add one or more roles to the security constraint. You are specifying the set of roles that are allowed to access the Web resource collection.

Authenticating Users of Web Resources

When you try to access a protected Web resource, the Web container activates the authentication mechanism that has been configured for that resource. You can configure the following authentication mechanisms for a Web resource:

- HTTP basic authentication
- Form-based authentication
- Client-certificate authentication

Basic Authentication

If you specify *HTTP basic authentication,* the Web server will authenticate a user by using the user name and password obtained from the Web client.

Form-Based Authentication

If you specify *form-based authentication*, you can customize the login screen and error pages that are presented to the end user by an HTTP browser.

Neither form-based authentication nor HTTP basic authentication is particularly secure. In form-based authentication, the content of the user dialog box is sent as plain text, and the target server is not authenticated. Basic authentication sends user names and passwords over the Internet as text that is uuencoded, but not encrypted. This form of authentication, which uses Base64 encoding, can expose your user names and passwords unless all connections are over SSL. If someone can intercept the transmission, the username and password information can easily be decoded.

Client-Certificate Authentication

Client-certificate authentication is a more secure method of authentication than either basic or form-based authentication. It uses HTTP over SSL (HTTPS), in which the server and, optionally, the client authenticate each other with Public Key Certificates. *Secure Sockets Layer* (SSL) provides data encryption, server authentication, message integrity, and optional client authentication for a TCP/IP connection. You can think of a *public key certificate* as the digital equivalent of a passport. It is issued by a trusted organization, which is called a *certificate authority* (CA), and provides identification for the bearer. If you specify client-certificate authentication, the Web server will authenticate the client using an *X.509 certificate*, a public key certificate that conforms to a standard that is defined by X.509 Public Key Infrastructure (PKI).

Configuring Web Resources' Authentication Mechanism

To configure the authentication mechanism that the Web resources in a WAR will use:

1. Select the WAR containing the Web resource.
2. Select the Security tab.
3. Choose one of the following authentication mechanisms from the User Authentication Method pull-down menu: None, Basic, Client-Certificate, or Form Based.
    a. If you choose form-based authentication, you must select Settings and fill in the Realm Name, Login Page, and Error Page fields in the Settings dialog box. The error page is displayed when the user cannot be logged in.
    b. If you choose basic authentication, you must select Settings and enter `Default` in the Realm Name field in the Settings dialog box.

Using SSL to Enhance the Confidentiality of HTTP Basic and Form-Based Authentication

Passwords are not protected for confidentiality with HTTP basic or form-based authentication. To overcome this limitation, you can run these authentication protocols over an SSL-protected session and ensure that all message content is protected for confidentiality.

To configure HTTP basic or form-based authentication over SSL:

1. Select the Web component. The Web Component inspector will be displayed.
2. From the Security tab, make sure that Basic or Form Based has been selected in the User Authentication Method pull-down menu.
3. Click on the Add button in the Security Constraint section.
4. Click on the security constraint that was added.
5. Select CONFIDENTIAL in the Network Security Requirement pull-down menu.

Using Programmatic Security in the Web Tier

Programmatic security is used by security-aware applications when declarative security alone is not sufficient to express the security model of the application. Programmatic security consists of the following methods of the `HttpServletRequest` interface:

- `getRemoteUser`
- `isUserInRole`
- `getUserPrincipal`

You can use the `getRemoteUser` method to determine the user name with which the client authenticated. The `isUserInRole` method is used to determine if a user is in a specific security role. The `getUserPrincipal` method returns a `java.security.Principal` object.

These APIs allow servlets to make business logic decisions based on the logical role of the remote user. They also allow the servlet to determine the principal name of the current user.

Unprotected Web Resources

Many applications feature unprotected Web content, which any caller can access without authentication. In the Web tier, unrestricted access is provided simply by not configuring an authentication mechanism.

EJB-Tier Security

The following sections describe declarative and programmatic security mechanisms that can be used to protect resources in the EJB tier. The protected resources include methods of enterprise beans that are called from the application clients, Web components, or other enterprise beans.

You can protect EJB-tier resources by doing the following:

- Declaring method permissions
- Mapping roles to J2EE users and groups

Declaring Method Permissions

After you've defined the roles, you can define the method permissions of an enterprise bean. Method permissions indicate which roles are allowed to invoke which methods.

Use the following procedure in `deploytool` to specify method permissions by mapping roles to methods.

1. Select the enterprise bean.
2. Select the Security tab.
3. In the Method Permissions table, select Sel Roles in the Availability column.
4. Then select a role's checkbox if that role should be allowed to invoke a method.

Using Programmatic Security in the EJB Tier

Programmatic security in the EJB tier consists of the `getCallerPrincipal` and the `isCallerInRole` methods. You can use the `getCallerPrincipal` method to determine the caller of the enterprise bean, and the `isCallerInRole` method to get the caller's role.

The `getCallerPrincipal` method of the `EJBContext` interface returns the `java.security.Principal` object that identifies the caller of the enterprise bean. (In this case, a principal is the same as a user.) In the following example, the `getUser` method of an enterprise bean returns the name of the J2EE user that invoked it:

```
public String getUser() {
   return context.getCallerPrincipal().getName();
}
```

You can determine whether an enterprise bean's caller belongs to a particular role by invoking the `isCallerInRole` method:

```
boolean result = context.isCallerInRole("Customer");
```

Unprotected EJB-Tier Resources

By default, the J2EE SDK assigns the `ANYONE` role to a method. The `guest` user, which is anonymous and unauthenticated, belongs to the `ANYONE` role. Therefore, if you do not map the roles, any user may invoke the methods of an enterprise bean.

Application Client-Tier Security

Authentication requirements for J2EE application clients are the same as the requirements for other J2EE components. Access to protected resources in either the EJB tier or the Web tier requires user authentication, whereas access to unprotected resources does not.

An application client can use the Java Authentication and Authorization Service (JAAS) for authentication. JAAS implements a Java version of the standard Pluggable Authentication Module (PAM) framework, which permits applications to remain independent from underlying authentication technologies. You can plug new or updated authentication technologies under an application without making any modifications to the application itself. Applications enable the authentication process by instantiating a `LoginContext` object, which, in turn, references a configuration to determine the authentication technologies or login modules that will be used to perform the authentication.

A typical login module could prompt for and verify a user name and password. Other modules could read and verify a voice or fingerprint sample.

In some cases, a login module needs to communicate with the user to obtain authentication information. Login modules use a `javax.security.auth.callback.CallbackHandler` for this purpose. Applications implement the `CallbackHandler` interface and pass it to the login context, which forwards it directly to the underlying login modules. A login module uses the callback handler both to gather input (such as a password or smart card PIN number) from users or to supply information (such as status information) to users. By allowing the application to specify the callback handler, an underlying login module can remain independent of the different ways applications interact with users.

For example, the implementation of a callback handler for a GUI application might display a window to solicit user input. Or, the implementation of a callback handler for a command line tool might simply prompt the user for input directly from the command line.

The login module passes an array of appropriate callbacks to the callback handler's `handle` method (for example, a `NameCallback` for the user name and a `PasswordCallback` for the password), and the callback handler performs the requested user interaction and sets appropriate values in the callbacks. For example, to process a `NameCallback`, the `CallbackHandler` may prompt for a name, retrieve the value from the user, and call the `setName` method of the `NameCallback` to store the name.

Specifying the Application Client's Callback Handler

Use the following procedure in `deploytool` to specify a callback handler for an application client.

1. Select the application client JAR.
2. Select the General tab.
3. From the CallbackHandler Class menu, select the `CallbackHandler` class that will be used as an interface to gather user authentication data.

EIS-Tier Security

In the EIS tier, an application component requests a connection to an EIS resource. As part of this connection, the EIS may require a sign-on to the resource. The application component provider has two choices for the design of the EIS sign-on:

- With the container-managed sign-on approach, the application component lets the container take the responsibility of configuring and managing the EIS sign-on. The container determines the user name and password for establishing a connection to an EIS instance.
- With the component-managed sign-on approach, the application component code manages EIS sign-on by including code that performs the sign-on process to an EIS.

The component provider can use `deploytool` to choose the type of sign-on.

Configuring Sign-On

Use the following procedure in deploytool to configure the type of sign-on.

1. Select the component.
2. Select the Resource Refs tab.
3. Click Add.
4. In the Authentication combo box, select either Container for container-managed sign-on or Application for component-managed sign-on.

Container-Managed Sign-On

With container-managed sign-on, an application component does not have to pass any security information for signing on to the resource to the getConnection() method. The security information is supplied by the container, as shown in the following example.

```
// Business method in an application component
Context initctx = new InitialContext();

// perform JNDI lookup to obtain a connection factory
javax.resource.cci.ConnectionFactory cxf =
     (javax.resource.cci.ConnectionFactory)initctx.lookup(
      "java:comp/env/eis/MainframeCxFactory");

// Invoke factory to obtain a connection. The security
// information is not passed in the getConnection method
javax.resource.cci.Connection cx = cxf.getConnection();
...
```

Component-Managed Sign-On

With component-managed sign-on, an application component is responsible for passing the security information that is needed for signing on to the resource to the getConnection() method. Security information could be a user name and password, for example, as shown here:

```
// Method in an application component
Context initctx = new InitialContext();

// perform JNDI lookup to obtain a connection factory
javax.resource.cci.ConnectionFactory cxf =
     (javax.resource.cci.ConnectionFactory)initctx.lookup(
       "java:comp/env/eis/MainframeCxFactory");
```

```
// Invoke factory to obtain a connection
com.myeis.ConnectionSpecImpl properties = //..

// get a new ConnectionSpec
properties.setUserName("...");
properties.setPassword("...");
javax.resource.cci.Connection cx =
  cxf.getConnection(properties);
...
```

Configuring Resource Adapter Security

In addition to configuring the sign-on, you must also configure the resource adapter security. To add security to a resource adapter, complete the following steps:

1. Select the resource adapter RAR (Resource Adapter Archive).
2. Select the Security tab. In the Authentication Mechanisms pane, select the authentication mechanisms that this resource adapter supports:
   - Password: A user and password is required to connect to an EIS.
   - Kerberos Version 5.0: The resource adapter supports the Kerberos authentication mechanism. See RFC-1510, The Kerberos Network Authentication Service (V5), for details. This specification can be found at `http://www.ietf.org/rfc/rfc1510.txt`.

   You can select no mechanism, one mechanism, or multiple mechanisms. If you do not select a mechanism, no security authentication will be supported.
3. Select Reauthentication Supported if the resource adapter supports performing reauthentication on an existing physical connection. Reauthentication will be performed when an application server calls the `getConnection()` method with a security context that is different from the one that was used to establish the connection.
4. In the Security Permissions pane, click the Add button to add a security permission that your resource adapter needs to access system resources in your operational environment. Specify only permissions that are not included in the default set, which are listed in Table 2 of Section 11.2 in the J2EE Connector Architecture Specification 1.0.
5. For each security permission, click the rightmost column labeled with a folded paper icon to enter a description for the permission.

To delete a security permission, select the permission in the table and click Delete.

Propagating Security Identity

When you deploy an enterprise bean or Web component, you can specify the security identity that will be propagated (illustrated in Figure 15–1) to enterprise beans invoked from within that component.

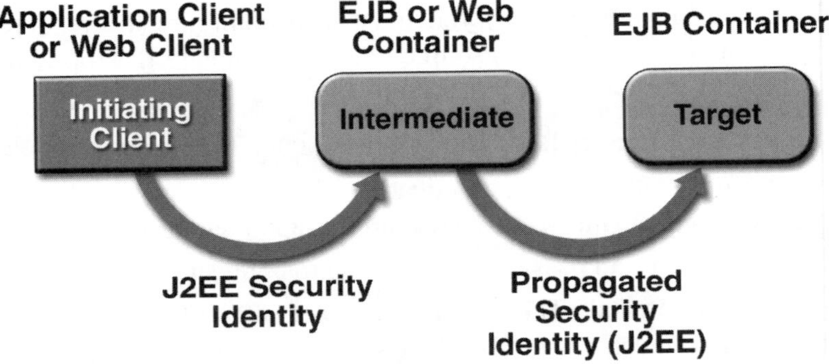

Figure 15–1 Security Identity Propagation

You can choose one of the following propagation styles:

- The caller identity of the intermediate component is propagated to the target enterprise bean. This technique is used when the target container trusts the intermediate container.
- A specific identity is propagated to the target enterprise bean. This technique is used when the target container expects access via a specific identity.

Configuring a Component's Propagated Security Identity

You use `deploytool` to select the type of security identity that is propagated from an enterprise bean or Web component.

To configure an enterprise bean or Web component to propagate the caller identity with which the component is running:

1. Select the component.
2. Select the Security tab.
3. In the Security Identity pane, select the Use Caller ID radio button.

To configure a component to propagate a security identity other than that with which the component is running:

1. Select the component.
2. Select the Security tab.
3. In the Security Identity pane, select the Run As Specified Role option.
4. Use the drop-down menu to select the role with which to run.
5. After you select the role, you can select a user from that role. To do this, select Deployment Settings.
6. From Run As Specified User, select the user name that the client will use to invoke the enterprise bean's methods.
7. Click OK.

Configuring Client Authentication

If an application component in an application client container accesses a protected method on a bean, use client authentication.

In `deploytool`, use the following procedure to configure client authentication:

1. Select the target enterprise bean.
2. Select the Security tab.
3. Select Deployment Settings to display the Security Deployment Settings dialog box.
4. Select the SSL Required checkbox to enable SSL.
5. In the Client Authentication pane, select Certificate as the method by which the server expects the client to authenticate itself to the server.
6. Click OK.

Trust between Containers

When an enterprise bean is designed so that either the original caller identity or a designated identity is used to call a target bean, the target bean will receive the propagated identity only; it will *not* receive any authentication data.

There is no way for the target container to authenticate the propagated security identity. However, since the security identity is used in authorization checks (for example, method permissions or with the `isCallerInRole()` method), it is vitally important that the security identity be authentic. Since there is no authentication data available to authenticate the propagated identity, the target must trust that the calling container has propagated an authenticated security identity.

By default, the J2EE SDK server is configured to trust identities that are propagated from different containers. Therefore, there are no special steps that you need to take to set up a trust relationship.

J2EE Users, Realms, and Groups

A J2EE user is similar to an operating system user. Typically, both types of users represent people. However, these two types of users are not the same. The J2EE authentication service has no knowledge of the user name and password you provide when you log on to the operating system. The J2EE authentication service is not connected to the security mechanism of the operating system. The two security services manage users that belong to different realms.

A *realm* is a collection of users that are controlled by the same authentication policy. The J2EE authentication service governs users in two realms: certificate and default.

Certificates are used with the HTTPS protocol to authenticate Web browser clients. To verify the identity of a user in the certificate realm, the authentication service verifies an X.509 certificate. For step-by-step instructions, see Setting Up a Server Certificate (page 350). The common name field of the X.509 certificate is used as the principal name.

In most cases, the J2EE authentication service verifies user identity by checking the default realm. This realm is used for the authentication of all clients except for Web browser clients that use the HTTPS protocol and certificates.

A J2EE user of the default realm can belong to a J2EE group. (A user in the certificate realm cannot.) A *J2EE group* is a category of users classified by common traits, such as job title or customer profile. For example, most customers of an e-commerce application might belong to the `CUSTOMER` group, but the big spenders would belong to the `PREFERRED` group. Categorizing users into groups makes it easier to control the access of large numbers of users. The section EJB-Tier Security (page 340) explains how to control user access to enterprise beans.

Managing J2EE Users and Groups

This section shows how to use `deploytool` to do the following:

- Display all users in the default realm
- Add a user to the default realm
- Add a user to the certificate realm
- Remove a user
- Add a group to the default realm (you cannot add a group to the certificate realm)
- Remove a group from the default realm

Use the following procedure to display all users in the default or certificate realm.

1. Select the server to which you want to add users or groups, or both.
2. Select Tools→Server Configuration to display the Configuration Installation screen.
3. Under J2EE Server in the tree view, select Users.
4. Select the realm (Default or Certificate).

Use the following procedure to add a user to the default realm.

1. Click Add User.
2. Enter a user name and a password in the appropriate fields.
3. In the Group Membership pane, select the group (from Available groups) to which the user you are adding will belong. To select multiple groups, repeat this step.
4. Click Add to move your selection(s) to Groups.
5. Click OK when done.

Use the following procedure to add a new group to the default realm.

1. Click Edit Groups.
2. From the Groups window, click Add.
3. Select the line you just added and enter the name of the group to add.
4. Click OK when done.

Use the following procedure to remove a group from the default realm.

1. Click Edit Groups.
2. From the Groups window, select the group to remove.

3. Click Delete.
4. Click Yes when prompted.
5. Click OK when done.

Use the following procedure to add a new user to the certificate realm.

1. Select the Certificate realm.
2. Click Add User.
3. Select the directory where the certificate is located.
4. Select the certificate file name.
5. Click OK when done.

Setting Up a Server Certificate

Certificates are used with the HTTPS protocol to authenticate Web clients. The HTTPS service of the J2EE server will not run unless a server certificate has been installed. Use the following procedure to set up a J2EE server certificate.

1. Generate a key pair and a self-signed certificate.

   The `keytool` utility enables you to create the certificate. The `keytool` utility that ships with the J2EE SDK has the same syntax as the one that ships with the J2SE software. However, the J2EE SDK version programmatically adds a Java Cryptographic Extension provider that has implementations of RSA algorithms. This provider enables you to import RSA-signed certificates.

   To generate the certificate, run the `keytool` utility as follows, substituting *<certificate-alias>* with the alias of your certificate and *<keystore-filename>* with the name of your keystore file:

   ```
   keytool -genkey -keyalg RSA -alias <certificate-alias>
      -keystore <keystore-filename>
   ```

2. The `keytool` utility prompts you for the following information:
   a. Keystore password: Enter a password. (You may want to use "`changeit`" to be consistent with the default password of the J2EE SDK keystore.)
   b. First and last name: Enter the fully qualified name of your server. This fully-qualified name includes the host name and the domain name.
   c. Organizational unit: Enter the appropriate value.

d. Organization: Enter the appropriate value.
e. City or locality: Enter the appropriate value.
f. State or province: Enter the unabbreviated name.
g. Two-letter country code: For the USA, the two-letter country code is US.
h. Key password for alias: Do not enter a password. Press the Return key.

3. Import the certificate.

   If your certificate will be signed by a CA other than Verisign, you must import the CA certificate. Otherwise, you may skip this step. (Even if your certificate will be signed by Verisign Test CA, you must import it.)

   To import the certificate, perform these tasks:

   a. Request the CA certificate from your CA. Store the certificate in a file.
   b. To install the CA certificate in the Java 2 Platform, Standard Edition, run the `keytool` utility as follows. (You must have the required permissions to modify the `$JAVA_HOME/jre/lib/security/cacerts` file.)

```
keytool -import -trustcacerts -alias <ca-cert-alias>
   -file <ca-cert-filename>
```

4. If you want to have your certificate digitally signed by a CA, do the following:

   a. Generate a Certificate Signing Request (CSR).

```
keytool -certreq -sigalg MD5withRSA -alias <cert-alias>
   -file <csr-filename>
```

   b. Send the contents of the *<csr-filename>* for signing. If you are using Verisign CA, go to `http://digitalid.verisign.com/`. Verisign will send the signed certificate via e-mail. Store this certificate in a file.
   c. Import the signed certificate that you received in email into the server:

```
keytool -import -alias <cert-alias> -file
   <signed-cert-file>
```

16

Resource Connections

Dale Green

BOTH enterprise beans and Web components can access a wide variety of resources, including databases, mail sessions, Java Message Service objects, and URLs. The J2EE platform provides mechanisms that allow you to access all of these resources in a similar manner. This chapter describes how to get connections to several types of resources. Although the code samples in this chapter are from enterprise beans, they will also work in Web components.

In This Chapter

JNDI Names and Resource References

First, let's define some terms.

JNDI is the acronym for the Java Naming and Directory Interface API. J2EE components locate objects by invoking the JNDI `lookup` method.

A *JNDI name* is a people-friendly name for an object. These names are bound to their objects by the naming and directory service that is provided by the J2EE server. Because J2EE components access this service through the JNDI API, we usually refer to an object's people-friendly name as its JNDI name. The JNDI name of the Cloudscape database is `jdbc/Cloudscape`. When it starts up, the J2EE server reads information from a configuration file and automatically adds JNDI database names such as `jdbc/Cloudscape` to the name space.

A *connection factory* is an object that produces connection objects that enable a J2EE component to access a resource. The connection factory for a database is a `javax.sql.DataSource` object, which creates a `java.sql.Connection` object.

A *resource reference* is an element in a deployment descriptor that identifies the component's coded name for the resource. More specifically, the coded name references a connection factory for the resource. In the example in the following section, the resource reference name is `jdbc/SavingsAccountDB`.

The JNDI name of a resource and the name of the resource reference are not the same. This approach to naming requires that you map the two names before deployment, but it also decouples components from resources. Because of this decoupling, if at a later time the component needs to access a different resource, you don't have to change the name in the code. This flexibility also makes it easier for you to assemble J2EE applications from preexisting components.

deploytool Tips for Resource References

The instructions that follow refer to the entity bean described in the section The SavingsAccountEJB Example (page 84). The `SavingsAccountEJB` code is in the `j2eetutorial/examples/src/ejb/savingsaccount` directory. A sample `SavingsAccountApp.ear` file is in the `j2eetutorial/examples/ears` directory.

Specifying a Resource Reference

1. In `deploytool`, select `SavingsAccountEJB` from the tree.
2. Select the Resource Refs tab.
3. Click Add.

4. In the Coded Name field, enter `jdbc/SavingsAccountDB`.

   The `SavingsAccountBean` code refers to the database as follows:

   ```
   private String dbName =
      "java:comp/env/jdbc/SavingsAccountDB";
   ```

   The `java:comp/env` prefix is the name of the JNDI context for the component. The `jdbc/SavingsAccountDB` string is the JNDI name for the resource reference. The JNDI names for JDBC `DataSource` objects are stored in the `java:comp/env/jdbc` subcontext.

5. In the Type combo box, select `javax.sql.DataSource`. A `DataSource` object is a factory for database connections.
6. In the Authentication combo box, select Container.
7. If you want other enterprise beans to share the connections acquired from the `DataSource`, select the Sharable checkbox.

If the preceding steps are followed, the Resource Refs tab will appear as shown in Figure 16–1.

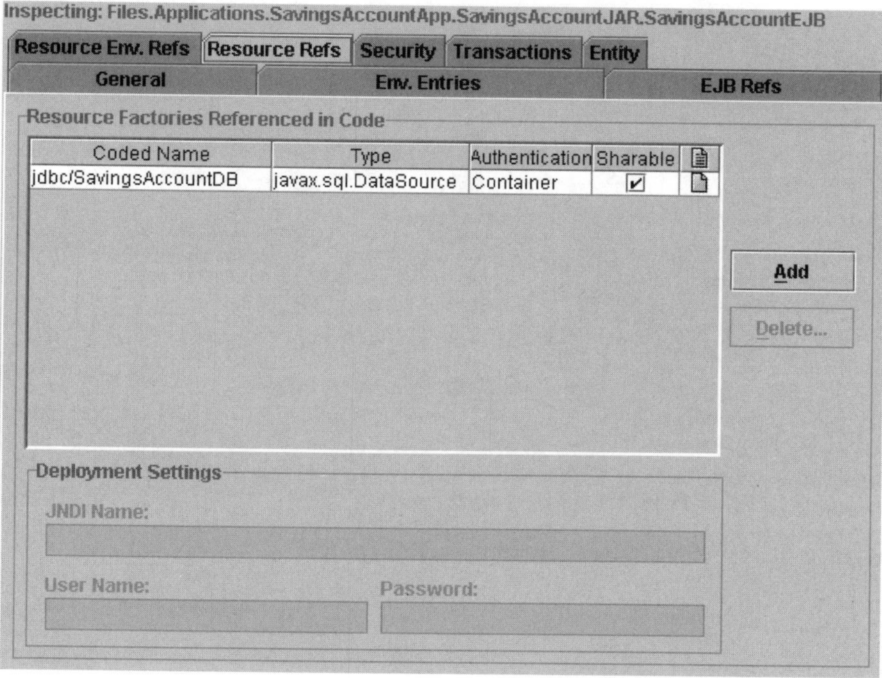

Figure 16–1 Resource Refs Tabbed Pane of `SavingsAccountEJB`

Mapping a Resource Reference to a JNDI Name

1. Select the J2EE application from the tree.
2. Select the JNDI Names tab.
3. In the References table, select the row containing the resource reference. For the `SavingsAccountEJB` example, the resource reference is `jdbc/SavingsAccountDB`, the name you entered in the Coded Name field of the Resource Refs tab.
4. In the row you just selected, enter the JNDI name. For the `SavingsAccountEJB` example, you would enter `jdbc/Cloudscape` in the JNDI Name field.

   The JNDI Names tab for `SavingsAccountApp` is shown in Figure 16–2.

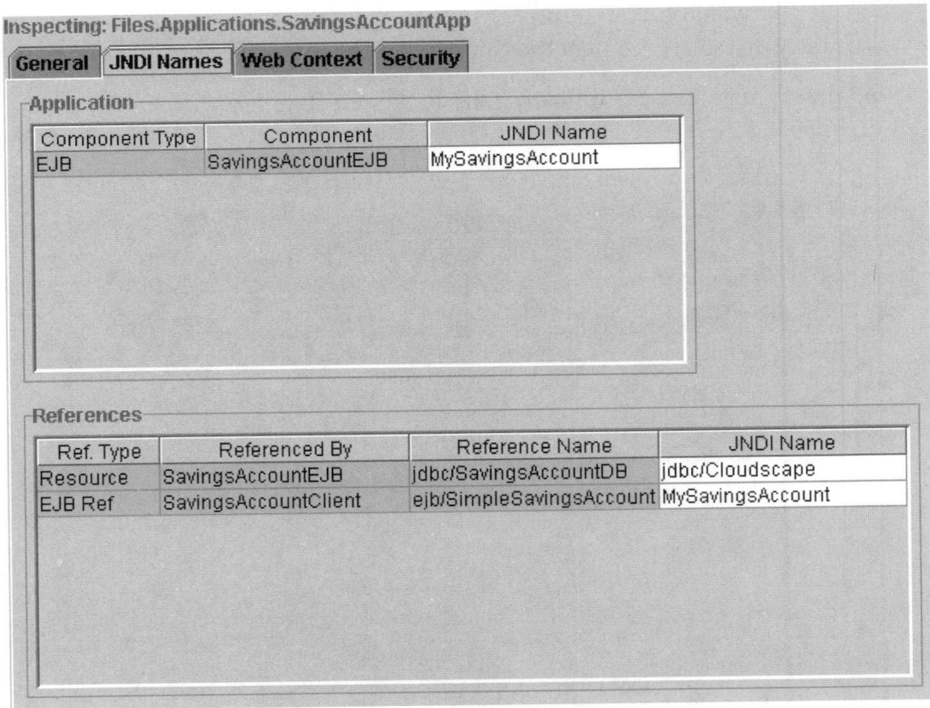

Figure 16–2 JNDI Names Tab of `SavingsAccountApp`

Database Connections for Enterprise Beans

The persistence type of an enterprise bean determines whether or not you code the connection routine. You must code the connection for enterprise beans that access a database and do not have container-managed persistence. Such beans include entity beans with bean-managed persistence and session beans. For entity beans with container-managed persistence, `deploytool` generates the connection routines for you.

Coded Connections

How to Connect

The code examples in this section are from the `SavingsAccountBean` class, which connects to the database via the following steps.

1. Specify the database name.

```
private String dbName =
   "java:comp/env/jdbc/SavingsAccountDB";
```

2. Obtain the `DataSource` associated with the logical name.

```
InitialContext ic = new InitialContext();
DataSource ds = (DataSource) ic.lookup(dbName);
```

3. Get the `Connection` from the `DataSource`.

```
Connection con =  ds.getConnection();
```

When to Connect

When coding an enterprise bean, you must decide how long it will retain the connection. Generally you have two choices: either hold the connection for the lifetime of the bean, or hold it only during each database call. Your choice determines the method (or methods) in which your bean connects to a database.

Long-Term Connections

You can design an enterprise bean that holds a database connection for its entire lifetime. Because the bean connects and disconnects just once, its code is slightly easier to write. But there's a trade-off—other components cannot acquire the connection. Session and entity beans issue the lifelong connections in different methods.

Session Beans

The EJB container invokes the ejbCreate method at the beginning of a session bean's life cycle and invokes the ejbRemove method at the end. To retain a connection for the lifetime of a session bean, you connect to the database in ejbCreate and disconnect in ejbRemove. If the session bean is stateful, you must also connect in ejbActivate and disconnect in ejbPassivate. A stateful session bean requires these additional calls because the EJB container may passivate the bean during its lifetime. During passivation, a stateful session bean is saved in secondary storage, but a database connection cannot be saved in this manner. Because a stateless session bean cannot be passivated, it does not require the additional calls in ejbActivate and ejbPassivate. For more information on activation and passivation, see The Life Cycle of a Stateful Session Bean (page 63). For an example of a stateful session bean with a long-term connection, see the TellerBean.java code in the j2eetutorial/examples/ejb/teller directory.

Entity Beans with Bean-Managed Persistence

After instantiating an entity bean and moving it to the pooled stage, the EJB container invokes the setEntityContext method. Conversely, the EJB container invokes the unsetEntityContext method when the entity bean leaves the pooled stage and becomes eligible for garbage collection. To retain a database connection for its entire life span, an entity bean connects in the setEntityContext method and disconnects in the unsetEntityContext method. To see a diagram of the life cycle, see Figure 3–5, (page 66). For an example of an entity bean with a long-term connection, see the SavingsAccountBean.java code in the j2eetutorial/examples/ejb/savingsaccount directory.

Short-term Connections

Briefly held connections allow many components to share the same connection. Because the EJB container manages a pool of database connections, enterprise beans can quickly obtain and release the connections. For example, a business method might connect to a database, insert a row, and then disconnect.

In a session bean, a business method that connects to a database should be transactional. The transaction will help maintain data integrity.

deploytool Tips for Specifying Database Users and Passwords

The instructions in this section do not apply to entity beans with container-managed persistence. For those entity beans, see the instructions in Specifying the Database JNDI Name, User Name, and Password (page 150).

To connect to the Cloudscape database bundled with this release, you do not specify a database user name and password; authentication is performed by a separate service. For more information about authentication, see Chapter 15.

However, some types of databases do require a user name and password during connection. For these databases, if the `getConnection` call has no parameters, you must specify the database user name and password with `deploytool`. To specify these values, perform these steps:

1. Select the enterprise bean in the tree view.
2. Select the Resource Refs tab.
3. Select the appropriate row in the table labeled Resource Factories Referenced in Code, and enter the database user name and password in the fields at the bottom.

If you wish to obtain the database user name and password programmatically, you do not need to specify them with `deploytool`. In this case, you include the database user name and password in the arguments of the `getConnection` method:

```
con = dataSource.getConnection(dbUser, dbPassword);
```

Connection Pooling

The EJB container maintains the pool of database connections. This pool is transparent to the enterprise beans. When an enterprise bean requests a connection, the container fetches one from the pool and assigns it to the bean. Because the time-consuming connection has already been made, the bean quickly gets a connection. The bean may release the connection after each database call, since it can rapidly get another connection. Because such a bean holds the connection for a short time, the same connection can be shared sequentially by many beans.

Mail Session Connections

If you've ever ordered a product from a Web site, you've probably received an e-mail confirming your order. The `ConfirmerBean` class demonstrates how to send e-mail from an enterprise bean.

The source code for this example is in the `j2eetutorial/examples/src/ejb/confirmer` directory. To compile the code, go to the `j2eetutorial/examples` directory and type `ant confirmer`. A sample `ConfirmerApp.ear` file is in the `j2eetutorial/examples/ears` directory.

In the sendNotice method of the ConfirmerBean class, the lookup method returns a Session object, which represents a mail session. Like a database connection, a mail session is a resource. As with any resource, you must link the coded name (TheMailSession) with a JNDI name. Using the Session object as an argument, the sendNotice method creates an empty Message object. After calling several set methods on the Message object, sendNotice invokes the send method of the Transport class to send the message on its way. The source code for the sendNotice method follows.

```
public void sendNotice(String recipient) {

   try {
       Context initial = new InitialContext();
       Session session =
         (Session) initial.lookup(
         "java:comp/env/TheMailSession");

       Message msg = new MimeMessage(session);
       msg.setFrom();

       msg.setRecipients(Message.RecipientType.TO,
          InternetAddress.parse(recipient, false));

       msg.setSubject("Test Message from ConfirmerBean");

       DateFormat dateFormatter =
         DateFormat.getDateTimeInstance(
         DateFormat.LONG, DateFormat.SHORT);

       Date timeStamp = new Date();

      String messageText = "Thank you for your order." + '\n' +
          "We received your order on " +
          dateFormatter.format(timeStamp) + ".";

       msg.setText(messageText);
       msg.setHeader("X-Mailer", mailer);
       msg.setSentDate(timeStamp);

       Transport.send(msg);

   } catch(Exception e) {
       throw new EJBException(e.getMessage());
   }
}
```

Running the ConfirmerEJB Example

Deploying the Application

1. In `deploytool`, open the `j2eetutorial/examples/ears/ConfirmerApp.ear` file (File→Open).
2. In the Resource Refs tab of the bean, specify the resource reference for the mail session with the values shown in Table 16–1.

Table 16–1 Resource Refs for the `ConfirmerEJB` Example

Field Name	**Value**
`Coded Name`	`TheMailSession`
`Type`	`javax.mail.Session`
`Authentication`	`Application`
`From`	`(your email address)`
`Host`	`(mail server host)`
`User Name`	`(user name for connecting to mail server)`

3. Deploy the `ConfirmerApp` application (Tools→Deploy). In the Introduction dialog box, make sure that you select the Return Client JAR checkbox.

Running the Client

1. In a terminal window, go to the `j2eetutorial/examples/ears` directory.
2. Set the `APPCPATH` environment variable to `ConfirmerAppClient.jar`.
3. Type the following command on a single line, replacing *<recipient>* with the e-mail address of the person who will receive the message.

```
runclient -client ConfirmerApp.ear -name ConfirmerClient
   -textauth <recipient>
```

4. At the login prompts, enter `guest` for the user name and `guest123` for the password.

Troubleshooting

If the application cannot connect to the mail server it will generate this exception:

```
javax.mail.MessagingException: Could not connect to SMTP host
```

To fix this problem, make sure that the mail server is running and that you've entered the correct name for the mail server host in the Resource Refs tab of the `deploytool`.

URL Connections

A Uniform Resource Locator (URL) specifies the location of a resource on the Web. The `HTMLReaderBean` class shows how to connect to a URL from within an enterprise bean.

The source code for this example is in the `j2eetutorial/examples/src/ejb/htmlreader` directory. To compile the code, go to the `j2eetutorial/examples` directory and type `ant htmlreader`. A sample `HTMLReaderApp.ear` file is in the `j2eetutorial/examples/ears` directory.

The `getContents` method of the `HTMLReaderBean` class returns a `String` that contains the contents of an HTML file. This method looks up the `java.net.URL` object associated with a coded name (`url/MyURL`), opens a connection to it, and then reads its contents from an `InputStream`. Before deploying the application, you must map the coded name (`url/MyURL`) to a JNDI name (a URL string). Here is the source code for the `getContents` method.

```
public StringBuffer getContents() throws HTTPResponseException
{

   Context context;
   URL url;
   StringBuffer buffer;
   String line;
   int responseCode;
   HttpURLConnection connection;
   InputStream input;
   BufferedReader dataInput;

   try {
      context = new InitialContext();
      url = (URL)context.lookup("java:comp/env/url/MyURL");
```

```
        connection = (HttpURLConnection)url.openConnection();
        responseCode = connection.getResponseCode();
    } catch (Exception ex) {
        throw new EJBException(ex.getMessage());
    }

    if (responseCode != HttpURLConnection.HTTP_OK) {
       throw new HTTPResponseException("HTTP response code: " +
          String.valueOf(responseCode));
    }

    try {
       buffer = new StringBuffer();
       input = connection.getInputStream();
       dataInput =
           new BufferedReader(new InputStreamReader(input));
       while ((line = dataInput.readLine()) != null) {
          buffer.append(line);
          buffer.append('\n');
       }
    } catch (Exception ex) {
        throw new EJBException(ex.getMessage());
    }
    return buffer;
}
```

Running the HTMLReaderEJB Example

Deploying the Application

1. In `deploytool`, open the `j2eetutorial/examples/ears/HTMLReaderApp.ear` file (File→Open).
2. Deploy the `HTMLReaderApp` application (Tools→Deploy). In the Introduction dialog box, make sure that you select the Return Client JAR checkbox.

Running the Client

1. In a terminal window, go to the `j2eetutorial/examples/ears` directory.
2. Set the `APPCPATH` environment variable to `HTMLReaderAppClient.jar`.
3. Type the following command on a single line:

```
runclient -client HTMLReaderApp.ear -name
  HTMLReaderClient -textauth
```

4. At the login prompts, enter `guest` for the user name and `guest123` for the password.
5. The client displays the contents of the `index.html` file that resides in the `public_html` directory of your J2EE SDK installation.

17

J2EE Connector Architecture

Dale Green and Beth Stearns

THE other chapters in this book are intended for business application developers, but this chapter is for advanced users such as system integrators and tools developers. The examples in this chapter demonstrate the J2EE Connector architecture by accessing relational databases. However, this technology is not a substitute for the JDBC API. Business application developers should continue to use the JDBC API to access relational databases.

The J2EE Connector architecture enables J2EE components such as enterprise beans to interact with enterprise information systems (EISs). EIS software includes various types of systems: enterprise resource planning (ERP), mainframe transaction processing, and non-relational databases, among others. The J2EE Connector architecture simplifies the integration of diverse EISs. Each EIS requires just one implementation of the J2EE Connector architecture. Because an implementation adheres to the J2EE Connector Specification, it is portable across all compliant J2EE servers.

In This Chapter

About Resource Adapters

A *resource adapter* is a J2EE component that implements the J2EE Connector architecture for a specific EIS. It is through the resource adapter that a J2EE application communicates with an EIS (see Figure 17–1).

Stored in a Resource Adapter Archive (RAR) file, a resource adapter may be deployed on any J2EE server, much like the EAR file of a J2EE application. A RAR file may be contained in an EAR file or it may exist as a separate file.

A resource adapter is analogous to a JDBC driver. Both provide a standard API through which an application can access a resource that is outside the J2EE server. For a resource adapter, the outside resource is an EIS; for a JDBC driver, it is a DBMS. Resource adapters and JDBC drivers are rarely created by application developers. In most cases, both types of software are built by vendors who sell products such as tools, servers, or integration software.

Resource Adapter Contracts

Figure 17–1 shows the two types of contracts implemented by a resource adapter. The application contract defines the API through which a J2EE component such as an enterprise bean accesses the EIS. This API is the only view that the component has of the EIS. The resource adapter itself and its system contracts are transparent to the J2EE component.

The system contracts link the resource adapter to important services—connection, transaction, and security—that are managed by the J2EE server.

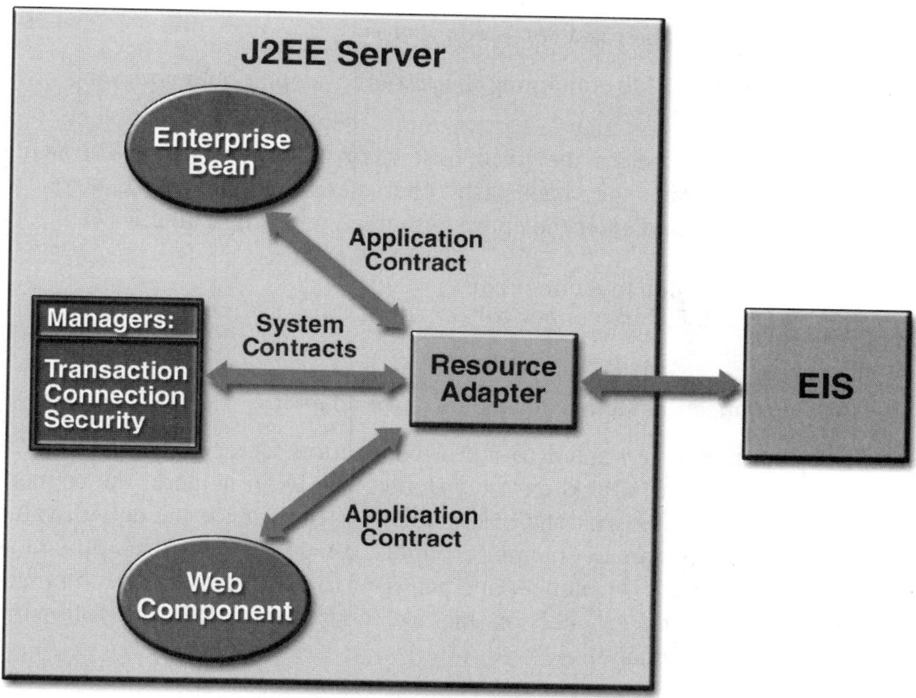

Figure 17–1 Accessing an EIS Through a Resource Adapter

The connection management contract supports connection pooling, a technique that enhances application performance and scalability. Connection pooling is transparent to the application, which simply obtains a connection to the EIS.

Because of the transaction management contract, a call to the EIS may be enclosed in an XA transaction. XA transactions are global—they may contain calls to multiple EISs, databases, and enterprise bean business methods. Although often appropriate, XA transactions are not mandatory. Instead, an application may use local transactions, which are managed by the individual EIS, or it may use no transactions at all.

To protect the information in an EIS, the security management contract provides these mechanisms: authentication, authorization, and secure communication between the J2EE server and the EIS.

Administering Resource Adapters

Installing a resource adapter is a two-step process:

1. Deploy the RAR file containing the resource adapter onto a server.

   The following command, for example, deploys a sample black box resource adapter onto the local host. (For Windows, in the following commands omit the backslash character, change `$J2EE_HOME` to `%J2EE_HOME%`, and enter the entire command on a single line.)

   ```
   deploytool -deployConnector \
      $J2EE_HOME/lib/connector/cciblackbox-tx.rar \
      localhost
   ```

2. Add a connection factory for the resource adapter.

   Suppose that you wanted to add a connection factory for the resource adapter in the `cciblackbox-tx.rar` file. The JNDI name of the connection factory will be `eis/MyCciBlackBoxTx`. To override the default value of the property named `ConnnectionURL`, you specify the URL of a database. (A *property* is a name-value pair used to configure a connection factory.) To add the connection factory, you might enter the following `j2eeadmin` command:

   ```
   j2eeadmin -addConnectorFactory \
      eis/MyCciBlackBoxTx \
      cciblackbox-tx.rar \
      -props \
      ConnectionURL=jdbc:oracle:thin:@myhost:1521:ACCTDB
   ```

For the full syntax of the `deploytool` and `j2eeadmin` commands, see Appendix B. These commands also list and remove resource adapters and connection factories.

To list the resource adapters that have been deployed, use the following command:

```
deploytool -listConnectors localhost
```

To list the connection factories that have been added, use the following command:

```
j2eeadmin -listConnectorFactory
```

To uninstall the resource adapter deployed in step 1, use the following command:

```
deploytool -undeployConnector cciblackbox-tx.rar localhost
```

To remove the connection factory added in step 2, use the following command:

```
j2eeadmin -removeConnectorFactory eis/MyCciBlackBoxTx
```

The Black Box Resource Adapters

The J2EE SDK includes several black box resource adapters for performing end-to-end and compatibility testing. The underlying EIS of these adapters is a relational DBMS. The client API is the JDBC 2.0 API and the `javax.sql.DataSource` interface. Underneath, the black box adapters use JDBC drivers to communicate with relational databases. For more information, see Configuring JDBC Drivers (page 371).

Note: Although the black box adapters use JDBC, resource adapters are not meant to replace JDBC for accessing relational databases. The black box adapters are for testing purposes only. Because they use JDBC, they can be plugged into existing tests that also use JDBC.

Transaction Levels

The black box resource adapters reside in the `$J2EE_HOME/lib/connector` (UNIX) or `%J2EE_HOME%\lib\connector` (Windows) subdirectory. Table 17–1 lists the black box RAR files and the different transaction levels that they support.

Table 17–1 Black Box Transaction Levels

File	Transaction Level
`blackbox-notx.rar`	`NO_TRANSACTION`
`blackbox-tx.rar`	`LOCAL_TRANSACTION`
`blackbox-xa.rar`	`XA_TRANSACTION`
`cciblackbox-tx.rar`	`LOCAL_TRANSACTION`

Table 17–1 Black Box Transaction Levels (Continued)

File	Transaction Level
cciblackbox-xa.rar	XA_TRANSACTION

For the XA_TRANSACTION level, the underlying JDBC driver must support the XA requirements as defined by the JDBC 2.0 API.

Properties

A resource adapter may contain properties, that is, name-value pairs containing information specific to the resource adapter and its underlying EIS. These properties are defined in the deployment descriptor of each black box RAR file. Because the EIS of a black box adapter is a relational database, the properties contain information required for connecting to a database. Table 17–2 lists the properties of the black box adapter files. Table 17–3 shows the default values for the black box properties.

Table 17–2 Black Box Properties

File	Property Name	Description
blackbox-notx.rar	ConnectionURL	URL of database
blackbox-tx.rar	ConnectionURL	URL of database
blackbox-xa.rar	XADataSourceName	JNDI name of XADataSource
cciblackbox-tx.rar	ConnectionURL	URL of database
cciblackbox-xa.rar	XADataSourceName	JNDI name of XADataSource

Table 17–3 Default Values for Black Box Properties

Property Name	Description
ConnectionURL	jdbc:cloudscape:rmi:CloudscapeDB;create=true
XADataSourceName	jdbc/XACloudscape_xa

To override a default property value, you set the value when adding a connection factory with the `j2eeadmin` command. See the section Administering Resource Adapters (page 368).

Configuring JDBC Drivers

If you are running the black box adapters against a Cloudscape database, you may skip this section. If you are using a database other than Cloudscape, you should perform the steps that follow.

The Non-XA Black Box Adapters

1. Set the JDBC driver class. Use the `j2eeadmin` tool with the `-addJdbcDriver` option and specify the driver class name. The syntax for this option is as follows:

   ```
   j2eeadmin -addJdbcDriver <class name>
   ```

2. Edit the `bin/userconfig.sh` (UNIX) or `bin\userconfig.bat` (Windows) file, setting the `J2EE_CLASSPATH` variable to the location of the JDBC driver classes.
3. Restart the J2EE server.

The XA Black Box Adapters

1. Set the `XADatasource` property. With the `j2eeadmin` tool and the `-addJdbcXADatasource` option, specify the JNDI name and class name for the `XADatasource` property. Optionally, you may specify the XA user name and password and you may override the default property value. The syntax follows:

   ```
   j2eeadmin -addJdbcXADatasource <jndi-name> <class-name>
      [<xa-user-name> <xa-password>]
      [-props (<name>=<value>)+]
   ```

   The preceding command results in two data sources. One is a `DataSource` object with the specified JNDI name from which the J2EE application gets a `Connection` instance. The other is an `XADatasource` object whose JNDI name is the *<jndi-name>* parameter appended with two underscores and `xa` (*<jndi-name>*`__xa`). Behind the scenes, the `DataSource` uses the `XADataSource` to create connections.

2. Restart the J2EE server.

Resource Adapter Tutorial

This tutorial shows how to deploy the black box resource adapter stored in the `blackbox-tx.rar` file. To test the resource adapter, you will modify the `examples/src/ejb/savingsaccount/SavingsAccountBean.java` file so that it accesses the Cloudscape database through the resource adapter. The `SavingsAccountBean.java` file is also used in another example; see Running the SavingsAccountEJB Example (page 97).

Setting Up

1. Start the J2EE server.

```
j2ee -verbose
```

2. Follow the instructions in the section Setting Up the Database (page 97).

Deploying the Resource Adapter

1. Deploy a black box resource adapter that is packaged in the `blackbox-tx.rar` file.

   UNIX

```
deploytool -deployConnector \
   $J2EE_HOME/lib/connector/blackbox-tx.rar localhost
```

   Windows (Enter the following and all subsequent Windows commands on a single line.)

```
deploytool -deployConnector
   %J2EE_HOME%\lib\connector\blackbox-tx.rar localhost
```

2. Add a connection factory for the resource adapter. The JNDI name for the connection factory is `eis/MyBlackBoxTx`.

   UNIX

```
j2eeadmin -addConnectorFactory \
   eis/MyBlackBoxTx blackbox-tx.rar
```

Windows

```
j2eeadmin -addConnectorFactory
   eis/MyBlackBoxTx blackbox-tx.rar
```

3. Verify that the resource adapter has been deployed.

```
deploytool -listConnectors localhost
```

The `deploytool` utility displays these lines:

```
Installed connector(s):
Connector Name: blackbox-tx.rar

Installed connection factories:
Connection Factory JNDI Name: eis/MyBlackBoxTx
```

Testing the Resource Adapter

1. If you are new to the J2EE SDK, you should first read the instructions in Chapter 2.
2. Locate the `SavingsAccountBean.java` source code, which resides in the `j2eetutorial/examples/src/ejb/savingsaccount` directory.
3. Edit the `SavingsAccountBean.java` source code, changing the value assigned to the `dbName` variable as follows:

```
private String dbName = "java:comp/env/MyEIS";
```

4. Compile the source code in the `savingsaccount` directory.
   a. Go to `j2eetutorial/examples`.
   b. Type `ant savingsaccount`.
5. Replace the new `SavingsAccountBean.class` file in the existing `SavingsAccountApp.ear` file.
   a. In the GUI `deploytool`, open the `j2eetutorial/examples/ears/SavingsAccountApp.ear` file.
   b. On the General tab of the `SavingsAccountJAR`, click Edit.
   c. In the Available Files field, locate the `j2eetutorial/examples/build/ejb/SavingsAccountBean.class` file.
   d. Drag and drop the `SavingsAccountBean.class` file from the Available Files field to the Contents field.

e. Click OK.

6. Change the resource factory reference.
   a. Select the Resource Refs tab of `SavingsAccountEJB`.
   b. Select the item whose Coded Name entry is `jdbc/SavingsAccountDB`.
   c. Click Delete.
   d. Click Add.
   e. Enter the values specified in Table 17–4.

Table 17–4 Resource References Values

Field	Value
Coded Name	`MyEIS`
Type	`javax.sql.DataSource`
Authentication	`Container`
JNDI Name	`eis/MyBlackBoxTx`

The `eis/MyBlackBoxTx` JNDI name matches the name of the connection factory that you added in step 2 of Deploying the Resource Adapter (page 372). The `MyEIS` value of the Coded Name field corresponds to this line in the `SavingsAccountBean.java` source code:

```
private String dbName = "java:comp/env/MyEIS";
```

Although it is included in the source code, the `java:comp/env/` subcontext is implicit in the Coded Name field of the Resource Refs tab.

7. Save the `SavingsAccountApp` application (File→Save).
8. Deploy the `SavingsAccountApp` application.
   a. Select Tools→Deploy.
   b. In the Introduction dialog box, select Return Client Jar.
   c. In the JNDI Names dialog box, verify that the JNDI names in Table 17–5 have been specified.
   d. To run the application, follow the directions in the section Running the Client (page 98).

Table 17–5 JNDI Names

Component or Reference Name	JNDI Name
`SavingsAccountEJB`	`MySavingsAccount`
`MyEIS`	`eis/MyBlackBoxTx`
`ejb/SimpleSavingsAccount`	`MySavingsAccount`

Common Client Interface

This section describes how components use the Connector architecture Common Client Interface (CCI) API and a resource adapter to access data from an EIS.

Overview of the CCI

Defined by the J2EE Connector Architecture specification, the CCI defines a set of interfaces and classes whose methods allow a client to perform typical data access operations. Our example `CoffeeEJB` session bean includes methods that illustrate how to use the CCI, in particular, the following CCI interfaces and classes:

- `ConnectionFactory`: Provides an application component with a `Connection` instance to an EIS.
- `Connection`: Represents the connection to the underlying EIS.
- `ConnectionSpec`: Provides a means for an application component to pass connection-request-specific properties to the `ConnectionFactory` when making a connection request.
- `Interaction`: Provides a means for an application component to execute EIS functions, such as database stored procedures.
- `InteractionSpec`: Holds properties pertaining to an application component's interaction with an EIS.
- `Record`: The superclass for the different kinds of record instances. Record instances may be `MappedRecord`, `IndexedRecord`, or `ResultSet` instances, which all inherit from the `Record` interface.

- `RecordFactory`: Provides an application component with a `Record` instance.
- `IndexedRecord`: Represents an ordered collection of `Record` instances based on the `java.util.List` interface.

A client or application component that uses the CCI to interact with an underlying EIS does so in a prescribed manner. The component must establish a connection to the EIS's resource manager, and it does so using the `ConnectionFactory`. The `Connection` object represents the actual connection to the EIS and is used for subsequent interactions with the EIS.

The component performs its interactions with the EIS, such as accessing data from a specific table, using an `Interaction` object. The application component defines the `Interaction` object using an `InteractionSpec` object. When the application component reads data from the EIS (such as from database tables) or writes to those tables, it does so using a particular type of `Record` instance, either a `MappedRecord`, `IndexedRecord`, or `ResultSet` instance. Just as the `ConnectionFactory` creates `Connection` instances, a `RecordFactory` creates `Record` instances.

Our example shows how a session bean uses a resource adapter to add and read records in a relational database. The example shows how to invoke stored procedures, which are business logic functions stored in a database and specific to an enterprise's operation. Stored procedures consist of SQL code to perform operations related to the business needs of an organization. They are kept in the database and can be invoked when needed, just as you might invoke a Java method. In addition to showing how to use the CCI to invoke stored procedures, we'll also explain how to pass parameters to stored procedures and how to map the parameter data types from SQL to those of the Java programming language.

Programming with the CCI

The code for the following example is in the `examples/src/connector/cci` directory.

To illustrate how to use a CCI resource adapter, we've written a session bean and a client of that bean. These pieces of code illustrate how clients invoke the different CCI methods that resource adapters built on CCI might make available. Our example uses the two sample CCI-specific resource adapters: `cciblackbox_tx.rar` and `cciblackbox_xa.rar`.

The `Coffee` session bean is much like any other session bean. It has a home interface (`CoffeeHome`), a remote interface (`Coffee`), and an implementation class (`CoffeeEJB`). To keep things simple, we've called the client `CoffeeClient`.

Let's start with the session bean interfaces and classes. The home interface, `CoffeeHome`, is like any other session bean home interface. It extends `EJBHome` and defines a `create` method to return a reference to the `Coffee` remote interface.

The `Coffee` remote interface defines the bean's two methods that may be called by a client.

```
public void insertCoffee(String name, int quantity)
throws RemoteException;
public int getCoffeeCount() throws RemoteException;
```

Now let's examine the `CoffeeEJB` session bean implementation class to see how it uses the CCI. To begin with, notice that `CoffeeEJB` imports the `javax.resource` CCI interfaces and classes, along with the `javax.resource.ResourceException` and the sample `cciblackbox` classes.

```
import javax.resource.cci.*;
import javax.resource.ResourceException;
import com.sun.connector.cciblackbox.*;
```

Prior to obtaining a database connection, the session bean does some set–up work in its `setSessionContext` method. (See the following code example.) Specifically, the `setSessionContext` method sets the user and password values, and instantiates a `ConnectionFactory`. These values and objects remain available to the other session bean methods. (In this and subsequent code examples, the numbers in the left margin correspond to the explanation that follows the code.)

```
    public void setSessionContext(SessionContext sc) {
        try {
            this.sc = sc;
1           Context ic = new InitialContext();
2           user = (String) ic.lookup("java:comp/env/user");
            password = (String) ic.lookup
               ("java:comp/env/password");
3           cf = (ConnectionFactory) ic.lookup
               ("java:comp/env/CCIEIS");
```

```
        } catch (NamingException ex) {
            ex.printStackTrace();
        }
    }
```

1. Establish a JNDI `InitialContext`.
2. Use the JNDI `InitialContext.lookup` method to find the user and password values.
3. Use the `lookup` method to locate the `ConnectionFactory` for the CCI black box resource adapter and obtain a reference to it.

`CoffeeEJB` uses its private method `getCCIConnection` to establish a connection to the underlying resource manager or database. A client of the `Coffee` session bean cannot invoke this method directly. Rather, the session bean uses this method internally to establish a connection to the database. The following code uses the CCI to establish a database connection.

```
    private Connection getCCIConnection() {
        Connection con = null;
        try {
1           ConnectionSpec spec =
                new CciConnectionSpec(user, password);
2           con = cf.getConnection(spec);
        } catch (ResourceException ex) {
            ex.printStackTrace();
        }
        return con;
    }
```

1. Instantiate a new `CciConnectionSpec` object with the user and password values obtained by the `setSessionContext` method. The `CciConnectionSpec` class is the implementation of the `ConnectionSpec` interface.
2. Call the `ConnectionFactory.getConnection` method to obtain a connection to the database. (The reference to the `ConnectionFactory` was obtained in the `setSessionContext` method.) Use the `CciConnectionSpec` object to pass the required properties to the `ConnectionFactory`. The `getConnection` method returns a `Connection` object.

The `CoffeeEJB` bean also includes a private method, `closeCCIConnection`, to close a connection. The method invokes the `Connection` object's `close` method from within a `try/catch` block. Like the `getCCIConnection` method, this is a private method intended to be called from within the session bean.

```
    private void closeCCIConnection(Connection con) {
        try {
            con.close();
        } catch (ResourceException ex) {
            ex.printStackTrace();
        }
    }
```

Database Stored Procedures

The sample CCI black box adapters call database stored procedures. It is important to understand stored procedures before delving into how to read or write data using the sample CCI black box adapters. The methods of these sample CCI adapters do not actually read data from a database or update database data. Instead, these sample CCI adapters enable you to invoke database stored procedures, and it is the stored procedures that actually read or write to the database.

A *stored procedure* is a business logic method or function that is stored in a database and is specific for the enterprise's business. Typically, stored procedures consist of SQL code, though in certain cases (such as with Cloudscape) they may contain code written in the Java programming language. Stored procedures perform operations related to the business needs of an organization. They are kept in the database, and applications can invoke them when needed.

Stored procedures are typically SQL statements. Our example calls two stored procedures: `COUNTCOFFEE` and `INSERTCOFFEE`. The `COUNTCOFFEE` procedure merely counts the number of coffee records in the `Coffee` table, as follows:

```
SELECT COUNT(*) FROM COFFEE
```

The `INSERTCOFFFEE` procedure adds a record with two values, passed to the procedure as parameters, to the same `Coffee` table, as follows:

```
INSERT INTO COFFEE VALUES (?,?)
```

Mapping to Stored Procedure Parameters

When you invoke a stored procedure from your application component, you may have to pass argument values to the procedure. For example, when you invoke the `INSERTCOFFEE` procedure, you pass it two values for the `Coffee` record elements. Likewise, you must be prepared to receive values that a stored procedure returns.

The stored procedure, in turn, passes its set of parameters to the database management system (DBMS) to carry out its operation and may receive values back from the DBMS. Database stored procedures specify, for each of their parameters, the SQL type of the parameter value and the mode of the parameter. Mode can be input (IN), output (OUT), or both input and output (INOUT). An input parameter only passes data in to the DBMS, and an output parameter only receives data back from the DBMS. An INOUT parameter accepts both input and output data.

When you use the CCI execute method to invoke a database stored procedure you also create an instance of an InputRecord, provided that you're passing a parameter to the stored procedure and that the stored procedure you're executing returns data (possibly an OutputRecord instance). The InputRecord and OutputRecord are instances of the supported Record types: IndexedRecord, MappedRecord, or ResultSet. In our example, we instantiate an InputRecord and an OutputRecord that are both IndexedRecord instances.

Note: The CCI black box adapters only support IndexedRecord types.

The InputRecord maps the IN and INOUT parameters for the stored procedure, and the OutputRecord maps the OUT and INOUT parameters. Each element of an input or output record corresponds to a stored procedure parameter. That is, there is an entry in the InputRecord for each IN and INOUT parameter declared in the stored procedure. Not only does the InputRecord have the same number of elements as the procedure's input parameters, but they also are declared in the same order as in the procedure's parameter list. The same holds true for the OutputRecord, though its list of elements matches only the OUT and INOUT parameters. For example, suppose you have a stored procedure X that declares three parameters. The first parameter is an IN parameter, the second is an OUT parameter, and the third is an INOUT parameter. Figure 17–2 shows how the elements of an InputRecord and an OutputRecord map to this stored procedure.

When you use the CCI black box adapter, you designate the parameter type and mode in the same way, though the underlying Oracle or Cloudscape DBMS declares the mode differently. Oracle designates the parameter's mode in the stored procedure declaration, along with the parameter's type declaration. For example, an Oracle INSERTCOFFEE procedure declares its two IN parameters as follows:

```
procedure INSERTCOFFEE (name IN VARCHAR2, qty IN INTEGER)
```

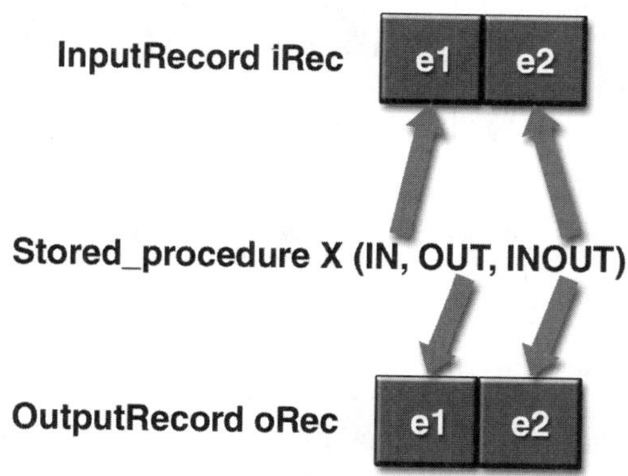

Figure 17–2 Mapping Stored Procedure Parameters to CCI Record Elements

An Oracle `COUNTCOFFEE` procedure declares its parameter `N` as an `OUT` parameter:

```
procedure COUNTCOFFEE (N OUT INTEGER)
```

Cloudscape, which declares a stored procedure as a method signature in the Java programming language, indicates an `IN` parameter using a single value, and an `INOUT` parameter using an array. The method's return value is the `OUT` parameter. For example, Cloudscape declares the `IN` parameters (`name` and `qty`) for `insertCoffee` and the `OUT` parameter (the method's return value) for `countCoffee` as follows:

```
public static void insertCoffee(String name, int qty)
public int countCoffee()
```

If `qty` were an `INOUT` parameter, then Cloudscape would declares it as

```
public static void insertCoffee(String name, int[] qty)
```

Oracle would declare it as

```
procedure INSERTCOFFEE (name IN VARCHAR2, qty INOUT INTEGER)
```

You must also map the SQL type of each value to its corresponding Java type. Thus, if the SQL type is an integer, then the `InputRecord` or `OutputRecord` element must be defined as an `Integer` object. If the SQL type is a `VARCHAR`, then the Java type must be a `String` object. Thus, when you add the element to the

Record, you declare it to be an object of the proper type. For example, add an integer and a string element to an InputRecord as follows:

```
iRec.add (new Integer (intval));
iRec.add (new String ("Mocha Java"));
```

Note: The JDBC Specification defines the type mapping of SQL and the Java programming language.

Reading Database Records

The getCoffeeCount method of CoffeeEJB illustrates how to use the CCI to read records from a database table. This method does not directly read the database records itself; instead, it invokes a procedure stored in the database called COUNTCOFFEE. It is the stored procedure that actually reads the records in the database table.

The CCI provides interfaces for three types of records: IndexedRecord, MappedRecord, and ResultSet. These three record types inherit from the base interface, Record. They differ only in how they map the record elements within the record. Our example uses IndexedRecord, which is the only record type currently supported. IndexedRecord holds its record elements in an ordered, indexed collection based on java.util.List. As a result, we use an Iterator object to access the individual elements in the list.

Let's begin by looking at how the getCoffeeCount method uses the CCI to invoke a database stored procedure. Again, note that the numbers in the margin to the left of the code correspond to the explanation after the code example.

```
     public int getCoffeeCount() {
         int count = -1;
         try {
1            Connection con = getCCIConnection();
2            Interaction ix = con.createInteraction();
3            CciInteractionSpec iSpec =
                new CciInteractionSpec();
4            iSpec.setSchema(user);
             iSpec.setCatalog(null);
             iSpec.setFunctionName("COUNTCOFFEE");
5            RecordFactory rf = cf.getRecordFactory();
6            IndexedRecord iRec =
                rf.createIndexedRecord("InputRecord");
7            Record oRec = ix.execute(iSpec, iRec);
8            Iterator iterator =
```

```
                ((IndexedRecord)oRec).iterator();
9           while(iterator.hasNext()) {
                Object obj = iterator.next();
                if(obj instanceof Integer) {
                    count = ((Integer)obj).intValue();
                }
                else if(obj instanceof BigDecimal) {
                    count = ((BigDecimal)obj).intValue();
                }
            }
10          closeCCIConnection(con);
        }catch(ResourceException ex) {
            ex.printStackTrace();
        }
        return count;
    }
```

1. Obtain a connection to the database.
2. Create a new `Interaction` instance. The `getCoffeeCount` method creates a new `Interaction` instance because it is this object that enables the session bean to execute EIS functions such as invoking stored procedures.
3. Instantiate a `CciInteractionSpec` object. The session bean must pass certain properties to the `Interaction` object, such as schema name, catalog name, and the name of the stored procedure. It does this by instantiating a `CciInteractionSpec` object. The `CciInteractionSpec` is the implementation class for the `InteractionSpec` interface, and it holds properties required by the `Interaction` object to interact with an EIS instance. (Note that our example uses a Cloudscape database, which does not require a catalog name.)
4. Set values for the `CciInteractionSpec` instance's fields. The session bean uses the `CciInteractionSpec` methods `setSchema`, `setCatalog`, and `setFunctionName` to set the required values into the instance's fields. Our example passes `COUNTCOFFEE` to `setFunctionName` because this is the name of the stored procedure it intends to invoke.
5. The `getCoffeeCount` method uses the `ConnectionFactory` to obtain a reference to a `RecordFactory` so that it can create an `IndexedRecord` instance. We obtain an `IndexedRecord` (or a `MappedRecord` or a `ResultSet`) using a `RecordFactory`.
6. Invoke the `createIndexedRecord` method of `RecordFactory`. This method creates a new `IndexedRecord` using the name `InputRecord`, which is passed to it as an argument.

7. The `getCoffeeCount` method has completed the required set-up work and can invoke the stored procedure `COUNTCOFFEE`. It does this using the `Interaction` instance's `execute` method. Notice that it passes two objects to the `execute` method: the `InteractionSpec` object, whose properties reference the `COUNTCOFFEE` stored procedure, and the `IndexedRecord` object, which the method expects to be an input `Record`. The `execute` method returns an output `Record` object.
8. The `getCoffeeCount` method uses an `Iterator` to retrieve the individual elements from the returned `IndexedRecord`. It casts the output `Record` object to an `IndexedRecord`. `IndexedRecord` contains an iterator method that it inherits from `java.util.List`.
9. Retrieve each element in the returned record object using the `iterator.hasNext` method. Each extracted element is an `Object`, and the bean evaluates whether it is an integer or decimal value and processes it accordingly.
10. Close the connection to the database.

Inserting Database Records

The `CoffeeEJB` session bean implements the `insertCoffee` method to add new records into the `Coffee` database table. This method invokes the `INSERTCOFFEE` stored procedure, which inserts a record with the values (`name` and `qty`) passed to it as arguments.

The `insertCoffee` method shown here illustrates how to use the CCI to invoke a stored procedure that expects to be passed argument values. This example shows the code for the `insertCoffee` method and is followed by an explanation.

```
    public void insertCoffee(String name, int qty) {
        try {
1           Connection con = getCCIConnection();
2           Interaction ix = con.createInteraction();
3           CciInteractionSpec iSpec =
               new CciInteractionSpec();
4           iSpec.setFunctionName("INSERTCOFFEE");
            iSpec.setSchema(user);
            iSpec.setCatalog(null);
5           RecordFactory rf = cf.getRecordFactory();
6           IndexedRecord iRec =
               rf.createIndexedRecord("InputRecord");
7           boolean flag = iRec.add(name);
            flag = iRec.add(new Integer(qty));
8           ix.execute(iSpec, iRec);
9           closeCCIConnection(con);
```

```
        }catch(ResourceException ex) {
            ex.printStackTrace();
        }
    }
```

1. Establish a connection to the database.
2. Create a new Interaction instance for the connection so that the bean can execute the database's stored procedures.
3. Instantiate a CciInteractionSpec object so that the bean can pass the necessary properties—schema name, catalog name, and stored procedure name—to the Interaction object. The CciInteractionSpec class implements the InteractionSpec interface and holds properties that the Interaction object requires to communicate with the database instance.
4. Set the required values into the new CciInteractionSpec instance's fields, using the instance's setSchema, setCatalog, and setFunctionName methods. Our example passes INSERTCOFFEE to setFunctionName, and user to setSchema.
5. Obtain a reference to a RecordFactory using the ConnectionFactory object's getRecordFactory method.
6. Invoke the RecordFactory object's createIndexedRecord method to create a new IndexedRecord with the name InputRecord.
7. Use the IndexedRecord add method to set the values for the two elements in the new record. Call the add method once for each element. Our example sets the first record element to the name value and the second element to the qty value. Notice that qty is set to an Integer object when it is passed to the add method. The CoffeeEJB session bean is now ready to add the new record to the database.
8. Call the Interaction instance's execute method to invoke the stored procedure INSERTCOFFEE. Just as we did when invoking the COUNTCOFFEE procedure, we pass two objects to the execute method: the InteractionSpec object with the correctly set properties for the INSERTCOFFEE stored procedure, and the IndexedRecord object representing an input Record. The execute method is not expected to return anything in this case.
9. Close the connection to the database.

Writing a CCI Client

A client application that relies on a CCI resource adapter is very much like any other J2EE client that uses enterprise bean methods. Our CoffeeClient application uses the methods of the CoffeeEJB session bean to access the Coffee table in the underlying database. `CoffeeClient` invokes the `Coffee.getCoffeeCount` method to read the `Coffee` table records and invokes `Coffee.insertCoffee` to add records to the table.

CCI Tutorial

This tutorial shows how to deploy and test the sample CCI black box adapter with the code described in the preceding sections. This code has been packaged into a J2EE application EAR file named `CoffeeApp.ear`, which is located in the `j2eetutorial/examples/ears` directory. The source code is in `j2eetutorial/examples/src/connector/cci`. To compile the source code, go to the `j2eetutorial/examples` directory and type `ant cci`.

Deploying the Resource Adapter

1. Use the `deploytool` utility to deploy the CCI black box resource adapter. Specify the name of the resource adapter's RAR file (`cciblackbox-tx.rar`), plus the name of the server (`localhost`).

   UNIX

   ```
   deploytool -deployConnector \
   $J2EE_HOME/lib/connector/cciblackbox-tx.rar localhost
   ```

   Windows (Note that this command and all subsequent Windows commands must be entered on a single line.)

   ```
   deploytool -deployConnector
   %J2EE_HOME%\lib\connector\cciblackbox-tx.rar localhost
   ```

2. Next, add a connection factory for the deployed CCI adapter. The connection factory supplies a data source connection for the adapter. Use `j2eeadmin` to create the connection factory, specifying the adapter's JNDI name plus the server name. Here, we add a connection factory for our CCI adapter whose JNDI name is `eis/CciBlackBoxTx` on the server `localhost`.

   UNIX

   ```
   j2eeadmin -addConnectorFactory \
     eis/CciBlackBoxTx cciblackbox-tx.rar
   ```

Windows

```
j2eeadmin -addConnectorFactory
   eis/CciBlackBoxTx cciblackbox-tx.rar
```

3. Verify that the resource adapter has been deployed.

```
deploytool -listConnectors localhost
```

The `deploytool` utility displays these lines:

```
Installed connector(s):
   Connector Name: cciblackbox-tx.rar
Installed connection factories:
   Connection Factory JNDI name: eis/CciBlackBoxTx
```

Setting Up the Database

For Cloudscape, use the following procedure.

1. Create the stored procedure.
   a. To compile the stored procedure, go to the `j2eetutorial/examples` directory and type `ant procs`. This command will put the `Procs.class` file in the `j2eetutorial/examples/build/connector/procs` directory.
   b. Locate the `bin/userconfig.sh` (UNIX) or `bin\userconfig.bat` (Windows) file in your J2EE SDK installation. Edit the file so that the `J2EE_CLASSPATH` variable points to the directory that contains the `Procs.class` file.
   c. Restart the Cloudscape server.
   d. Go to the `j2eetutorial/examples` directory and type `ant create-procs-alias`. This command creates aliases for the methods in `Procs.class`. Cloudscape uses method aliases to simulate stored procedures.
2. To create the `Coffee` table, go to the j2eetutorial/`examples` directory and type `ant create-coffee-table`.

For Oracle, use the following procedure.

1. Start the database server.
2. Run the `j2eetutorial/examples/sql/oracle.sql` script, which creates both the stored procedures and the `Coffee` table.

Browsing the CoffeeApp Application

1. In the GUI `deploytool`, open the `j2eetutorial/examples/ears/CoffeeApp.ear` file.
2. Select the Resource Refs tab of the `CoffeeBean` component and note the following (Figure 17–3).
   - The Coded Name of `CCIEIS` corresponds to the following line in the `CoffeeEJB.java` source code:

     ```
     cf = (ConnectionFactory)
        ic.lookup("java:comp/env/CCIEIS");
     ```

   - The JNDI Name of `eis/CciBlackBoxTx` matches the name of the connection factory you added in step 2 of Deploying the Resource Adapter (page 386).
   - The User Name and Password fields contain dummy values (XXX), since this EAR file was tested with a Cloudscape database. For other types of databases, you may be required to insert actual values in these fields. For these databases, you should also insert actual values in the Env. Entries tab of `CoffeeBean`.
3. Select the JNDI Names tab of `CoffeeApp` (Figure 17–4). Note that the CCIEIS value in the Reference Name field has been mapped to the `eis/CciBlackBoxTx` value in the JNDI Name field.

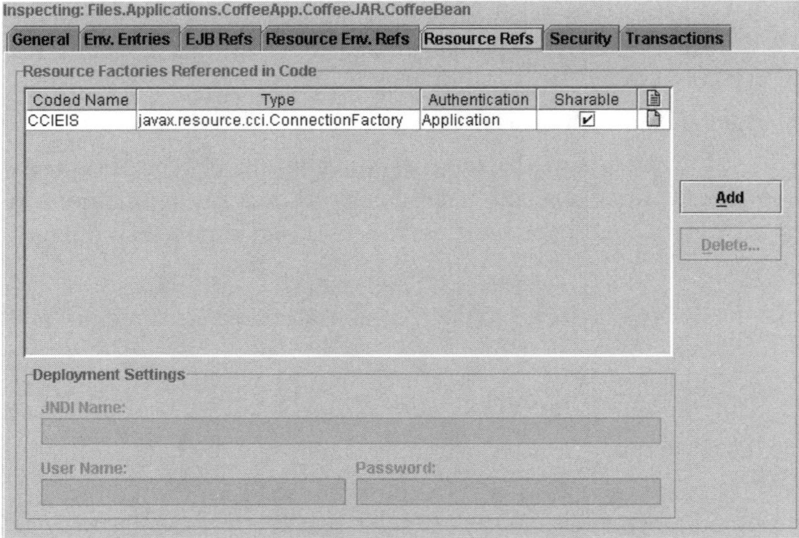

Figure 17–3 Resource Refs Tab of the `CoffeeApp` Application

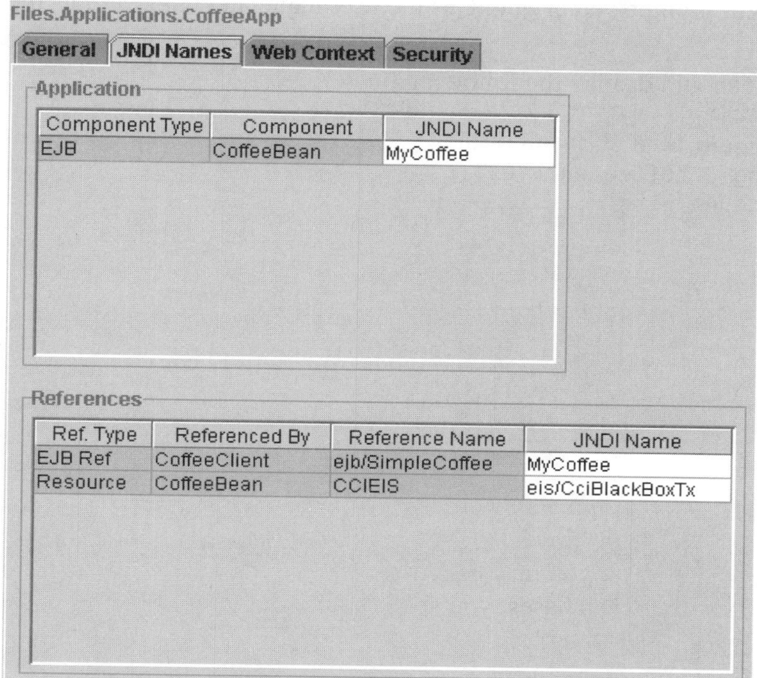

Figure 17–4 JNDI Tab of the `CoffeeApp` Application

Deploying and Running the CoffeeApp Application

1. Deploy the application.
   a. In the GUI `deploytool`, select Tools→Deploy.
   b. In the Introduction dialog box, select Return Client Jar.
2. In a terminal window, go to the `j2eetutorial/examples/ears` directory.
3. Set the `APPCPATH` environment variable to the name of the stub client JAR file: `CoffeeAppClient.jar`.
4. Run the client by typing the following on one line.

```
runclient -client CoffeeApp.ear -name CoffeeClient
   -textauth
```

5. At the login prompts, enter `guest` as the user name and `guest123` as the password.
6. The client should display the following lines:

```
Coffee count = 0
Inserting 3 coffee entries...
Coffee count = 3
```

18

The Duke's Bank Application

Stephanie Bodoff, Dale Green, Eric Jendrock, and Monica Pawlan

THIS chapter describes the Duke's Bank application, an online banking application. Duke's Bank has two clients: a J2EE application client used by administrators to manage customers and accounts, and a Web client used by customers to access account histories and perform transactions. The clients access the customer, account, and transaction information maintained in a database through enterprise beans. The Duke's Bank application demonstrates how all the component technologies—enterprise beans, J2EE application clients, and Web components—presented in this tutorial are put together to provide a simple but functional application.

Figure 18–1 gives a high-level view of how the components interact. This chapter looks at each of the component types in detail and concludes with a discussion of how to build, deploy, and run the application.

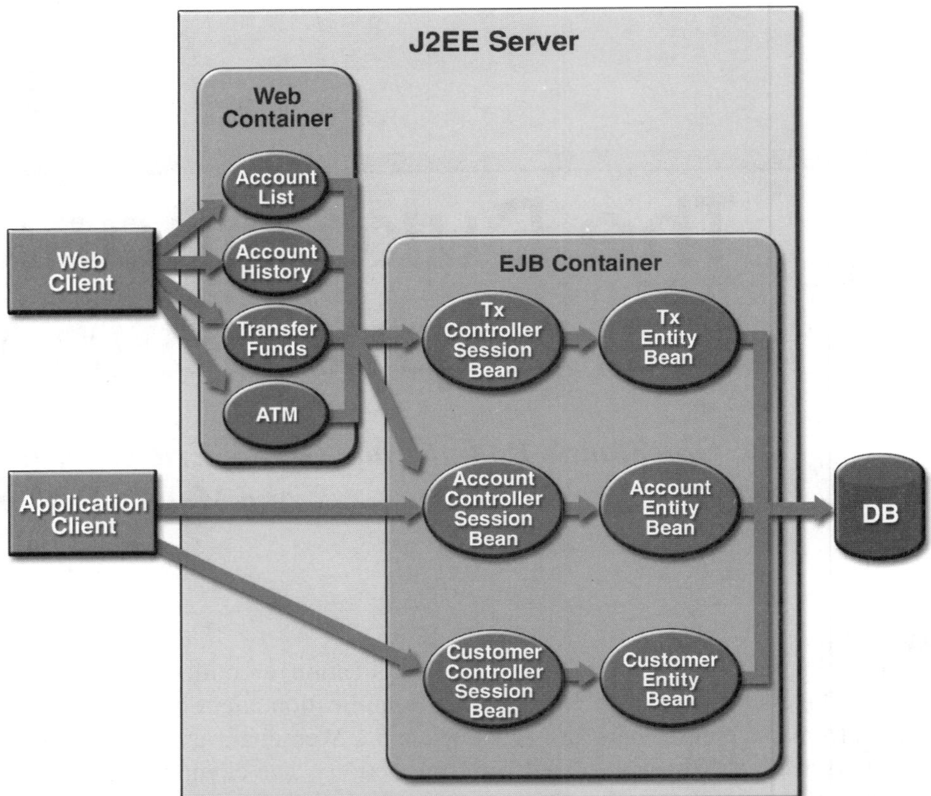

Figure 18–1 Duke's Bank Application

In This Chapter

Enterprise Beans

Figure 18–2 takes a closer look at the access paths between the clients, enterprise beans, and database tables. As you can see, the end-user clients (Web and J2EE application clients) access only the session beans. Within the enterprise bean tier, the session beans are clients of the entity beans. On the back end of the application, the entity beans access the database tables that store the entity states.

The source code for these enterprise beans is in the `j2eetutorial/bank/src/com/sun/ebank/ejb` subdirectory.

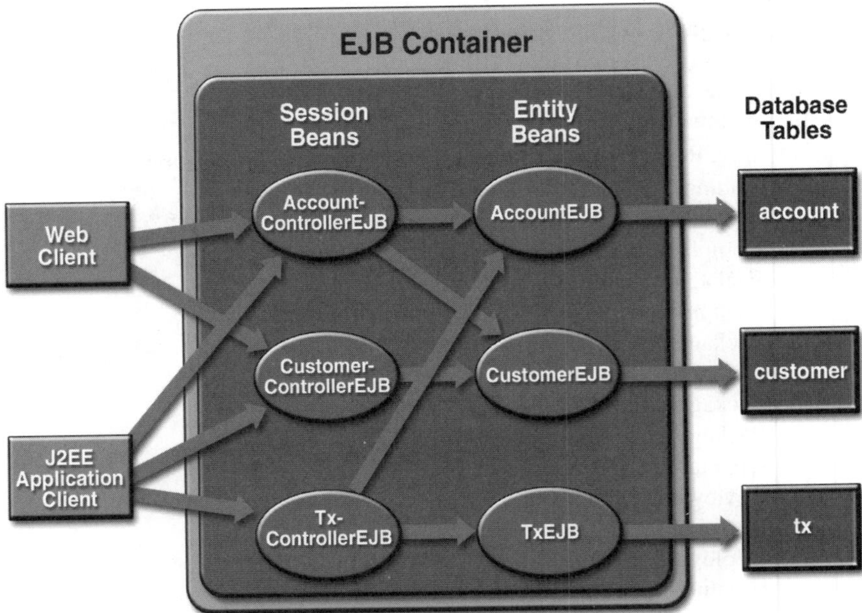

Figure 18–2 Enterprise Beans in the Duke's Bank Application

Session Beans

The Duke's Bank application has three session beans: `AccountControllerEJB`, `CustomerControllerEJB`, and `TxControllerEJB`. (`Tx` stands for a business transaction, such as transferring funds.) These session beans provide a client's view of the application's business logic. Hidden from the clients are the server-side routines that implement the business logic, access databases, manage relationships, and perform error checking.

AccountControllerEJB

The business methods of the `AccountControllerEJB` session bean perform tasks that fall into the following categories: creating and removing entity beans, managing the account-customer relationship, and getting the account information.

The following methods create and remove entity beans:

- `createAccount`
- `removeAccount`

These methods of the AccountControllerEJB session bean call the create and remove methods of the AccountEJB entity bean. The createAccount and removeAccount methods throw application exceptions to indicate invalid method arguments. The createAccount method throws an IllegalAccountTypeException if the type argument is neither Checking, Savings, Credit, nor Money Market. The createAccount method also verifies that the specified customer exists by invoking the findByPrimaryKey method of the CustomerEJB entity bean. If the result of this verification is false, the createAccount method throws a CustomerNotFoundException.

The following methods manage the account-customer relationship:

- addCustomerToAccount
- removeCustomerFromAccount

The AccountEJB and CustomerEJB entity beans have a many-to-many relationship. A bank account may be jointly held by more than one customer, and a customer may have multiple accounts. Because the entity beans use bean-managed persistence, there are several ways to manage this relationship. For more information, see Mapping Table Relationships for Bean-Managed Persistence (page 99).

In the Duke's Bank application, the addCustomerToAccount and removeCustomerFromAccount methods of the AccountControllerEJB session bean manage the account-customer relationship. The addCustomerToAccount method, for example, starts by verifying that the customer exists. To create the relationship, the addCustomerToAccount method inserts a row into the customer_account_xref database table. In this cross-reference table, each row contains the customerId and accountId of the related entities. To remove a relationship, the removeCustomerFromAccount method deletes a row from the customer_account_xref table. If a client calls the removeAccount method, then all rows for the specified accountId are removed from the customer_account_xref table.

The following methods get the account information:

- getAccountsOfCustomer
- getDetails

The AccountControllerEJB session bean has two get methods. The getAccountsOfCustomer method returns all of the accounts of a given customer by invoking the findByCustomer method of the AccountEJB entity bean. Instead of implementing a get method for every instance variable, the AccountControllerEJB has a getDetails method that returns an object (AccountDetails) that encapsulates the entire state of an AccountEJB bean. Because it can invoke a single method to retrieve the entire state, the client avoids the overhead associated with multiple remote calls.

CustomerControllerEJB

Because it is the `AccountControllerEJB` bean that manages the customer-account relationship, `CustomerControllerEJB` is the simpler of these two session beans. A client creates a `CustomerEJB` entity bean by invoking the `createCustomer` method of the `CustomerControllerEJB` session bean. To remove a customer, the client calls the `removeCustomer` method, which not only invokes the `remove` method of `CustomerEJB`, but also deletes from the `customer_account_xref` table all rows that identify the customer.

The `CustomerControllerEJB` session bean has two methods that return multiple customers: `getCustomersOfAccount` and `getCustomersOfLastName`. These methods call the corresponding finder methods—`findbyAccountId` and `findByLastName`—of `CustomerEJB`.

TxControllerEJB

The `TxControllerEJB` session bean handles bank transactions. In addition to its `get` methods, `getTxsOfAccount` and `getDetails`, the `TxControllerEJB` bean has several methods that change the balances of the bank accounts:

- `withdraw`
- `deposit`
- `makeCharge`
- `makePayment`
- `transferFunds`

These methods access an `AccountEJB` entity bean to verify the account type and to set the new balance. The `withdraw` and `deposit` methods are for non-credit accounts, whereas the `makeCharge` and `makePayment` methods are for credit accounts. If the `type` method argument does not match the account, these methods throw an `IllegalAccountTypeException`. If a withdrawal were to result in a negative balance, then the `withdraw` method throws an `InsufficientFundsException`. If a credit charge attempts to exceed the account's credit line, the `makeCharge` method throws an `InsufficientCreditException`.

The `transferFunds` method also checks the account type and new balance; if necessary, it throws the same exceptions as the `withdraw` and `makeCharge` methods. The `transferFunds` method subtracts from the balance of one `AccountEJB` instance and adds the same amount to another instance. Because both of these steps must complete, the `transferFunds` method has a `Required` transaction attribute. If either step fails, the entire operation is rolled back and the balances remain unchanged.

Entity Beans

For each business entity represented in our simple bank, the Duke's Bank application has a matching entity bean:

- `AccountEJB`
- `CustomerEJB`
- `TxEJB`

The purpose of these beans is to provide an object view of these database tables: `account`, `customer`, and `tx`. For each column in a table, the corresponding entity bean has an instance variable. Because they use bean-managed persistence, the entity beans contain the SQL statements that access the tables. For example, the `create` method of the `CustomerEJB` entity bean calls the SQL `INSERT` command.

Unlike the session beans, the entity beans do not validate method parameters (except for the primary key parameter of `ejbCreate`). During the design phase, we decided that the session beans would check the parameters and throw the application exceptions, such as `CustomerNotInAccountException` and `IllegalAccountTypeException`. Consequently, if some other application were to include these entity beans, its session beans would also have to validate the method parameters.

Helper Classes

The EJB JAR files include several helper classes that are used by the enterprise beans. The source code for these classes is in the `j2eetutorial/bank/src/com/sun/ebank/util` subdirectory. Table 18–1 briefly describes the helper classes.

Table 18–1 Helper Classes for the Application's Enterprise Beans

Class Name	Description
AccountDetails	Encapsulates the state of an AccountEJB instance. Returned by the getDetails methods of AccountControllerEJB and AccountEJB.
CodedNames	Defines the strings that are the logical names in the calls of the lookup method. (For example: java:comp/env/ejb/account). The EJB-Getter class references these strings.
CustomerDetails	Encapsulates the state of a CustomerEJB instance. Returned by the getDetails methods of CustomerControllerEJB and Customer-EJB.
DBHelper	Provides methods that generate the next primary keys (for example, getNextAccountId).
Debug	Has simple methods for printing a debugging message from an enterprise bean. These messages appear on the stdout of the J2EE server if it's run with the -verbose option.
DomainUtil	Contains validation methods: getAccountTypes, checkAccount-Type, and isCreditAccount.
EJBGetter	Has methods that locate (by invoking lookup) and return home interfaces (for example, getAccountControllerHome).
TxDetails	Encapsulates the state of a TxEJB instance. Returned by the getDe-tails methods of TxControllerEJB and TxEJB.

Database Tables

A database table of the Duke's Bank application may be categorized by its purpose: representing business entities and holding the next primary key.

Tables Representing Business Entities

Figure 18–3 shows relationships between the database tables. The customer and account tables have a many-to-many relationship: A customer may have several bank accounts, and each account may be owned by more than one customer. This many-to-many relationship is implemented by the cross–reference table named customer_account_xref. The account and tx tables have a one-to-many relationship: A bank account may have many transactions, but each transaction refers to a single account.

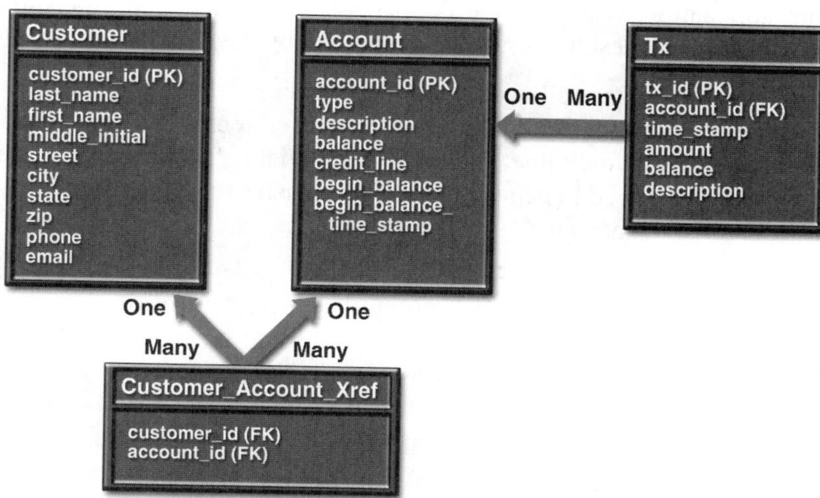

Figure 18–3 Database Tables in the Duke's Bank Application

Figure 18–3 makes use of several abbreviations. PK stands for primary key, the value that uniquely identifies a row in a table. FK is an abbreviation for foreign key, which is the primary key of the related table. Tx is short for transaction, such as a deposit or withdrawal.

Tables That Hold the Next Primary Key

These tables have the following names:

- next_account_id
- next_customer_id
- next_tx_id

Each of these tables has a single column named id. The value of id is the next primary key that is passed to the create method of an entity bean. For example, before it creates a new AccountEJB entity bean, the AccountControllerEJB session bean must obtain a unique key by invoking the getNextAccountId method of the DBHelper class. The getNextAccountId method reads the id from the next_account_id table, increments the id value in the table, and then returns the id.

Protecting the Enterprise Beans

In the J2EE platform, you can protect an enterprise bean by specifying the security roles that can access its methods (see EJB-Tier Security, page 340). In the Duke's Bank application, two roles are defined—`BankCustomer` and `BankAdmin`—because two categories of operations are defined by the enterprise beans.

A user in the `BankAdmin` role is allowed to perform administrative functions: creating or removing an account, adding a customer to or removing a customer from an account, setting a credit line, and setting an initial balance. A user in the `BankCustomer` role is allowed to deposit, withdraw, transfer funds, make charges and payments, and list the account's transactions. Notice that there is no overlap in functions that users in either role can perform.

Access to these functions was restricted to the appropriate role by setting method permissions on selected methods of the `CustomerControllerEJB`, `AccountControllerEJB`, and `TxControllerEJB` enterprise beans. For example, by allowing only users in the `BankAdmin` role to access the `createAccount` method in the `AccountControllerEJB` enterprise bean, you have denied users in the `BankCustomer` role or any other role permission to create bank accounts. To see the method permissions that have been set, in `deploytool` locate the `CustomerControllerEJB`, `AccountControllerEJB`, and `TxControllerEJB` enterprise beans in the tree view. For each bean, select the Security tab and examine the method permissions.

Application Client

Sometimes, enterprise applications use a stand-alone client application for handling tasks such as system or application administration. For example, the Duke's Bank application uses a J2EE application client to manually administer customers and accounts. This capability is useful in the event the site becomes inaccessible for any reason or a customer prefers to communicate things such as changes to account information by phone.

A J2EE application client is a standalone program launched from the command line or desktop; it accesses enterprise beans running on the J2EE application server.

The application client shown in Figure 18–4 handles basic customer and account administration for the banking application through a Swing user interface. The bank administrator can perform any of the following functions by making menu selections.

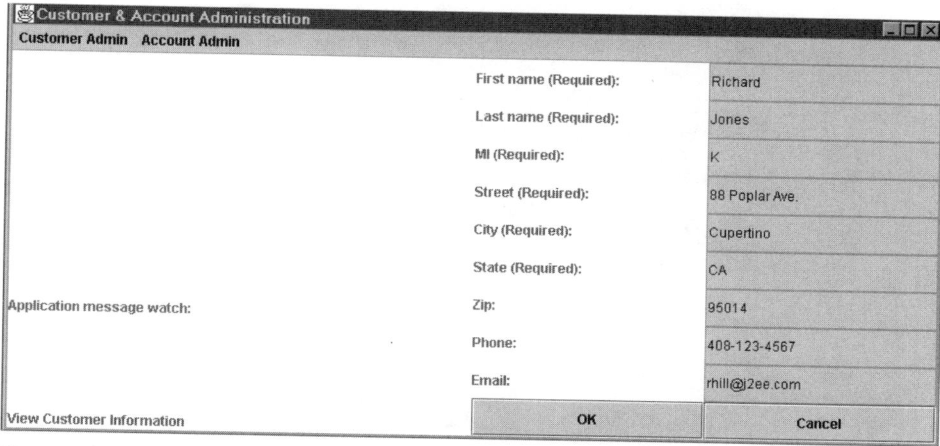

Figure 18–4 Application Client

Customer Administration

- View customer information
- Add a new customer to the database
- Update customer information
- Find customer ID

Account Administration

- Create a new account
- Add a new customer to an existing account
- View account information
- Remove an account from the database

Error and informational messages appear in the left pane under `Application Message Watch:`, and data is entered and displayed in the right pane.

The Classes and Their Relationships

The J2EE application client is divided into three classes: `BankAdmin`, `EventHandle`, and `DataModel`; the relationships among the classes are depicted in Figure 18–5.

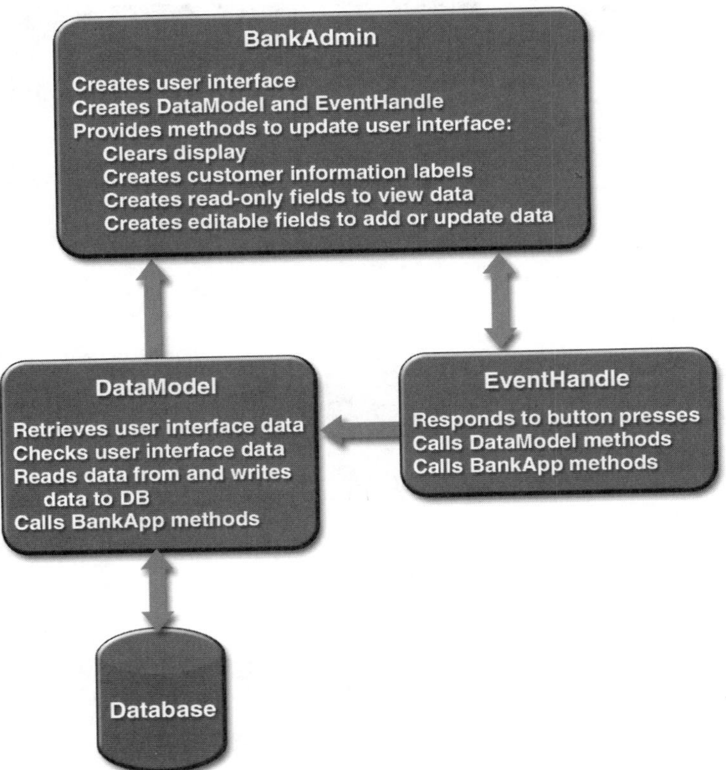

Figure 18–5 Relationships among Classes

`BankAdmin` builds the initial user interface, creates the `EventHandle` object, and provides methods for the `EventHandle` and `DataModel` objects to call to update the user interface.

`EventHandle` listens for button clicks by the user, takes action based on which button the user clicks, creates the `DataModel` object, calls methods in the `DataModel` object to write data to and read data from the underlying database, and calls methods in the `BankAdmin` object to update the user interface when actions complete.

`DataModel` retrieves data from the user interface, performs data checks, writes valid data to and reads stored data from the underlying database, and calls methods in the `BankAdmin` object to update the user interface based on the success of the database read or write operation.

BankAdmin Class

The BankAdmin class, which creates the user interface, is the class with the main method, and provides protected methods for the other BankAdmin application classes to call.

main Method

The main method creates instances of the BankAdmin and EventHandle classes. Arguments passed to the main method are used to initialize a locale, which is passed to the BankAdmin constructor.

```
public static void main(String args[]) {
   String language, country;
   if(args.length == 1) {
      language = new String(args[0]);
      currentLocale = new Locale(language, "");
   } else if(args.length == 2) {
      language = new String(args[0]);
      country = new String(args[1]);
      currentLocale = new Locale(language, country);
   } else
      currentLocale = Locale.getDefault();
   frame = new BankAdmin(currentLocale);
   frame.setTitle(messages.getString("CustAndAccountAdmin"));
   WindowListener l = new WindowAdapter() {
      public void windowClosing(WindowEvent e) {
         System.exit(0);
      }
   };
   frame.addWindowListener(l);
   frame.pack();
   frame.setVisible(true);
   ehandle = new EventHandle(frame, messages);
   System.exit(0);
   }
}
```

Constructor

The BankAdmin constructor creates the initial user interface, which consists of a menu bar and two panels. The menu bar contains the customer and account menus, the left panel contains a message area, and the right panel is a data display or update area.

Class Methods

The `BankAdmin` class provides methods that other objects call when they need to update the user interface. These methods are as follows:

- `clearMessages`: Clears the application messages that appear in the left panel
- `resetPanelTwo`: Resets the right panel when the user selects OK to signal the end of a data view or update operation
- `createPanelTwoActLabels`: Creates labels for account fields when account information is either viewed or updated
- `createActFields`: Creates account fields when account information is either viewed or updated
- `createPanelTwoCustLabels`: Creates labels for customer fields when customer information is either viewed or updated
- `createCustFields`: Creates customer fields when account information is either viewed or updated
- `addCustToActFields`: Creates labels and fields for when an add customer to account operation is invoked
- `makeRadioButtons`: Makes radio buttons for selecting the account type when a new account is created
- `getDescription`: Makes the radio button labels that describe each available account type

EventHandle Class

The `EventHandle` class implements the `ActionListener` interface, which provides a method interface for handling action events. Like all other interfaces in the Java programming language, `ActionListener` defines a set of methods, but does not implement their behavior. Instead, you provide the implementations because they take application-specific actions.

Constructor

The constructor receives an instance of the `ResourceBundle` and `BankAdmin` classes and assigns them to its private instance variable so that the `EventHandle` object has access to the application client's localized text and can update the user interface as needed. Lastly, the constructor calls the `hookupEvents` method to create the inner classes to listen for and handle action events.

```
public EventHandle(BankAdmin frame, ResourceBundle messages) {
    this.frame = frame;
    this.messages = messages;
    this.dataModel = new DataModel(frame, messages);
    //Hook up action events
    hookupEvents();
}
```

actionPerformed Method

The `ActionListener` interface has only one method, the `actionPerformed` method. This method handles action events generated by the `BankAdmin` user interface when users create a new account. Specifically, it sets the account description when a bank administrator selects an account type radio button and sets the current balance to the beginning balance for new accounts when a bank administrator presses the Return key in the Beginning Balance field.

hookupEvents Method

The `EventHandle` class uses inner classes to handle menu and button press events. An inner class is a class nested or defined inside another class. Using inner classes in this way modularizes the code, making it easier to read and maintain. `EventHandle` inner classes manage the following application client operations:

- View customer information
- Create new customer
- Update customer information
- Find customer ID by last name
- View account information
- Create new account
- Add customer to account
- Remove account
- Clear data on Cancel button press
- Process data on OK button press

DataModel Class

The `DataModel` class provides methods for reading data from the database, writing data to the database, retrieving data from the user interface, and checking that data before it is written to the database.

Constructor

The constructor receives an instance of the BankAdmin class and assigns it to its private instance variable so that the DataModel object can display error messages in the user interface when its checkActData, checkCustData, or writeData method detects errors. It also receives an instance of the ResourceBundle class and assigns it to its private instance variable so that the DataModel object has access to the application client's localized text.

Because the DataModel class interacts with the database, the constructor also has the code to establish connections with the remote interfaces for the CustomerController and AccountController enterprise beans, and to use their remote interfaces to create an instance of the CustomerController and AccountController enterprise beans.

```
//Constructor
public DataModel(BankAdmin frame, ResourceBundle messages) {
  this.frame = frame;
  this.messages = messages;
//Look up and create CustomerController bean
    try {
      CustomerControllerHome customerControllerHome =
        EJBGetter.
        getCustomerControllerHome();
      customer = customerControllerHome.create();
    } catch (Exception NamingException) {
      NamingException.printStackTrace();
    }
//Look up and create AccountController bean
    try {
      AccountControllerHome accountControllerHome =
        EJBGetter.getAccountControllerHome();
      account = accountControllerHome.create();
    } catch (Exception NamingException) {
      NamingException.printStackTrace();
    }
}
```

Methods

The getData method retrieves data from the user interface text fields and uses the String.trim method to remove extra control characters such as spaces and returns. Its one parameter is a JTextfield so that any instance of the JTextfield class can be passed in for processing.

```
private String getData(JTextField component) {
    String text, trimmed;
    if(component.getText().length() > 0) {
      text = component.getText();
      trimmed = text.trim();
      return trimmed;
    } else {
      text = null;
      return text;
    }
}
```

The `checkCustData` method stores customer data retrieved by the `getData` method, but first checks the data to be sure all required fields have data, the middle initial is no longer than one character, and the state is no longer than two characters. If everything checks out, the `writeData` method is called. If there are errors, they are printed to the user interface in the `BankAdmin` object. The `checkActData` method uses a similar model to check and store account data.

The `createCustInf` and `createActInf` methods are called by the `EventHandle` class to refresh the Panel 2 display in the event of a view, update, or add action event.

Create Customer Information

- For a view or update event, the `createCustInf` method gets the customer information for the specified customer from the database and passes it to the `createCustFields` method in the `BankAdmin` class. A Boolean variable is used to determine whether the `createCustFields` method should create read-only fields for a view event or writable fields for an update event.
- For create event, the `createCustInf` method calls the `createCustFields` method in the `BankAdmin` class with null data and a Boolean variable to create empty editable fields for the user to enter customer data.

Create Account Information

- For a view or update event, the `createActInf` method gets the account information for the specified account from the database and passes it to the `createActFields` method in the `BankAdmin` class. A Boolean variable is used to determine whether the `createActFields` method should create read-only fields for a view event or writable fields for an update event.

- For a create event, the `createActInf` method calls the `createActFields` method in the `BankAdmin` class with null data and a Boolean variable to create empty editable fields for the user to enter customer data.
- Adding a customer to an account or removing an account events operate directly on the database without creating any user interface components.

Web Client

In the Duke's Bank application, the Web client is used by customers to access account information and perform operations on accounts. Table 18–2 lists the functions the client supports, the URLs used to access the functions, and the components that implement the functions. Figure 18–6 shows an account history screen.

Table 18–2 Web Client

Function	URL Aliases	JSP Pages	JavaBeans Components
Home page	`/main`	`main.jsp`	

Log on or off the application	`/logon`
	`/logonError`
	`/logoff`
		`logon.jsp`
		`logonError.jsp`
		`logoff.jsp`	

List account	`/accountList`	`accountList.jsp`	
List the history of an account	`/accountHist`	`accountHist.jsp`	`AccountHistory-Bean`
Transfer funds between accounts	`/transferFunds` `/transferAck`	`transferFunds.jsp` `transferAck.jsp`	`TransferBean`
Withdraw and deposit funds	`/atm` `/atmAck`	`atm.jsp` `atmAck.jsp`	`ATMBean`
Error handling	`/error`	`error.jsp`	

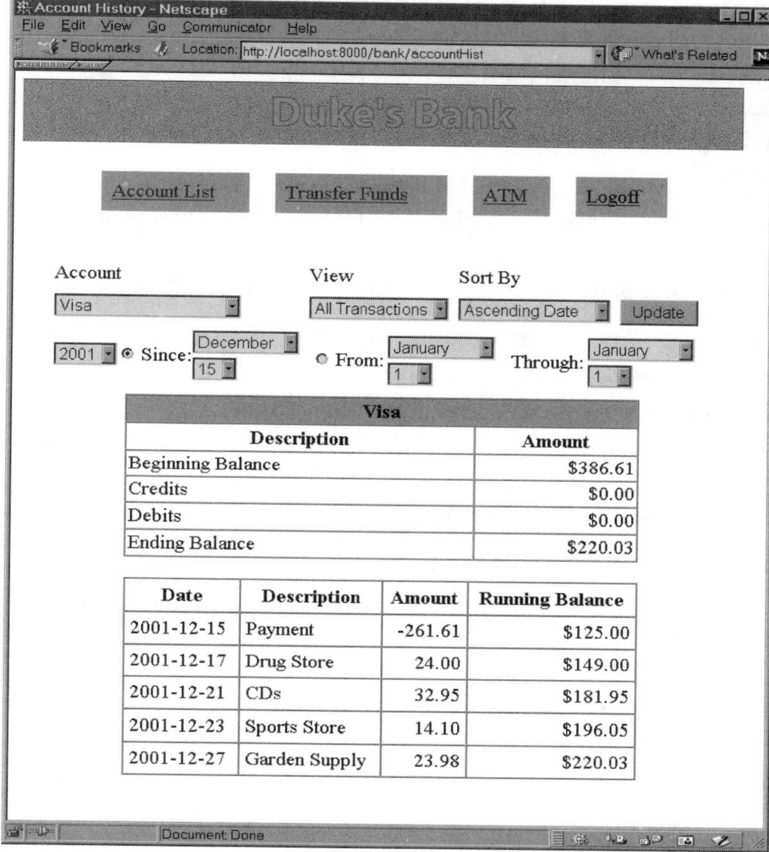

Figure 18–6 Account History

Design Strategies

The main job of the JSP pages in the Duke's Bank application is presentation. A strategy for developing maintainable JSP pages is to minimize the amount of scripting embedded in the pages. In order to achieve this, most dynamic processing tasks are delegated to enterprise beans, custom tags, and JavaBeans components.

In the Duke's Bank application, the JSP pages use enterprise beans to handle interactions with the database. In addition, the JSP pages rely heavily on JavaBeans components for interactions with the enterprise beans. In the Duke's Bookstore application, presented in chapters 10 to 13, the `BookDB` JavaBeans component acted as a front end to a database or as a facade to the interface provided by an enterprise bean. In the Duke's Bank application, TransferBean plays the same role. However, the other JavaBeans components have much richer functionality. ATMBean invokes enterprise bean methods and sets acknowledgement strings according to customer input, and AccountHistoryBean massages the data returned from the enterprise beans in order to present the view of the data required by the customer.

The Web client uses a template mechanism implemented by custom tags (discussed in A Template Tag Library, page 308) to maintain a common look across all the JSP pages. The template mechanism consists of three components:

- template.jsp determines the structure of each screen. It uses the insert tag to compose a screen from subcomponents.
- screendefinitions.jsp defines the subcomponents used by each screen. All screens have the same banner, but different title and body content (specified by the JSP Pages column in Table 18–2).
- Dispatcher, a servlet, processes requests and forwards to template.jsp.

Finally, the Web client uses three logic tags—iterate, equal, and notEqual—from the Struts tag library discussed in the section The Example JSP Pages (page 281) to perform flow control.

Web Client Life Cycle

Initializing the Client Components

Responsibility for managing the enterprise beans used by the Web client rests with the BeanManager class. It creates customer, account, and transaction controller enterprise beans and provides methods for retrieving the beans.

When instantiated, BeanManager retrieves the home interface for each bean from the helper class EJBGetter and creates an instance by calling the create method of the home interface. Because this is an application-level function, BeanManager itself is created and stored as a context attribute by a ContextListener (see Handling Servlet Life-Cycle Events, page 216) when the client is first initialized.

```
public class BeanManager {
   private CustomerController custctl;
   private AccountController acctctl;
   private TxController txctl;
   public BeanManager() {
      if (custctl == null) {
         try {
```

```
            CustomerControllerHome home =
               EJBGetter.getCustomerControllerHome();
            custctl = home.create();
         } catch (RemoteException ex) {
            System.out.println("...");
         } catch (CreateException ex) {
            System.out.println();
         } catch (NamingException ex) {
            System.out.println();
      }
   }
   public CustomerController getCustomerController() {
      return custctl;
   }
   ...
}

public final class ContextListener
   implements ServletContextListener {
   private ServletContext context = null;
   ...
   public void contextInitialized(ServletContextEvent event) {
      this.context = event.getServletContext();
      context.setAttribute("beanManager",
         new BeanManager());
      context.log("contextInitialized()");
   }
   ...
}
```

Request Processing

All requests for the URLs listed in Table 18–2 are mapped to the `dispatcher` Web component, which is implemented by the `Dispatcher` servlet:

```
public class Dispatcher extends HttpServlet {
   public void doPost(HttpServletRequest request,
      HttpServletResponse response) {
   ...
   String selectedScreen = request.getServletPath();

   request.setAttribute("selectedScreen", selectedScreen);
   BeanManager beanManager = getServletContext().getAttribute(
      "beanManager");
   ...
   if (selectedScreen.equals("/accountHist")) {
      ...
   } else if (selectedScreen.equals("/transferAck")) {
```

```
            String fromAccountId =
               request.getParameter("fromAccountId");
            String toAccountId =
               request.getParameter("toAccountId");
            if ( (fromAccountId == null) || (toAccountId == null)) {
               request.setAttribute("selectedScreen", "/error");
               request.setAttribute("errorMessage",
                  messages.getString("AccountError"));
            } else {
               TransferBean transferBean = new TransferBean();
               request.setAttribute("transferBean",
               transferBean);
               transferBean.setMessages(messages);
               transferBean.setFromAccountId(fromAccountId);
               transferBean.setToAccountId(toAccountId);
               transferBean.setBeanManager(beanManager);
               try {
                  transferBean.setTransferAmount(new
                     BigDecimal(request.
                        getParameter("transferAmount")));
                  String errorMessage = transferBean.populate();
                  if (errorMessage != null) {
                     request.setAttribute("selectedScreen", "/error");
                     request.setAttribute("errorMessage",
                        errorMessage);
                  }
               } catch (NumberFormatException e) {
                  request.setAttribute("selectedScreen", "/error");
                  request.setAttribute("errorMessage",
                     messages.getString("AmountError"));
               }
            }
            ...
            try {
            request.getRequestDispatcher("/template.jsp").
               forward(request, response);
            } catch(Exception e) {
            }
         }
      }
```

When a request is delivered, `Dispatcher` does the following:

1. Retrieves and saves the incoming request URL in the request attribute `selectedScreen`. This is done because the URL will be modified when the request is later forwarded to the application's template page.
2. Creates a JavaBeans component and stores the bean as a request attribute.

3. Parses and validates the request parameters. If a parameter is invalid, `Dispatcher` may reset the request alias to an error page. Otherwise, it initializes the JavaBeans component.
4. Calls the `populate` method of the JavaBeans component. This method retrieves data from the enterprise beans and processes the data according to options specified by the customer.
5. Forwards the request to `template.jsp`.

As mentioned earlier, `template.jsp` generates the response by including the responses from subcomponents. If the request is a `GET`, the body subcomponent usually retrieves data from the enterprise bean directly; otherwise it retrieves data from the JavaBeans component initialized by `Dispatcher`.

Figure 18–7 depicts the interaction between these components.

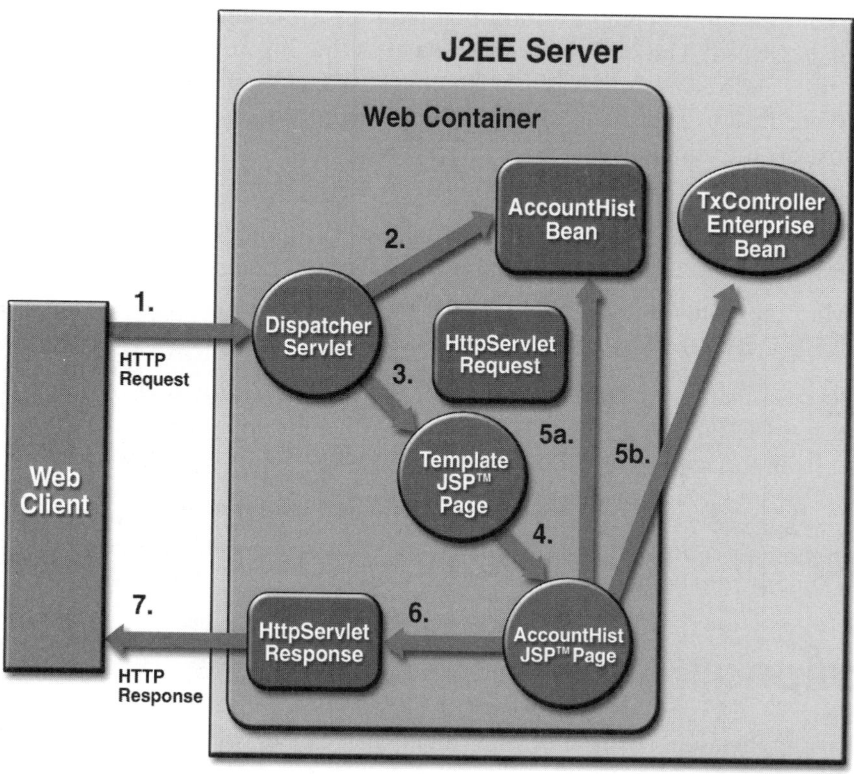

Figure 18–7 Web Component Interaction

Protecting the Web Resources

In the J2EE platform, a Web resource is protected from anonymous access by specifying which security roles can access the resource (see Controlling Access to Web Resources, page 338). This is known as a *security constraint*. The Web container guarantees that only certain users acting in roles specified in the security constraint can access the resource. In order for the Web container to enforce the security constraint, the application must specify a means for users to identify themselves (described in Authenticating Users of Web Resources, page 338) and the Web container must support mapping a role to a user.

In the Duke's Bank Web client, all of the URLs listed in Table 18–2 are restricted to the security role `BankCustomer`. The application requires users to identify themselves via the form-based login mechanism. When a customer tries to access a Web client URL, and has not been authenticated, the Web container displays the form-based login URL `/logon`, which is mapped to the JSP page `logon.jsp`. This page contains a form that requires a customer to enter an identifier and password. The Web container retrieves this information, maps it to a security role, and verifies that the role matches that specified in the security constraint. Note that in order for the Web container to check the validity of the authentication information and perform the mapping, you must perform these two steps when you deploy the application:

1. Add the customer's group, ID, and password to the default realm of the container (see J2EE Users, Realms, and Groups, page 348).
2. Map the `BankCustomer` role to the customer *or* customer's group (see J2EE Users, Realms, and Groups, page 348).

Once the customer has been authenticated, the identifier provided by the customer is used as a key to identify the customer's accounts. The identifier is retrieved from the request as follows:

```
<% ArrayList accounts =
beanManager.getAccountController().getAccountsOfCustomer(
   request.getUserPrincipal().getName()); %>
```

Internationalization

The J2EE application client and Web client distributed with the Duke's Bank application are internationalized. All strings that appear in the user interfaces are retrieved from resource bundles. The administration client uses resource bundles named `AdminMessages_*.properties`. The Web client uses resource bundles named `WebMessages_*.properties`. Both clients are distributed with English and Spanish resource bundles.

The application client retrieves locale information from the command line. For example, to use the Spanish resource bundle, invoke the application like this:

```
runclient -client BankApp.ear -name BankAdmin es
```

The administration client class `BankAdmin` creates a `ResourceBundle` with a locale created from the command-line arguments:

```
//Constructor
public BankAdmin(Locale currentLocale) {
   //Internationalization setup
   messages = ResourceBundle.getBundle("AdminMessages",
      currentLocale);
```

The Web client `Dispatcher` component retrieves the locale (set by a browser language preference) from the request, opens the resource bundle, and then saves the bundle as a session attribute:

```
ResourceBundle messages = (ResourceBundle)session.
   getAttribute("messages");
   if (messages == null) {
      Locale locale=request.getLocale();
      messages = ResourceBundle.getBundle("WebMessages",
         locale);
      session.setAttribute("messages", messages);
   }
```

In the Web client, each JSP page first retrieves the resource bundle from the session:

```
<% ResourceBundle messages =
   (ResourceBundle)session.getAttribute("messages"); %>
```

and then looks up any string that it needs in the bundle. For example, here is how `accountHist.jsp` generates the headings for the transactions table:

```
<td><b><%=messages.getString("TxDate")%></b></td>
<td><b><%=messages.getString("TxDescription")%></b></td>
<td><b><%=messages.getString("TxAmount")%></b></td>
<td><b><%=messages.getString("TxRunningBalance")%></b></td>
```

Building, Packaging, Deploying, and Running the Application

To build the Duke's Bank application, you must have downloaded and unzipped the tutorial bundle as described in Downloading the Examples (page xxii). When you install the bundle, the Duke's Bank application files are placed in the following directory structure of the `j2eetutorial` directory:

```
/bank
   /dd - deployment descriptors
      account-ejb.xml
      app-client.xml
      customer-ejb.xml
      runtime-ac.xml
      runtime-app.xml
      tx-ejb.xml
      web.xml
   /src
      /com - component classes
         /sun/ebank/appclient
         /sun/ebank/ejb
         /sun/ebank/web
      /web - JSP pages, images
   /sql - database scripts
      create-table.sql
      insert.sql
```

To simplify building, packaging, and deploying the Duke's Bank application, the tutorial bundle includes deployment descriptors, source code, and a `build.xml` file that contains the automated `ant` tasks. If you haven't run `ant` yet, please see How to Build and Run the Examples (page xxii).

After you compile the source code, the resulting class files will reside in the `j2eetutorial/bank/build` subdirectory. When you package the components and the application, the resulting archive files are placed in the `j2eetutorial/bank/jar` subdirectory.

Adding Groups and Users to the Realm

To run the J2EE application and Web clients, you must add groups and users to the default security realm. To create the `Customer` and `Admin` groups, add the user `200` to the `Customer` group, and add the user `admin` to the `Admin` group in `deploytool`:

1. Select Tools→Server Configuration
2. In the tree, select the Users node.
3. Make sure that Default is selected in the Realm combo box.
4. Click Add User.
5. Click Edit Groups.
6. Click Add.
7. Enter `Customer`.
8. Click Add.
9. Enter `Admin`.
10. Click OK.
11. Enter `200` for User Name: and `j2ee` for Password:
12. Select the `Customer` group from the Available Groups list.
13. Click Add.
14. Click Apply.
15. Enter `admin` for User Name and `j2ee` for Password.
16. Select the `Admin` Group from the Available Groups list.
17. Click Add.
18. Click OK.

You can perform the same tasks with the `realmtool` command-line utility:

1. `realmtool -addGroup Customer`
2. `realmtool -add 200 j2ee Customer`
3. `realmtool -addGroup Admin`
4. `realmtool -add admin j2ee Admin`

Starting the J2EE Server, deploytool, and Database

J2EE Server

Start the J2EE server:

```
j2ee -verbose
```

Deploytool

After the J2EE server reports `startup complete`, run `deploytool`:

1. If the `deploytool` utility is not running, launch it from the command line:

   ```
   deploytool
   ```

2. If `deploytool` is already running, reconnect to the J2EE server:

   a. Select File→Add Server

   b. In the Add Server dialog box, enter `localhost` in the Server Name field.

   c. Click OK.

Cloudscape

Start the Cloudscape database server:

```
cloudscape -start
```

Compiling the Enterprise Beans

In a different window, go to the `j2eetutorial/bank` subdirectory of the tutorial distribution and type this command:

```
ant compile-ejb
```

Packaging the Enterprise Beans

To package the enterprise beans, type the following:

```
ant package-ejb
```

The preceding command packages the class files and the deployment descriptors into the following EJB JAR files, which reside in the `j2eetutorial/bank/jar` subdirectory.

```
account-ejb.jar
customer-ejb.jar
tx-ejb.jar
```

When packaging a component in this chapter, `ant` may report that it cannot find a file (such as `account-ejb.jar`) to delete. You may ignore these messages.

Compiling the Web Client

To compile the Web client, go to the `j2eetutorial/bank` directory of the tutorial distribution and execute the following:

```
ant compile-web
```

Packaging the Web Client

The Web client uses the Struts tag library discussed in The Example JSP Pages (page 281). Before you can package the Web client, you must download and install Struts version 1.0 from

```
http://jakarta.apache.org/builds/jakarta-struts/release/v1.0/
```

Copy `struts-logic.tld` and `struts.jar` from `jakarta-struts-1.0/lib` to `j2eetutorial/bank/jar`. Then change to the `j2eetutorial/bank` directory and type the following:

```
ant package-web
```

This command packages the servlet class, JSP pages, JavaBeans component classes, tag libraries, and the Web application deployment descriptor into `web-client.war` and puts this file in `j2eetutorial/bank/jar`.

Compiling the J2EE Application Client

To compile the application client, go to the `j2eetutorial/bank` subdirectory and run this command:

```
ant compile-ac
```

Packaging the J2EE Application Client

1. Go to the `j2eetutorial/bank` directory and run this command:

   ```
   ant package-ac
   ```

   This command creates the `app-client.jar` file in the `j2eetutorial/bank/jar` directory.

2. From the same directory, type the following:

   ```
   ant setruntime-ac
   ```

This command adds a runtime deployment descriptor (`j2eetutorial/bank/dd/runtime-ac.xml`) to `app-client.jar`.

Packaging the Enterprise Archive File

1. To create the Duke's Bank enterprise archive file, go to the `j2eetutorial/bank` directory and run this command:

   ```
   ant assemble-app
   ```

   This command creates the `DukesBankApp.ear` file in the `j2eetutorial/bank/jar` directory.

2. From the same directory, type the following:

   ```
   ant setruntime-app
   ```

   This command adds a runtime deployment descriptor (`j2eetutorial/bank/dd/runtime-app.xml`) to `DukesBankApp.ear`.

Opening the Enterprise Archive File

In `deploytool`, open the EAR as follows:

1. Select File→Open.
2. Go to the `j2eetutorial/bank/jar` subdirectory.
3. Select `DukesBankApp.ear`.
4. Click Open Object.

You should see the screen shown in Figure 18–8 in `deploytool`.

Reviewing JNDI Names

With `DukesBankApp` selected, click the JNDI Names tab. The JNDI Name column is shown in Figure 18–9. The order may be a little different on your own display.

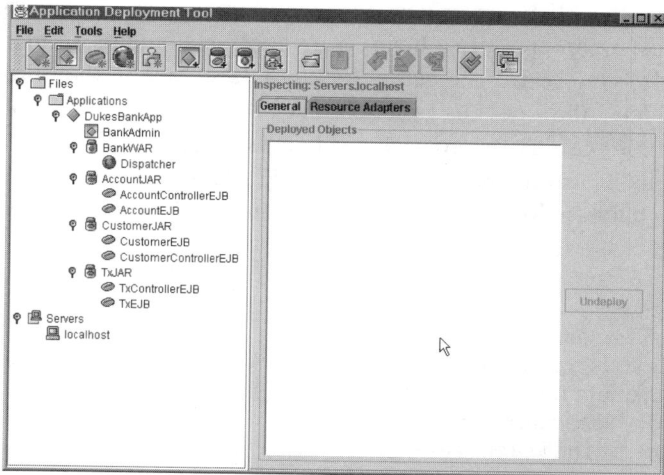

Figure 18–8 Application Archives and Components

Inspecting: Files.Applications.DukesBankApp

General | JNDI Names | Web Context | Security

Application

Component Type	Component	JNDI Name
EJB	AccountControllerEJB	MyAccountController
EJB	AccountEJB	MyAccount
EJB	CustomerControllerEJB	MyCustomerController
EJB	CustomerEJB	MyCustomer
EJB	TxEJB	MyTx
EJB	TxControllerEJB	MyTxController

References

Ref. Type	Referenced By	Reference Name	JNDI Name
Resource	AccountControllerEJB	jdbc/BankDB	jdbc/Cloudscape
EJB Ref	AccountControllerEJB	ejb/account	MyAccount
EJB Ref	AccountControllerEJB	ejb/customer	MyCustomer
Resource	AccountEJB	jdbc/BankDB	jdbc/Cloudscape
Resource	CustomerControllerEJB	jdbc/BankDB	jdbc/Cloudscape
EJB Ref	CustomerControllerEJB	ejb/customer	MyCustomer
Resource	CustomerEJB	jdbc/BankDB	jdbc/Cloudscape
Resource	TxEJB	jdbc/BankDB	jdbc/Cloudscape
Resource	TxControllerEJB	jdbc/BankDB	jdbc/Cloudscape
EJB Ref	TxControllerEJB	ejb/tx	MyTx
EJB Ref	TxControllerEJB	ejb/account	MyAccount
EJB Ref	BankWar	ejb/accountController	MyAccountController
EJB Ref	BankWar	ejb/customerController	MyCustomerController
EJB Ref	BankWar	ejb/txController	MyTxController
EJB Ref	BankAdmin	ejb/customerController	MyCustomerController
EJB Ref	BankAdmin	ejb/accountController	MyAccountController

Figure 18–9 JNDI Names

A *JNDI name* is the name the J2EE server uses to look up enterprise beans and resources. When you look up an enterprise bean, you supply statements similar to those shown in the following code. The actual lookup takes place in the third line of code, in which the `getCustomerControllerHome` method of `com.sun.ebank.utilEJBGetter` is called. `EJBGetter` is a utility class that retrieves a coded JNDI name from `com.sun.ebank.util.CodedNames`. In this example, the application client is looking up the coded name for the `CustomerController` remote interface:

```
try {
   customerControllerHome =
      EJBGetter.getCustomerControllerHome();
   customer = customerControllerHome.create();
} catch (Exception NamingException) {
   NamingException.printStackTrace();
}

public static CustomerHome getCustomerHome() throws
NamingException {
   InitialContext initial = new InitialContext();
   Object objref = initial.lookup(
      CodedNames.CUSTOMER_EJBHOME);
```

`BankAdmin` (the display name for the main class of the application client) references `ejb/customerController`, which is the coded name defined in `CodedNames` for the `CustomerController` remote interface.

The JNDI name is stored in the J2EE application deployment descriptor, and the J2EE server uses it to look up the `CustomerControllerEJB` bean. In Figure 18–9 you see that `CustomerControllerEJB` is mapped to the same JNDI name as is `ejb/customerController`. It does not matter what the JNDI name is, as long as it is the same name for the remote interface lookup as you use for its corresponding bean. So, looking at the table, you can say that the application client (`BankAdmin`) looks up the `CustomerController` remote interface, which uses the JNDI name of `MyCustomerController`, and the J2EE server uses the `MyCustomerController` JNDI name to find the corresponding `CustomerControllerEJB` object.

The other rows in the table have the mappings for the other enterprise beans. All of these beans are stored in the JAR files you added to the J2EE application during assembly. Their implementations have coded names for looking up either other enterprise beans or the database driver.

The JNDI name for the database driver is `jdbc/Cloudscape`. This name is the default coded name supplied in a configuration file of your J2EE SDK installation. For more information, see the *Configuration Guide* of the J2EE SDK.

Mapping the Security Roles to Groups

To map the `BankAdmin` role to the `Admin` group and the `BankCustomer` role to the `Customer` group:

1. In `deploytool`, select `DukesBankApp`.
2. In the Security tab, select the `BankAdmin` role from the Role Name list.
3. Click Add.
4. In the User Groups dialog box, select the `Admin` group in the Group Name list.
5. Click OK.
6. In the Security tab, select the `BankCustomer` role from the Role Name list.
7. Click Add.
8. In the User Groups dialog box, select the `Customer` group in the Group Name list.
9. Click OK.
10. From the main menu, select File→Save.

Figure 18–10 shows the `BankCustomer` role selected and the `Customer` group to which it is mapped.

Deploying the Duke's Bank Application

To deploy the application:

1. Select the `DukesBankApp` application.
2. Select Tools→Deploy.
3. Select the checkbox labeled Return Client Jar. By default, the directory for the returned JAR file is the same as where the EAR file is stored. The default name of the client JAR file is the application name with `Client.jar` appended, in this case, `DukesBankAppClient.jar`.
4. Click Finish.

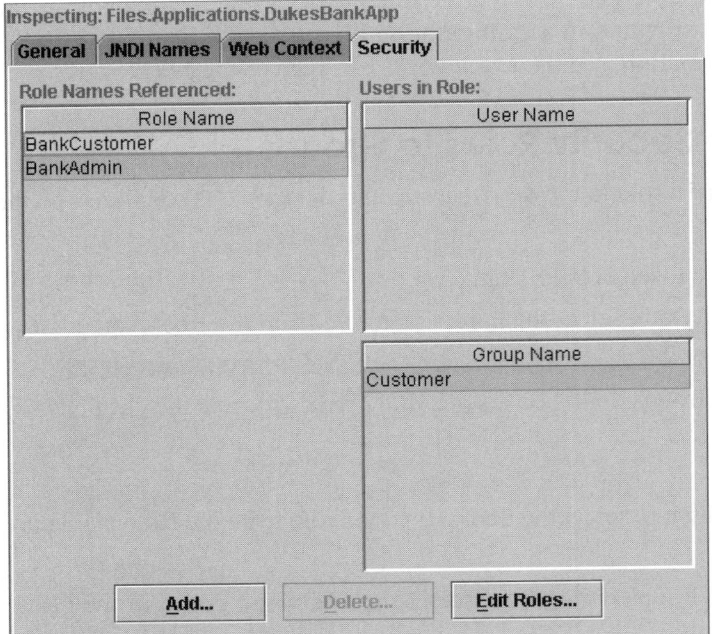

Figure 18–10 `BankCustomer` Role Mapped to `Customer` Group

Creating the Bank Database

You have to create and enter data into the appropriate tables so that the enterprise beans have something to read from and write to the database. To create and populate the database tables, in a terminal window go to the `j2eetutorial/bank` directory and type the following commands:

1. `ant db-create-table`
2. `ant db-insert`

Running the J2EE Application Client

To run the J2EE application client:

1. In a terminal window, go to `j2eetutorial/bank/jar`.
2. Set the `APPCPATH` environment variable to `DukesBankAppClient.jar`.
3. To run the English version of the client, execute the following command:

```
runclient -client DukesBankApp.ear -name BankAdmin
```

4. To run the Spanish version, include the `es` language code:

```
runclient -client DukesBankApp.ear -name BankAdmin es
```

   The `DukesBankApp.ear` parameter is the name of the J2EE application EAR file, and the `BankAdmin` parameter is the display name of the application client.

5. At the login prompts, type in `admin` for the user name and `j2ee` for the password. The next thing you should see is the application shown in Figure 18–11.

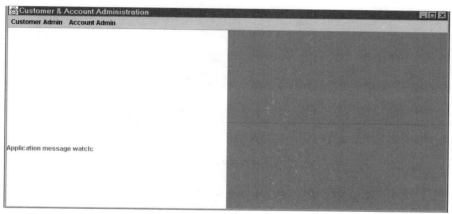

Figure 18–11 `BankAdmin` J2EE Application Client

Running the Web Client

To run the Web client:

1. Open the bank URL, `http://<host>:8000/bank/main`, in a Web browser. If your J2EE server is running on the same host as your Web browser, replace *<host>* with `localhost`. To see the Spanish version of the application, set your browser language preference to any Spanish dialect.
2. The application will display the login page. Enter `200` for the customer ID and `j2ee` for the password. Click Submit.

3. Select an application function: Account List, Transfer Funds, ATM, or Logoff. Once you have a list of accounts, you can get an account history by selecting an account link.

Note: The first time you select a new page, particularly a complicated page like an account history, it takes some time to display because the J2EE server must translate the page into a servlet class and compile and load the class.

If you select Account List, you will see the screen shown in Figure 18–12.

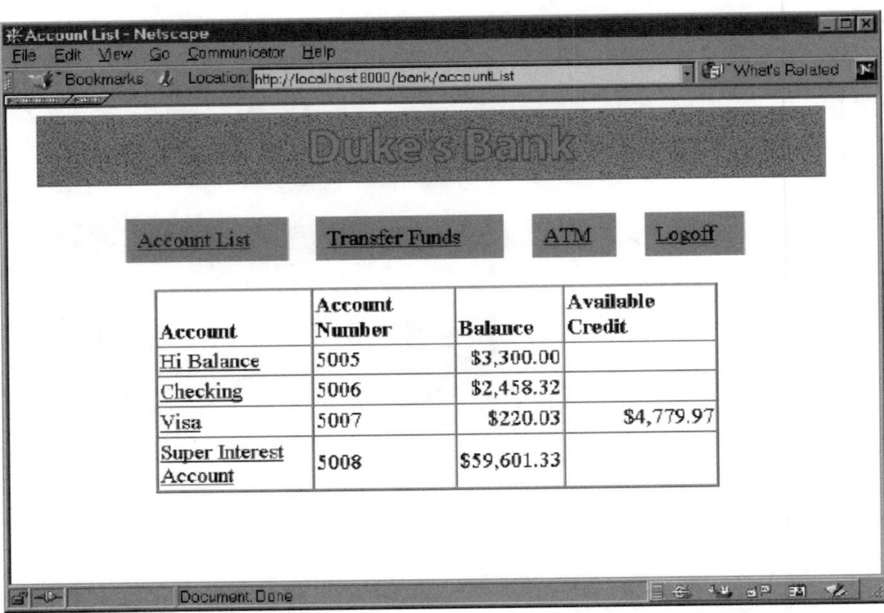

Account	Account Number	Balance	Available Credit
Hi Balance	5005	$3,300.00	
Checking	5006	$2,458.32	
Visa	5007	$220.03	$4,779.97
Super Interest Account	5008	$59,601.33	

Figure 18–12 Account List

A

HTTP Overview

Stephanie Bodoff

MOST J2EE Web clients use the HTTP protocol to communicate with a J2EE server. HTTP defines the requests that a client can send to a server and the responses that the server can send in reply. Each request contains a URL, which is a string that identifies a Web component or a static object such as an HTML page or image file.

The J2EE server converts an HTTP request to an HTTP request object and delivers it to the Web component identified by the request URL. The Web component fills in an HTTP response object, which the server converts to an HTTP response and sends to the client.

This appendix provides some introductory material on the HTTP protocol. For further information on this protocol, see the Internet RFCs 1945 (HTTP/1.0) and 2616 (HTTP/1.1), which can be downloaded from

```
http://www.rfc-editor.org/rfc.html
```

In This Appendix

HTTP Requests

An HTTP request consists of a request method, a request URL, header fields, and a body. HTTP 1.1 defines the following request methods:

- `GET`: Retrieves the resource identified by the request URL
- `HEAD`: Returns the headers identified by the request URL
- `POST`: Sends data of unlimited length to the Web server
- `PUT`: Stores a resource under the request URL
- `DELETE`: Removes the resource identified by the request URL
- `OPTIONS`: Returns the HTTP methods the server supports
- `TRACE`: Returns the header fields sent with the `TRACE` request

HTTP 1.0 includes only the `GET`, `HEAD`, and `POST` methods. Although J2EE servers are only required to support HTTP 1.0, in practice many servers, including the one contained in the J2EE SDK, support HTTP 1.1.

HTTP Responses

An HTTP response contains a result code, header fields, and a body. The HTTP protocol expects the result code and all header fields to be returned before any body content.

Some commonly used status codes include the following:

- `404`: Indicates that the requested resource is not available
- `401`: Indicates that the request requires HTTP authentication
- `500`: Indicates an error inside the HTTP server which prevented it from fulfilling the request
- `503`: Indicates that the HTTP server is temporarily overloaded, and unable to handle the request

B

J2EE SDK Tools

THE J2EE SDK includes a number of tools, which are described in this appendix.

In This Appendix

J2EE Administration Tool

The `j2eeadmin` tool is a command-line script that enables you to add and remove these resources: JDBC drivers and data sources, JMS destinations and connection factories, and resource adapter connection factories.

Table B–1 `j2eeadmin` Options

Option	Description
`-addConnectorFactory` *<jndi-name>* [*<app-name>*:] *<rar-filename>* [*<xa-user-name>* *<xa-password>*] [-props (*<name>*=*<value>*)+]	Adds a connection factory with the specified *<jndi-name>*. The connection factory is contained in the RAR file specified by *<rar-filename>*. The *<rar-filename>* must be the base name of the file; it cannot include any prefix ending in / (UNIX) or \ (Windows). If the RAR file is contained in an EAR file, then the name of the J2EE application name must be specified by *<app-name>*, followed by a colon. Optionally, a user name and password for the factory may be specified. Also optional is the `-props` flag, followed by one or more name-value pairs that specify properties for this factory. To prevent the shell from interpreting characters in the values, enclose the values in single or double quotes.
`-addJdbcDriver` `<class-name>`	Adds the JDBC driver specified by its fully qualified *<class-name>*. You must also update the `J2EE_CLASSPATH` environment variable in the file `bin\userconfig.bat`. Then you must restart the J2EE server.
`-addJdbcDatasource` *<jndi-name>* *<url>*	Adds the JDBC `DataSource` with the specified *<jndi-name>* and *<url>*.
`-addJdbcXADatasource` *<jndi-name>* *<class-name>* [*<xa-user-name>* *<xa-password>*] [-props *<name>*=*<value>*)+]	Adds the JDBC `XADataSource` with the specified *<jndi-name>* and fully-qualified *<class-name>*. Optionally, a user name and password for the `DataSource` may be specified. Also optional is the `-props` flag, followed by one or more name-value pairs that specify properties for this `DataSource`.
`-addJmsDestination` `<jndi-name>` `(queue|topic)`	Adds a JMS destination with the specified *<jndi-name>* and declares the destination as either a `queue` or `topic`.

Table B–1 `j2eeadmin` Options (Continued)

Option	Description
`-addJmsFactory <jndi-name> (queue|topic) [-props (<name>=<value>)+]`	Adds a JMS connection factory with the specified *<jndi-name>* and destination type, either queue or topic. Optionally, one or more properties may be specified with name-value pairs.
`-list<resource-type>`	Lists resources of the specified *<resource-type>*, either `ConnectorFactory`, `JdbcDriver`, `JdbcDatasource`, `JdbcXADatasource`, `JmsDestination`, or `JmsFactory`. There is no space between `-list` and *<resource-type>*.
`-remove<resource-type> <jndi-name>`	Removes the resource of the specified *<resource-type>* and *<jndi-name>*. (See the description of `-list` for the allowed *<resource-type>* elements.)
`-removeAll<resource-type>`	Removes all resources of the specified *<resource-type>*. (See the description of `-list` for the allowed *<resource-type>* elements.)

Cleanup Tool

The `cleanup` tool is a command-line script that removes all deployed applications from your J2EE server. It will not delete the component files (JAR, WAR, EAR).

Note: Use this utility with care!

Cloudscape Server

The examples in this manual have been tested with the Cloudscape DBMS, which is included in the J2EE SDK.

Starting Cloudscape

Before your enterprise beans can access a Cloudscape database, you must run the Cloudscape server from the command line:

```
cloudscape -start
```

You should see output similar to the following:

```
Mon Aug 09 11:50:30 PDT 1999: [RmiJdbc]
COM.cloudscape.core.JDBCDriver registered in DriverManager
Mon Aug 09 11:50:30 PDT 1999: [RmiJdbc] Binding . . ..
Mon Aug 09 11:50:30 PDT 1999: [RmiJdbc] No installation of
RMI Security Manager...
Mon Aug 09 11:50:31 PDT 1999: [RmiJdbc] RmiJdbcServer
bound in rmi registry
```

Stopping Cloudscape

To stop the server type the following command:

```
cloudscape -stop
```

You should see output similar to the following:

```
Attempting to shutdown RmiJdbc server
RmiJdbc Server RmiAddr is: //buzz/RmiJdbcServer
WARNING: Shutdown was successful!
```

Note: If you stop the server with Control-c, files will not be closed properly. When the server is started the next time, it must perform recovery by rolling back noncommitted transactions and possibly applying the forward log.

Running the Interactive SQL Tool

The Cloudscape product includes a text-based, interactive tool called `ij`. (This tool is not supported by Sun Microsystems, Inc.) You can run the `ij` tool by typing this command:

```
cloudscape -isql
```

Within the tool, each command you type must end in a semicolon. The commands in the next example display all rows from the `orders` table, execute a SQL script named `myscript.sql`, and end the tool session:

```
ij> select * from orders;
ij> run 'myscript.sql';
ij> exit;
```

The following example runs a SQL script from the command line:

```
cloudscape -isql < myscript.sql
```

This command lists the names of all user tables in the database:

```
ij> select tablename from sys.systables
    where tabletype = 'T';
```

The next example displays the column names of the `orders` table:

```
ij> select columnname from sys.syscolumns
    where referenceid =
          (select tableid from sys.systables
           where tablename = 'orders');
```

Before you deploy an entity bean with container-managed persistence, you use `deploytool` to generate the bean's SQL statements. Because the table names in these SQL statements are case sensitive, you must enclose them in double quotes:

```
ij> select * from "TeamBeanTable";
```

For more information on the `ij` tool, please refer to the online documentation on the Cloudscape Web site:

```
http://www.cloudscape.com
```

Cloudscape Server Configuration

The default database used by the Cloudscape server is named `CloudscapeDB`. This database will reside in the `cloudscape` directory of your J2EE SDK installation. The `CloudscapeDB` database will be created automatically the first time it is accessed. The driver for the Cloudscape server is already configured in the `config/default.properties` file. No further changes by you are necessary.

Deployment Tool

The `deploytool` utility has two versions: GUI and command line. The GUI version enables you to package components and to deploy applications. If you run the `deploytool` script with no options, the GUI version is launched.

The GUI version includes online help information that is context sensitive. To access a help topic for a particular dialog box or tab, press F1.

The command-line version of the tool enables you to deploy and undeploy applications. To package components from the command line, use the `packager` tool.

Table B–2 `deploytool` Options

Option	Description
`-deploy` *`<ear-filename>`* `<server-name>` [*`<client-stub-jar>`*]	Deploys the J2EE application contained in the EAR file specified by *`<ear-filename>`* onto the J2EE server running on the machine specified by *`<server-name>`*. Optionally, a JAR file for a stand-alone Java application client may be created by specifying *`<client-stub-jar>`*.
`-deployConnector` *`<rar-filename>`* `<server-name>`	Deploys the resource adapter contained in the RAR file specified by *`<rar-filename>`* onto the J2EE server running on the machine specified by *`<server-name>`*.
`-generateSQL` *`<ear-filename>`* *`<server-name>`* `[noOverWrite]`	Generates SQL statements for all entity beans with container-managed persistence. These beans are in the EAR file specified by *`<ear-filename>`* that has been deployed on the J2EE server running on the machine specified by *`<server-name>`*. If the `noOverWrite` option is specified, then existing SQL statements are not overwritten.
`-listApps` `<server-name>`	Lists the J2EE applications that are deployed on the J2EE server running on the machine specified by *`<server-name>`*.
`-listConnectors` `<server-name>`	Lists the resource adapters that are deployed on the J2EE server running on the machine specified by *`<server-name>`*.

Table B–2 `deploytool` Options (Continued)

Option	Description
`-undeployConnector` *`<rar-filename>`* `<server-name>`	Undeploys the resource adapter contained in the file specified by *`<rar-filename>`* from the J2EE server running on the machine specified by *`<server-name>`*.
`-uninstall` `<app-name>` `<server-name>`	Undeploys the J2EE application whose name is *`<app-name>`* from the J2EE server running on the machine specified by *`<server-name>`*.
`-help`	Displays options.
`-ui`	Runs the GUI version (default).

J2EE Server

To launch the J2EE server, run the `j2ee` script from the command-line prompt.

Table B–3 `j2ee` Options

Option	Description
`-verbose`	Redirects all logging output to the current shell.
`-version`	Displays the version number.
`-stop`	Stops the J2EE server.

To run the HTTPS service of the J2EE server, you must install a server certificate. For instructions, see Chapter 15.

Key Tool

The `keytool` utility creates public and private keys and generates X.509 self-signed certificates. The J2EE SDK version of the `keytool` utility has the same options as the version distributed with the J2SE SDK. For more information, see Chapter 15 and the J2EE SDK Configuration Guide.

Packager Tool

The `packager` tool is a command-line script that enables you to package J2EE components. This tool is for advanced users who do not want to use `deploytool` to package J2EE components. With `packager`, you can create the following component packages:

- EJB JAR file
- Web application WAR file
- Application client JAR file
- J2EE application EAR file
- Resource adapter RAR file

The `packager` tool also enables you to set the runtime deployment information of an application EAR file.

Note: To make them easier to read, the examples that follow contain line breaks within the commands. When typing these commands, do not include the line breaks.

EJB JAR File

Syntax

```
packager -ejbJar <root-directory> <file-list>
<ejb-dd> <ejb-jar>
```

Example

The following command packages the three `Hello` classes and the `hello-jar.xml` deployment descriptor into the `HelloEJB.jar` file:

```
packager -ejbJar /home/duke/classes/
HelloHome.class:HelloEJB.class:HelloRemote.class
hello-jar.xml HelloEJB.jar
```

Web Application WAR File

Syntax

```
packager -webArchive
[-classpath <root-directory> [-classFiles <file-list>]]
<content-root> [-contentFiles <file-list>] <web-dd> <web-war>
```

Example

The following command packages helper classes and JSP pages into the bookstore2.war file:

```
packager -webArchive -classpath .
-classFiles
   cart\ShoppingCart.class:cart\ShoppingCartItem.class:
   database\BookDB.class:util\Currency.class
.
-contentFiles
   banner.jsp:bookdetails.jsp:bookstore.jsp:cashier.jsp:
   catalog.jsp:DigitalClock.class:duke.books.gif:
   errorpage.jsp:initdestroy.jsp:receipt.jsp:showcart.jsp
web.xml bookstore2.war
```

Application Client JAR File

Syntax

```
packager -applicationClient <root-directory> <file-list>
<main-class> <appclient-dd> <appclient-jar>
```

Example

The following command creates the appClient.jar file:

```
packager  -applicationClient classes
hola:hello/HelloUtil.class
package.Main client.xml appClient.jar
```

J2EE Application EAR File

Syntax

```
packager -enterpriseArchive <file-only-list>
[-alternativeDescriptorEntries <file-only-list>]
[-libraryJars <file-list>] <app-name> <app-ear>
```

Example

In the following command, the optional `-alternativeDescriptorEntries` flag allows you to specify the external descriptor entry name of each component as you wish it to appear in the EAR file:

```
packager -enterpriseArchive
myWeb.war:myEJB.jar:appClient.ear
-alternativeDescriptorEntries
myWeb/web.xml:myEjb/myEjb.xml:client/client.xml
myAppName myApp.ear
```

Specifying the Runtime Deployment Descriptor

The preceding example specified the `-enterpriseArchive` flag to create a portable J2EE application EAR file. This file is portable because you can import it into any J2EE environment that conforms to the J2EE Specification. Although you can import the file into the `deploytool`, you cannot deploy it on the J2EE server until it contains a runtime deployment descriptor. This deployment descriptor is an XML file that contains information such as the JNDI names of the application's enterprise beans.

Syntax

```
packager -setRuntime <app-ear>|<appclient-jar> <runtime.xml>
[-o <output-file>]
```

Example

In the following command, the `-setRuntime` flag instructs `packager` to insert the runtime deployment descriptor (`sun-j2ee-ri.xml`) into the `myApp.ear` file:

```
packager -setRuntime MyApp.ear sun-j2ee-ri.xml
```

The following command copies `MyApp.ear` to `OtherApp.ear`, inserts the deployment descriptor into the `OtherApp.ear` file, and leaves `MyApp.ear` unchanged:

```
packager -setRuntime MyApp.ear sun-j2ee-ri.xml -o OtherApp.ear
```

To obtain an example of the runtime deployment descriptor, extract it from an EAR file that you've already deployed:

```
jar -xvf SomeApp.ear
```

The DTD of the runtime deployment descriptor is in the `lib/dtds/sun-j2ee-ri-dtd` file of your J2EE SDK installation.

Note: The runtime deployment descriptor (`sun-j2ee-ri-<version>.xml`) is not required by the J2EE Specification. This descriptor is unique to the J2EE SDK and may change in future releases.

Resource Adapter RAR File

Syntax

```
packager -connector <root-directory> <file-list>
ra.xml myConnector.rar
```

Example

In this example, the `jar` command packages the files under the `com` directory into `myfiles.jar`. The packager command creates a RAR file named `theConnector.rar` that contains `myfiles.jar` and the `myra.xml` deployment descriptor:

```
jar -cvf myadapter.jar com
packager -connector . myadapter.jar myra.xml theConnector.rar
```

Realm Tool

The `realmtool` utility is a command-line script that enables you to add and remove J2EE users and to import certificate files.

Table B–4 `realmtool` Options

Option	Description
`-show`	Lists the realm names.
`-list` *<realm-name>*	Lists the users in the specified realm. This release has two realms: `default` and `certificate`.
`-listGroups`	Lists the groups in the `default` realm.
`-userGroups` *<user-name>*	Lists the groups in the `default` realm to which the specified user belongs.
`-add` *<user-name password group[,group]>*	Adds the specified user to the `default` realm.
`-addGroup` *<group>*	Adds a group to the `default` realm.
`-import` *<certificate-file>*	Adds a user to the `certificate` realm by importing a file containing an X.509 certificate.
`-remove` *<realm-name user-name>*	Removes a user from the specified realm.
`-removeGroup` *<group>*	Removes a group.

Examples

To display all users in the default realm, type this command:

```
realmtool -list default
```

To add a user to the default realm you specify the `-add` flag. The following command will add a user named `robin` who is protected by the password `red`, and will include `robin` in the `bird` and `wing` groups:

```
realmtool -add robin red bird,wing
```

To add a user to the certificate realm, you import a file containing the X.509 certificate that identifies the user:

```
realmtool -import certificate-file
```

To remove a user, you specify the `-remove` flag. For example, to remove a user named `sparrow` from the default realm, you would type the following command:

```
realmtool -remove default sparrow
```

To add a group to the default realm you specify the `-addGroup` flag. The following command adds the `wing` group:

```
realmtool -addGroup wing
```

(You cannot add a group to the certificate realm.)

To remove a group from the default realm, you specify the `-removeGroup` flag:

```
realmtool -removeGroup wing
```

runclient Script

To run a J2EE application client, you execute the `runclient` script from a command-line prompt.

Syntax

```
runclient -client <appjar> [-name <name>]
[-textauth] [<app-args>]
```

Table B–5 `runclient` Options

Option	Description
`-client <appjar>`	The J2EE application EAR file
`-name <name>`	The display name of the J2EE application client component
`-textauth`	Causes the client container to prompt for the user name and password from the command line, not from a pop-up window

Table B–5 `runclient` Options (Continued)

Option	Description
`<app-args>`	Any arguments required by the J2EE application

Example

Before executing the `runclient` command, you must set the `APPCPATH` environment variable to the name of the client JAR stub file that is generated during deployment. The following example shows how to set `APPCPATH` on a Windows machine. The `runclient` command that follows launches a client named `FabulousClient`. The J2EE application of this client resides in the `FabulousApp.ear` file.

```
set APPCPATH=FabulousAppClient.jar
runclient -client FabulousApp.ear -name FabulousClient
```

Accessing a Remote Server

If the J2EE application client will reside on a different machine than the J2EE server, before executing `runclient` you must do the following:

1. Install the J2EE SDK on the remote client's machine. The SDK must be on the client's machine so that you can run its `runclient` script. You do not need to start the J2EE server on the client's machine.
2. Copy the EAR file to the remote client's machine.
3. Copy the client JAR stub file to the remote client's machine.
4. Set the `APPCPATH` environment variable to the name of the client JAR stub file.
5. Set the `VMARGS` environment variable to the following value:

```
-Dorg.omg.CORBA.ORBInitialHost=<remote-host>
```

For example, if the remote host were named `murphy`, you would set the `VMARGS` variable on a Windows machine as follows:

```
set VMARGS=-Dorg.omg.CORBA.ORBInitialHost=murphy
```

Preventing the User Name and Password Prompts

During iterative development, you may find it convenient to prevent the client container from prompting for the user name and password. To prevent these prompts, set the VMARGS environment variable to the following value:

```
-Dj2eelogin.name=guest -Dj2eelogin.password=guest123
```

Verifier Tool

The `verifier` tool validates J2EE archive files (EAR, WAR, JAR).

You can run `verifier` three ways:

- From within the `deploytool` GUI
- As a command-line utility
- As a stand-alone GUI utility

To run `verifier` from within the `deploytool` GUI, choose Verifier from the Tools menu. The following sections explain how to run the verifier the other two ways.

Command-Line Verifier

The command-line `verifier` tool has the following syntax:

```
verifier [options] <filename>
```

The *`filename`* argument is the name of a J2EE component file.

Table B–6 `verifier` Options

Syntax	Description
`-v`	Displays a verbose version of output.
`-o <output-file>`	Writes the results to the specified *<output-file>*, overriding the default `Results.txt` file.
`-u`	Runs the stand-alone GUI version.

Table B–6 `verifier` Options (Continued)

Syntax	Description
`-<report-level>`	Determines whether warnings or failures are reported. The `<report-level>` may be either `a`, `w`, or `f`: `a` (all results) `w` (warnings only) `f` (failures only) By default, only warnings and failures are reported.

Stand-Alone GUI Verifier

To run the stand-alone GUI `verifier` tool, follow these steps:

1. From the command-line prompt, type:

   ```
   verifier -u
   ```

2. To select a file for verification, click Add.
3. Select the radio button to indicate the report level:
   - All Results
   - Failures Only
   - Failures and Warnings Only
4. Click OK.
5. The `verifier` tool lists the details in the lower portion of the screen.

C
Examples

Table C–1 lists the examples in the tutorial and specifies the chapter or section in which each is discussed.

Table C–1 Examples

Chapter or Section	**Directory** (`examples/src`)	**Features**
Container-Managed Transactions (page 316)	`ejb/bank`	Rolling back a container-managed transaction, synchronizing a session bean's instance variables with the database values
The CartEJB Example (page 70)	`ejb/cart`	A stateful session bean
Accessing Environment Entries (page 78)	`ejb/checker`	A session bean with environment entries
Container-Managed Persistence Examples (page 119), Example Queries (page 167)	`ejb/cmproster`	An application with container-managed entity beans and relationships
Mail Session Connections (page 359)	`ejb/confirmer`	Sending e-mail from an enterprise bean

Table C–1 Examples (Continued)

Chapter or Section	Directory (examples/src)	Features
Getting Started (page 21)	ejb/converter	Step-by-step instructions for building a simple application with a session bean, JSP page, and J2EE application client
Many-to-Many Relationships (page 110)	ejb/enroller	Mapping a many-to-many relationship between database tables to a pair of entity beans with bean-managed persistence
URL Connections (page 362)	ejb/htmlreader	Connecting to a URL from an enterprise bean
A Helper Class for the Child Table (page 103)	ejb/order	Mapping a one-to-many relationship between database tables to a helper class and an entity bean with bean-managed persistence
An Entity Bean for the Child Table (page 107)	ejb/salesrep	Mapping a one-to-many relationship between database tables to a pair of entity beans with bean-managed persistence
The SavingsAccountEJB Example (page 84), Database Connections for Enterprise Beans (page 357)	ejb/savingsaccount	An entity bean with bean-managed persistence
A Message-Driven Bean Example (page 155)	ejb/simplemessage	A simple message-driven bean that listens to a JMS queue
One-to-One Relationships (page 99)	ejb/storagebin	Mapping a one-to-one relationship between database tables to a pair of entity beans with bean-managed persistence

Table C–1 Examples (Continued)

Chapter or Section	Directory (examples/src)	Features
JTA Transactions (page 325)	`ejb/teller`	Bean-managed transactions with the `javax.transaction.UserTransaction` interface
JDBC Transactions (page 324)	`ejb/warehouse`	Bean-managed transactions with the `java.sql.Connection` interface
Java Servlet Technology (page 209)	`web/bookstore1`	Servlet-based Web application
JavaServer Pages Technology (page 245)	`web/bookstore2`	JSP technology-based Web application, with one enterprise bean
Custom Tags in JSP Pages (page 279)	`web/bookstore3`	JSP technology-based Web application, with JSP custom tags and one enterprise bean
JavaServer Pages Technology (page 245)	`web/date`	Simple JSP pages
Web Clients and Components (page 193)	`web/hello1`	Simple servlet
Web Clients and Components (page 193)	`web/hello2`	Simple JSP pages
Programming with the CCI (page 376)	`connector/cci`	Connecting to a resource adapter through the Common Client Interface (CCI) API of the J2EE Connector architecture
The Duke's Bank Application (page 391)	`bank`	Full-featured J2EE application including J2EE application client, entity and session beans, servlet, JSP pages, and JSP custom tags.

Glossary

abstract schema
The part of an entity bean's deployment descriptor that defines the bean's persistent fields and relationships.

abstract schema name
A logical name that is referenced in Enterprise JavaBeans Query Language queries.

access control
The methods by which interactions with resources are limited to collections of users or programs for the purpose of enforcing integrity, confidentiality, or availability constraints.

ACID
The acronym for the four properties guaranteed by transactions: atomicity, consistency, isolation, and durability.

activation
The process of transferring an enterprise bean from secondary storage to memory. (See *passivation*.)

applet
A component that typically executes in a Web browser, but can execute in a variety of other applications or devices that support the applet programming model.

applet container
A *container* that includes support for the applet programming model.

application assembler
A person that combines *components* and *modules* into deployable application units.

application client
A first-tier client component that executes in its own Java virtual machine. Application clients have access to some (JNDI, JDBC, RMI-IIOP, JMS) J2EE platform APIs.

application client container
A *container* that supports application client components.

application client module
A software unit that consists of one or more classes and an application client deployment descriptor.

application component provider
A vendor that provides the Java classes that implement components' methods, JSP page definitions, and any required deployment descriptors.

authentication
The process by which an entity proves to another entity that it is acting on behalf of a specific identity. The J2EE platform requires three types of authentication: *basic*, *form-based*, and *mutual*, and supports *digest* authentication.

authorization
The process by which access to a method or resource is determined. Authorization in the J2EE platform depends upon the determination of whether the principal associated with a request through authentication is in a given security role. A security role is a logical grouping of users defined by an Application Component Provider or Assembler. A Deployer maps security roles to security identities. Security identities may be principals or groups in the operational environment.

authorization constraint
An authorization rule that determines who is permitted to access a Web resource collection.

basic authentication
An authentication mechanism in which a Web server authenticates an entity with a user name and password obtained using the Web client's built-in authentication mechanism.

bean-managed persistence
Data transfer between an entity bean's variables and a resource manager managed by the entity bean.

bean-managed transaction
A transaction whose boundaries are defined by an enterprise bean.

business logic
The code that implements the functionality of an application. In the Enterprise JavaBeans model, this logic is implemented by the methods of an enterprise bean.

business method
A method of an enterprise bean that implements the business logic or rules of an application.

callback methods
Component methods called by the container to notify the component of important events in its life cycle.

caller
Same as *caller principal.*

caller principal
The principal that identifies the invoker of the enterprise bean method.

cascade delete
A deletion that triggers another deletion. A cascade delete may be specified for an entity bean with container-managed persistence.

client certificate authentication
An authentication mechanism in which a client uses an X.509 certificate to establish its identity.

commit
The point in a transaction when all updates to any resources involved in the transaction are made permanent.

component
An application-level software unit supported by a *container.* Components are configurable at deployment time. The J2EE platform defines four types of components: *enterprise beans*, *Web components*, *applets*, and *application clients*.

component contract
The contract between a component and its container. The contract includes: life cycle management of the component, a context interface that the instance uses to obtain various information and services from its container, and a list of services that every container must provide for its components.

connection
See *resource manager connection.*

connection factory
See *resource manager connection factory.*

connector

A standard extension mechanism for containers to provide connectivity to enterprise information systems. A connector is specific to an enterprise information system and consists of a *resource adapter* and application development tools for enterprise information system connectivity. The resource adapter is plugged in to a container through its support for system-level contracts defined in the Connector architecture.

Connector architecture

An architecture for integration of J2EE products with *enterprise information systems*. There are two parts to this architecture: a resource adapter provided by an enterprise information system vendor and the J2EE product that allows this resource adapter to plug in. This architecture defines a set of contracts that a resource adapter has to support to plug in to a J2EE product, for example, transactions, security, and resource management.

container

An entity that provides life-cycle management, security, deployment, and runtime services to *components*. Each type of container (*EJB*, *Web*, *JSP*, *servlet*, *applet*, and *application client*) also provides component-specific services.

container-managed persistence

Data transfer between an entity bean's variables and a resource manager managed by the entity bean's container.

container-managed transaction

A transaction whose boundaries are defined by an EJB container. An *entity bean* must use container-managed transactions.

context attribute

An object bound into the context associated with a servlet.

context root

A name that gets mapped to the *document root* of a Web client.

conversational state

The field values of a session bean plus the transitive closure of the objects reachable from the bean's fields. The transitive closure of a bean is defined in terms of the serialization protocol for the Java programming language, that is, the fields that would be stored by serializing the bean instance.

CORBA

Common Object Request Broker Architecture. A language-independent distributed object model specified by the Object Management Group (OMG).

`create` **method**

A method defined in the *home interface* and invoked by a client to create an *enterprise bean*.

credentials

The information describing the security attributes of a *principal*.

CSS

Cascading Style Sheet. A stylesheet used with HTML and XML documents to add a style to all elements marked with a particular tag, for the direction of browsers or other presentation mechanisms.

CTS

Compatibility Test Suite. A suite of compatibility tests for verifying that a J2EE product complies with the J2EE platform specification.

delegation

An act whereby one *principal* authorizes another principal to use its identity or privileges with some restrictions.

deployer

A person who installs modules and J2EE applications into an operational environment.

deployment

The process whereby software is installed into an operational environment.

deployment descriptor

An XML file provided with each module and application that describes how they should be deployed. The deployment descriptor directs a deployment tool to deploy a module or application with specific container options and describes specific configuration requirements that a deployer must resolve.

destination

A JMS administered object that encapsulates the identity of a JMS queue or topic. See *point-to-point messaging system*, *publish/subscribe messaging system*.

digest authentication

An authentication mechanism in which a Web client authenticates to a Web server by sending the server a message digest along with its HTTP request message. The digest is computed by employing a one-way hash algorithm to a concatenation of the HTTP request message and the client's password. The digest is typically much smaller than the HTTP request and doesn't contain the password.

distributed application
An application made up of distinct components running in separate runtime environments, usually on different platforms connected via a network. Typical distributed applications are two tier (client and server), three tier (client and middleware and server), and multitier (client and multiple middleware and multiple servers).

document root
The top-level directory of a *WAR*. The document root is where JSP pages, client-side classes and archives, and static Web resources are stored.

DOM
Document Object Model. A tree of objects with interfaces for traversing the tree and writing an *XML* version of it, as defined by the W3C specification.

DTD
Document type definition. A description of the structure and properties of a class of *XML* files.

durable subscription
In a JMS *publish/subscribe messaging system*, a subscription that continues to exist whether or not there is a current active subscriber object. If there is no active subscriber, JMS retains the subscription's *messages* until they are received by the subscription or until they expire.

EAR file
Enterprise Archive file. A JAR archive that contains a J2EE application.

EJB
See *Enterprise JavaBeans*.

EJB container
A container that implements the EJB component contract of the J2EE architecture. This contract specifies a runtime environment for enterprise beans that includes security, concurrency, life cycle management, transactions, deployment, naming, and other services. An EJB container is provided by an *EJB* or *J2EE* server.

EJB container provider
A vendor that supplies an EJB container.

EJB context
An object that allows an enterprise bean to invoke services provided by the container and to obtain the information about the caller of a client-invoked method.

EJB home object

An object that provides the life cycle operations (create, remove, find) for an enterprise bean. The class for the EJB home object is generated by the container's deployment tools. The EJB home object implements the enterprise bean's home interface. The client references an EJB home object to perform life-cycle operations on an EJB object. The client uses JNDI to locate an EJB home object.

EJB JAR file

A JAR archive that contains an EJB module.

EJB module

A software unit that consists of one or more enterprise beans and an EJB deployment descriptor.

EJB object

An object whose class implements the enterprise bean's remote interface. A client never references an enterprise bean instance directly; a client always references an EJB object. The class of an EJB object is generated by a container's deployment tools.

EJB server

Software that provides services to an *EJB container*. For example, an EJB container typically relies on a transaction manager that is part of the EJB server to perform the two-phase commit across all the participating resource managers. The J2EE architecture assumes that an EJB container is hosted by an EJB server from the same vendor, so it does not specify the contract between these two entities. An EJB server may host one or more EJB containers.

EJB server provider

A vendor that supplies an EJB server.

enterprise bean

A component that implements a business task or business entity and resides in an EJB container; either an *entity bean*, *session bean*, or *message-driven bean*.

enterprise bean provider

An application programmer who produces enterprise bean classes, remote and home interfaces, and deployment descriptor files, and packages them in an EJB JAR file.

enterprise information system

The applications that comprise an enterprise's existing system for handling company-wide information. These applications provide an information infrastructure for an enterprise. An enterprise information system offers a well-defined set of services to its clients. These services are exposed to clients as local or remote interfaces or both. Examples of enterprise information systems include enterprise resource planning systems, mainframe transaction processing systems, and legacy database systems.

enterprise information system resource

An entity that provides enterprise information system-specific functionality to its clients. Examples are: a record or set of records in a database system, a business object in an enterprise resource planning system, and a transaction program in a transaction processing system.

Enterprise JavaBeans™ (EJB™)

A component architecture for the development and deployment of object-oriented, distributed, enterprise-level applications. Applications written using the Enterprise JavaBeans architecture are scalable, transactional, and secure.

Enterprise JavaBeans Query Language ("EJB QL")

Defines the queries for the finder and select methods of an entity bean with container-managed persistence. A subset of SQL92, EJB QL has extensions that allow navigation over the relationships defined in an entity bean's abstract schema.

entity bean

An enterprise bean that represents persistent data maintained in a database. An entity bean can manage its own persistence or can delegate this function to its container. An entity bean is identified by a primary key. If the container in which an entity bean is hosted crashes, the entity bean, its primary key, and any remote references survive the crash.

filter

An object that can transform the header or content or both of a request or response. Filters differ from *Web components* in that they usually do not themselves create responses but rather modify or adapt the requests for a resource, and modify or adapt responses from a resource. A filter should not have any dependencies on a Web resource for which it is acting as a filter so that it can be composable with more than one type of Web resource.

finder method

A method defined in the *home interface* and invoked by a client to locate an *entity bean*.

form-based authentication

An authentication mechanism in which a Web container provides an application-specific form for logging in.

group

A collection of principals within a given security policy domain.

handle

An object that identifies an enterprise bean. A client may serialize the handle, and then later deserialize it to obtain a reference to the enterprise bean.

home handle

An object that can be used to obtain a reference of the home interface. A home handle can be serialized and written to stable storage and deserialized to obtain the reference.

home interface

One of two interfaces for an *enterprise bean*. The home interface defines zero or more methods for managing an enterprise bean. The home interface of a session bean defines `create` and `remove` methods, while the home interface of an entity bean defines `create`, finder, and `remove` methods.

HTML

Hypertext Markup Language. A markup language for hypertext documents on the Internet. HTML enables the embedding of images, sounds, video streams, form fields, references to other objects with URLs, and basic text formatting.

HTTP

Hypertext Transfer Protocol. The Internet protocol used to fetch hypertext objects from remote hosts. HTTP messages consist of requests from client to server and responses from server to client.

HTTPS

HTTP layered over the SSL protocol.

IDL

Interface Definition Language. A language used to define interfaces to remote CORBA objects. The interfaces are independent of operating systems and programming languages.

IIOP

Internet Inter-ORB Protocol. A protocol used for communication between CORBA object request brokers.

impersonation

An act whereby one entity assumes the identity and privileges of another entity without restrictions and without any indication visible to the recipients of the impersonator's calls that delegation has taken place. Impersonation is a case of simple *delegation*.

initialization parameter
A parameter that initializes the context associated with a servlet.

ISV
Independent software vendor.

J2EE
See *Java 2 Platform, Enterprise Edition.*

J2ME
See *Java 2 Platform, Micro Edition.*

J2SE
See *Java 2 Platform, Standard Edition.*

J2EE application
Any deployable unit of J2EE functionality. This can be a single module or a group of modules packaged into an EAR file with a J2EE application deployment descriptor. J2EE applications are typically engineered to be distributed across multiple computing tiers.

J2EE product
An implementation that conforms to the J2EE platform specification.

J2EE product provider
A vendor that supplies a J2EE product.

J2EE server
The runtime portion of a J2EE product. A J2EE server provides *EJB* or *Web* containers or both.

JAR
Java Archive. A platform-independent file format that permits many files to be aggregated into one file.

Java™ 2 Platform, Enterprise Edition (J2EE™)
An environment for developing and deploying enterprise applications. The J2EE platform consists of a set of services, application programming interfaces (APIs), and protocols that provide the functionality for developing multitiered, Web-based applications.

Java™ 2 Platform, Micro Edition (J2ME™)
A highly optimized Java runtime environment targeting a wide range of consumer products, including pagers, cellular phones, screenphones, digital set-top boxes, and car navigation systems.

Java™ 2 Platform, Standard Edition (J2SE™)
The core Java technology platform.

Java 2 SDK, Enterprise Edition (J2EE SDK)
Sun's implementation of the J2EE platform. This implementation provides an operational definition of the J2EE platform.

Java IDL
A technology that provides CORBA interoperability and connectivity capabilities for the J2EE platform. These capabilities enable J2EE applications to invoke operations on remote network services using the Object Management Group IDL and IIOP.

Java Message Service ("JMS")
An API for using enterprise messaging systems such as IBM MQ Series, TIBCO Rendezvous, and so on.

Java Naming and Directory Interface™ ("JNDI")
An API that provides naming and directory functionality.

Java Transaction API ("JTA")
An API that allows applications and J2EE servers to access transactions.

Java Transaction Service ("JTS")
Specifies the implementation of a transaction manager which supports JTA and implements the Java mapping of the Object Management Group Object Transaction Service (OTS) 1.1 specification at the level below the API.

JavaBeans™ component
A Java class that can be manipulated in a visual builder tool and composed into applications. A JavaBeans component must adhere to certain property and event interface conventions.

JavaMail™
An API for sending and receiving e-mail.

JavaServer Pages™ (JSP™)
An extensible Web technology that uses template data, custom elements, scripting languages, and server-side Java objects to return dynamic content to a client. Typically the template data is HTML or XML elements, and in many cases the client is a Web browser.

JDBC™
An API for database-independent connectivity between the J2EE platform and a wide range of data sources.

JMS
See *Java Message Service*.

JMS administered object

A preconfigured JMS object (a *resource manager connection factory* or a *destination*) created by an administrator for the use of *JMS clients* and placed in a *JNDI* namespace.

JMS application

One or more *JMS clients* that exchange *messages*.

JMS client

A Java language program that sends or receives *messages*.

JMS provider

A messaging system that implements the *Java Message Service* as well as other administrative and control functionality needed in a full-featured messaging product.

JMS session

A single-threaded context for sending and receiving JMS *messages*. A JMS session can be non transacted, locally transacted, or participating in a distributed transaction.

JNDI

See *Java Naming and Directory Interface*.

JSP

See *JavaServer Pages*.

JSP action

A JSP element that can act on implicit objects and other server-side objects or can define new scripting variables. Actions follow the XML syntax for elements with a start tag, a body, and an end tag; if the body is empty it can also use the empty tag syntax. The tag must use a prefix.

JSP action, custom

An action described in a portable manner by a tag library descriptor and a collection of Java classes and imported into a JSP page by a `taglib` directive. A custom action is invoked when a JSP page uses a custom tag.

JSP action, standard

An action that is defined in the JSP specification and is always available to a JSP file without being imported.

JSP application

A stand-alone Web application, written using the JavaServer Pages technology, that can contain JSP pages, servlets, HTML files, images, applets, and JavaBeans components.

JSP container

A *container* that provides the same services as a *servlet container* and an engine that interprets and processes JSP pages into a servlet.

JSP container, distributed

A JSP container that can run a Web application that is tagged as distributable and is spread across multiple Java virtual machines that might be running on different hosts.

JSP declaration

A JSP scripting element that declares methods, variables, or both in a JSP file.

JSP directive

A JSP element that gives an instruction to the JSP container and is interpreted at translation time.

JSP element

A portion of a JSP page that is recognized by a JSP translator. An element can be a *directive*, an *action*, or a *scripting element*.

JSP expression

A scripting element that contains a valid scripting language expression that is evaluated, converted to a `String`, and placed into the implicit `out` object.

JSP file

A file that contains a JSP page. In the Servlet 2.2 specification, a JSP file must have a `.jsp` extension.

JSP page

A text-based document using fixed template data and JSP elements that describes how to process a request to create a response.

JSP scripting element

A JSP *declaration*, *scriptlet*, or *expression*, whose tag syntax is defined by the JSP specification, and whose content is written according to the scripting language used in the JSP page. The JSP specification describes the syntax and semantics for the case where the language page attribute is `"java"`.

JSP scriptlet

A JSP scripting element containing any code fragment that is valid in the scripting language used in the JSP page. The JSP specification describes what is a valid scriptlet for the case where the language page attribute is `"java"`.

JSP tag
A piece of text between a left angle bracket and a right angle bracket that is used in a JSP file as part of a JSP element. The tag is distinguishable as markup, as opposed to data, because it is surrounded by angle brackets.

JSP tag library
A collection of custom tags identifying custom actions described via a tag library descriptor and Java classes.

JTA
See *Java Transaction API*.

JTS
See *Java Transaction Service*.

life cycle
The framework events of a component's existence. Each type of component has defining events which mark its transition into states where it has varying availability for use. For example, a servlet is created and has its `init` method called by its container prior to invocation of its service method by clients or other servlets that require its functionality. After the call of its `init` method it has the data and readiness for its intended use. The servlet's `destroy` method is called by its container prior to the ending of its existence so that processing associated with winding up may be done, and resources may be released. The `init` and `destroy` methods in this example are *callback methods*. Similar considerations apply to all J2EE component types: enterprise beans, Web components (servlets or JSP pages), applets, and application clients.

message
In the *Java Message Service*, an asynchronous request, report, or event that is created, sent, and consumed by an enterprise application, not by a human. It contains vital information needed to coordinate enterprise applications, in the form of precisely formatted data that describes specific business actions.

message-driven bean
An enterprise bean that is an asynchronous message consumer. A message-driven bean has no state for a specific client, but its instance variables may contain state across the handling of client messages, including an open database connection and an object reference to an *EJB object*. A client accesses a message-driven bean by sending messages to the destination for which the bean is a message listener.

`MessageConsumer`
An object created by a *JMS session* that is used for receiving *messages* sent to a *destination*.

`MessageProducer`
An object created by a *JMS session* that is used for sending *messages* to a *destination*.

method permission
An authorization rule that determines who is permitted to execute one or more enterprise bean methods.

module
A software unit that consists of one or more J2EE components of the same container type and one deployment descriptor of that type. There are three types of modules: *EJB*, *Web*, and *application client*. Modules can be deployed as stand-alone units or assembled into an application.

mutual authentication
An authentication mechanism employed by two parties for the purpose of proving each other's identity to one another.

naming context
A set of associations between unique, atomic, people-friendly identifiers and objects.

naming environment
A mechanism that allows a component to be customized without the need to access or change the component's source code. A container implements the component's naming environment, and provides it to the component as a *JNDI naming context*. Each component names and accesses its environment entries using the `java:comp/env` JNDI context. The environment entries are declaratively specified in the component's deployment descriptor.

non-JMS client
A messaging client program that uses a message system's native client API instead of the *Java Message Service*.

ORB
Object request broker. A library that enables CORBA objects to locate and communicate with one another.

OS principal
A principal native to the operating system (OS) on which the J2EE platform is executing.

OTS
Object Transaction Service. A definition of the interfaces that permit CORBA objects to participate in transactions.

passivation
The process of transferring an enterprise bean from memory to secondary storage. (See *activation*.)

persistence
The protocol for transferring the state of an entity bean between its instance variables and an underlying database.

persistent field
A virtual field of an entity bean with container-managed persistence; it is stored in a database.

POA
Portable Object Adapter. A CORBA standard for building server-side applications that are portable across heterogeneous ORBs.

point-to-point messaging system
A messaging system built around the concept of message queues. Each *message* is addressed to a specific queue; clients extract messages from the queue(s) established to hold their messages.

primary key
An object that uniquely identifies an entity bean within a home.

principal
The identity assigned to a user as a result of authentication.

privilege
A security attribute that does not have the property of uniqueness and that may be shared by many principals.

publish/subscribe messaging system
A messaging system in which clients address *messages* to a specific node in a content hierarchy. Publishers and subscribers are generally anonymous and may dynamically publish or subscribe to the content hierarchy. The system takes care of distributing the messages arriving from a node's multiple publishers to its multiple subscribers.

queue
See *point-to-point messaging system*.

RAR
Resource Adapter Archive. A JAR archive that contains a resource adapter.

realm
See *security policy domain*. Also, a string, passed as part of an HTTP request during *basic authentication*, that defines a protection space. The protected resources on a server can be partitioned into a set of protection spaces, each with its own authentication scheme or authorization database or both.

re-entrant entity bean
An entity bean that can handle multiple simultaneous, interleaved, or nested invocations which will not interfere with each other.

Reference Implementation
: See *Java 2 SDK, Enterprise Edition*.

relationship field
: A virtual field of an entity bean with container-managed persistence; it identifies a related entity bean.

remote interface
: One of two interfaces for an *enterprise bean*. The remote interface defines the business methods callable by a client.

`remove` **method**
: Method defined in the *home interface* and invoked by a client to destroy an *enterprise bean*.

resource adapter
: A system-level software driver that is used by an EJB container or an application client to connect to an enterprise information system. A resource adapter is typically specific to an enterprise information system. It is available as a library and is used within the address space of the server or client using it. A resource adapter plugs into a container. The application components deployed on the container then use the client API (exposed by the adapter) or tool-generated high-level abstractions to access the underlying enterprise information system. The resource adapter and EJB container collaborate to provide the underlying mechanisms—transactions, security, and connection pooling—for connectivity to the enterprise information system.

resource manager
: Provides access to a set of shared resources. A resource manager participates in transactions that are externally controlled and coordinated by a transaction manager. A resource manager is typically in a different address space or on a different machine from the clients that access it. Note: An *enterprise information system* is referred to as a resource manager when it is mentioned in the context of resource and transaction management.

resource manager connection
: An object that represents a session with a resource manager.

resource manager connection factory
: An object used for creating a resource manager connection.

RMI
: Remote Method Invocation. A technology that allows an object running in one Java virtual machine to invoke methods on an object running in a different Java virtual machine.

RMI-IIOP
A version of RMI implemented to use the CORBA IIOP protocol. RMI over IIOP provides interoperability with CORBA objects implemented in any language if all the remote interfaces are originally defined as RMI interfaces.

role (development)
The function performed by a party in the development and deployment phases of an application developed using J2EE technology. The roles are: *application component provider*, *application assembler*, *deployer*, *J2EE product provider*, *EJB container provider*, *EJB server provider*, *Web container provider*, *Web server provider*, *tool provider*, and *system administrator*.

role (security)
An abstract logical grouping of users that is defined by the application assembler. When an application is deployed, the roles are mapped to security identities, such as *principals* or *groups*, in the operational environment.

role mapping
The process of associating the groups or principals or both, recognized by the container to security roles specified in the *deployment descriptor*. Security roles have to be mapped by the deployer before the component is installed in the server.

rollback
The point in a transaction when all updates to any resources involved in the transaction are reversed.

SAX
Simple API for *XML*. An event-driven, serial-access mechanism for accessing XML documents.

security attributes
A set of properties associated with a principal. Security attributes can be associated with a principal by an authentication protocol or by a J2EE product provider, or both.

security constraint
A declarative way to annotate the intended protection of Web content. A security constraint consists of a *Web resource collection*, an *authorization constraint*, and a *user data constraint*.

security context
An object that encapsulates the shared state information regarding security between two entities.

security permission

A mechanism, defined by J2SE, used by the J2EE platform to express the programming restrictions imposed on application component providers.

security permission set

The minimum set of security permissions that a J2EE product provider must provide for the execution of each component type.

security policy domain

A scope over which security policies are defined and enforced by a security administrator. A security policy domain has a collection of users (or principals), uses a well defined authentication protocol or protocols for authenticating users (or principals), and may have groups to simplify setting of security policies.

security role

See *role (security)*.

security technology domain

A scope over which the same security mechanism is used to enforce a security policy. Multiple security policy domains can exist within a single technology domain.

security view

The set of security roles defined by the application assembler.

server principal

The OS principal that the server is executing as.

servlet

A Java program that extends the functionality of a Web server, generating dynamic content and interacting with Web clients using a request-response paradigm.

servlet container

A *container* that provides the network services over which requests and responses are sent, decodes requests, and formats responses. All servlet containers must support HTTP as a protocol for requests and responses, but may also support additional request-response protocols, such as HTTPS.

servlet container, distributed

A servlet container that can run a Web application that is tagged as distributable and that executes across multiple Java virtual machines running on the same host or on different hosts.

servlet context

An object that contains a servlet's view of the Web application within which the servlet is running. Using the context, a servlet can log events, obtain

URL references to resources, and set and store attributes that other servlets in the context can use.

servlet mapping
Defines an association between a URL pattern and a servlet. The mapping is used to map requests to servlets.

session
An object used by a servlet to track a user's interaction with a Web application across multiple HTTP requests.

session bean
An enterprise bean that is created by a client and that usually exists only for the duration of a single client-server session. A session bean performs operations, such as calculations or accessing a database, for the client. Although a session bean may be transactional, it is not recoverable should a system crash occur. Session bean objects can be either stateless or can maintain conversational state across methods and transactions. If a session bean maintains state, then the EJB container manages this state if the object must be removed from memory. However, the session bean object itself must manage its own persistent data.

SQL
Structured Query Language. The standardized relational database language for defining database objects and manipulating data.

SQL/J
A set of standards that includes specifications for embedding SQL statements in methods in the Java programming language and specifications for calling Java static methods as SQL stored procedures and user-defined functions. An SQL checker can detect errors in static SQL statements at program development time, rather than at execution time as with a JDBC driver.

SSL
Secure Socket Layer. A security protocol that provides privacy over the Internet. The protocol allows client-server applications to communicate in a way that cannot be eavesdropped upon or tampered with. Servers are always authenticated and clients are optionally authenticated.

stateful session bean
A session bean with a conversational state.

stateless session bean
A session bean with no conversational state. All instances of a stateless session bean are identical.

system administrator
The person responsible for configuring and administering the enterprise's computers, networks, and software systems.

tool provider
An organization or software vendor that provides tools used for the development, packaging, and deployment of J2EE applications.

topic
See *publish-subscribe messaging system*.

transaction
An atomic unit of work that modifies data. A transaction encloses one or more program statements, all of which either complete or roll back. Transactions enable multiple users to access the same data concurrently.

transaction attribute
A value specified in an enterprise bean's deployment descriptor that is used by the EJB container to control the transaction scope when the enterprise bean's methods are invoked. A transaction attribute can have the following values: `Required`, `RequiresNew`, `Supports`, `NotSupported`, `Mandatory`, or `Never`.

transaction isolation level
The degree to which the intermediate state of the data being modified by a transaction is visible to other concurrent transactions and data being modified by other transactions is visible to it.

transaction manager
Provides the services and management functions required to support transaction demarcation, transactional resource management, synchronization, and transaction context propagation.

URI
Uniform Resource Identifier. A compact string of characters for identifying an abstract or physical resource. A URI is either a *URL* or a *URN*. URLs and URNs are concrete entities that actually exist; a URI is an abstract superclass.

URL
Uniform Resource Locator. A standard for writing a textual reference to an arbitrary piece of data in the World Wide Web. A URL looks like this: `protocol://host/localinfo` where `protocol` specifies a protocol for fetching the object (such as HTTP or FTP), `host` specifies the Internet name of the targeted host, and `localinfo` is a string (often a file name) passed to the protocol handler on the remote host.

URL path
The URL passed by a HTTP request to invoke a servlet. The URL consists of the context path + servlet path + path info, where

- Context path is the path prefix associated with a servlet context of which this servlet is a part. If this context is the default context rooted at the base of the Web server's URL namespace, the path prefix will be an empty string. Otherwise, the path prefix starts with a / character but does not end with a / character.
- Servlet path is the path section that directly corresponds to the mapping that activated this request. This path starts with a / character.
- Path info is the part of the request path that is not part of the context path or the servlet path.

URN
Uniform Resource Name. A unique identifier that identifies an entity but doesn't tell where it is located. A system can use a URN to look up an entity locally before trying to find it on the Web. It also allows the Web location to change while still allowing the entity to be found.

user data constraint
Indicates how data between a client and a Web container should be protected. The protection can be the prevention of tampering with the data or prevention of eavesdropping on the data.

WAR file
Web Archive file. A JAR archive that contains a Web module.

Web application
An application written for the Internet, including those built with Java technologies such as JavaServer Pages and servlets, as well as those built with non-Java technologies such as CGI and Perl.

Web application, distributable
A Web application that uses J2EE technology written so that it can be deployed in a Web container distributed across multiple Java virtual machines running on the same host or different hosts. The deployment descriptor for such an application uses the distributable element.

Web component
A component that provides services in response to requests; either a *servlet* or a *JSP page*.

Web container
A *container* that implements the Web component contract of the J2EE architecture. This contract specifies a runtime environment for Web components

that includes security, concurrency, life-cycle management, transaction, deployment, and other services. A Web container provides the same services as a *JSP container* as well as a federated view of the J2EE platform APIs. A Web container is provided by a *Web* or *J2EE* server.

Web container, distributed
A Web container that can run a Web application that is tagged as distributable and that executes across multiple Java virtual machines running on the same host or on different hosts.

Web container provider
A vendor that supplies a Web container.

Web module
A unit that consists of one or more Web components, other resources, and a Web deployment descriptor.

Web resource
A static or dynamic object contained in a Web application archive that can be referenced by a URL.

Web resource collection
A list of URL patterns and HTTP methods that describe a set of resources to be protected.

Web server
Software that provides services to access the Internet, an intranet, or an extranet. A Web server hosts Web sites, provides support for HTTP and other protocols, and executes server-side programs (such as CGI scripts or servlets) that perform certain functions. In the J2EE architecture, a Web server provides services to a *Web container*. For example, a Web container typically relies on a Web server to provide HTTP message handling. The J2EE architecture assumes that a Web container is hosted by a Web server from the same vendor, so does not specify the contract between these two entities. A Web server may host one or more Web containers.

Web server provider
A vendor that supplies a Web server.

XML
Extensible Markup Language. A markup language that allows you to define the tags (markup) needed to identify the content, data, and text in XML documents. It differs from *HTML*, the markup language most often used to present information on the internet. HTML has fixed tags that deal mainly with style or presentation. An XML document must undergo a transformation into a language with style tags under the control of a stylesheet before it can be presented by a browser or other presentation mechanism. Two types

of style sheets used with XML are *CSS* and *XSL*. Typically, XML is transformed into HTML for presentation. Although tags may be defined as needed in the generation of an XML document, a document type definition (*DTD*) may be used to define the elements allowed in a particular type of document. A document may be compared with the rules in the DTD to determine its validity and to locate particular elements in the document. J2EE deployment descriptors are expressed in XML with DTDs defining allowed elements. Programs for processing XML documents use *SAX* or *DOM* APIs. J2EE *deployment descriptors* are expressed in XML.

XSL

Extensible Stylesheet Language. An *XML* transformation language used for transforming XML documents into documents with flow object tags for presentation purposes. The transformation aspect of XSL has been abstracted into *XSLT,* with the XSL name now used to designate the presentation flow language. XSL is a direct descendent of the DSSSL style language for SGML (Standard Generalized Markup Language), the language from which XML was subsetted. It was designed to have all the capabilities of *CSS*, the stylesheet often used with *HTML*. XSL flow objects can be presented by specialized browsers and can themselves be transformed into PDF documents.

XSLT

XSL Transformation. An XML file that controls the transformation of an XML document into another XML document or HTML. The target document often will have presentation-related tags dictating how it will be rendered by a browser or other presentation mechanism. XSLT was formerly part of XSL, which also included a tag language of style flow objects.

About the Authors

Web Technology

Stephanie Bodoff is a staff writer at Sun Microsystems. In previous positions she worked as a software engineer on distributed computing and telecommunications systems and object-oriented software development methods. Since her conversion to technical writing, Stephanie has documented object-oriented databases, application servers, and enterprise application development methods. She is a co-author of *Designing Enterprise Applications with the Java™ 2 Platform, Enterprise Edition,* and *Object-Oriented Software Development: The Fusion Method.*

Enterprise JavaBeans Technology, Transactions, Resource Connections

Dale Green is a staff writer with Sun Microsystems, where he documents the J2EE platform. In previous positions he programmed business applications, designed databases, taught technical classes, and documented RDBMS products. He wrote the internationalization and reflection trails for *The Java™ Tutorial Continued.* In his current position he writes about Enterprise JavaBeans technology and the J2EE SDK.

Message-Driven Beans

Kim Haase is a staff writer with Sun Microsystems, where she documents the J2EE platform. In previous positions she has documented compilers, debuggers, and floating-point programming. She currently writes about the Java Message Service and J2EE SDK tools.

Security

Eric Jendrock is a staff writer with Sun Microsystems, where he documents the J2EE platform. Previously, he documented middleware products and standards. Currently, he writes about the J2EE Compatibility Test Suite and J2EE security.

Overview

Monica Pawlan is a staff writer for the Java Developer Connection (JDC), and was a contributing author for *The Java™ Tutorial*. She is the author of *Essentials of the Java Programming Language: A Hands-On Guide* and co-author of *Advanced Programming for the Java 2 Platform*. She has a background in 2D and 3D graphics, security, and database products, and loves to study and write about emerging technologies. When not writing, she spends her spare time gardening, studying classical piano, and dreaming of far away places—some of which she occasionally visits.

J2EE Connector Architecture

Beth Stearns is the president of Computer Ease Publishing, a computer consulting firm she founded in 1982. Her client list includes Sun Microsystems Inc., Silicon Graphics Inc., Oracle Corporation, and Xerox Corporation, among others. Her *Understanding EDT*, a guide to Digital Equipment Corporation's text editor, has sold throughout the world. She received her B.S. degree from Cornell University and a master's degree from Adelphi University. Beth wrote the JNI trail for *The Java™ Tutorial Continued*. She is a co-author of *Applying Enterprise JavaBeans: Component-Based Development for the J2EE Platform*.

Index

E

F

J

R

S

The Java™ Series

ISBN 0-201-63456-2

ISBN 0-201-70433-1

ISBN 0-201-31005-8

ISBN 0-201-79168-4

ISBN 0-201-70393-9

ISBN 0-201-48558-3

ISBN 0-201-74622-0

ISBN 0-201-75280-8

ISBN 0-201-76810-0

ISBN 0-201-31002-3

ISBN 0-201-31003-1

ISBN 0-201-48552-4

ISBN 0-201-71102-8

ISBN 0-201-70329-7

ISBN 0-201-30955-6

ISBN 0-201-31000-7

ISBN 0-201-31008-2

ISBN 0-201-78472-6

ISBN 0-201-31009-0

ISBN 0-201-70502-8

ISBN 0-201-32577-2

ISBN 0-201-43294-3

ISBN 0-201-70267-3

ISBN 0-201-74627-1

ISBN 0-201-70456-0

ISBN 0-201-77580-8

ISBN 0-201-78790-3

ISBN 0-201-71041-2

ISBN 0-201-77582-4

ISBN 0-201-43321-4

ISBN 0-201-43328-1

ISBN 0-201-70969-4

ISBN 0-201-72617-3

Please see our web site (http://www.awl.com/cseng/javaseries) for more information on these titles.

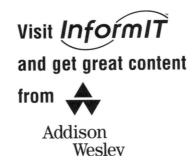

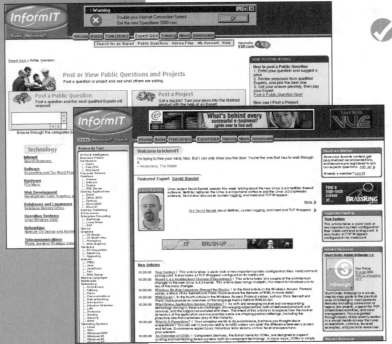

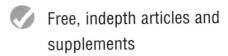

CD-ROM Warranty

Addison-Wesley warrants the enclosed disc to be free of defects in materials and faulty workmanship under normal use for a period of ninety days after purchase. If a defect is discovered in the disc during this warranty period, a replacement disc can be obtained at no charge by sending the defective disc, postage prepaid, with proof of purchase to:

Editorial Department

Addison-Wesley Professional

Pearson Technology Group

75 Arlington Street, Suite 300

Boston, MA 02116

Email: AWPro@awl.com

Addison-Wesley makes no warranty or representation, either expressed or implied, with respect to this software, its quality, performance, merchantability, or fitness for a particular purpose. In no event will Addison-Wesley, its distributors, or dealers be liable for direct, indirect, special, incidental, or consequential damages arising out of the use or inability to use the software. The exclusion of implied warranties is not permitted in some states. Therefore, the above exclusion may not apply to you. This warranty provides you with specific legal rights. There may be other rights that you may have that vary from state to state. The contents of this CD-ROM are intended for personal use only.

More information and updates are available at:

http://www.awl.com/cseng/titles/0201791684